I0053224

FUTURE VALUE

MONEY LESSONS FOR LIFE

Mark DiGiovanni

THE LESSONS

Various Charts and Tables

INTRODUCTION - MISSING PIECES

Are you young? Have you recently had a milestone event like a graduation? Were you given this book in recognition of your milestone? If you answered yes to these questions, congratulations – you're my target market. (If you didn't answer yes, you're still valued, so please keep reading.)

Whether you graduated recently or some time ago, in your twelve or sixteen or twenty years of formal education, how much time was spent teaching you about money? If you're like most graduates, the answer is little to none.

It costs roughly $150,000 to take a child from pre-K through high school. It can cost that much again to earn a college degree. Some claim noble reasons for all this education – love of learning, personal growth, etc. The main reason is economic. Parents spend all this money giving their children a good education so those children will get good jobs. And the main indicator of a good job is how much it pays. **You learn to earn.**

There is nothing wrong with wanting your children to become well-educated and to have good-paying jobs in adulthood. Parents, politicians, and school systems agree on this point. But there's a problem. While an enormous amount of time, effort, and money has been spent to enable you to earn money, almost nothing has been spent to teach you about money itself or what to do with it once you earn it. **Money is a tool. As with any tool, it makes no sense to teach someone how to *make* the tool if you don't also teach them how to *use* the tool.**

Parents and schools have been shortsighted when it comes to teaching you about money. In some cases, the parents assume the schools are teaching you, and the schools assume the parents have it covered. In many cases, neither the parents nor the schools feel confident enough on the subject of money to properly teach their children about it.

Teachers don't become teachers for the money; they become teachers for the love of learning. Some schools may believe that teaching about money puts too much emphasis on money at the expense of more "worthy" subjects like science and math. Teaching about money would acknowledge the economic reasons for education, which might make some educators uncomfortable.

There's another, more pressing reason schools don't teach about money. Standardized testing has become the measure of a school's effectiveness. Schools now teach to the test. If a subject like money isn't being tested, it won't be taught. If colleges encouraged or even required incoming students to take money classes in high school, money classes would start being taught there. Since most high school students hope to attend college, colleges can influence high school curricula more than parents, teachers, or politicians.

Everyone would benefit if new college students had some basic money education before arriving on campus. **Young people today have more access to money and less knowledge about money than any previous generation.** An eighteen-year-old with a new credit card, ample student loans, no money education and no supervision is dangerous. That combination often leads to parents paying off huge credit card debts, a college that loses a student, and a young person who loses an education but gains a mountain of debt. A cycle of money mistakes begins that may last a lifetime.

It wouldn't take much to give students the knowledge they need about money. A one-semester class in 8th, 10th, and 12th grades could give them the knowledge they need, and it would only consume about 2% of their total school time. It would be a small investment with a big return.

Until such changes occur, a book like this will have to try to fill the gap.

You'll probably spend forty or more years working before you retire. Those forty years are on top of at least a dozen years you spent in school. Most people devote the single biggest chunk of their time from ages 5 to 65 learning job skills and earning money. If these people (including you) learned about money early on, they would likely have to work less, and they would accumulate more wealth while working. They would also better understand money's possibilities and its limitations, avoiding a lot of the crises adults bring on themselves.

Even if you're not young, you're never too old to benefit from these lessons. **Their future value will be determined not just by how long you can apply them, but how well.**

HOW MONEY SERVES YOU

When Yvonne and Quentin got married, one of their first goals was to buy a house. They calculated how much house they could afford, based on incomes and existing debts. They calculated their down payment and how much they needed to save monthly to accumulate it within three years. They then opened a separate savings account at their bank just for their down payment.

Yvonne and Quentin were disciplined about saving for their down payment, and within three years they had saved enough. They had also studied the real estate market in their area for those three years. They knew what they could afford in their area. They eventually found a three-bedroom, two-bath, Cape Cod house on a quiet street with good schools nearby.

There was the usual back-and-forth between buyer and seller about price, repairs, maintenance, closing costs, etc. Everyone eventually agreed on all these issues, and the closing itself went smoothly. Three weeks later, Yvonne and Quentin hosted their first party in their new home for all the friends and relatives who helped them move from their cramped apartment.

Lots of moving parts had to work well together for Yvonne and Quentin's dream of home ownership to come true. Wife and husband worked as a team to sacrifice, save, and find just the right property. Family and friends were supportive during times when it seemed the dream wouldn't come true. Bankers, realtors, and attorneys all had to coordinate their efforts. Finally, buyer and seller had to come to agreement on many different aspects of the sale – disagreement on any of which could have killed the deal.

There was another moving part to Yvonne and Quentin's home buying adventure that was absolutely essential; yet no one gave it a thought because they didn't have to. That ignored moving part was money.

Money serves four basic functions. Here are those functions and how they worked for Yvonne and Quentin:

Unit of account – **Money can express the market value of different goods and services.** If something can be valued in money, its value can be compared to other things that can be valued in money. Even your time can be valued in money, so you can calculate how much time you must pay to get something you want.

The market value of the house Yvonne and Quentin wanted was expressed in money (in this case, dollars). Money could accurately express what both buyer and seller thought the house was worth, so they knew how far apart they were when negotiating. Imagine trying to value this house in livestock, steel, or even your time. When trying to value something, money is the common language spoken and understood by everyone.

Store of Value – Wealth can be held in many forms (stocks, real estate, etc.), but **no form of wealth is as flexible as money.** Money can also be accumulated over time, with no upper limits and stored where only inflation can harm its value.

When Yvonne and Quentin were saving for their down payment, they knew exactly how much they had by checking their bank statement. The money was ready when they were. They didn't have to sell it or convert it. The only worry was if home prices increased while they were saving up their down payment. Inflation would have reduced the value of their money, weakening it as a store of value. They would have needed a bigger down payment if inflation raised home prices.

Medium of exchange – Without money, people would have to barter to exchange goods and services. **Money eliminates the need for a *coincidence of wants*.** Money encourages trade because people agree on its value and because it's widely accepted as payment for anything.

Yvonne and Quentin weren't saving money just to have money. They were going to exchange their money for a house. The seller didn't want to be paid in money just to have money, either. At some point, the seller would use the money from the sale to buy necessities and luxuries, possibly even another house.

A house is expensive. Yvonne and Quentin had only money as an acceptable form of payment. They had nothing that valuable to barter or exchange. They couldn't work directly for the seller, either. It would take too long, and they didn't have skills the seller needed. Even though money was the only acceptable payment method, Yvonne and Quentin needed more money than they had saved to make the deal.

Standard of deferred payments – Because so much of the modern economy is based on credit markets, money is critical for the stability of those markets. **Only money can be maintained in such a way that neither lenders nor borrowers stand to lose.**

Yvonne and Quentin worked hard and sacrificed to save up their down payment. Even so, their down payment was only ten percent of the cost of the house. They had to borrow the rest in the form of a thirty-year fixed-rate mortgage.

No bank would make a loan for a large amount, with a payment schedule lasting three decades, if they weren't sure what they would actually be getting back. The bank that handled the mortgage first checked out Yvonne and Quentin to make sure they were good credit risks. Then they entered the loan amount, the interest rate, and the repayment period to calculate the monthly payment. The bank could approve the loan because they knew how they would be paid, how much they would be paid, and for how long they would be paid. No other method of payment but money would be as accurate, and accuracy is essential in such a deal.

Money served Yvonne and Quentin in many ways and very well. Money stands ready to serve you, too. You have to be careful, though. Just because money can serve you in certain circumstances, that doesn't mean it should.

Unit of Account Pitfall - Things that should not be valued in money or have their value compared to other things have it done because money is our default method of assessing value.

Store of Value Pitfall - The ability to store wealth through money can lead to a disconnection between the individual and other people and between the individual and God.

Medium of Exchange Pitfall - The ability of money to enable the exchange of goods and services can lead to goods and services that should not be valued in money being exchanged for money.

Standard of Deferred Payments Pitfall - By stabilizing credit markets, money makes credit more tempting and more available, leading to major financial problems for many.

11

MONEY ISN'T

Money Isn't the Cause

You don't work for money. You should work for two reasons. First, work gives meaning to your life by contributing; you provide society with needed goods and services. Second, you work to provide you and your family with all the necessities and a few luxuries.

Money has nothing to do with the first reason for working. If your work has no meaning, no amount of money can fill that void. As for the second reason, money is a medium of exchange. It enables you to convert your work into necessities, luxuries, and anything else money can buy.

Money Isn't (a) God

When money is desired for its own sake, the worship of money begins. The Bible mentions money more than any other topic because money is mankind's first choice as a substitute for the supernatural.

Wealth can create a delusion of self-sufficiency. We can come to believe we don't need other people and we don't need God. Such pride is considered a sin. It weakens the bonds of a society and weakens the bonds between individuals and God. Money is not evil. The material world is not evil; it is merely secondary to the spiritual world.

Money Isn't Power

It's easy to think money is power when we see people with money exerting influence on those without it. Money is the most obvious difference between the people, so we conclude money is the reason for the difference in power.

The ability to be controlled by people with money comes from a failure to control money in one's own life. You must understand money and have self-discipline about money. It will protect you from those who would use money to control you. Money is power against you only if you are under the power of money.

Money Isn't a Weapon

When people attempt to use money as a weapon, it's usually done by withholding money, not by providing it. To be vulnerable, you have to need money from others, and they control its flow.

This is not about earning an income. That money comes from a fair and voluntary exchange of labor. If you lose your job, you can still get another. This is about someone who receives money from others without giving something in return.

Money Isn't Character

Most wealthy people also possess high character. Most wealthy people in America made it through hard work and sacrifice. Their character is an asset and a large reason for their financial success.

Money isn't character, but it can reveal character. How people earn money and how they spend it reveals their priorities. Priorities reveal character. Someone of high character earns money honestly, saves it seriously, spends it carefully, and gives it generously. Man makes the money; money doesn't make the man, or the woman.

Money Isn't Happiness

Money can buy pleasure but not happiness in the same way that money can buy books but not wisdom.

Several studies confirm certain correlations between money and happiness. It's harder to be happy when you're poor. Your ability to give is hampered and you're focused on survival. Once basic needs are met, more money barely moves the happiness meter. Buying more stuff brings short-lived pleasure, then disappointment. The disappointment of no happiness is compounded by the disappointment of less money.

Money Isn't Human

With the invention of money, we created the ability to quantify almost every aspect of life. Money enables us to have greater contact with the outside world, though largely on a superficial transactional basis.

We don't give of ourselves if it's easier to give money. We don't owe gratitude; we just owe money. Money greatly enabled and simplified transactions. A consequence is we can come to think of relationships as transactions. We try to put a price on everything, even those things that money can't buy.

MONEY IS

Money Is the Effect

We've become accustomed to spending money we haven't earned yet. As a result, we tend to see money as cause rather than effect. Effect follows cause. It's hard to see money as the effect of your work if the money is spent before the work to earn it has been performed.

At work, this misperception can create this mindset: If my boss would pay me more, I would work harder. This is backward. You must create value before you can receive value.

Money Is a Tool

Money used to destroy is a weapon. Money used to build is a tool - the greatest building tool ever devised.

Money is unsurpassed at building a future. When used properly, money does not deteriorate over time like most things we build. When properly used and managed, money becomes bigger and better over time. Money can build a future we can't even imagine today.

Money Is Dignity

The status that money may create isn't the same as dignity. Status is conveyed by other people to an individual. Dignity is conveyed by individuals to themselves.

Dignity is a synonym for self-respect. It must be earned by you, and it can't be taken away by others. Few things generate self-respect like a dollar earned through honest labor. The ability to accumulate money from earnings is a great source of dignity.

Money Is Freedom

Money spent can be a prison, but money saved can be freedom. Smaller financial liabilities and larger financial assets equal greater freedom. Money that generates an income can free you from the task of generating an income. Money's ability to make money is also greater than yours.

The time may come when you don't want to work. The time will almost certainly come when you can't work. Money can give you the freedom to stop working when that time comes. Money can also give you the freedom to leave on your own terms.

Money Is Hope

Hope is the ultimate motivator. Hope enables you to work hard, delay gratification, set priorities, and remain disciplined. Hope motivates you to act in ways that enable the accumulation of wealth.

In addition to hard work, sacrifice, determination and optimism, many of your hopes will require money to be fulfilled. Your hopes will require money because they will require outside assistance to be fulfilled. Money motivates the outside world to provide that assistance.

Money Is Love

Money is excellent as an *expression* of love.

Money is horrible as a *substitute* for love.

Money-is-love has no time frame. You can express love to those who have died by establishing a memorial fund for a cause they supported. You can express love in the present by the simple act of buying a gift for someone for no special reason. You can express love in the future by providing money in the future to help those who will live there, even if you aren't one of them.

Money Is a Mirror

Many people contend that how we allocate our time reflects our priorities and our character. It's a valid contention, but it doesn't go far enough.

How we allocate our money offers an even more accurate reflection. While both time and money are valuable resources, your money balance is known, while your time balance is not. This difference makes a unit of money more valuable than a unit of time. How you allocate the more valuable resource says the most about your priorities and who you are.

MONEY MOVER I – GREED

In Southeast Asia, there is an effective way to capture monkeys. A hole about an inch-and-a-half in diameter is bored into a coconut. The milk is drained, and fruits and nuts monkeys like are inserted into the coconut. The coconut is then placed where it can be observed.

Before long a monkey gets the scent. The monkey inserts its hand into the coconut and grabs a handful. The monkey's open hand fits into the hole; the monkey's fist, filled with food, doesn't fit. The monkey can't run and carry the heavy coconut. A tossed net seals its fate.

The monkey had time to let go of the food, remove its hand and run away before being caught. But it didn't. Greed clouded its judgment, even to the point of risking capture. It's a trait they share with humans.

Greed is an excessive desire to acquire or possess more than what one needs or deserves. Avarice is extreme greed for material wealth.

Brain studies show financial rewards stimulate the nucleus accumbens. The nucleus accumbens is one of the most primitive parts of our brain. Almost all animals have one. Generosity stimulates the posterior superior temporal sulcus. These two parts of the brain can't function at the same time. **We can be greedy or we can be generous, but not simultaneously.**

Greed is one of our most primitive emotions because it comes from one of the most primitive parts of our brain. Generosity is one of our highest emotions because it comes from a highly developed part of our brain.

Our greedy part has an unfair advantage over our generous part. The nucleus accumbens releases dopamine, the pleasure chemical we crave. **Generosity gives us warm fuzzies, but greed gives us a rush.**

Even for generous people, when the stakes rise, greed can overpower generosity. Donating blood makes you feel generous. That feeling is worth more to you than $50 you might receive if you sold blood. If the price rose to $1,000, you would likely stop being so generous. You're willing to give away $50 worth of blood, but not $1,000 worth, even if it's the same blood.

There are several characteristics of money that make it useful in feeding greed:

- *Money is compact.* If the product of greed is money, millions can be stored on a few financial statements.
- *Money is anonymous.* Money can enable greed without evidence. Money doesn't reveal its owner or even its existence. Possessions can betray one's greed; money doesn't.
- *Money is precise.* Competition often stokes greed, especially competition to have the most. Money's precise value makes it easy to make comparisons and keep score.
- *Money is portable.* Cash is more portable than most items it can buy. Even cash is cumbersome compared to cyber-money. A mouse click or screen tap can move money quickly and easily to maximize greed.
- *Money is respectable.* If you become rich enough, people are willing to ignore many flaws, including greed. Sufficient wealth can buy respectability, which is why so many crave it.
- *Money is universal.* Money is the best tool for getting more money because people are so lured by it. One of the best ways to get rich without earning it is to appeal to the greed of others.

- *Money is insulating*. Greed often results from a desire to be insulated from the outside world. With sufficient wealth, you can insulate yourself from poor schools, neighbors, have-nots, and whatever else annoys you.
- *Money is multi-faceted*. A public display of charity prompts the public to disregard many transgressions. "Good Money" sanitizes "Bad Money." Goodwill buys protection from scrutiny.

Greed moves money, even if the greed is not for money specifically. Almost everything one could be greedy for can be bought. **Whether money is the means to an end or an end itself, greed moves it.**

Greed leads to wanting more than one needs. *Need* is subjective. If you grew up in extreme poverty, you might never feel you could be rich enough. You would always fear a return to poverty. **Greed is sometimes as much a psychological disorder as a sin.**

Greed is also fueled by confusing wants with needs. You wouldn't want to be accused of being greedy over something you merely wanted. But you can't be greedy over something you need. **Reclassifying a want to a need insulates you from the label of greed**, at least in your own mind.

Greed leads to wanting more than one deserves. *Deserve* is subjective, too. As with need, what you think you deserve may not match what others think you deserve.

What someone deserves is often determined by law. Greed can become so overpowering that the law is no longer an impediment. Greed is most harmful to others when someone is willing to cross that line.

Greed causes resources like money to move in only one direction – to the greedy person. Money in the economy is like blood in your body. It needs to circulate to be useful. **Greed takes money out of circulation and pools it where it serves no purpose.**

Greed is unhealthy for the economy, but it's unhealthy for the greedy, too. They can never feel successful because whatever they have, it isn't enough. They will always want more.

They can't be happy, either. Happiness doesn't come from material possessions or wealth. It can come from generosity, but that avenue is blocked by their greed. **The desire for success and happiness fuels most greed. But greed makes success or happiness impossible.**

The greedy are like Tantalus, a king in Greek mythology. Tantalus was a son of Zeus and enjoyed great privilege. Despite such privilege, he fell victim to greed. He stole ambrosia and nectar from Zeus' table, brought it back to his kingdom, and revealed the secrets of the gods.

For his punishment, Tantalus was forced to stand in a pool of water with the branches of a fruit tree hanging just overhead. Whenever he reached for the fruit, the branches receded just out of reach. Whenever he bent down to take a drink, the water receded before he could drink.

To the greedy, the fruit tree is success; the water is happiness. They will be forever tantalized by them, yet will never attain them.

MONEY MOVER II – FEAR

How would a man from the Dark Ages, the 600-year period following the fall of the Roman Empire, perceive our society today? The first thing he might notice is almost everything that caused fear in his time is no longer a problem.

Talking with us, our visitor from the past might become dismayed. He might wonder why, after eliminating so many major fears, we've replaced them with so many minor fears. How could a few cases of the flu constitute a national emergency? He saw half a continent killed off by the plague. Why do people worry about the quality of a school lunch program? He lost children to starvation and malnutrition. Why do people worry about Social Security? He never knew anyone who lived past fifty. He might remind us of our progress and tell us to stop fearing things that don't merit fear.

Fear is an emotion experienced in anticipation of pain or danger. Fear is also an uneasiness of the mind. The first kind of fear is physical and instinctual. It's the fear you experience when you hear a sudden crash of thunder or step in front of an oncoming car. The second kind of fear, the kind that dwells in your head, is very different.

The first kind of fear, instinctual, is a healthy fear. Instinctual fear is a survival tool. Fear is an unpleasant emotion and you try to avoid it. Your desire to avoid fear helps you avoid harm.

The second kind of fear, the one in your head, is unhealthy fear. This fear is based on *thoughts* of potential future trouble. It is unique to humans because we are the only species that contemplates the future. It can consume your thoughts, paralyze you, cause you to act irrationally, and can even lead to phobias and paranoia.

The response to fear can take one of two paths – think of them as gut vs. head. Gut response is "Shoot first and ask questions later." Head response calculates the danger, and then develops an appropriate response. The gut response's advantage is speed; the head response's advantage is accuracy.

Instinctual fears require a gut response. Speed is primary because these dangers are immediate. Our body instinctively creates a gut response to instinctual fears.

Thought-based fears require a head response. The danger is not immediate and may not even exist. Our bodies still want to create a gut response because that's all it knows how to do. The head must override the gut response, assess the danger and develop an appropriate action, if one is even needed. These fears are created in the head; it's the head's job to deal with them.

Here are some modern fears that relate to money:
- fear of change (and of the process of change)
- fear of uncertainty about the future
- fear of regression from current prosperity
- fear of making mistakes
- fear of failure on our part
- fear of missing an opportunity
- fear of loss of control over our lives
- fear of losing out to others
- fear of being exploited by others
- fear of the big disaster

Money-related fears are thought-based. They require a head response. A gut response to thought-based money fears is an invitation to financial disaster.

Once we have a stake in something, we worry about loss. The entire insurance industry is based on reducing risk of financial loss by transferring your risk to them. If you total all the insurance premiums you pay, you realize you pay a lot to avoid a potentially much bigger loss. **Insurance is a tool for controlling risk, but its greatest benefit may be as a tool for controlling fear.**

Once people begin to save and invest, they begin to worry about two things – the return *on* their money and the return *of* their money. If money is going into a bank, there is no worry about the return of the money.

People use banks for security for savings. Savings is defined as money set aside for the short-term, five years or less. Investing has a longer time frame. Investments typically generate higher long-term returns than savings; they also have higher short-term volatility. **Investing can create fears about the return on the money *and* the return of the money.**

Nothing scares retirees more than the thought of outliving their money. Most retirees are careful not to spend money at a rate that could cause them to run out. But they fear a drop in the value of the investments that can't be recovered before they need to sell them. This fear is the main reason retirees hold safe investments like bank CDs and government bonds.

Of all our money fears, one is justified but few people have. It's **fear of inflation**. Most people don't think about inflation's effects on their purchasing power.

When retirees fear a drop in the value of their investments, they limit themselves to investments that won't drop, but can't grow enough to offset inflation. They worry a drop in value will leave them with less money. Inflation guarantees they will have less money, as measured in purchasing power.

24

It is fear more than greed that prompts people to move in and out of the stock market – especially out. Greed is less likely than fear to be harmful in market timing. **Greed is proactive** and can promote courage. **Fear is reactive** and is more typically the reason for moving in and out of the market, especially at the worst possible times.

Studies over more than two decades have measured the cost of fear selling. These studies showed that missing *only the best forty days* of market gains over a twenty-year period would reduce gains by *almost half*. Forty days was less than 1% of the total trading days during the periods studied.

Irrational fears of the mind have two major consequences – they reduce your chances of success in the future, and they reduce your chances for happiness in the present.

Fear of change, uncertainty, regression, mistakes, failure, missed opportunities, loss of control, losing, exploitation, and the big disaster can cause you to freeze. Potentially worse, these and other fears can cause you to act in ways that can be financially fatal. They can make you miserable in the present and even more miserable in the future.

MONEY MOVER III – LOVE

A child born is born to a middle class American family in 2016. The parents are both thirty years old. If they're typical parents, they will spend roughly $300,000 getting their child to voting age. A bachelor's degree at a public university will cost another $400,000. If they're lucky, the expenses will end there.

These new parents knew raising a child would be expensive. They may have even seen these estimates of the cost. But they only know part of the cost.

If these parents took all the money they would spend on their child over the next 22 years and invested it at a 7% annual return, when they retired at age 67 they would have over *$3 million*. That $3 million is an *opportunity cost*. An opportunity cost is what you give up when you choose something else. A child carries a huge opportunity cost for the parents.

Throughout almost all of human history, parents had children out of self-interest. Children were their only old age security. Parents had many children, hoping one or two might survive and care for them in old age.

Today we can save and invest. We have professional, high-quality elder care. Having children isn't necessary for old age security. **Having children today is more selfless; it's more an act of love.**

Greed, fear, and love are all emotions that move money. Greed and fear are self-centered emotions. When they move money it rarely benefits anyone. Love is a selfless emotion. When love moves money, it's almost always done to benefit others.

As stated before, **money is excellent as an expression of love, but it is horrible as a substitute for**

love. Money possesses no human characteristics. Money is incapable of substituting for our most human characteristic, love. Giving money instead of your love is like giving a clock instead of your time.

If you buy a gift for someone, you are using money as an expression of love. If you donate to a charity, you are using money as an expression of love. If you buy life insurance for the benefit of others, you are using money as an expression of love. **If you use your money to benefit others, love is moving that money.**

While money should never be used as a substitute for love, there is a financial component to some of our strongest expressions of love.

The payment of a dowry is a four-thousand-year-old practice. The wife provides financial assets to begin the marriage. One of its main purposes is to protect the wife against ill treatment by the husband or his family. The dowry system is still practiced in parts of south Asia.

Modern western marriages begin with a major financial component, too - the engagement ring. The ring symbolizes the partners' commitment, though it has also come to symbolize the financial strength of the groom-to-be.

Because money can be an expression of love, it can also be misinterpreted as a measure of love. If you measure someone's love by how much they spend on you, you're misinterpreting money for love. The giver may then begin to misinterpret money for love, too. It's a short trip from misinterpreting money for love to substituting money for love.

There are four ancient Greek words for love: *eros*, *philia*, *storge*, and *agape*. Each is a different type of love, though all use money as an expression of love.

Eros refers to intimate or romantic love. The term *erotic* is derived from eros. Eros love burns intensely, though often briefly. The intensity of eros love can cloud judgment.

Under the spell of eros love, you might find yourself buying expensive gifts, taking trips, or providing financial support to a lover. These expressions of love can hurt your own finances when carried to extremes.

Eros love has a short life expectancy. When it dies, there are often regrets about money spent in the heat of the moment.

Philia love is often translated as brotherly love, friendship, or affection. The name *Philadelphia* comes from philia.

Aristotle divided philia friendships into three types. **Friendships of utility are typically transactional,** such as a buyer and seller. Money is a key component in these friendships; without money, the relationship would not likely exist.

Friendships of pleasure are based on the pleasure of another person's company. They are often based on a shared activity or experience. Reciprocity is a key component in these relationships. Money is usually a component only if it provides mutual benefit.

Friendships of the good are based on respect for another's character. This is the highest level of friendship, what some call true friendship. People willingly spend money on the other person. Recipients take care that givers don't give too much.

Storge love is a natural affection. It is also called familial love, especially the love between parents and children. It is also the love between committed partners.

Eros love does not evolve into storge love, though it might be replaced by it over time. Eros love is looking into each other's eyes; storge love is looking in the same direction.

Because storge love involves deep, long-term commitments, the financial commitments are also deep and long-term. Whether the commitment is to a spouse, a parent, or a child, it's one that can cover decades or even a lifetime. Storge love often carries the biggest price tags, but also has the highest potential return.

Agape love is considered the highest form of love. It is the love of God for man and of man for God. It is also the love that is reflected in charity. Agape is a selfless love, one committed to the well-being of another.

When people give to their place of worship, they express agape love with money. When people put money in a Salvation Army kettle or directly into the hands of a homeless person, they express agape love with money.

Because agape love is the highest love, money is not given with any expectation of reciprocity or recognition. It is not given out of any sense of duty or obligation. Agape love is the highest love, and **money moved by agape love is money serving its highest purpose.**

Love makes you selfless and brave. **Where money is concerned, love is a powerful antidote to greed and fear.** Money moved by love rarely moves in the wrong direction. It also prevents a lot of money from moving in the wrong direction.

SHARE/SAVE/SPEND

The word *share* has many meanings in the English language. It's a portion of something; it's often used to mean an equitable portion. Ownership of a company is divided into shares of stock; owners are shareholders. It can mean to take part in something. *Share* has positive connotations, unless it's your parents commanding you to share your toys with siblings.

All the major religions endorse sharing. One of the five pillars of Islam is *Zakat*, which is charitable giving, especially to the poor. In Judaism, *Tzedakah* is the obligation to be charitable. In Hinduism, one of the ten Niyamas, or observances, is *Dana*, the practice of charity. Buddhism professes that wealth provides four kinds of happiness, one of them happiness from sharing wealth. The Bible has numerous passages urging Christians to share what God has provided them. Corinthians II reminds us: "God loves a cheerful giver."

Greed involves taking more than your fair share. Greed is considered sinful by all these religions.

Greed follows the law of diminishing returns. An extra dollar acquired through greed has little value. In contrast, sharing has no diminishing returns. Sharing feels as good the thousandth time as it does the first.

The best antidote for greed is sharing. Greed hurts everyone, but no one more than the greedy. They rarely gain financially in the long run, and they sacrifice almost everything money can't buy in the interim. Sharing helps everyone, perhaps no one more than the person sharing.

Many people put sharing last instead of first. They want to see what they will have left before deciding what they will share. **When sharing is left for last, there will never be money left to share.**

Many people wait to see what they will have before deciding what they will share. But all the faiths remind us that God waits to see what we will share before deciding what we will have.

Even if you don't believe in God, sharing is therapeutic. Money can cause us to disconnect from our fellow man; sharing it helps us reconnect. Even if you're ruled by self-interest, sharing still makes sense. People prefer doing business with people who put others first. If nothing else, sharing is good for business. **First you give, then you get, whether it's personal or business.**

If sharing is the antidote for greed, **saving is the antidote for fear.**

There are many different kinds of money fears. All these fears really come down to one – we fear we won't have money when we need it. Based on the high debt and low savings of most Americans, these money fears are well-founded.

The best way to reduce the fear of not having money when you need it is to save money for when you do need it. Saving more does require spending less. Spending less is the price of reducing money fears. The ability to reduce your money fears is at least within your control – it merely requires some self-discipline.

Fear incites panic; panic leads to mistakes. Saving money reduces fear; it also reduces money mistakes that increase fear and trigger panic, leading to more money mistakes and even more fear and panic.

In a financial emergency, using savings can be the best option. Borrowing money is costly; it also adds the stress of paying off additional debt. Using savings may mean not having to sell valued possessions during an emergency. Selling inherited jewelry would be bad; selling your car would be a catastrophe.

Saving money also proves you can live below your means. Living below your means makes a pay cut easier to handle. Savings can help you endure a period of unemployment. Simply knowing you have the discipline to save builds confidence and reduces your fear of the unexpected. You believe you can handle anything.

By sharing and saving first, you enable guilt-free spending. Your first spending priorities are necessities and obligations – food, mortgage, utilities, medical, transportation, etc. Even with necessities, you have some control over how much you spend. By taking care of sharing, saving, and necessary spending first, you may have less discretionary spending, but you'll actually enjoy it more. You'll replace quantity with quality, both in what you buy and the process of buying it.

So, how much should you share, save, and spend? **A good share-save-spend ratio is 10/10/80.** (Saving here also includes long-term investing.) If you're not sharing or saving anything now, start by moving 1-2% of your income into each category. Raise it 1-2% each year. In just a few years, you'll have built a great immune system to greed and fear, the two biggest threats to your financial health.

SHARE THIS

SAVE THIS

SPEND THIS

THE GOOD STEWARD

The *Broken Windows Theory* was first introduced in an article titled "Broken Windows", which appeared in *The Atlantic Monthly* in 1982. The title comes from the following example:

"Consider a building with a few broken windows. If the windows are not repaired, the tendency is for vandals to break a few more windows. Eventually, they may even break into the building, and if it's unoccupied, perhaps become squatters or light fires inside."

A successful strategy for preventing vandalism is to fix the problems while they're still small. Making repairs quickly shows good stewardship. Good stewardship thwarts damage and deterioration.

Stewardship originally referred to the servant's duties to bring food and drink. Stewardship responsibilities eventually expanded to include all of the domestic, service, and management needs of the household. **Stewardship today is the acceptance of responsibility to shepherd and safeguard the property of others.**

A saying attributed to Native-Americans reflects the essence of stewardship: "We do not inherit the earth from our ancestors. We borrow it from our children." This saying reminds us that, **while we possess some things temporarily, we own nothing permanently.** Much of what we possess existed before us. And it will all have to be left behind when we die.

In the United States, with our emphasis on individual property rights, it can be difficult to accept that we are merely stewards of what we may legally own. If you own something, you can do what you want with it, even destroy it. If you're a steward of something, you have a

33

duty to care for it, even if you don't benefit from that care. **Stewardship implies more responsibilities and fewer rights than ownership.**

In addition to being a steward of money and material things, you are also steward of your mind, your body, and your time. Your stewardship of these greatly affects how much money and material things will eventually come under your stewardship.

Time is your most valuable resource. Unless you're a good steward of your time, you're unlikely to be a good steward of anything else. **The proper stewardship of time is the first ingredient of wealth.**

In addition to wasting the present time, too many people deplete their reserves of time. They reduce the quality and quantity of their future time by not taking proper care of themselves. Proper stewardship of time includes taking time to care for your body and mind. **Your body and mind are the tools you use to convert time into wealth.**

We have all known people who lost what they legally owned through neglect, carelessness, or abuse. Whether you consider it a law of economics, of nature, or of God, **a prerequisite to getting more is taking care of what you already have.** People want to be assured that, if they entrust something to you, it will be in good hands.

Humans have a natural instinct to want to own things. The concept of stewardship goes against that instinct, which is why it can be difficult to adopt. **Adopting a stewardship mentality is often the result of a higher calling.**

Becoming a parent is one of those higher callings. When you have children of your own, you transition from inheriting from your ancestors to borrowing from your children. You transition from owner to steward.

As we enter our twilight years, we also adopt a stewardship mentality. Even if we spent decades acquiring all we could, we come to realize we can't take any of it with us. At that point, we plan our estate so that everything we leave behind will be entrusted to those who have demonstrated good stewardship.

A higher calling may actually be a literal higher calling. All the major religions profess that we are merely stewards of God's gifts. Those who accept that everything is God's, and that they are merely stewards, embrace the role of steward as an honor, not a burden.

A stewardship mindset can be liberating. It frees you from competitive materialism; you stop keeping score. You care for possessions, but they don't possess you. You fear loss less. You see the bigger picture.

Paul Harvey offered many words of wisdom over six decades in broadcasting. One of his bits of advice was "Leave the woodpile higher than you found it."

For thousands of years, wood was our primary source of fuel. For many, it was as essential to survival as food and water. Community woodpiles made sure everyone had enough wood to survive. Citizens were expected to not exploit this public asset and to add to it as were able.

No one owned the woodpile, yet everyone had a responsibility to it. No one wanted to see the woodpile abandoned because there were more takers than givers. Everyone was a steward of the woodpile.

The metaphorical woodpile that benefits everyone was built by your ancestors. Leaving it higher than you found it is your tribute to your ancestors and your responsibility to your children.

(DIS)CONNECTIONS

In the opening scene of *The Godfather*, Bonasera the undertaker offers Don Corleone money to kill the men who violated his daughter. The Don replies, "What have I done to make you treat me so disrespectfully? You don't ask this favor out of friendship. Instead you come to my house on the day of my daughter's wedding and ask me to do murder for money."

In our world, we have *social norms* and *market norms*. **Social norms are an unwritten code of behavior between people.** They're about helping each other and getting along. They're the glue that holds a society together. They're biological.

Market norms are transaction-based. They involve a bottom line. They can be precisely measured. They're mechanical. Bonasera's offense to Don Corleone was inserting market norms where social norms belonged.

When social norms collide with market norms, social norms almost always lose. This collision usually occurs when market norms invade the world of social norms. Don Corleone refused to let market norms usurp social norms in his world.

In social relationships, social norms should rule. When you're invited to a friend's house for dinner, you bring a bottle of wine as a gift; you don't offer to "pay the tab" at the end of the evening. When your neighbor asks to borrow your lawn mower, you lend it with the expectation he will return the favor; you don't charge him rent. Reciprocity is part of social norms and market norms. **With social norms, reciprocity is expected; with market norms, reciprocity is required.**

With a higher calling, social norms should prevail. People are more inclined to donate blood than sell it. If people want to do something for altruistic reasons, you'll offend them and risk losing their support if you bring money into the equation. Blood donors are offered cookies and juice as a thank-you; they're not offered cash as compensation. The good feeling we get from giving is priceless; never attempt to put a price on it.

Adhering to social norms requires courtesy and patience. Many potentially romantic relationships were never consummated because the man commented that he had spent a good bit of money and wasn't receiving anything in return.

It's considered rude to put market norms ahead of social norms. It gives the impression you care more about the money than the person. Many business deals were never consummated because one party began talking business prematurely. For example, in golf there are certain social norms. Never discuss business the first time you play with a customer or client. Never discuss business before the third hole, after the fifteenth, on the green, or when someone is preparing to shoot.

People prefer doing business with people they like. Social norms create an environment for others to get to like you. Adhering to social norms shows you like or at least respect the other person enough to be courteous.

If you introduce market norms where social norms belong, market norms will almost always win. But **inserting market norms too soon almost always ends up killing the business deal *and* damaging the social relationship.**

Money enables us to have more relationships. But those relationships are based on market norms, and they exist only as long as there's a financial component.

Social relationships should avoid having a financial component. When a financial component is introduced, it often does serious damage to the relationship. More than one friendship ended when money was borrowed and wasn't repaid. **If you let it, money is more likely to disconnect you to others than to connect you.**

For many, nothing represents the material world with all its flaws more than money. This belief is formed because they've seen too many cases where money has brought out the worst in people. Money has that ability, but it's not money's fault. Money merely reflects the qualities of those who possess it.

If you want to become less materialistic and more spiritual, one of the best places to begin conversion is through your use of money.

Money incorporates many of the characteristics of the material and the spiritual. You can see it and touch it. Money is precise and measurable. Almost anything in the material world can be attained with a sufficient amount of money. If you had to pick one thing to represent the material world, money would be an excellent choice.

Money also mimics characteristics of the spiritual. Money is only of value to those who believe in its value. After the Confederacy was defeated in the Civil War, Confederate money became worthless because no one believed in its value any longer. **Money, like God, requires a certain element of faith in it.**

Money can bring out the worst in our earthly selves; it can also bring out the best in our spiritual selves. Every time we use money to benefit others, we reveal our spirituality.

Money not only works well in both the earthly and spiritual realms, it can also work between the earthly and the spiritual. Money can bridge the gap between them and reconcile the two to each other. You can turn greed into generosity by simply turning money from an inward to an outward direction. Making a will is recognition that money is merely an earthly creation. It can also remind you that you are more than merely an earthly creation.

Money was created for a noble purpose. Money is an inspired invention of people who understood the play of forces in human life. It was created as a way of recognizing that humans have property rights, but that no human is self-sufficient.

Money enabled people to establish connections they could never establish without money. The invention of money greatly facilitated trade. Throughout history, trade has increased connections within cultures and between cultures, reducing the risk of war.

Money used rightly connects people. Money used wrongly disconnects people. **Money can be either a wedge or a bridge between people.** But it's people, not money, who make that call.

MEASURES AND PLEASURES

In 2011, the United Nations General Assembly invited member countries to measure the happiness of their people and use the findings to help guide their public policies. The now-annual *World Happiness Report* is the result of that invitation.

Residents of these countries rank their happiness on a scale of 1-10 in such areas as GDP, social support, health, freedom, generosity, and government. The happiest countries have overall scores above 7; most of them are in northern Europe. The unhappiest countries have overall scores under 4; most of them are in Africa.

Wealth was certainly a factor in peoples' perceptions of happiness. The countries at the top are far wealthier than those at the bottom. But wealth was only one of many factors. Health, freedom, and social support were ranked more important to happiness than money. The U.S. ranked 15th out of 158 countries; only two of the higher-ranked countries had a higher per-capita GDP.

Most people, at least in the U.S., believe more money will make them happier. Studies conducted in many countries over several decades have reached some interesting conclusions. First, it is harder to be happy if you are living in poverty, though many manage to be. Second, once you reach the average income for your society, there is little additional happiness from more money. Third, the sacrifices necessary to raise your income well above the average can lead to unhappiness and regret.

We seek success, happiness, and pleasure. We often fail to acquire them because we confuse the three. Specifically, we get the connection between

success and happiness wrong. We also confuse pleasure and happiness.

Author Dale Carnegie said, "Success is getting what you want; happiness is wanting what you get." Nobel Peace Prize recipient Dr. Albert Schweitzer said, "Success is not the key to happiness; happiness is the key to success." These quotes make two important points: **First, happiness is not something you find; it's something you create. Second, happiness makes a better starting point than a destination.**

People equate success with happiness; they see happiness as the inevitable result of success. Achieving success can often prove disappointing, though.

For example, a young woman equates success (and happiness) with becoming a partner at her firm. She works long hours and makes sacrifices to make partner. Once promoted, she experiences more emptiness than elation. She has success, but the happiness she expected is missing; happiness was not automatic with success. She might actually feel sadness because her expectations of happiness were so unmet.

The most common measure of success is money. In any given field, the person who is paid more is considered more successful. **If we equate success with money, and if we equate success with happiness, it's easy to then equate money with happiness.**

Do you know of anyone who is successful, wealthy, and unhappy? Do you know of anyone who is happy, despite no typical or obvious success or wealth? If you do, those people disprove money equating with happiness.

Money is our default measure of success because it is precise and familiar. Success is also easy to measure in most cases because it involves the achievement of

41

measurable goals. Happiness varies greatly by the person; it is far less definable and harder to measure, especially with money.

The happiness that success brings lies not in the achievement or the rewards, but in the effort made to reach the achievement. If you think about your past successes, the journey to success was probably more fulfilling than the destination. Money may have been a byproduct of your success, but if money was your motivation to succeed, you probably felt a letdown from success. **The kind of success that leads to happiness doesn't need a financial component. A financial component might actually impede happiness.**

It's easier to generate negative emotions than positive ones. We expect to feel sad when we fail, so failure usually generates sadness. Success generating happiness is trickier and less reliable.

Success and failure are two sides of the same coin. They are also nouns, not adjectives. You *realize* success or failure; you *are not* a success or a failure. **The less you depend on success for happiness, the less failure will burden you with sadness.**

Because we incorrectly equate money with happiness, we then think we can buy happiness. **We think we can buy happiness because we confuse happiness with pleasure.**

Pleasure is a sensual gratification or indulgence. Pleasure is triggered by an external stimulus. People seeking happiness often look for it down the path of pleasure. Sex, drugs, rock 'n roll, a new Mercedes, a house at the beach, and a Mediterranean vacation can all bring pleasure; none of them can bring happiness.

Pleasure is externally generated; happiness is internally generated. Happiness does not depend on external circumstances or material wealth for its existence and growth.

Money can buy pleasure, but not happiness, in the same way that money can buy books, but not wisdom. **Pleasure involves receiving. Happiness involves giving.** Money can bring pleasure in its accumulation and on the external stimuli it can buy. But it brings happiness through its voluntary sharing with someone or something that benefits others.

It's not only more blessed to give than receive, it also brings greater happiness. In one research study, people were given $100. The first group was instructed to spend it on themselves; the second group was instructed to spend it on others or to give it away. The second group reported happiness measures resulting from their actions that were *four times higher* than the first group.

Money may buy pleasure, but pleasures often deliver more bad than good. Most pleasures come at a price beyond money. Pleasures also fade quickly, while the money spent on them stays gone forever.

Money can't buy the kind of success that's of value. Money is a poor motivation to succeed. And money as a reward for success leads to disappointment.

Money can't buy happiness, though it can improve conditions to create happiness. If you're successful enough to have a lot of money, your money can remove some impediments to happiness and allow you to indulge in a few pleasures. Beyond that, the best way to attain happiness from money is to create happiness for others.

INPUTS AND OUTCOMES

Charles Van Doren, Marion Jones, Atlanta Teachers, 1919 Chicago White Sox, Volkswagen, Rosie Ruiz, Lance Armstrong, Bernie Madoff, Enron, Ben Johnson, Harvard Students, Ivan Boesky.

The list above is varied, but they have one thing in common. They are some of the more notorious cheaters in history. Whether it's cheating in business, education, or sports, the cheaters listed above have one thing in common with all cheaters – **they tried to change the outcome without changing the inputs.** The outcomes here involve numbers – sports scores, test scores, race results, or dollars on a financial statement. In every case, the cheaters tried to create a result they had not earned.

Almost everyone cheats at some time. Most times it's small, like cheating in a children's game or claiming higher deductions on a tax return. Almost everyone gets cheated at some time, too. When we know someone has cheated us, it taints the relationship. Cheaters rarely consider the consequences of their actions. They're among the worst examples of the ends justifying the means.

People want to believe that inputs and outcomes are connected. We want to believe that greater effort will lead to greater rewards. We know it won't always work out that way; we just want to know the system isn't rigged against it working out that way.

Employers use outcomes to motivate employees to contribute their inputs. One outcome employers want is higher profits. The quality and quantity of employee inputs greatly affects profits.

Employees seek two types of rewards – intrinsic and extrinsic. Intrinsic rewards are desired for their own sake, like autonomy and a sense of accomplishment. Extrinsic rewards can be status or money, or simply avoiding punishment. Intrinsic and extrinsic rewards are employees' desired outcomes. They motivate employees to increase input.

High inputs are the result of high motivation. To be highly motivated, you have to believe that higher effort will lead to higher performance and that higher performance will lead to your desired outcome. When these connections exist, you see the connection between inputs and outcomes. You're motivated to do your best, and you're not motivated to cheat.

If you don't see a connection between your effort and your performance, you'll lose motivation and eventually quit. Effort is important, but talent can play a role in outcomes, too. If you're low on talent, it's hard to stay motivated; you may work harder but perform worse than those with more talent.

If you don't see a connection between your performance and outcomes, you'll lose motivation. **If others are cheating, they're stealing the outcomes you worked for.** When the boss takes credit for your ideas or gives the promotion you earned to his nephew, it's easy to doubt the connection between inputs and outcomes. When that happens, there can be a strong temptation to stop trying, or worse, to join the ranks of cheaters.

In your work, the desired outcomes of your employer may not match your desired outcomes. If the two are far apart, you won't be motivated, and your input will be low. In that case, it's in your interest to find a place where you and your employer want the same outcomes.

In your personal life, it's easier to maintain the connection between inputs and outcomes. If you eat less and exercise more, you will lose weight. If you enroll in college and study hard, you will earn a degree. If you save money every month, you will be wealthier at the end of the year.

Sometimes we misjudge the connection between inputs and outcomes. The misjudging is almost always a case of underestimating inputs and overestimating outcomes. You won't lose thirty pounds in a month by walking one mile a day, and you won't be a millionaire in ten years by saving $10 a week. It's natural to seek maximum outcomes from minimum inputs. Reality checks help align behavior and expectations.

When it comes to inputs and outcomes, what stresses people and drives them crazy (or to cheat) is thinking they have control over outcomes they can't control. It's a helpless feeling when you can't control an outcome, yet others hold you responsible for it. It's a frustrating feeling when you can't control an outcome you want. In the first case, you may be tempted to cheat out of fear. In the second case, you may be tempted to cheat out of greed.

Some examples where you might think you control the outcome, but don't:

- Your spouse. Whether you want your spouse to change or not change, prepare to be disappointed.
- Your kids. You may do everything you can to raise them into certain types, but they will be who they are.
- Everyone else you know. The best you can do is to be a good role model and hope some of it rubs off.
- Winning any competition. You can control your play; you can't control others' play. Some days someone else just plays better.

- Your work. Even if you're self-employed, there may be unstoppable outside forces that can destroy a business.
- Your investments. You can set aside the necessary amount and choose appropriate investments, but how they will perform is up to the market, not you.
- Your expiration date. You can live a healthy lifestyle, but fate is never far away.

Knowing you actually control few of your desired outcomes can be frustrating. It can make it easy to give up on the input side. But your inputs still have more of an effect on your desired outcomes than any other factor. There may not be a perfect correlation between inputs and outcomes, but the correlation is still high.

Knowing you control inputs but not outcomes can be liberating. That knowledge reduces the temptation to cheat. Knowing you control inputs but not outcomes frees you to do your best without worrying about being the best.

THE TWO YOUS

In the movie *The Shawshank Redemption*, Morgan Freeman plays Red, a man who has spent forty years in prison for a murder he committed at age twenty. Red is up for parole for the umpteenth time. Whenever he's been asked at these hearings if he's sorry for his crime, he's told the parole board what he thought they wanted to hear. This time he speaks from the heart:

*"**Not a day goes by I don't feel regret**, and not because I'm in here or because you think I should. I look back on myself the way I was – a stupid kid who did that terrible crime. I wish I could talk sense to him. Tell him how things are. But I can't. **That kid's long gone and this old man is all that's left.** And I have to live with that."*

You're unlikely to do anything that will land you in prison for forty years. But you are likely to do many things you will regret later in life.

There are two yous – present-you and future-you. Just like Red, future-you will pay the penalty for what present-you does or doesn't do.

Another actor, John Barrymore, said, "A man is not old until regrets take the place of dreams." By that definition, one can be old without having lived a long time. **The more things you do that create regret and crush dreams, the faster you become old.**

You've probably heard the old saying – "Eat, drink, and be merry, for tomorrow we die." The saying is based on verses from the books of Ecclesiastes and Isaiah. Many people live by this motto. If you're actually going to die tomorrow, this is excellent advice. If you're not, tomorrow you'll just be fatter, hungover, and depressed.

If you're wondering if you're the type of person whose future-you will be punished by present-you, there are ways of telling. If you binge eat or drink, present-you is getting the pleasure while future-you is getting the pain. If you buy things on impulse even though you don't have the money, present-you is sticking future-you with the bill. If you ignore saving for retirement because you'd rather have a good time now, present-you is stealing from future-you. **If you know an action has long-term consequences and you do it anyway, you're guilty of elder abuse in the future.**

If you've already experienced the consequences of a past action, you can't claim ignorance if you do it again. Many of your actions have long-term consequences you haven't yet experienced. In those cases, you may be more guilty of ignorance than of future-you abuse.

This ignorance is partly due to a lack of imagination. It's hard to imagine being older. A single twenty-five-year-old struggles to imagine being forty-five, married with kids, a mortgage, and a boring job. To imagine being seventy-five, sick, broke, alone, and living in public housing is asking a lot. But it's necessary because not being able to imagine it makes it more likely to happen. **If you ignore future-you, a poor, unhealthy, unhappy future-you is your default scenario.**

Taking care of future-you requires present-you to make some sacrifices; there's no avoiding it. It may mean staying home and studying instead of going out with friends. It may mean not taking a trip to fund your 401(k) plan at work. It may mean getting serious about losing weight. All of these ask present-you to give up something now to benefit future-you. **Sacrifices made in the present pay future dividends. Sacrifices not made in the present exact future penalties.**

Health and wealth are two important areas of focus. Poor health habits in the present don't just create future health issues. The cost of trying to restore health in the future can destroy wealth.

Examples of poor health choices are all around you. People who smoked, drank, didn't exercise etc. pay the price in old age, assuming they get there. Their care also exacts a price from the rest of us.

Poor financial choices may not be as obvious as poor health choices, but they can be more devastating. If you think money is important when you're young, it's nothing compared to when you're old. When you're old, you can do fewer things for yourself, including making money. **A lack of money in old age makes everything harder when you're least able to handle it.**

You may not be able to create a conversation between future-you and present-you, but it's worth trying. Ask future-you what present-you is doing that will penalize future-you. You may already know many of the answers.

If you can't manage that conversation, ask some older people what they would want to tell their younger selves. What advice would they give? What would they say was most important to do, or not do? What past actions had the biggest rewards and the biggest consequences? Use their experiences to guide you.

Future-you will be your own creation. Work to create a future-you who can live in dignity, someone who is worthy of respect. And **a future-you worthy of respect begins with respect from present-you.**

THE MONEY FOLLOWS THE MISSION

If you've ever researched a company or interviewed for a job, you've certainly come across a mission statement or two. Most of them come across as a car wreck of corporate-speak. They could apply to almost any organization. There's even a web site called *Mission Statement Generator*. It offers a menu of pre-packaged mission statements, as well as lists of adjectives, adverbs, verbs, and nouns to "customize" your mission statement. Here's just one example of their product:

Our vision is to continue to collaboratively synergize market-driven intellectual capital while continuing to synergistically administrate enterprise-wide leadership skills to meet customers' needs.

You're probably also familiar with TED Talks. TED began in 1984 as a conference converging Technology, Entertainment, and Design (hence, TED). Today, TED Talks cover a wide variety of topics in more than 100 languages. TED's mission statement is: *Spread Ideas*.

In two words **you know what TED is all about. You also know it's an organization you can probably support. That's the mission of the mission statement.**

Do you have a mission statement? Do you even have a mission? You'll want both. **Your mission will be the sail that pulls you through life in general and through rough waters in particular. Your mission statement will be how you convey your mission to others so they will enthusiastically offer their support.**

A good mission statement:
- Uses understandable language
- Is emotionally stirring
- Communicates "Why", not just "What" or "How"

51

- Is a single, concise, powerful sentence
- Sounds good when spoken
- Is memorable, actionable, and specific.

You will likely have several personal missions throughout your life. Most of these may require moral, rather than financial support from others. **You will also have professional missions. Those will require financial support.**

People don't give to need; they give to vision. Giving to need can become endless. People are willing to give based on temporary need. But if need is seen as endless, or if there's no plan to overcome need, they won't continue giving.

Even your strongest supporters won't support you indefinitely just because you have a need. They need to know their support is leading to something better. Your mission is the something better, and your mission statement tells them about it. **It assures people their financial support is not the end, but the means to an end.**

One of your first professional missions is to get the necessary education to enable you to fulfill future professional missions. To that end, you pursue degrees, get technical training, and serve internships. Most people need the support of others to fulfill even this first mission.

If you're seeking financial support, the "Why" is more important than the "What". For example, you may need money for tuition, but you would tell supporters about your plans to use your degree to become more self-sufficient and make the world a better place through your chosen profession. If you were seeking seed money for a new business, you wouldn't talk about the need to rent space or buy equipment. You would talk about how the products or services you will produce will have a positive impact on people's lives. **If people believe in your mission, in your "Why", they will give more freely. They will also leave the details, the "What, How, When, and Where", up to you.**

One professional mission that isn't verbalized (but is always there) is the mission to make money. It isn't verbalized because **money should not be the cause of a mission, but rather the effect of a mission accomplished.**

Few people take the time and make the effort to develop a personal or professional mission statement. They don't do it because few people have a personal or professional mission to make a statement about. Taking the time and making this effort has several benefits. It helps you to **clarify** what is most important to you and it helps you to **concentrate** your efforts on what's important. It also makes it easier to gain support – moral as well as financial - for your mission.

There's a lot of competition out there for limited funds. Many people competing for financial support aren't good communicators. They may have noble missions, but if they can't articulate those missions to the people with money, they won't get any. If you have a mission people can support and you can articulate it with an effective mission statement, you will be way ahead of the competition. And the money will follow your mission.

GOAL-TENDING

"If your only goal is to become rich, you will never achieve it."

-John D. Rockefeller Sr.

John D. Rockefeller knew something about becoming rich. He was the founder of Standard Oil Company, which, at its peak, controlled 90% of all oil in the U.S. Adjusted for inflation, his fortune upon his death in 1937 stood at $336 *billion*, more than the five richest people in the world today combined.

Rockefeller's statement is true for a couple of reasons. First, **becoming rich in any endeavor is, or should be, a by-product, not a goal.** Riches, honestly made, come from providing something of value to others. If customers will buy enough of, and pay enough for, what you provide, you can become rich.

Second, how do you define rich? It's a sliding scale. **We frequently think of being rich in relative terms.** Even poor Americans are considered rich by the standards of many countries. We compare our wealth to others to determine if we're rich. As we become richer, we keep changing our reference group. If we hang out with richer and richer people, we feel less and less rich.

While we frequently judge our wealth compared to others, we also judge our wealth by what we don't yet have. If your net worth were ten-thousand dollars, you would classify rich as having half-a-million. Once you got there, the bar would move to one million; then five; then ten; then fifty. You might never consider yourself rich because your definition of rich would keep changing. People frequently realize how rich they were only after they lose their fortune.

The purpose of this lesson is not to discourage you from becoming rich. The purpose is to encourage you to set goals you can achieve to become rich if you want to.

If your mission is your sail, your goals are your rudder. Goals, like a rudder, keep you going in the right direction.

In recent years, American business has embraced the concept of **SMART** goals. The acronym stands for *Specific, Measurable, Achievable, Realistic, and Time-targeted*. The concept of SMART goals contends that specific, challenging goals increase performance more than goals that are not.

SMART goals affect outcomes in four ways:
- They focus attention to goal-relevant activities.
- They increase effort if a goal exceeds current levels.
- Pursuing a goal increases persistence through setbacks.
- They can change long-term behavior for the better.

Imagine you're a runner on your school's track team. Your specialty is the one-mile run. If your coach set a goal to "run faster", how would you respond? Is one second faster sufficient? Are ten seconds insufficient? You need more guidance.

Instead of telling you to run faster, your coach makes this your goal: run one-mile in competition in less than 5 minutes before the end of the season in two months. You now know exactly what you have to do. This goal is *specific* (one-mile run), *measurable* (less than five minutes), and *time-targeted* (by the end of the season).

What's still unknown is if this goal is *achievable* and *realistic*. A good coach would set goals that were both, but that were also a challenge. **Goals that are too easy**

don't enable you to reach your potential. Goals that are too hard may discourage you from even trying.

While coaches and others may set goals for you, **you have to embrace a goal if you're going to reach it.** Parents often set goals for a child that the child doesn't embrace. The parents are then disappointed when the child doesn't achieve those goals. Once you embrace a general goal (being the best runner you can be), others can help you with the specifics. Other people, like parents and coaches, may actually be the better judges of your potential.

Some people think that setting small goals leads to less success because you aren't pushing yourself. That's not the case. Small goals that get accomplished spur us on. Large goals always seem to be over the horizon. **The positive reinforcement from achieving small goals enables continued progress toward larger goals.**

If you were a recent college graduate and were told you will need $4 million in order to retire comfortably at age 67, that goal might seem so impossible you would never even try. On the other hand, if you were told that investing 12% of your income in the S&P 500 every paycheck between now and 67 would get you to $4 million, that would seem quite doable. It was a matter of taking one enormous goal and breaking it down into about 2,000 little ones.

Goals should lift you up, but not hold you back. Goals that are set too low can hold you back. In saving for retirement, you might find you can easily save 15% of your income. If so, you need to raise your goal. **Goals should have enough flexibility that you can raise them to keep you challenged and lower them if they're impossibly high.**

The path to achieving your goals will not be a straight line. We typically start out with great enthusiasm, excited by this new challenge. We also end with great enthusiasm, knowing victory is at hand. It's the long slog in the middle that can undo everything. Realize there will be setbacks along the way. Realize your enthusiasm will wane when you're a long way from the beginning and the end. Realizing these conditions will enable you to face them head on and overcome them. **To achieve most of your goals, the only tool you really need is persistence.**

Goals involving money are easy to make because of money's characteristics. Money is very *specific* and *measurable*. Money can be very *time-targeted* because savings and growth rates can be precisely calculated.

Goals involving money also need to be *achievable* and *realistic*, which are judgment calls. Whatever your money goal, you can accurately calculate what needs to be done to achieve it. The only question that remains is - are you willing to do what needs to be done?

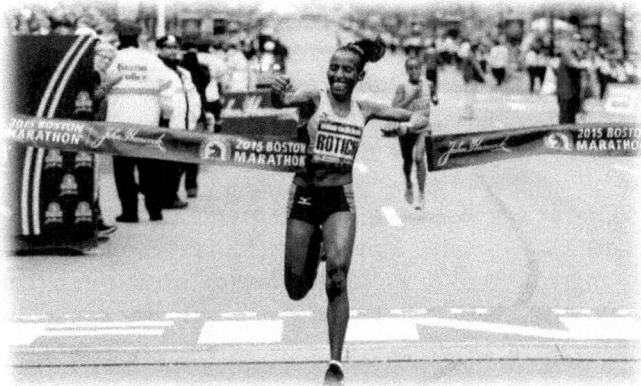

WEALTH'S NOT-SO-MAGIC FORMULA

If you're looking for some quick and easy ways to get rich, *Bloomberg Business* has offered these possibilities:
- Be born rich.
- Inherit a fortune.
- Marry rich.
- Divorce a rich person.
- Have an affair with a bigwig.
- Win the lottery.
- Discover oil on your property.
- Unearth gold with a metal detector.
- Find treasure in your basement.
- Get lucky at a yard sale.
- Catch a record-breaking home run ball.
- Your bank adds extra zeroes to your account.

Most of these are possible; none are remotely probable. If there were a high-probability method of quick and easy (and legal) riches, it would be the world's worst-kept secret.

If you want to get rich quickly and easily, the best way may be selling people ways to get rich quickly and easily. There will never be a shortage of people looking for shortcuts to wealth. The quicker and easier the method, the more people will be attracted to it. But any method you may devise will almost certainly be deemed a fraud by the courts, so proceed cautiously.

There are two essential ingredients to creating wealth. Any wealth formula that doesn't include these two ingredients is a transfer of wealth, or worse, a theft of wealth. **These two essential ingredients are *Work* and *Delayed Gratification.*** Any claim that wealth can be created without these two ingredients is a lie.

Most people are willing to do the work. Most people aren't willing to do the delayed gratification. Delaying gratification requires discipline and a long-term perspective, two traits in short supply.

Delaying gratification is difficult under the best of circumstances. There are many demands and temptations in the present to spend money. Delaying gratification cuts against the grain of our consumer culture. Ours is also not a patient culture. We are always looking for faster ways to do something, especially getting rich.

Work creates money, but delayed gratification turns it into wealth. Delayed gratification requires self-control. Delayed gratification is also more than a wealth-building skill; it's a survival skill.

Even if your goal isn't wealth, delayed gratification is essential when you're young to avoid poverty when you're old. Unless you pull off one of the quick and easy ways to get rich listed earlier, **the money you will spend when you don't work is the money you didn't spend when you did work.**

Delayed gratification protects something of value from being consumed in the present. It provides the opportunity to grow it into something more substantial in the future.

Here is the not-so-magic formula for creating wealth: Work/Earn/Invest/Repeat. That's it. It's not complicated, merely hard, which is why so few people are wealthy.

WORK. You will almost certainly never become rich by your labor alone. But **your labors, mental or physical, are the seeds of wealth.** In the 21st century, mental labor dominates. Even if you work with your hands, you have to work with your head, too. Your hands can also be replaced easier than your head.

EARN. If you're going to work, you want to earn all you're worth. That does not mean you settle for the highest-paying job. You want to earn a higher income and earn it for a long time. **Your best chance to earn more and for longer is to work at something you both enjoy and are good at.** The less your work feels like work, the better you will do it, the longer you will want to do it, and the more people will pay you to do it.

INVEST. This is where delayed gratification comes in. One definition of *invest* is to spend or utilize for future advantage or benefit. **Investing requires giving up something good now for something better later**; that's pretty much the definition and purpose of delayed gratification.

Investing is a broad term here. It can be money in stocks; it can also be money in your own business or money in self-improvement, like further education. It's also the investment of time. Investing time for a better future usually requires sacrificing some pleasures in the present.

REPEAT. A process is an ongoing series of actions. Building wealth is a process. **Maintaining the process of building wealth will be easier if you make a habit of it.** Getting started is the biggest challenge in creating a habit. Make the effort to start the process and develop it into a habit. It won't take long before work-earn-invest becomes a habit you don't even have to think about.

For centuries, people have sought a magic formula for wealth. Those people were often lazy or impatient or both. There is no magic formula, but there is a formula. It's amazingly simple, incredibly effective, and anyone can do it. Anyone can do it, but few will. Will you?

FROM NOT-RICH TO RICH

The rich are probably the most reviled *and* the most envied people on earth. Oddly, many of those who most revile the rich would quickly join their ranks if given the chance. False and negative stereotypes of the rich don't help. The not-rich also believe they would never become the stereotypical rich person if they became rich.

In truth, the rich are different from the stereotypes. They're also different from the not-rich, but not in ways you might not think. If you want to go from not-rich to rich, you'll want to know how the rich are different.

The rich prefer opportunity over security. Opportunities almost always involve risks, but the rich know that risk and reward move in tandem. The rich are comfortable being uncomfortable. The rich rarely work for someone else. At some point, they made the decision that the security of a paycheck was not worth losing the opportunity for an unlimited income. The rich will give up a floor of security to remove a ceiling on opportunity.

The rich live below their means – always. Even before they became rich, the soon-to-be-rich saved and invested a large percentage of their incomes. That habit didn't change when they eventually became rich; it merely got easier. Even after they become rich, the rich continue to live below their means as a tribute of sorts. They know that living below their means was the single biggest reason they became rich, so they appreciate its power and continue its practice.

The rich don't climb the ladder; they own it. Even if you're well on your way to the top in the corporate world, you're still working for someone else. The CEOs of the biggest corporations still have bosses – the board of directors. The board of directors is made up of the biggest stockholders of the corporation. They don't need to work for money because their money works for them. If you work for someone else, you let others tell you what you will do and how much you will be paid for it. The rich refuse to accept such restrictions.

The rich choose their friends carefully. People gravitate to the level of their associates. Most people have an income equal to the average of their three closest friends. The rich learned early on to gravitate upward. They began associating with people they admired – not because of their wealth but because of their work ethic and their record of success that led to their wealth. The soon-to-be-rich learned what it really took to be successful and they put it to use in their own lives.

The rich know that work is more about learning than earning. The not-rich can be persuaded to change jobs for a small pay raise. Those job changes are often lateral moves that don't provide the opportunity to learn new skills. Especially in the early years of their careers, the rich looked for opportunities to learn the most, not earn the most. They then parlayed that knowledge into the career or business that helped make them rich. The rich also recognize that learning never ends because you can never know all you need to know.

The rich prefer having money more than the things money can buy. Few things that can be bought with money appreciate in value. Most things we buy depreciate quickly. Money that's invested can grow. Money that's readily available can be tapped when an opportunity to buy something that will appreciate in value comes along. The rich value the opportunity *and* security that ready money affords them.

The rich focus on their earning power first. Saving is good. Investing is good. Living below your means is good. The rich realize the more you earn, the more you can save and invest and the easier it is to live below your means. They devote huge amounts of time and energy figuring out how to maximize their earning power.

The rich are less emotional about money. That statement may not seem logical, but logical is what the rich are when it comes to money. When the stock market is booming and prices are high and everyone is frantically buying, who's doing the selling? The rich. When the stock market tanks and everyone is frantically selling, who's doing the buying? The rich again. The rich make money off the not-rich because the not-rich are emotional about money while the rich are logical. The rich are logical about money; they're passionate about it too, and that's a potent combination.

The rich set audacious goals. One young man set a goal of building a company that would be worth $100 million in twenty years. Another young man set a goal of earning $100,000 in ten years. One goal was audacious; the other was realistic. The second young man would probably reach his goal. The first young man might fail miserably at his goal. His company might only be worth $20 million after twenty years. Even so, he would have grown his wealth by a million dollars a year over that time. Not bad for a failure. The risk is not in setting goals that are too high; it's in setting goals that aren't high enough.

The rich know that work alone will not make you rich. Unless you're a famous athlete or entertainer, income from your work is limited. The rich know two more things. The first thing is that their money can earn more than they can. Money never sleeps, and it's always out there making more money. One way to know you're rich is you can't earn as much money in a year as your money can.

The second thing the rich know is that it's better to make a small amount from a lot of people than to try to make a lot from you alone. One reason most rich people are business owners is they make something from each person who works for them. If you own a business that employs 1,000 people and you make $1,000 a year from each employee's labor, you've made a million dollars that year.

The rich live in the future. They have ideas. They have vision. Their biggest pleasure in the present is working to make the future better for themselves and others. The rich like living in the future because they're optimistic about the future. They're optimistic about the future because they plan to have a positive impact on it. Even if they have it good now, the rich believe the best is yet to come.

The rich believe in themselves. Success begets success, but success needs a starting point. At some point in the early years, the rich made a bet on themselves and they worked to make the bet pay off. That first success led to future successes. The rich know the odds are with them when they try something new. Even if they fail, they will learn from the experience and be more likely to succeed in their next venture.

The rich believe in more than themselves. Most of the rich marry only once. Most of the rich practice a faith. Most of the rich have strong ties with family and friends. Most of the rich know that, while being rich is better than being poor, it doesn't make them better people. And the rich also know, even more than the not-rich, that the best things in life can't be bought.

GOING THE DISTANCE

Throughout most of history, humans practiced *persistence hunting* - a group of hunters would literally run their prey to death. Our survival as a species depended on our ability to pursue prey, even fast prey, until it collapsed. It was the most efficient form of hunting until firearms appeared.

Persistence hunters never knew if they were going to run 10, 20, or 50 miles on a hunt. The hunt ended when the prey collapsed. The human body evolved incredible endurance to undertake such hunts.

This evolution is still with us. Almost no animal can run for as long or as far as humans. A world-class marathon runner can run over 26 miles at an average speed of over 12 miles per hour. We not only run long distances, we can run for decades. Marathon runners in their sixties are often faster than they were in their teens.

Aesop's fable of the tortoise and the hare offers many timeless lessons. Persistence is better than speed. Slow and steady wins the race. Talent without discipline is useless. Run your own race.

Imagine you're training for a marathon. You find a 10-minute-mile pace will enable you to finish the 26.2 mile race. What would happen if you ran the first third of the race at an 8-minute-mile pace? Around the 9-mile mark you'd be nearly 20 minutes ahead of your target. You'd be feeling pretty good at that point.

That fast pace would start taking its toll soon after. About halfway through the race, your per-mile pace would be slower than your 10-minute target. Before you finished 20 miles, you would "hit the wall". At that point, your system would be depleted and you couldn't take another step. You sacrificed endurance for speed. It cost you any chance of accomplishing your goal, of reaching the finish line.

Meeting your financial goals, especially building wealth, requires endurance, persistence, and discipline. **Meeting your financial goals doesn't require speed because it's not a sprint; it's a marathon.**

Meeting your financial goals is a marathon, but your only competition is the clock (actually, the calendar). **Your financial goals have nothing to do with anyone else's financial goals or performance.** A major reason people fail to meet their goals is they get competitive. They also let others set the pace.

If your financial goals are a marathon, your goal for the marathon is not to win. Winning isn't a goal because you're not in competition with anyone else. **Your goal is to finish the marathon.** Finishing is accomplishment enough. You won't finish this marathon if you start sprinting in the middle trying to catch someone else.

Humans require endurance far more than speed. Our lives are long. We pay few penalties for lack of speed. We pay major penalties for lack of endurance. Doing well financially in your twenties won't mean much in your sixties if you don't maintain the effort through your thirties, forties, and fifties. The hare took an early lead, but then slacked off. The tortoise maintained a consistent pace.

The value of endurance over speed shows up early in school. There are no prizes for being the first one to complete a test. Earning a high school diploma is a thirteen-year marathon itself. Those who don't complete it face severe financial penalties later. Employers say a major reason they recruit college graduates is their degree demonstrates they have endurance, persistence, and the ability to finish what they started.

The creation of wealth takes time. Overnight wealth is almost always the result of a transfer of wealth, not the creation of wealth. Sometimes the wealth was transferred legally, such as by inheritance. Sometimes it's transferred illegally, such as by fraud.

The desire for quick riches leads to shortcuts. A business may overcharge customers or produce inferior merchandise. A taxpayer may cheat on his taxes. An investor may borrow heavily to play the market. There is no shortage of shortcuts.

Shortcuts can't be sustained for very long. Customers leave. The IRS runs an audit. The stock market takes all your money, including the money you borrowed.

Shortcuts don't lead to your goal. You end up having to backtrack to the regular path. **Shortcuts don't save time or make money – they exact a penalty of both.**

If your goal were to retire at 50, you'd have to make a choice – make extraordinary sacrifices or take shortcuts. Sacrifice is hard and shortcuts don't work. If neither were true, then everyone would be retired at 50.

Investments that tout speed over endurance end up giving neither. A legitimate long-term investment might double your money in eight or nine years. An investment claiming it can double your money in two years is either a fraud or so risky it will likely to be worthless by then.

Two of the biggest financial goals people have are a worry-free retirement and something to leave for children and grandchildren. You will likely have similar goals. These goals get met late in life, but they require effort throughout life. See these goals as a marathon and not a sprint if you hope to reach them.

CHECKBOOK EXPOSE'

If you were developing a serious relationship, would a Checkbook Expose' help you, or hurt you?

If you were running for elected office, would a Checkbook Expose' gain votes, or lose votes for you?

If you were in the job market, would a Checkbook Expose' get you hired, or fired?

Checkbook Expose' is an expression for publicizing your spending habits and money management skills. Even if you never write a check, you have bank and credit card statements that tell your money story. For many, it's a story they would not want told.

A Chief Financial Officer (CFO) is the person responsible for a company's finances. As controller, the CFO presents accurate information about the *past* to stockholders. As treasurer, the CFO is responsible for the corporation's *present* financial condition and use of funds. As a strategist, the CFO is responsible for identifying the best uses of resources in the *future*.

You are the CFO of You, Inc.

As CFO, you are responsible for your financial past, present, and future. You can't change your financial past, but any past problems must be fixed in the present. What you do in the present determines your financial future. Also, negative actions have an impact faster than positive actions.

Money is valued by everyone, and almost everyone feels they don't have enough. **Because of money's importance and scarcity, how people use their money says more about their priorities than anything else.** A Checkbook Expose' lets everyone know what's most important to you – more than anything you might say.

What would a Checkbook Expose' reveal about you? The first thing it might reveal is your ability to live within your means. Are you frequently overdrawn in your bank accounts? That could indicate poor record-keeping at a minimum; it could also indicate spending that's out of control. The severe bank charges for being overdrawn only compound the problem.

You may not be overdrawing your bank account, but does your credit card balance continue to rise each month? If so, it's a signal that expenses are exceeding income. As the outstanding balance rises, more money each month goes to paying interest instead of principal, worsening the problem.

One of the most important responsibilities of a CFO is cash flow management. Cash flow is the life blood of a corporation. A corporation or an individual that has more cash going out than coming in will bleed to death before long. Every CFO knows **positive cash flow leads to wealth; negative cash flow leads to bankruptcy.**

Beyond the basic money management of cash flow, a Checkbook Expose' can reveal important details about you. What do you spend your money on every month? Do you spend a lot on entertainment, but have a car that is unreliable? Does spending on cigarettes and alcohol leave less money for healthy food? Do you take nice vacations, but don't have needed insurance? Every good CFO knows how to prioritize. **The first priority is business always comes before pleasure.**

Your Checkbook Expose' reveals your spending priorities; **it also reveals your values.** Did more of your money go to vices than to charity? Did you spend money on others, or just on yourself? Did you support causes you believe in with your money as well as your mouth? CFOs know profit is important, but so are other things.

In a corporation, the CFO often has to be the voice of dispassionate reason. The CEO and board of directors may get excited about a merger or acquisition. Their excitement can blind them to potential pitfalls. They may not look closely into the financials of their potential partner. The CFO must perform due diligence to make sure the board clearly sees what they're getting into.

The CFO also makes sure business associates are financially solid and well-respected. The corporation does not want its credit or reputation damaged by poorly managed suppliers, customers, or other associates.

You have the same responsibilities as CFO of You, Inc. Your merger may involve wedding vows. **A marriage should be a merger of equals; it should not be an acquisition.** It should not be a financially responsible person acquiring the financial baggage of a financially irresponsible person. If you're a financially responsible CFO, **you have a duty to perform due diligence before merging with anyone.**

If you're not a financially responsible person, you'll have problems with any merger. Merge with a financially responsible person and you'll have to make major improvements or risk ruining the marriage. Merge with an equally irresponsible person and you'll likely drag each other down further.

You also have a responsibility as CFO to associate only with financially responsible people. You may not have legal liability for financially irresponsible friends, but they can still create a mess for you.

Would your Checkbook Expose' inspire confidence from others? Would others want to associate with you? Would the trends be positive?

Or would a Checkbook Expose' reveal you're not qualified to be your own CFO?

RISK AND REWARD

Go back in time more than 70,000 years. You're a homo sapien living in the Great Rift Valley of east Africa, about the only place on earth your species currently occupies. Persistent drought is making it harder to survive there. One day your leader indicates it's time to look for another place to live. So you start walking.

You walk just a few miles a day. Sometimes you encounter another species, Neanderthals. They're not glad to see you. You encounter new plants and animals. Every day brings new and unexpected risks.

You will only live to be thirty, but over the next 3,000 generations your descendants will travel to every continent, becoming the planet's dominant species.

Humans became the dominant species because we were risk-takers. It's in your genes. It's in your nerves, too. Specifically, your nerve cells emit dopamine, a chemical we really like. It's dopamine that gives us a sense of satisfaction when we accomplish a task. And the riskier the task, the bigger the dopamine hit.

For some people, the rush of dopamine is enough to engage in risky behavior. For the more practical of us, we need more tangible rewards, too.

People spend a good part of their lives evaluating risk and reward. **Nearly every action a person takes with benefits or consequences begins by evaluating the risk-reward tradeoff.** These evaluations can determine the course of our lives more than anything else we do, so it's important to do them right.

Of course, there are some people who choose to ignore risk and see only rewards. And there are those who seek risk for its own sake. They tend to get thinned from the herd early.

When we think of rewards, we think first of financial gain. **Rewards can also include the absence of financial loss.** In fact, when faced with the prospect of financial loss, people engage in riskier behavior than they do for a similar financial gain.

If you were given $100, and then offered a double-or-nothing coin flip, you would likely turn it down and keep the $100. But if you had to give up $100, and then were offered a coin flip to get your $100 back or pay another $100, you likely accept that risk. **If it will feel like punishment, we'll take greater risks to avoid it.**

Everyone evaluates risk and reward differently. Your personality plays a big part in how you evaluate them. In general, an optimist is likely to underestimate risk and overestimate reward. A pessimist is likely to do the opposite.

Previous experiences also affect our evaluations. A good experience (maybe just good luck) can lead to underestimating risk. A bad experience (maybe just bad luck) can lead to overestimating risk.

It's easy to look at a situation and see only the rewards but not the risks. You may read about a successful, famous, rich entrepreneur. You want those rewards, so you plan to quit your job and follow in that person's footsteps. But you didn't read the fine print. Your successful entrepreneur may have had several previous failures, including bankruptcy. There were years of struggles and many times when the new enterprise was on life support. You also forgot that for every successful entrepreneur like this one, there were dozens or hundreds who went down in flames.

It's important to honestly evaluate both risk and reward. It's also important to know which one is doing the driving. Risk tolerance is the horse. The reward is the cart. The size of the cart you can pull is determined by the size of the horse. In other words, **the reward you get is determined by your risk tolerance, not the other way around.** You can't expect a small horse to pull a big cart. You can't ratchet up your risk tolerance simply because you want a bigger reward, either.

Our risk tolerance can be hard to gauge. When the risk isn't obvious, we don't give it much thought and can overestimate our risk tolerance. But when the risk is staring us in the face, we find out just how brave we are. In a bull market, many investors are fearless. Then a bear market comes and their investments drop by 25%. Many of those fearless investors flee the market like they were being chased by an actual bear.

More reward always requires taking on more risk. Free markets make sure that correlation always exists. There is a price to be paid for more reward – that price is more risk. The markets give nothing away.

If you've ever been offered an investment promising high returns with no-risk, it's a scam. It is simply impossible in a free market system to get something for nothing honestly, which is what is being promised with high returns and no risk. While scammers promise high reward-no risk, in reality it's no reward-high risk.

While more reward requires more risk, more risk does not automatically mean more reward. Activities like bungee jumping and Russian Roulette are high risk, but the only possible reward is the rush from not dying.

A low risk tolerance is often the product of fear. Fear is most often the product of ignorance.

Knowledge reduces fear. The best way to increase your risk tolerance is to better understand the actual risks.

Many people don't invest in stocks because they see them as too risky. They watch the markets go up and down or they hear stories of people who lost money in stocks and they conclude the risk is too high for the reward.

Stocks can be risky in the short-term. No one knows what the markets will do from one week or month to the next. Short term market swings often have little to do with what's going on in the world. However, over longer periods of time, the markets become much more predictable and far less risky. And stocks are supposed to be long-term investments, not short-term gambles.

Market volatility is not the same as risk of loss. Knowing the difference can raise risk tolerance and the rewards that can follow. The bigger risks for many investors are "safe" investments that will never grow enough to meet their owners' needs later in life.

Whether it's investments, careers, or relationships, we all try to balance risk and reward. The better you can look objectively at both, the better your chances of getting the balance right for you.

LOANERS AND OWNERS

George Lucas of *Star Wars* fame is a very rich man. How he got to be so rich is a lesson for us all.

In 1973, Lucas directed *American Graffiti*. It was a big hit, and Lucas was paid $150,000 for directing. He was entitled to a salary of $500,000 to direct his next movie, *Star Wars*. 20th Century Fox Studios had doubts about the movie's commercial potential. Lucas had no such doubts. Lucas went to the studio with a proposition. He would keep his salary at $150,000, but he would retain all the merchandising rights and the rights to any sequels. Since the studio saw little potential in either merchandising or sequels for this movie, they quickly accepted the offer.

Through 2015, the sequels and merchandising rights Lucas bought for $350,000 in reduced salary have generated over $30 billion in revenue. Lucas' personal net worth is conservatively estimated at over $8 billion, almost all of it *Star Wars* money. By ***owning*** his movies instead of merely ***loaning*** his talent to them, Lucas turned each dollar he gave up on the front end into more than twenty-thousand dollars.

Investing can be broken down into two broad categories – loaning and owning. There are pros and cons to each. Whether it's better to be a loaner or an owner depends on the investment itself, your goals for the investment, as well as your own personality and personal goals.

Loaners typically invest in bonds. Bonds are used by corporations and governments to borrow money. When you purchase a bond, you loan money to the issuer of the bond. Bonds are issued with a face value, the amount typically paid for the bond. The bond also has a stated interest rate it pays and a time until the bond matures.

As an example, you purchase a $1,000 10-year bond from ABC Corp. that pays 6% annual interest. You pay $1,000 for the bond. Each year for the next ten years, ABC Corp. will pay you $60 interest (6% of $1,000). At the end of ten years, ABC Corp. repays you the original $1,000.

The pros of being a bondholder are you stand near the front of the line to get paid. The issuer has to pay all their bondholders before they can give any money to the owners. You also know how much you will get each year and when you'll get it. If you need steady income from investments, bonds can help provide that income.

The cons are you will never get more than is stated on the bond. Your $1,000 6% bond will pay you $60 per year and never a penny more. When the bond matures after ten years, you will get your $1,000 back and not a penny more. If interest rates rise and you have to sell your bond before the ten years are up, the market price for the bond will be less than $1,000. Also, if the issuer of the bond goes out of business, you might lose all your money.

Owners typically invest in stocks. When you own stock in a corporation, you own a piece of that corporation. Your shares of stock entitle you to vote for the board of directors for the corporation.

The pros of being a stockholder are you get all the profits after the obligations to everyone else have been paid. Some of the profits may be paid directly to you as dividends. Some of the profits will be retained by the corporation for future growth. That growth will help

76

raise the value of your stock. The rise in the stock's value isn't taxable until you sell it, either.

The cons are you stand at the end of the line to get paid. If there are no profits, you get nothing. If the company is losing money and falls behind on payments to bondholders and others, you won't get anything until all those debts are caught up. The value of your stock can go up and down a lot – usually a lot more than bonds do. Sometimes those price swings have nothing to do with the corporation but are caused by swings in the stock market itself. Finally, all your money is at risk. If the company declares bankruptcy, your stock can become worthless. Even if it doesn't declare bankruptcy, if the corporation isn't likely to make a profit, the market may determine the stock is worthless. A stock's price is determined mostly by that corporation's expected future profits.

As an investment, a corporation is either good enough or it isn't, whether we're talking loaning or owning. If the corporation is good enough to loan to, they should be good enough to own, too. If you don't think they're good enough to own, you shouldn't loan to them, either.

Whether you're a loaner or an owner will depend on your needs and goals. If you need current income, bonds usually pay more in income, though they also don't grow like stocks can. If your goal is long-term growth, stocks have a better chance of providing that. Most investors own some combination of stocks and bonds because they need some combination of growth, income, and diversification.

Finally, your personality can determine whether you should be a loaner or an owner, or at least how much of each you should be. Stocks typically have more risks than bonds. Because of that higher risk, stocks typically have higher rewards, too. You may like the thought of higher rewards, but if your personality doesn't handle risk well, you may panic and sell your stocks at the worst time. Even if you hang on, you may make yourself sick worrying about your investments.

Being a loaner offers greater security than being an owner. Being an owner offers greater opportunity than being a loaner. Everyone would like ample helpings of security *and* opportunity, but one comes at the expense of the other. Whether you're a loaner or an owner, and in what proportion, will be determined by your needs, goals, and what you can live with.

MARKET MOVERS

Various studies over the years have shown that economists' predictions are wrong more than half the time. Their failure rate makes them less useful for forecasting than a coin toss, yet they still make forecasts. How can so many experts be wrong so often?

Economists are rational thinkers. What they don't take into account when they make predictions is how irrational humans can be. Our irrationality makes predicting what we'll do a coin toss at best.

It's been said that **in the short-term, the stock market is a voting mechanism; in the long-term, it's a weighing mechanism.** This description reflects the human aspect of markets. In the short-term, people vote their money in or out of various markets. Which way they vote is often based on their emotions of the moment. In the long-term, the markets measure the actual value of investments. This discrepancy makes markets unpredictable in the short-term, but quite reliable in the long-term.

Whether the product being sold is stocks, bonds, oil, or real estate, **price is affected greatly in the short-term by supply and demand.** When the economy is strong and stocks are up (the weighing part), demand for stocks also rises, pushing prices even higher (the voting part). When the economy is weak and stocks are down (the weighing part), people move from stocks to the relative safety of bonds. They push stock prices even lower and raise bond prices (the voting part).

In the long-term, the supply and demand for stocks and bonds balances at particular price levels. When demand is higher, the price level will be higher until supply catches up. When demand drops, supply shrinks until price levels rebound. **The ability to adjust supply to demand helps make long-term predictions more reliable.** Many people try to make quick money betting on the effects of short-term imbalances; most fail.

What everyone wants is a good return on investment. **What determines a "good" return is subjective.** A good return for a risk-free government bond may be nothing more than the rate of inflation. In bad times, a good return might only mean not losing value. A good return for an S&P 500 company might be five percent more than government bonds, to account for the higher risk. A good return for an even riskier investment, like a start-up company, might be three or four times the return for an S&P 500 company.

The quality of an investment's return is measured against investment alternatives; it is also bounded by your risk tolerance. **Whether you're receiving a good return on an investment is determined by how much risk you have to accept to get that return, and by how much return is provided by investments with similar risks.** Investments with similar risks should offer similar returns.

There is a time value to money. A dollar today is worth more than dollar tomorrow. The longer you have to wait for a dollar, the less that dollar will be worth when you finally get it. Inflation will whittle away that dollar's purchasing power over time. There is also personal value to using a dollar now instead of later.

Investments that tie up money for long periods should offer better returns than more liquid investments. Long-term bonds pay higher interest than short-term bonds. The longer you have to wait for your money, the more money you should receive for waiting.

Bond prices are determined by two factors. In the short-term, they're affected by demand. **Whenever the stock market has a sharp decline, people turn to bonds for safety.** This increased demand pushes up bond prices. Bonds are essentially loans paying a fixed interest rate to the lender (bondholder); the higher the bond price, the lower the interest rate.

For example, XYZ Corp. issues a $1,000 bond that pays 6% interest, or $60 a year. Soon after, a bear market in stocks increases demand for bonds. The market price of the XYZ bond rises to $1,200. XYZ pays their bondholder $60 interest a year; that payment doesn't change. If you bought the bond for $1,200, you would only earn 5% interest - $60 interest payment divided by your $1,200 purchase price.

The bond market could go the other way, too. If demand for XYZ bonds dropped, the market price might fall to $800. If you bought the bond at that price, the $60 interest payment would equal 7.5%.

In the long-term, bond prices are affected mostly by the inflation rate. People delay spending and invest money now only if they expect to have more money (purchasing power) in the future. Delaying spending and having *less* money makes no sense.

When the XYZ bond was issued, inflation was 3% per year; the bond paid 3% over the inflation rate. Since then, inflation rose to 6%. New, similar bonds are paying 9%, 3% over the inflation rate. In order to sell, the market price of the XYZ bond has to fall so the $60 interest payment equals 9%. That price is $667.

In this example, a 3% rise in the inflation rate drove the price of the bond down by a third. **Inflation can move bond prices a lot, and not in a good way.**

People don't buy stocks to own the hard assets (buildings, equipment, etc.) of a company. **People buy stocks to own a piece of the future profits (earnings) of a company.**

Whether a stock is a good buy or not is determined in large part by its price-earnings (P/E) ratio. This ratio is the market price of the stock divided by its earnings over the past year. **A stock's price-earnings ratio is a useful tool, though it measures past performance.**

Since investors are buying a piece of future earnings, they want to know the future P/E ratio. Companies and analysts offer future P/E ratios to potential investors, but they are only predictions, not guarantees of anything.

What's a good P/E ratio? **For the broad stock market, the P/E ratio has historically been in the 15-20 range;** you would pay $15-20 to get $1 of earnings. At the height of some bull markets, the P/E ratio climbed to over 30. At the bottom of some bear markets, the P/E ratio fell to below 8. At 30, the market was overpriced; stocks soon fell dramatically. At 8, there were bargains galore. Smart shoppers started buying and moved prices and price-earnings ratios higher.

Companies with bigger growth potential usually have higher P/E ratios. The growth potential for a bio-engineering firm is greater than for an automaker. Profits for the automaker may be stable, but they won't rise dramatically. The bio-engineering firm might – might – have a breakthrough that makes profits explode. People will pay more for that potential.

Money and markets never sleep. Events halfway around the world can move markets back home. In the short-term, no one can know if a market – any market – will move up or down. The one certainty is that markets are always moving.

DESIRE vs. REQUIRE

"I just have to have it!"

That statement has been the prelude to countless personal financial disasters. That statement takes something desired and turns it, in the speaker's mind, into something required. Nearly every time it's made, the more correct statement might be, "I really want it."

Why do so many people seem to confuse want with need? Usually, it's not confusion; it's reclassification. By claiming you need something, rather than merely want it, you promote it from luxury to necessity, from desired to required. By definition, no one needs a luxury. There are lots of reasons, many of them financial, why getting a luxury might be a bad idea. **But if a luxury is reclassified as a necessity, denying yourself isn't merely wrong – it's inhumane.**

The outside world is no help, either. One of the best ways to sell something is to convince people they have to have it – that it's a necessity. Advertising has been doing this since advertising first appeared. Even if you're immune to advertising's lure, peer pressure may effectively convince you that you "have to have it." Your peers may mean no harm, but their pressure can still be harmful.

More often, the pressure is internal. One way to ease the guilt of making a luxury a necessity is to make others responsible. If you convince yourself that a purchase is a necessity to maintain relationships or social standing, any blame shifts from you to them.

If you ask people what are truly necessities, the most common answers are food, clothing, and shelter. These are necessities because no one can live without them, at least not for long.

Food, clothing, and shelter have been necessities for thousands of years. In the 21st century, there are new priorities, and new priorities create new necessities.

The first new necessity is *medical*. Access to proper medical care is likely to save your health, and possibly your life, more than once. That life-saving care may only be available if you're insured. Medical insurance is a necessity because the consequences of not having it are too great to risk.

The next new necessity is *transportation*. Five-hundred years ago, when someone's entire world was within walking distance, transportation wasn't a necessity. In the 21st century, it is.

Even if transportation is only needed to get to and from work, it's a necessity because your job is a necessity of a different kind. Your job provides money to pay for all your material necessities, which makes your job the biggest necessity of all. If your job is your biggest necessity, by extension, every necessity to keep your job is a necessity, too.

The next new necessity is *communication*. Your family may be spread out over continents and your job may require you to be available at any moment. Accessibility is a necessity in the 21st century.

The final 21st century necessity is a *retirement fund*. This may not seem to meet the definition of a necessity because it deals with a future necessity, not a present one. But a retirement fund is a future necessity that can only be funded in the present. Any future necessity that must be funded in the present is a present necessity.

Just because something is a necessity doesn't mean there are no spending limits on it. For example:

- Food is a necessity; dining out is not.
- Clothing is a necessity; eighty pairs of shoes are not.
- Shelter is a necessity; a 5,000 square foot home is not.
- Medical is a necessity; plastic surgery is not.
- Transportation is a necessity; a Mercedes is not.
- Communication is a necessity; anything beyond a cell phone and internet is not.
- A retirement fund is a necessity; overfunding it is not, especially if you don't meet other necessities first.

It's important not to overspend by raising necessities to luxuries. It's equally important to adequately cover necessities. Adequate coverage can include:

- Eating healthy foods, even if it costs a little more;
- Buying clothing that serves its purpose;
- Living in a home that's well-maintained and safe;
- Medical insurance that promotes good health, too;
- Reliable, safe, environmentally-friendly transportation;
- Communication that promotes positive relationships;
- Retirement funding that maximizes employer matches.

There is nothing wrong with spending on luxuries, once your necessities are fully covered. Your rewards for hard work are the luxuries of life, not merely life's necessities. But necessities are necessities because they must be covered first, including covering necessities for those who depend on you. **If you put what's required before what's desired, you can expect financial peace. If you put what's desired before what's required, you can expect financial disaster.**

OPPORTUNITY vs. SECURITY

In the 1930's, during the Great Depression, the federal government created the Social **Security** Administration. In the 2000's, after the attacks of September 11, 2001, the federal government created the Department of Homeland **Security**.

Crisis creates fear. When we're afraid, we seek security. The federal government responded by creating agencies to deal with crises, but also to reduce public fears. The word *Security* in the titles was no accident.

America is the land of opportunity, but we expect our government, first and foremost, to keep us secure. Federal spending reflects this priority:

- 18% goes to Defense and Homeland Security.
- 24% goes to Social Security.
- 24% goes to Medicare and Medicaid.
- 11% goes to programs classified as "Safety Net".

Our government isn't merely giving the people what they want. They recognize that **people need to feel secure before they can pursue opportunity.**

Studies with small children have shown that when children feel secure with their parents present, they will try new things and meet new friends. When the parents leave, these same children become withdrawn and stressed. The children needed security before they could pursue opportunity. Adults are no different.

While opportunity is pursued more when there's a foundation of security, **opportunity and security are often in competition.** Security can provide a floor of protection, but usually also imposes a ceiling of limitations. Opportunity removes the ceiling of limitations, but usually removes the floor, too. We want a floor of protection *and* no ceiling of limitations. Unfortunately, we usually have to choose between the two.

For centuries, the work people did changed very little. The Industrial Revolution totally changed the world of work. The Technological Revolution has increased the rate of change even more. These changes create opportunities, but they also reduce security.

In 1942, the term *Creative Destruction* was coined. It referred to the process of replacing outdated products, technologies, and jobs with newer, improved versions. The creative part provides opportunities and benefits to society as a whole. The destructive part mostly destroys the security of those whose livelihoods disappear.

Someone with a marketable skill often has a choice of working for a large company or starting their own business. Working for a large company provides a higher level of security. The company can pay a steady income and provide other benefits. The company will likely be in business for the foreseeable future. While opportunities there exist, they are limited and there is more competition for those opportunities.

Starting a company provides many opportunities, but no real security. Success or failure rests with very few people, maybe just one. Income may fluctuate and not even exist in the early stages. Getting established will be difficult. But while security is nil, the opportunities are far greater. Many *Fortune 500* companies were started by one or two people.

Investing involves similar trade-offs between opportunity and security. If you want your investments to have no risk of loss, their return will be very small – so small it probably won't keep up with inflation.

The investments that provide greater opportunities for growth also come with less security. Stocks provide greater opportunities for growth than bonds, but they also have greater risks – another way of saying they're less secure. Small companies have greater opportunities for rapid growth than large companies, but their profits and even their existence are less secure than large companies. The prices of these investments reflect their levels of opportunity and security.

When we're feeling optimistic, we value opportunity over security. When we're feeling pessimistic, we value security over opportunity. When the economy is strong, people feel optimistic. They buy more stocks and buy riskier stocks like small companies with little profit history. When a crisis hits, people feel afraid. They will sell their riskier investments and put their money in risk-free investments like bank CDs and government bonds.

Whether it's the job market or the stock market, each person has to make choices between opportunity and security. Some people are natural risk-takers. They will choose opportunity over security every time. They don't want to be blocked by the ceiling. Some people are very risk-averse. They look for as much security as they can find. They want that floor under them, even if the ceiling is right on top of them, too.

Most of us are in the middle. Whether we favor opportunity or security depends on several factors. The size of the opportunity and the quality of the security both play a part. Age also plays a part. The young favor opportunity; the old favor security. The need to provide security for others, like children, also affects our choices.

Whether it's their careers or their investments, people run into trouble when they misjudge levels of opportunity and security. **Optimists are likely to overestimate an opportunity and underestimate the importance of security. Pessimists are likely to underestimate an opportunity and overestimate the level of security.**

Overestimating opportunity and ignoring security can lead to disaster. A person might leave a good job to start a company without looking at the pitfalls. In a short time, the business fails and the person is unemployed. Investors who overestimate opportunity will overpay for an investment and will be shocked by the downside. They can be in denial about misjudging the investment and will hang on until it's worthless.

Overestimating security and ignoring opportunity can also lead to disaster, though maybe slower. A secure job with a large company might get eliminated in reorganization. Making only secure investments usually means having to save a lot more and for a lot longer to reach your goals. Sometimes the desire for present security can compromise future security as well as future opportunities.

It's actually risky to expect security from others. Your family and your government may have an interest in keeping you secure, but no one else does. **The only reliable source of security is you**. And the best way to create security is to make the most of every opportunity.

STABLE vs. STAGNANT

Have you ever heard of a "Kodak Moment"? If you're less than a certain age, you may not have, though you may create more Kodak Moments than people familiar with the term.

A Kodak Moment was a term for an occasion that deserved to be preserved with a photo. The Eastman Kodak Company began in 1888 and created personal photography for the masses. Kodak became one of the largest companies in America. For decades it was one of thirty companies comprising the Dow Jones Industrial Average. As late as 1976, 90% of the film and 85% of the cameras sold in the U.S. were made by Kodak.

In 1975, a Kodak engineer invented the first digital camera. Kodak didn't pursue development because they felt it would threaten their film business. By the 1990's, Kodak accepted that digital photography was inevitable. By then, they were well behind the market. Kodak's sales and profits fell as digital cameras got better and cheaper. People stopped buying film, and they avoided inferior Kodak digital cameras. In 2012, 124 years after its founding, Kodak filed for bankruptcy.

Imagine if Kodak had been able to keep photography stagnant in order to keep their business model stable. Photography would be more limited (no phone cameras), more expensive (costly film/developing), and more harmful to the environment (chemicals from the manufacture and processing of film). But Kodak's mistakes were not unique, merely large-scale. Regular people make similar mistakes.

***Stable* is defined as resistant to sudden change of position or condition; maintaining equilibrium; self-**

restoring; consistently dependable. *Stagnant* **is defined as not moving or flowing; foul from standing still; lacking liveliness or briskness.** In seeking to be stable, Kodak became stagnant instead.

Stable means self-restoring; stagnant means not flowing. The two are incompatible. A lake may have a stable water level, but it isn't stagnant. Water flows in and out constantly, restoring the lake. If the water flow stopped, the water level might remain stable, but the lake itself would become stagnant. Stagnancy breeds instability. Letting something become stagnant in the quest for stability almost guarantees instability.

The S&P 500 Index is composed of 500 stocks of large U.S. companies. In its present form, it has been around since 1957. While the S&P 500 is a consistent indicator of stock prices, the companies in the index change constantly. In a typical year, 20 to 25 companies move in and out of the S&P 500. If the S&P 500 wasn't "self-restoring", it would still include stocks like Pan Am, Woolworth's, and Kodak. By not becoming stagnant, the S&P 500 Index remains stable – and relevant.

People seek stability because they too resist "sudden change of position or condition". The technical term for this resistance is *status quo bias*. Change involves risk. Risk triggers fear. **The biggest fear for most people is that change will make things worse.** Fear of moving backward leads to no movement at all, including moving forward. No movement is one definition of stagnant.

The world is not stagnant, though. The world is always moving forward, though not always smoothly. Staying in the same position means falling behind the world as it moves forward. Stability is measured relative to the world, not in absolute terms. Absolute stability is another definition of stagnant.

This desire for stability shows up in investing. Risk and reward move together. Avoiding risk means avoiding reward, too.

If you were afraid to see your investments drop in value, you could put your money in insured CDs at the bank or in government-guaranteed bonds. The risk would be very low, but so would the reward. Such investments earn so little that inflation eats away their gains. After five years, you would have more dollars, but they would buy less than they could five years ago. You didn't get stability; you didn't even get stagnation; you just got poorer.

Think about your investments, your career, your relationships, even your life, like a lake. On the surface and along the shore, the lake appears to be unchanging. But the lake is never the same from one minute to the next. Water enters and exits. There's constant activity below the surface. The lake's visible stability is the result of invisible, constant changes. Without those invisible constant changes, the lake would change in ways that would be visible and unpleasant – it would become stagnant.

Real stability - financial, professional, and even emotional - comes from imitating the lake. Set boundaries, remain calm on the surface, and constantly restore what you're made of.

MAXIMUM vs. OPTIMUM

Everyone loves an underdog success story, and the story of David and Goliath is the most famous of all. The small shepherd David defeated the giant warrior Goliath and saved Israel. But there's more to the story than that.

David was an experienced shepherd. Shepherds and soldiers both used a sling as a weapon. This sling was not a slingshot as we know it. It was a leather pouch that held a stone or lead ball, with two long strings from which the sling would spin. A skilled slinger could release a projectile at over 100 miles per hour and could be accurate up to 200 yards. An equivalent modern weapon is a 9mm handgun.

Goliath was 6'9", at least a foot-and-a-half taller than the average man of that time. He was also covered in a hundred pounds of armor, making an imposing figure on the battlefield. Goliath's size was caused by acromegaly, a benign tumor near the pituitary gland that results in too much growth hormone. The tumor presses on the optic nerves, impairing vision. The abnormal growth rate also makes a person slower and clumsier than normal. While an imposing figure, Goliath was actually a semi-blind, immobile, immense target facing a trained marksman at close range. He never stood a chance.

Maximum *can be an adjective, a noun, or a verb. In all cases, it is synonymous with the greatest, the highest, the most.* **Optimum** *is defined as the most favorable condition for success. It is synonymous with best. Maximum focuses on quantity; optimum focuses on quality.*

Goliath was the maximum warrior. David was the optimum warrior.

There is a natural tendency to seek maximum, rather than optimum. One reason is our belief that, if a certain amount of something is good, then more is better, and the most is the best. **If we see *most* and *best* as synonymous, we will see *maximum* and *optimum* as synonymous, too.**

It also takes some effort to determine what the optimum is without assuming it's just the maximum. Sometimes the maximum is also the optimum (love being the best example). Usually though, optimum shows up well before maximum. It's a skill to know how far to go without going too far.

Going beyond optimum to maximum can be harmful on its own. An all-you-can-eat buffet is a monument to the maximum, but when you look at America's obesity rate, it's hard to argue that it's the optimum way to eat. Even for something as essential as food, optimum and maximum are not the same.

Defaulting to the maximum instead of calculating the optimum is also wasteful. Whether the resource is time, effort, food, or money, consuming more and achieving less isn't just wasteful; it's stupid.

People tend to fall into one of two groups – *maximizers* and *optimizers*.

Maximizers seek perfection in everything they do. While that approach may seem admirable, it's not very sensible. Because perfection is almost never attainable, maximizers tend to be frustrated and unhappy. They will spend resources seeking perfection that go way past the point of diminishing returns. Maximizers also suffer greater buyer's remorse. Whatever they do or buy, they always wonder if there wasn't a better possible outcome. Nothing is ever good enough. Maximizers' obsession with quality reduces the quantity of their achievements.

Optimizers don't expect perfection and don't seek it. They look for the best overall outcomes, not the best individual outcomes. Optimizers don't suffer from tunnel vision like maximizers do. Optimizers recognize the point of diminishing returns and will reallocate their resources to another project when they reach that point. Optimizers can be satisfied when something is good enough because that frees them to start something new.

While maximum is associated with quantity and optimum is associated with quality, it's a bit opposite when talking about maximizers and optimizers. Maximizers focus on the quality of their efforts while optimizers focus on quantity. The end results still align optimizers with quality, though. By being more efficient in the allocation of all their resources, optimizers get more done and add more to their quality of life. They also have more fun and less stress in the process.

Even with money, maximum and optimum are not the same. Great wealth also makes great demands. Beyond a certain amount, more money will not change your life for the better. Studies have shown that once you make a little more than the average, more money does not raise your level of happiness. Sacrifices must be made to accumulate and preserve wealth. **The optimum amount of wealth is when the benefits of additional wealth are less than the sacrifice needed to obtain and maintain it.** You'll know you've reached your optimum wealth when your response to getting more is, "It's not worth it."

The optimum is almost always less than the maximum. But, as David proved with Goliath, less is more. And getting more from less is an excellent way to create the most favorable condition for success.

OWNERSHIP vs. POSSESSION

It happens along beautiful stretches of beach. It happens on mountains with majestic views. It happens by a beautiful stream or a peaceful lake. "It" is a conversation. It starts after a couple has settled into their temporary lodgings at the beach or mountain or lake. Regardless of who starts the conversation, it usually contains some version of the following:

"Isn't his place magnificent?"

"Wouldn't you just love to own a place here?"

And so it begins.

When we come across something we really like, there is a natural tendency to want to own it. This tendency has led to some of the most horrible acts in history. Most wars started because one group wanted to own what others already owned. While no one is going to war for a beachfront condo, that doesn't mean harmful things won't be done trying to own one.

Because of our natural tendency to want to own things, our perceptions about ownership can get skewed. They get skewed when we only see the pros but go blind to the cons of owning something.

People often fall in love with something and they'll move heaven and earth to own it. Once they own it, they find ownership is a burden. That burden can kill the love they once had for the thing.

Ownership **is the legal right to possess something.** ***Possession*** **is a state of having or controlling something.** Ownership and possession both convey rights. Ownership also conveys responsibilities. If you own a cabin in the mountains, you are responsible for paying taxes, utilities, and other expenses to maintain your property. If you rent your cabin, you retain ownership and all the responsibilities, but you turn possession with all its benefits over to someone else.

Many people sacrifice a lot of money and time to own a second home at the beach or the mountains. They then feel they have to spend all their spare time at their second home to justify the sacrifice. When they're at their getaway, they don't get away – they spend time doing repairs and other chores. They may rent the house out part-time to defray some of the costs, even though they don't like having strangers in their home.

In such cases, **the owner often gets all the responsibilities and few of the benefits, while the possessor (renter) gets all of the benefits and none of the responsibilities.** The renter gets to enjoy the property and simply leave when time is up. The renter is also free to go someplace else next time.

It's true the possessor pays rent to the owner. The renter feels the rent is reasonable to possess the property for that time; if not, he/she wouldn't rent it. The owner, on the other hand, may not get enough rental income to justify the expense and reduced use of the property.

Very often, in the overwhelming desire to own something, we find ourselves owned by that very thing. This is often the case when we make great sacrifices to own something we merely want but don't need. This is especially true if these things carry big price tags, like second homes or luxury cars.

How can you know when it's better to opt for possession over ownership? The first step is to recognize that possession may be what you're really after most of the time. When you think about a condo at the beach, what attracts you? Is it the views and sounds and peaceful walks at sunset? Or is it seeing your name on the deed (and mortgage) and bragging that you own a condo at the beach? Your answer can tell you whether ownership or possession is really what you want.

Speaking of bragging, being able to tell everyone "It's mine!" is a big motivation to own something. It's also a poor reason to take on the burdens of ownership. When contemplating buying something, ask yourself a question. Would you want to take on the expense and responsibility of owning it if you couldn't tell a soul about it? Your answer can tell you whether ownership or possession - or neither - is really what you want.

If something appreciates in value, ownership may be better; if it depreciates in value, possession may be all you want. You want to own stocks because they should appreciate in value, making ownership profitable. You may not want to own an expensive car that will lose half its value in the first two years.

Owning a home, as opposed to renting, makes sense if owning it will be better financially in the long run. Knowing the answer requires calculating all the costs of ownership and estimating how much equity you will build over time. Those numbers have to be compared with what you would pay in rent over that same time. The differences will help determine whether renting or owning is better for you.

Ownership can offer many benefits, psychological and financial. Ownership can provide a sense of security along with a way to build wealth. But ownership has costs that go beyond money – costs in time, stress, and lost opportunities.

Before you pay all those costs to own something, take a critical look at *why* you want to own it. You may find that, while you thought you wanted to own something, mere possession will really make you happier.

CURRENCY vs. PURCHASING POWER

If you're old enough to read this, you've probably seen *The Wizard of Oz*. The movie was adapted from a book written by Frank Baum in 1900. While the movie is well-known and well-loved, much of its symbolism is less well-known.

In 1900, the U.S. was just emerging from a period of depression and deflation. Prices had fallen by 22% in the previous 16 years. Farmers were hit especially hard.

The U.S. was operating on a gold standard - it tied the value of the dollar to gold and tied the money supply to the gold supply. Farmers wanted a dual standard - money backed by gold *and* silver. A dual standard would have increased the money supply, raising prices and reducing farmers' debt burden.

Some of *The Wizard of Oz*'s symbolism includes:

- Dorothy: Everyday American
- Scarecrow: Farmer
- Tin Man: Industrial Worker
- Lion: William Jennings Bryan, politician of the era
- Wizard of Oz: U.S. presidents of the era
- Emerald City: Washington, D.C.
- Oz: short for ounce, a measure of silver and gold
- Yellow Brick Road: Gold standard
- Ruby Slippers: They were silver in the book; ruby looked better for a technicolor movie

The dual standard was never adopted, and the U.S. went off the gold standard in 1971. Today, money supply is determined by the Federal Reserve. A bigger supply can stimulate the economy, but cause inflation; a smaller supply has the opposite effect. The government manages the economy by managing the money supply.

The only restrictions on our money supply today come from people, not natural resources. Today, no major world currency is backed by gold. The benefit is economies are not restricted by their gold supplies. The risk is governments will finance spending by printing money, which they prefer over tax increases. Inflation can result if the money supply increases faster than goods or services available for purchase.

The ancient Romans extended their empire further and facilitated trade within the empire with a standard currency. It is said that the coins used to flow from the Roman mint in a constant stream. The Latin word *currere*, which means to flow, was used to describe the stream. Our word *currency* comes from it.

We tend to equate money and money supply with currency. It's better to equate money with *purchasing power*. Money, currency, and purchasing power may seem synonymous, but purchasing power can change drastically, even when the currency is unchanged.

Seeing money as currency and not as purchasing power can lead to mistakes. You may end up sacrificing the purchasing power of your money in order to protect the currency that represents it.

Here's an illustration. You have $100 that you can either spend now or save for a year. Saving earns 3% interest; in a year you will receive $103. Inflation is 4%; what costs $100 now will cost $104 in a year.

You decide to save to get the increase from $100 to $103. Even though you will have more currency in a year, you will have less purchasing power. You will need $104 to buy what $100 bought a year ago, but you only have $103. You also waited a year to enjoy what you bought. Delaying gratification to have more currency is senseless if delay decreases purchasing power. **Saving should be done to increase purchasing power, not just currency.**

In uncertain economic times, people look for "safe" places to put their money. By safe, they mean the preservation of their currency. In many cases, they pay a high price for safety.

The difference between $103 and $104 isn't much. It's the decline of purchasing power over decades that can really cost you.

Retirees often have a choice between "safe" options that have a stable amount and options that can fluctuate. If someone were retired for 25 years and their income were a "stable" amount, their purchasing power might be cut in half over that time. The currency they received every year was unchanged, but their purchasing power got hammered. Stable money isn't stable if it buys less over time. **The only measure of money's stability is its purchasing power over time.**

The cost of living varies widely around the U.S and around the world. If you were offered jobs in Des Moines, Iowa and San Francisco, the San Francisco job would likely pay more. The higher pay would be tempting, until you looked at what you could buy.

The San Francisco job might pay 30% more. But the cost of housing might be 300% more. Taxes might be 180% more. Almost everything would cost significantly more in San Francisco than Des Moines. You would receive less currency in Des Moines; you would have less purchasing power in San Francisco.

Wealth is not pieces of paper or digits in a ledger. Wealth is what the paper or digits can obtain for you. Currency is a representation; purchasing power is the real thing. **Wealth is not measured by currency; it's measured by purchasing power.**

HABITUAL OFFENDER

Every day over 100 million women do more physical work to avoid doing more mental work. These women are on "the pill". The birth control pill has been available since 1960. It is the most successful contraceptive in history. The prescription requires taking a combination of estrogen and progestin in pill form daily for 21 days, then discontinuing dosage for 7 days. Almost all prescriptions are packaged with 28 pills - 21 active pills and 7 placebos, identified by different colors.

Women can choose not to take the placebos, though most do. It's easy to take a pill a day for a week. It's harder to remember to start taking the active pills after a week off. The mental effort to remember combined with the consequences of forgetting make taking the placebo the smart choice. Taking the pill daily is easier because it becomes a *habit*.

Humans think in two different ways - one intuitive and automatic, the other rational and reflective.

The automatic system relies on instinct rather than thought. When you react to a clap of thunder or a baby's laugh, you're using your automatic system. **The reflective system is thoughtful and deliberate.** You're using it now to read this sentence. When you develop a skill, an unstated goal is to raise the exercise of that skill from reflective to automatic. Skills at that level appear instinctive because they've become instinctive.

Habits are controlled by our automatic system. We develop habits so we don't have to think about what we're doing. Almost by definition, if you have to think about doing something, it isn't a habit. Tasks you do automatically (brushing teeth, making coffee, etc.) are habits. They're handled by your automatic system.

More than forty percent of your actions are habits, yet nothing ever begins as a habit. At some point, you made conscious decisions about everything you do that's now a habit. You chose a particular action and repeated it. In time, it became automatic. Once the behavior became automatic, a habit was born.

Habits develop so we can think less. Anything that enables the brain to work less will automatically be endorsed by the body. Habits also develop automatically without conscious thought. You don't have to give your approval for a habit to form.

The habit will form as long as there is:
- **a routine that can be followed**
- **something to cue that routine**
- **positive reinforcement or the absence of negative reinforcement.**

Your body doesn't distinguish between good and bad habits. Unfortunately, bad habits usually have better immediate rewards than good habits. Watching TV feels better than jogging. Spending feels better than saving. Bad habits form because we like their rewards. We go after the reward again and again until we've created a habit.

Good habits also have rewards. Unfortunately, most good habits have rewards on a time-delay. Exercising makes you look and feel great, but it doesn't happen overnight. A donut tastes good right now. Saving money gives you a feeling of independence and security, but it takes time to save enough to get that feeling. Spending money feels good right now.

Bad habits have downsides; it's why they're bad. The downsides rarely occur immediately; if they did, you wouldn't repeat the behavior and create a habit. The downsides (obesity, alcoholism, bankruptcy, divorce, etc.) occur later. By then, even though you want to break the bad habit, it's so ingrained that breaking it requires extraordinary effort.

One of the best ways to break a bad habit is to replace it with a good habit. We seek rewards, including rewards that may be harmful in the long term. Breaking a bad habit may remove a long-term negative, but it also removes a short-term positive. A bad habit is more likely to stay broken if a new positive is added.

A habit starts with a cue, such as the alarm clock going off. The cue is followed by a routine, such as eating a donut. Positive reinforcement follows, such as savoring something tasty.

Bad habits can be replaced with good habits by changing the routine in the middle. The cue (alarm clock) is still there. Eating something tasty *that's also healthy* is the change in routine. The positive reinforcement of savoring something tasty is still there. It's easier to break the morning donut habit by eating something better than eating nothing at all. Replacing is more effective than removing.

Some habits matter more than others. Some habits are capable of changing other habits. These are known as *keystone habits.* **A positive change in a keystone habit can pay unexpected benefits in seemingly unrelated areas.**

Physical exercise is considered a keystone habit. Once people begin an exercise habit, they reconsider other habits that can undo the progress made by exercise. Financial exercise is another keystone habit. Financial exercise does for your finances what physical exercise does for your body.

You can create your own financial exercise routine. You might begin by saving 1% of your income. Then you work to pay off all credit card debt. Then you develop a budget. You follow that by getting properly insured for life, health, and disability. Your financial exercise routine, like your physical exercise routine, should be designed to provide the maximum benefit for the effort. It should enable you to keep the routine going until it becomes a habit. And like physical exercise, you can increase your effort as you get better at it.

Financial keystone habits not only provide benefits on their own, they also deter you from developing bad financial habits. If you're proud of your habit of saving regularly, you are less likely to raid savings for an impulse purchase. If you've paid off your credit cards, you are less likely to succumb to new credit card debt. If you developed a budget, you'll monitor your spending more closely. If you have health, life, and disability insurance, you are less likely to engage in behavior that would increase their cost or lead to cancellations.

It doesn't take any more effort to create a good habit than a bad one. However, **bad habits give a small reward now and exact a large price later. Good habits exact a small price now and give a large reward later.**

We are creatures of habit. Habit can be your greatest helper or your heaviest burden. It can push you on or drag you down. It can lead you to profit or to ruin. You're a creature of habit, but you choose what kind of creature you will be.

THINKING ABSOLUTELY; NOT RELATIVELY

More than a half-century has passed since President Johnson declared a "War on Poverty". In the six years before the 1965 start of this war, the poverty rate in the U.S. had declined from 22% to 15%. Since then, the poverty rate has never been below 12% and still hovers around 15% most years. More than fifty years of effort hasn't moved the needle.

These figures are for *absolute poverty*, which measures poverty against a fixed standard. Those defending current anti-poverty programs prefer to look at *relative poverty*. They cite economist John Kenneth Galbraith, who said, "People are poverty stricken when their income, even if adequate for survival, falls markedly behind that of their community."

Relative poverty really measures income inequality. Relative poverty could drop by making the rich poorer. Relative poverty could drop even if *everyone* has less money, including the poor. If everyone is getting richer, absolute poverty falls. But, if the rich are getting richer faster (which is typical), relative poverty rises while absolute poverty falls. With relative poverty, rising tides do not lift all boats.

The poor today may feel unhappy when they look at their relative position. However, of those classified as poor today, 99% have electricity, running water, a refrigerator, and flush toilets; 97% have a television and a telephone; 78% have a car and air conditioning.

Cornelius Vanderbilt was one of the first railroad tycoons of the 19th century. He built Grand Central Station in New York. He was worth $100 million when he died in 1877 and is considered the third richest man in American history. He had none of the items listed previously. Neither did many Americans in the Eisenhower era. A deeper look at relative poverty finds that the poor in America actually live better than 99.9% of humanity throughout history.

Despite one of the highest standards of living, Americans are not measurably happier than people in other countries. We're happier than people in Egypt, but not Mexico. Our higher standard of living does not lead to a higher level of happiness.

If you compare your situation to those with more, you'll feel resentful; compare to those with less, you'll feel grateful. People let happiness hinge less on what they have in absolute terms and more on what they have relative to others - typically family, friends, and peers.

Possessions help orient us in our social worlds because they imply status and wealth. When we view someone's possessions, we form impressions and calculate how to interact with them. We defer to those with greater wealth, or at least the appearance of greater wealth.

As we climb the socio-economic ladder, we change our peer group, and we spend more to keep up with them. The goal is to seem better off, but moving upscale works against that.

Your sense of financial security largely emerges from how you appraise three gaps in your life:
- the gap between what you have and what you want;
- the gap between what you have and what you think others have;
- the gap between what you have and the best of what you had in the past.

The larger the gaps, the greater your insecurity.

Your sense of financial security can be improved in several ways. You can simply want less by being grateful and content with what you have. You can close the gap between what you have and what you think others have by recognizing their fraud. Boasting is easier than confessing, so people parade their assets and bury their liabilities. You can close the gap between your past and present by looking closer at the negatives of your past and the positives of your present.

University of California professor of psychology Sonja Lyubomirsky studied how happy and unhappy people react differently if they compare themselves to others. Her findings are revealing.

When working with a peer on a project, happy people were only slightly affected by their performance relative to a peer. If they did better than their peer, they felt slightly better about their performance. If they did worse than their peer, it did not affect whether the person felt good about his/her performance. The happy person could still appreciate an improvement in their performance of a task, even if someone else performed better.

Unhappy people, by contrast, did not feel better about an improved performance if a peer had a better performance. **Unhappy people were too busy comparing themselves to their peers**, instead of to their own previous performance. **Happy people focused almost exclusively on how they compared to themselves**, not how they compared to others.

These studies showed that unhappy people spend a lot of time comparing themselves to other people, which is probably why they're unhappy. Happy people realize the only person they have to be better than is the person they are right now. To sum up:

Thinking Absolutely ⇨ Happy
Thinking Relatively ⇨ Unhappy

Most millionaires are millionaires because they don't care what other people assume about their wealth or lifestyle. They don't compare themselves to others, and they ignore those who do. Spending time making comparisons to others won't improve your performance. You will only frustrate yourself when you compare to "superiors," and delude yourself when you compare to "inferiors". **Don't worry about *being* the best. *Doing* your best is more than enough.**

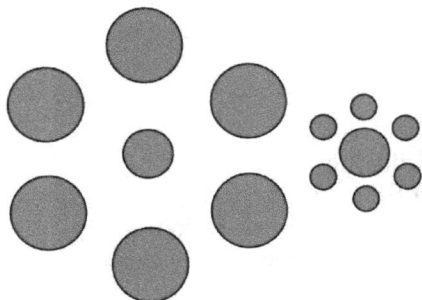

The
center dots
are
ABSOLUTELY
the
same size.

A BUCK IS A BUCK

Laura and Anthony weren't having much luck in Vegas. In two days they had lost more than $1,000 in the casino. After Laura had gone to bed, Anthony was packing and discovered a $20 chip in a pocket. He decided to take one last crack at the roulette table.

He placed his chip on number 14. The ball hit 14 and the bet paid $700 at 35-1 odds. Anthony let it ride on 14 and it hit 14 again. He was up to $24,500. He then bet it all on number 23. It hit 23. Anthony was now up to $857,500. This time he bet it all on number 6. It hit 28. Anthony was crushed - and broke once again.

"Where'd you go?" Laura asked when he returned.

"I was playing roulette."

"How'd you do?"

"I lost $20."

Anthony reasoned that he only lost $20 as a defense. The thought of losing fifteen years' salary in one spin of the wheel might have made his head explode.

Anthony's reasoning is one reason why casinos are so profitable. In gambling parlance, the casino is known as the house, and the house always wins. The house wins in large part because **people are much more careless with their winnings than they are about money they worked for.** Gamblers like Anthony think of their winnings as "house money", not their own. They are far more reckless with it, which is why it almost always ends up back with the house.

Anthony was guilty of ***mental accounting.*** He saw the money he won as different from the money he brought with him to Vegas. He was probably more upset about losing the $1,000 he worked for than the $857,500 that luck handed him. Anthony couldn't imagine betting even one percent of $857,500 if it was his own hard-earned money. But he didn't give a thought about betting a fortune when it didn't feel like *his* fortune.

It's easy to criticize Anthony, but we're all guilty of mental accounting to various degrees. Money is, to use an accounting term, *fungible*. Fungible means identical items can be substituted for each other. Any dollar bill can substitute for another dollar bill. It also means that **a dollar won at the roulette table, a dollar Grandma gave you, and a dollar earned digging ditches all have the same value. If they all have the same value, they should all be treated the same.** But they rarely are.

Most of us are careful about spending our paycheck. We know how hard we work for that money and we don't want to be stupid with it. But if we get a big tax refund, we're much more likely to do something stupid with it. The tax refund feels like found money; we weren't planning on it so we didn't make plans for it. We give ourselves permission to be stupid, even though that money is part of the money we worked hard for. Because that money spent time with the government, we now think about it differently. More important, we treat it with less respect.

It's even easier to do mental accounting with money from the future; in this case, credit cards. Not only do people buy things on credit that they wouldn't buy for cash, they also pay an average of 17% more for items bought on credit compared to paying cash. When you buy something with a credit card, you don't pay for it until later. You also get the credit card back. When you pay cash, you have to hand over bills. You feel the cost right away, which can make you stop and think if you really want that item and at that price.

If you have money sitting in a bank earning 1% interest, and you also have credit card debt at 12% interest, you're guilty of mental accounting. If you saw the dollars in each as the same, you wouldn't loan your money at 1% interest and then borrow it back at 12%. That can only happen if you see the dollars differently.

Size matters, too. Studies have shown people are more careless with small windfalls than big ones. If you received a $500 windfall, you might blow it over a weekend. If you received a $50,000 windfall, you might pause and think about the long-term impact the money could have. You'd be less inclined to be frivolous with it, even though you had far more to be frivolous with.

Mental accounting can cause us to be too careful with money, as well as being too frivolous. Money that is earmarked for a specific purpose may not get invested properly for fear of losing it. A child's college fund, a retirement account, an inheritance from Grandma - we may be so worried about losing these funds that we never give them the chance to go to work on our behalf.

If you're inclined to be careless with money, to spend some dollars more frivolously than others, try this. Imagine every dollar you're spending is the dollar you worked hardest for in your life. Remember the dirtiest job for the lowest pay you ever had and treat your dollars like they came from that.

If you already treat every dollar like you sweated blood to earn it, try designating some portion of your money for frivolous purposes. Your money, like your time, should be allocated to meet your needs but fulfill some wants, too. A buck is a buck. Treat them all with equal respect and they'll reward you equally in whatever way they serve you.

NUMERATORS AND DENOMINATORS

If you were alive during World War II, in which of these countries would you be most likely to die?

- China – 20,000,000 deaths
- Japan – 3,000,000 deaths
- India – 2,000,000 deaths
- Greece – 700,000 deaths
- Latvia – 220,000 deaths

You quickly notice many more Chinese than Latvians died in World War II – about 90 to 1. China would seem the most likely place to die and by a wide margin.

You don't yet have all the information you need to answer the question. The question wasn't which country had the most deaths; it was where you would be *most likely* to die. You need more information. You need to know the countries' populations at that time:

- China – 518,000,000
- Japan – 72,000,000
- India – 378,000,000
- Greece – 7,200,000
- Latvia – 2,000,000

You now have enough information to calculate where you would be most likely to die. Here are the odds of dying by country:

- China – 1 in 26
- Japan – 1 in 24
- India – 1 in 189
- Greece – 1 in 10
- Latvia – 1 in 9

A Latvian was almost three times more likely to die during World War II than a Chinese. The number of deaths was the numerator. The population was the denominator. To know your odds of dying, you had to know both numbers. (FYI – the odds of an American dying in WWII were 1 in 312.)

Whether talking about fractions, ratios, or odds, they're made with numerators and denominators.

We tend to pay more attention to numerators than denominators. Numerators are like the flashy hype you see in a commercial. Denominators are like the legal disclaimers they throw in later. **Numerators excite. Denominators clarify.**

Because numerators excite, they can cause us to overreact. We hear a news story of a random murder and we buy a gun for protection. The odds are about 1 in 90,000 that you would be killed by a stranger this year. The odds are about three times greater that you would be killed by someone you know. For each person murdered by a stranger, more than a hundred people will die from smoking. The murder numerator is much smaller, but it screams louder and frightens us more.

Ignoring the denominator can cost us when it comes to purchases like insurance. People often buy flight insurance which pays a death benefit, but only if their flight crashes and they die. The odds are much greater they would die driving to the airport than they would in a plane crash. People also buy life insurance but don't buy disability insurance. Even though they're fifteen times more likely to become disabled than to die before they retire, it doesn't motivate them. Death is a scary numerator and a strong motivator.

Most of us live in states with lotteries. The weekly lotto jackpot is broadcast to lure players. You buy a ticket thinking your odds are as good as anyone's. Your odds may be as good as anyone's, but your odds are also about 1 in 175,000,000. **The numerator giveth; the denominator taketh away.**

You may look around and see dozens of successful businesses started by people just like you. You decide, if they can succeed, so can you. You may very well be right, but you've only looked at the numerator. The denominator would tell you that, for every successful business you see, nine businesses failed in the first three years. Knowing the denominator might actually increase your chances for success. You now know what you're up against and what it will take to succeed. **Denominators help kill delusions created by the numerator.**

You may be considering a job with two different pay options. One pays a straight salary of $60,000 per year. The other pays a commission ranging from $30,000 to $90,000. Which one should you take? To answer, you need to know the odds of earning the various commissions. As a start, if the odds are better than 50/50 that you'll make more than $60,000, the commission job is probably the better choice.

Numerators and denominators, in the form of ratios, are some of the most important tools in financial analysis. If you were thinking of investing in a company, you would want to look at several financial ratios: price ratios, profitability ratios, liquidity ratios, debt ratios, and efficiency ratios. Perhaps the most important of all ratios is the *price-earnings ratio* - the price of the stock divided by the past year's earnings. It can indicate if a stock is overpriced or underpriced. It's a good starting point.

Others use numerators and denominators to evaluate you. If you apply for a loan, especially a mortgage, a lender will look closely at your debt to income ratio. The numerator is your monthly debt payments; the denominator is your monthly income. If the ratio is more than 36%, you may be turned down or have to pay a higher interest rate.

When seeking a target ratio between numerator and denominator, changing either will change the ratio. For your debt to income ratio, you can lower your ratio (and improve your chances for a loan) by reducing debt or by increasing income. If your income isn't rising, you would use income as a denominator and calculate the numerator that gets the ratio to 36%. Your goal would be to reduce your monthly debt payments to that number.

You can't calculate the odds if you don't know the numerator and the denominator. When we want something badly, we're inclined to bend the facts to our favor. By tweaking numerator and denominator, we can bend the facts and make the odds appear better. But even though you can torture numbers until they say what you want, that doesn't make it the truth.

Looking at numerator and denominator lets you calculate the odds and make comparisons. Looking at numerator and denominator lets you know what you have to do to reach certain financial goals. Perhaps more important, **looking at both numerator *and* denominator enables you to reduce numerator noise and put it into proper perspective.**

LOSS AVERSION

Your football team is leading by ten points late in the game. They built this lead with consistent offense and aggressive defense. They've blitzed the opposing quarterback and disrupted his passing game all day. But with five minutes to play, your team shifts to the "prevent" defense. They stop blitzing. They focus on preventing a long run after a short completion. The other team scores a quick touchdown, then holds your team to three-and-out. The opponent then moves down the field with a series of short sideline passes your defense willingly concedes. They score the winning touchdown on the final play. Once again, your team has snatched defeat from the jaws of victory.

What prompts a coach to change what worked and replace it with a strategy that prevents nothing but victory? **Coaches and the rest of us may love to win, but we hate, hate, HATE to lose. It's painful.**

There are actually two kinds of pain at work here – the pain of losing and the pain of loss.

The pain of losing is fairly simple. Certain activities, like competitive sports, require a winner and a loser. If you choose to compete, you accept the possibility of losing. Other than in wars, the pain of losing is a risk we usually accept freely. It's not nice, but it's not unexpected.

If the pain of losing is unbearable to you, you can:
- not compete
- drive yourself to always be the best (not realistic)
- cheat (not recommended)

It hurts more to see your team blow a late lead than it does to see them mount a comeback that falls just short.

It hurts more because blowing a late lead not only brings the pain of losing; it brings the pain of loss.

The pain of loss is felt when we had something and then we didn't. When our team blows a late lead, we feel that victory was ours and then it wasn't. We didn't feel that way with the comeback that fell short.

Even those who aren't fans of poetry are familiar with the words of Alfred Lord Tennyson: "Tis better to have loved and lost than never to have loved at all." It's a romantic notion. It's also wrong.

If you ask people who've loved and lost if the pain was worth the experience, you'll get mixed answers. In the midst of the pain though, most would remove the experience if it would remove the pain. Tennyson was also referring only to lost love and nothing more. Certainly, it's not better to have loved and lost a child than to never have had a child to love at all.

Loss aversion can affect us whenever we feel we have something to lose. **Loss aversion is a major reason why people resist change.** Change might make things better, but it might also make things worse. Making something worse is felt as loss. We also feel worse about a change we made that didn't work than a change we didn't make that did work. **We feel greater responsibility for our actions than our inactions.**

Our feelings about gains and losses affect decisions more than the amount of gain or loss. **The more we sacrifice for something, the more we resist losing it and the greater the feeling of loss if we do.** In most wars, the losing side continues fighting well after defeat is inevitable. Losses also escalate toward the end. Loss aversion by the losing side leads to even bigger losses.

People are cautious when it comes to gains. Given the choice of a sure $100 gain or double-or-nothing on a coin toss, the great majority will choose the sure $100. They view the coin toss, not as a chance to win $200, but as a chance to lose a sure $100 gain.

In a reverse situation, people become risk takers. Given the choice of a sure $100 loss or double-or-nothing on a coin toss, the great majority will choose the coin toss. They view the coin toss, not as a chance to lose $200, but as a chance to avoid a sure $100 loss.

People feel the pain of loss more than they feel the pleasure of gain. Some studies estimate that **losses have twice the psychological impact of comparable gains.**

When it comes to investing, loss aversion can be a two-edged sword. When investments drop in value because the market has dropped, the fear of seeing it drop further causes many people to sell at a loss. Oddly, they accept a sure loss to reduce the possibility of further loss. Of course, until they sold, it wasn't loss; it was only price fluctuation.

The other edge of the sword comes from hanging on to an investment that has tanked. This is more common with an investment the investor personally selected. People can get emotionally as well as financially invested in something. If the investment turns out to be a mistake, the investor may be in denial about its condition and deluded about its prospects.

With investing, loss aversion leads many people to sell their winners and keep their losers. This is not a formula for financial success.

Loss aversion leads people to throw good money after bad. A business venture that isn't making it can feel like an army losing a war. A realistic view would see the futility of wasting more resources on a lost cause. But the emotional investment taints the view of the financial investment. Money gets spent until the money runs out.

Loss aversion can be good in many situations. In the early stages of mankind, loss aversion was a necessary trait for survival. The gains to be made from taking risks were small compared to the potential loss of life. Loss aversion is still important today when it keeps you from taking unnecessary risks.

When it comes to money, loss aversion can hurt us more than it helps us. It can cause us to bail on a good thing that's going through a bad spell. It can cause us to hang on to a good thing gone bad because we want it to be good again. It can cause us to go when we should stop and to stop when we should go. It can cause us to change strategies that have worked, like the coach switching to the prevent defense. It can snatch defeat from the jaws of victory.

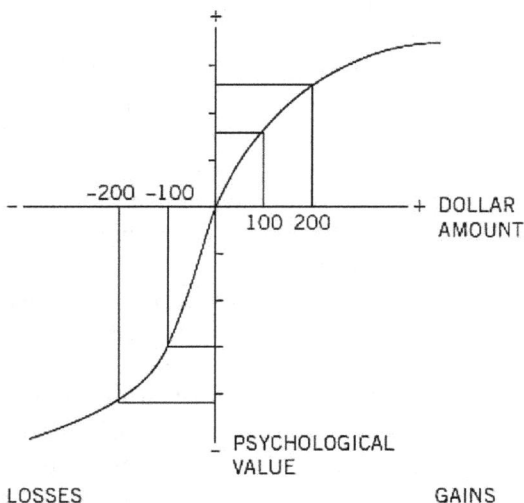

LOSSES   GAINS

FRAMING ANCHORS

Pakistan and Bangladesh are two countries that straddle India. They were known as West Pakistan and East Pakistan until Bangladesh broke off and became independent in 1971. Pakistan has a population of 200 million as of 2015 and an area of 796,095 square miles. Bangladesh has an area of 143,998 square miles. What is the population of Bangladesh?

Chevrolet priced the 2016 base Corvette sports car with 460 horsepower at $56,000. They also offered a 650 horsepower model for $80,000. Porsche priced the 2016 base 911 sports car with 350 horsepower at $82,000. They also offered a 560 horsepower model. What was the price for this model?

How did you estimate Bangladesh's population? You probably assumed Bangladesh's population density is similar to Pakistan's. That would make their population about 1/5th of Pakistan's, or about 40 million. Is that close to your estimate?

How did you estimate the Porsche's price? Porsche charged $228 per horsepower for the base model. If they charged that much for each additional horsepower, the price for the higher model would be $127,680. Is that close to your estimate?

The population of Bangladesh is 170 million. The price of the 560 horsepower Porsche 911 was $183,000.

You probably underestimated both numbers. If you did, you were affected by *anchoring*. **Anchoring occurs when people are influenced by a number that may have no bearing on the number they actually seek.** If you adjusted your estimates when you saw my estimates, you anchored a second time.

Most people would use the population of Pakistan and its relative size to Bangladesh as anchors to estimate Bangladesh's population. Similarities were assumed that weren't there. Most people would use the per-horsepower cost of the base Porsche as an anchor to calculate the cost of the higher model. That would seem logical, especially since the Corvette's per-horsepower costs were consistent from model to model.

We're subjected to anchors all the time. On Ebay, you'll see a "Buy It Now" price. That's an anchor. If you shop for a house, you'll see a listing price. That's an anchor. If you look at a wine list, you may see one wine that's much more expensive than the others. That's an anchor. These and hundreds of other anchors influence what you think a number should be.

Sellers will set a high anchor even though they don't expect to get that price. The high anchor forces the buyer to pull down harder on that price to get close to a "fair" price. Most people don't pull down enough before giving in.

For example, a man is selling a classic car. The price range for this car is $40-60,000. He offers it for sale for $70,000, though its value is $50,000. Buyer and seller finally agree at $55,000. The buyer paid more than its value, but he's happy because he paid far less than the asking price, the anchor. The seller is happy because a high anchor netted him an additional $5,000.

Anchors are strong influencers when people give to charities. In one study, people who had no anchor said they would give an average of $64 to a particular cause. When a $5 anchor was suggested, the average donation dropped to $20; when a $400 anchor was suggested, the average donation rose to $143.

Anchors can have an unintended effect, too. Some courts put a cap on awards. Setting a $1 million cap on jury awards does reduce huge awards. It also increases the smaller awards because $1 million becomes the anchor in smaller cases.

An anchor can work against us when we sell something. If you paid $200,000 for a house, that's your anchor. If the market price is less, it will be hard to sell at that lower price. If your neighbor just sold a similar house for $300,000, that will become your anchor. **Sellers look for high anchors; buyers for low ones.**

Anchoring is common in investing, too. It's hard to sell a stock for $35 a share when you paid $50. It's also hard to sell it for $60 a share, even when you paid $50, if last month it was selling for $70. Which anchor you choose determines whether you'll see the sale as a $10 gain or a $10 loss per share.

Let's return to the Corvette-Porsche comparison. Suppose you really wanted a new Corvette, but your significant other was not on board. To make your case, you compared the Corvette to the Porsche. You pointed out the high-horsepower Corvette cost less than the base Porsche, so it was really a good deal. The answer was still no. You then offered to "settle" for the base Corvette (which is what you really wanted all along).

You *framed* your argument to make your case. **Framing takes a situation and puts it in a certain context. When we practice framing, we put something in a context to best serve our purpose.**

Your significant other had been building frames, too. Your Corvette was now compared to a Honda Civic. The Civic was more fuel efficient, cost about one-third of the Corvette, and even came with a back seat. Practical frames like this are particularly hard to break.

Framing involves taking carefully selected anchors and using them to bolster our case. The Porsche was an anchor to frame the Corvette as a bargain. The Civic was an anchor to frame the Corvette as an extravagance.

Framing is used to make risks seem larger or smaller. For medical treatments, saying the survival rate is 90% sounds much better than saying the mortality rate is 10%. The statements say the same thing, but the first one is encouraging; the second one is frightening.

Framing is important in your finances, too. You're more likely to maintain a regular investment program if you're told that your chances of reaching your goal are 90%, rather than saying your chances of failure are 10%.

The anchors you choose and the frames you make will have a large effect on both your financial and overall well-being. Being aware of anchors and framing is a good start. Awareness enables you to use anchors and framing to make your case and get what you want. Awareness also enables you to spot when others are using anchors and framing to get what they want at your expense.

Finally, anchors are used to restrain and frames are used to enclose. Their symbolism is valid here. **Anchors and frames can restrain our thinking and enclose us from other perspectives.** There is potential for damage when others use them against you. The greater potential damage may come from your own anchors and frames.

VALUE VALUE

Value *(verb)*: to consider someone or something to be important or beneficial; to have a high opinion of.

Value *(noun)*: the regard that something is held to deserve; the importance, worth, or usefulness of something.

In Oscar Wilde's play, *Lady Windermere's Fan*, Cecil Graham and Lord Darlington have a conversation:
Cecil Graham: *What is a cynic?*
Lord Darlington: *A man who knows the price of everything, and the value of nothing.*
Cecil Graham: *And a sentimentalist, my dear Darlington, is a man who sees an absurd value in everything and doesn't know the market price of any single thing.*

Although Wilde's play was first produced in 1893, people are still the same. We still have cynics, people who see only price, but not value. And we still have sentimentalists, people who refuse to recognize price as one measure of value.

Value is very subjective; price is much less so. Value can also be expressed in terms other than money. When someone says "I would sacrifice my life for my child." they are valuing their child with the most valuable thing they have – their own life. They probably wouldn't make such a sacrifice for a stranger.

Value and price intersect when transactions occur. Buyer and seller don't usually start with equal values. They need to find a price acceptable to both. Money as a medium of exchange makes it easier to find that acceptable price. Everyone is familiar with money - it doesn't require conversion or translation.

A big obstacle to finding an acceptable price is the seller's perspective. **We value what is ours more than others do - a condition known as the** *endowment effect.* One example was just given about the value given to one's own children, but not to a stranger.

A better example is your home. When you live in a house for a while, it becomes *your home*. When you offer it for sale, others will value it as a house for sale, not as *their home*. Different perspectives lead to different perceptions of value and different offer and bid prices. Unless the seller reconciles the value as home with the market's value as a house, no sale will occur.

When Cecil Graham describes a sentimentalist, he's actually describing people under the endowment effect. We're sentimental about things that touch us personally, and many of our possessions are very personal. We will place an "absurd value" on something that touches us personally (a photo, a gift, a home). That value has no relationship to the "market price" others give it.

When Lord Darlington is describing a cynic, he's describing people who can only evaluate something based on market price. These people have the opposite problem of the sentimentalist. The sentimentalist assigns value by personal assessment, ignoring outside opinions. The cynic can't or won't assign a value and uses market price alone.

A sentimentalist might continue to own a stock that fell in price and was expected to fall more. The sentimentalist couldn't ignore the original value and focus on current value. The cynic, on the other hand, might rely on the current price as the final word on the stock's value. The cynic would sell the stock when the price fell, even if long-term prospects for the stock were excellent. In both cases, their perceptions of value can cost them.

When price is confused with value, one of two problems can occur. The first one is overpaying for something because it has a high price. High price is associated with equally high value, which may not be the case. It's easier to raise the price than to raise the quality; it's more profitable too, at least in the short run.

The other problem is the opposite – looking only at price and thinking the best value is the one with the lowest price. Another term for lowest price is cheapest. *Cheap* is defined with terms like small value, poor quality, inferior, devalued, and not worthy of respect. If someone calls you or something you own cheap, it's not a compliment.

For many items, value is better measured in utility than price. For example, a man is shopping for a suit. He narrows his choice to two; both are three-button, single-breasted, navy blue. They're made of different materials and by different manufacturers. One suit is $200; the other is $400. Which is the better value?

If our shopper only uses price to determine value, he would only consider the $200 suit. Price alone doesn't tell him all he needs to know. There's probably a good reason why one suit costs more.

The more expensive suit uses much better materials that maintain color and shape and don't wear as quickly. The stitching is straighter and stronger. The fit is better. The superior quality of the more expensive suit means it is good for 500 wearings; the cheaper suit is only good for 200.

The suit's purpose is to make its wearer look as good as possible as often as possible. The higher quality of the

$400 suit guarantees he will look better. He will also look better at a cost of $.80 per wearing; the cheaper suits costs $1.00 per wearing. Which is the better value now?

There are parts of your life that shouldn't have assigned values. Relationships and experiences come to mind. For things we negotiate in the marketplace, determining value requires looking at quality, expected utility, and yes, price. Value is determined where these three intersect.

In the long run, it's better to pay a fair price for something good than to pay a good price for something fair. And in the long run, the cheapest is usually the most expensive.

THE COSTS

It may have happened to you already. If it hasn't happened to you yet, there's still a chance it will. If you're smart and a little lucky, it won't happen to you more than once.

"It" is a bad relationship. You invest a lot of time and effort in it. Despite your efforts, you reach a point where you doubt the relationship will ever become what you hoped it would. You begin to consider your options.

You consider all the time invested in your current relationship. If you end it, all that time and effort will seem wasted. You wonder if more time invested can salvage the relationship.

You consider the possibility of other relationships. You know other relationships are possible, and that some of them would have to be better than your current one. But that's all you know.

"In for a penny, in for a pound" is an old English saying with more than one meaning. It originally meant if you owed a penny (pence), you might as well owe a pound; the penalties for non-payment of either were about the same. The more common meaning is once you start something you should finish it, regardless of cost. It's known as perseverance, a trait we admire. But it's worth remembering that **perseverance in a good cause is stubbornness in a bad one.**

Stubbornness is the usual result when you succumb to *sunk-cost fallacy.* **A sunk cost is a cost that has already been incurred and can't be recovered; it's a fallacy to think it can be.** Sunk costs are in the past; they should have no impact on future plans. But they do, and to an alarming extent.

It is unlikely that investing more time will turn a bad relationship into a good one. The time already invested is a sunk cost – it will never be recovered no matter how much additional time is invested. It's called a *sunk* cost for a reason.

There's another saying – Don't throw good money after bad. Even the best and brightest do it, though.

Max Bazerman, a professor at the Harvard Business School, created a unique auction. His students could bid on a $20 bill. Normally, such an auction would end when the bid reached $20. Dr. Bazerman added a twist. While the winner got the $20, the runner-up was also required to honor his/her bid. If the winning bid was $20 and the second highest bid was $19, that bidder had to pay $19, while receiving nothing.

Inevitably, the bidding went past $20; neither bidder wanted the sure loss. Every bid was a sunk cost for the bidders. This mindset pushed the bidding to where both parties suffered big losses. This auction has been conducted over 200 times. The lowest winning bid was $39; the highest was $437. The best and brightest at Harvard succumbed to sunk-cost fallacy. They threw astonishing amounts of good money after bad.

If you've held on to a money-losing investment too long, you've succumbed to sunk-cost fallacy. The sunk cost feels like an anchor around your neck. You delude yourself about the investment's prospects. You sink additional money into it, hoping to turn it around. You would've been better off selling at a loss and moving the money into something more productive.

Every choice we make comes with an *opportunity cost.* For everything we choose, there is something we don't choose. **The choice we don't make is the opportunity cost.**

If you continued in a bad relationship, the opportunity cost would be all the relationships you could have instead. Even if you weren't considering another relationship, the opportunity cost could also be the peace of mind of not being in a bad relationship.

There is an opportunity cost in money associated with each possession. Your financial resources are limited. **For everything you own, you forego the opportunity to own something else.**

You also pay an opportunity cost in time for each possession. You spend time earning money to buy, protect, and maintain a possession. You also spend time using that possession. **For everything you do, you forego the opportunity to do something else.**

Impulsive people are likely to ignore opportunity costs. When there is something they want to own or do, they act impulsively without considering all the costs. **Patient, contemplative people consider opportunity costs and have fewer regrets about their decisions.**

Patient, contemplative people also suffer less from sunk-cost fallacy. By investing time and research into something before investing money, these people have fewer delusions about their investment. Their investment is less likely to disappoint them. If it does, they can be objective enough to recognize the money is sunk and there's no point in throwing good money after bad.

Sunk costs are about the past. If a sunk cost turns out to be a mistake, leave it in the past. Don't compound the mistake by dragging it into the present. Don't throw good money after bad.

Opportunity costs are about the future. Carefully consider the opportunity costs before any investment of time and money. You don't want to spend the future lamenting missed opportunities of the past.

THE SUM IS ZERO

Warren Buffett probably knows more about investing than anyone ever. His ranking as one of the world's richest people testifies to his skill. He also knows the difference between investing and gambling. In a speech to MBA students, Buffett recalled an early lesson: "On my honeymoon I traveled out West. When I visited the casino and saw all these smart, well-dressed people participating in a game with the odds against them, it was then I realized I won't have a problem getting rich!"

Over the 2,500-year history of money, **one of humanity's biggest errors is mistaking gambling for investing, and vice versa.**

Misunderstanding the difference between gambling and investing is a two-edged sword. Mistaking gambling for investing leads to greater risks and greater losses. Mistaking investing for gambling leads to fewer risks and fewer gains.

Most people understand the concept of gambling if they've ever placed a bet. Whether the gambling occurs at a Friday night poker game or a Super Bowl bet, such bets have one thing in common – they're *zero-sum games*.

Zero-sum games create no wealth; they merely transfer wealth from one person to another. When six friends get together for an evening of poker, some will leave richer and some will leave poorer, but the total amount of money among them won't change.

In a zero-sum game like friendly poker among friends, the total odds for the group are even. If one player's odds of winning are 2 to 1, some other player or players' odds of winning are 1 to 2. Every cent of gain for one involves a cent of loss for another.

In a zero-sum game, you can tip the odds in your favor if you're better at the game than your opponents. However, it's hard for most people to accurately judge their skill level. Most people overestimate it, leading to losses.

Most zero-sum games are games of chance, not skill. **It's only a game of skill if *your* skill affects the outcome.** When two football teams play, it's a game of skill for the players only. For everyone else, they're betting on a zero-sum game of chance - a sucker bet because they have no control over the outcome.

With both investing and betting, you can gain or lose, but the similarity ends there. **With betting, someone *has* to lose.** There may also be many more losers than winners, lotteries being one example. **With investing, no one *has* to lose** because investing isn't a zero-sum game.

Investing is putting money to work with the opportunity to make more. **The key difference between gambling money and investment money is investment money works while gambling money doesn't.** That difference enables every potential investment to be a winner.

When people like Henry Ford and Bill Gates created multi-billion-dollar enterprises, those billions weren't transferred; they were created by creating products that benefitted billions of people over many decades. Such enterprises show **investing is designed to be win-win. Gambling is designed to be win-lose.**

Another difference between gambling and investing is addiction. For compulsive gamblers, winning at gambling activates the brain like cocaine does for cocaine addicts. Gambling gives the gambler a rush. If an investor gets a rush from investing, what passes for investing might actually be gambling.

Success in investing requires nothing more than fair amounts of skill and patience. You can increase your levels of skill and patience to become a better investor. Success in betting requires huge amounts of luck. By definition, luck is not something you can control. Luck also evens out over time. A winning streak today will be followed by a losing streak tomorrow. Very few gamblers have the discipline to quit in the middle of a winning streak. Fewer still have the discipline to quit during a losing streak, until they're wiped out.

There's nothing wrong in trying to be as efficient as possible in building wealth. There is also no escaping the correlation between risk and reward. Investing can mutate into gambling when it's done for similar reasons - the desire for quick riches and the thrill of making it happen.

Gambling creates risk where none existed before. With a zero-sum game, the floor of risk and the ceiling of reward are the same. In contrast, investing does not create risk; it spreads risk among those seeking the rewards of investing. Investment risk is also reduced by diversifying – not putting all your eggs in one basket.

There's one other very important difference between gambling and investing. **There is an upper limit to how much reward you can get from a bet.** Even if you're lucky enough to win a $1 bet with 100 to 1 odds, you'll only receive $100. If you're patient, **there is no upper limit on how large a $1 investment can grow.**

A $1 investment fifty years ago in Warren Buffett's Berkshire Hathaway Company would be worth over $10,000 today. In order to have a similar gain from

gambling, you would need to win 100 consecutive $1 bets, each with 100 to 1 odds against you. To put that in perspective, the odds of winning all 100 bets are:
1 in 100,000,000,000,000,000,000,000,000,000,000,000,000, 000,000,000,000,000,000,000,000,000,000,000,000,000,000, 000,000,000,000,000,000,000,000,000,000,000,000,000,000, 000,000,000,000,000,000,000,000,000,000,000,000,000,000, 000,000,000,000,000,000,000,000,000,000,000,000.

That number is a 1 followed by 200 zeroes. If you want to name it, say "one-hundred" and then "billion" twenty-two times. If you try generating it in a calculator, it reads "Error", a perfect summary of gambling on zero-sum games.

Match		Prize	Odds
⊙ ⊙ ⊙ ⊙ ⊙ + ⊙		Jackpot	1 in 175,223,510.00
⊙ ⊙ ⊙ ⊙ ⊙		$1,000,000	1 in 5,153,632.65
⊙ ⊙ ⊙ ⊙ + ⊙		$10,000	1 in 648,975.96
⊙ ⊙ ⊙ ⊙		$100	1 in 19,087.53
⊙ ⊙ ⊙ + ⊙		$100	1 in 12,244.83
⊙ ⊙ ⊙		$7	1 in 360.14
⊙ ⊙ + ⊙		$7	1 in 706.43
⊙ + ⊙		$4	1 in 110.81
⊙		$4	1 in 55.41

THE RESERVOIR

In 1930, the population of Las Vegas, Nevada was 5,000; today it is 2 million. In 1930, the population of Phoenix, Arizona was less than 50,000; today it is 4.5 million.

Many factors enabled these desert cities to grow over a hundred-fold in under a hundred years. No factor determines a city's size more than a reliable water supply. No factor determines a reliable water supply more than a reservoir.

The Colorado River is the closest major water source to Las Vegas and Phoenix. In 1930, the river was wild, its flow uncontrolled and unpredictable. In the 1930s, Hoover Dam was built on the Colorado. The dam created Lake Mead, the largest U.S. reservoir by water volume. Lake Mead can hold two years' river flow. It took five years to fill.

Hoover Dam provided electricity for Las Vegas and Phoenix to grow. But Lake Mead provided essential water to enable millions to live in a desert. The reservoir insured survival first and growth opportunities second.

Your money moves like the waters of the Colorado. Most of the time, its flow is adequate, predictable and manageable. Occasionally, there is high volume. More often, there is low volume. The periods of low volume are the problem.

Everyone needs a money reservoir. A money reservoir can be used for emergencies and more. But before a money reservoir can be used, it has to be built.

Lake Mead was filled by retaining part of the river's flow. The amount retained had to balance the needs of those downstream with the need to fill the reservoir in a reasonable amount of time. Above-average flows could shorten the time to fill, but they couldn't be assumed in the planning.

In building a money reservoir, you would take the same approach. **Unexpected inflows of money should be sent directly to the reservoir.** Such inflows may not occur at all, and they can't be counted on to meet your goals. They're merely a pleasant surprise and a chance to reach your goal ahead of schedule. A bonus from work, an inheritance, or a lucky weekend in Las Vegas are examples of unexpected inflows. When money falls into your lap, pour it into your money reservoir.

Most of your money reservoir would be filled with money diverted from other uses. **Filling your money reservoir would mean spending less during the time the reservoir is filling.** You would have to make adjustments to outflows. Some discretionary spending would have to be curtailed. It doesn't have to be permanent, though. Once you reached your goal for your money reservoir, you wouldn't need to continue diverting funds to it. However, if you established the habit, it's a good one to maintain. You don't know how much you'll need from your reservoir in hard times.

How big should your money reservoir be? For starters, it can't be too big. Lake Mead's size is limited by the height of Hoover Dam. Your money reservoir has no such limitations. As long as you're meeting your financial obligations and you have money you can add to your reservoir, keep adding to it.

If you're a single-income household, a good goal for your money reservoir is six months of living expenses. If the only wage earner becomes unemployed, six months of living expenses in the reservoir should be enough until a new job can be found.

A two-income household runs a smaller risk of having no income. For that reason, three months of living expenses is a good goal for the reservoir. If one income is substantially larger, a larger reserve may be needed. The goal should be to have enough in the reservoir to cover the expenses paid for by the higher income for six months.

Saving six months of living expenses is no small task. It would require setting aside ten percent of income for five years for a single household; two to three years for a two-income household. The burden could be made easier by designating all pay raises and all money from non-work to go into the reservoir.

The benefits of a money reservoir are worth the sacrifice to build it. **The reservoir creates security against the unexpected.** The unexpected might be a job loss, a medical emergency, or an uninsured loss. Borrowing to deal with the unexpected might be expensive and might not even be possible. An unexpected loss and no money reservoir might require selling assets at fire-sale prices to raise cash.

A money reservoir also enables you to seize opportunities. Whether it's a business venture or an asset at a great deal, some opportunities are only available to those with ready cash.

Even if a money reservoir is never needed, it pays for itself by providing peace of mind. Knowing a potential disaster doesn't also have to become a financial disaster makes it easier to handle whatever comes along.

Your money reservoir probably won't benefit you as much as Lake Mead did for Las Vegas and Phoenix. It doesn't have to. Your money reservoir will provide you with security and opportunity, which is all we should expect money to do.

THE PRICE OF PROCRASTINATION

Jean and Sue were best friends in high school. When they graduated in 1953, they both landed typist jobs at the same company. Part of their new employee orientation was a presentation by a mutual fund salesman. He talked about the advantages of investing early and regularly. Jean decided to invest $600 per year into an S&P 500 mutual fund, a collection of 500 stocks of the biggest American corporations. Sue decided to wait. She preferred to use her earnings to enjoy herself and make herself appealing to eligible young bachelors at her company.

A decade went by. Jean got married and left work to start a family. She stopped regular investing, but left her money in the mutual fund. By this time, Sue was pushing thirty and realized she needed to start investing. She feared she might be working another thirty-five years - she hadn't yet snagged a husband. Sue followed Jean's lead and started investing $600 per year in the S&P 500 mutual fund. Sue did this faithfully for the next thirty-five years.

Neither woman ever took any money out of her investment. Jean and Sue had remained friends over the years. One day they were having lunch and talking about the upcoming forty-five-year high school reunion. The topic drifted to their first jobs after high school and to their choices - Jean's to invest now and Sue's to invest later. They decided to compare notes on how their investments had done.

Sue went first. She had invested $600 per year every year for the last thirty-five years. Her investment had grown to an impressive $458,446*. Then it was Jean's turn. She had started forty-five years ago, invested $600 per year for ten years, and then stopped when she got married. Her investment had grown to an even more impressive $726,828*.

Sue was shocked. "How could you have more money than me? I invested for thirty-five years and you only invested for ten!" Jean didn't have a technical answer. All she could say was, **"I guess my ten-year head start was too hard to overcome."** She could have said a ten-year delay is also hard to overcome, but Sue already realized that.

Imagine your goals are a prize that awaits you at the top of a long set of steps. You have to climb the steps, but you have a limited amount of time because water will soon begin flooding the area. Some people look at the steps; they decide they'll never make it to the top in the given time, so they don't even try. These people refuse to acknowledge the coming flood. To do nothing is to be doomed, so any progress is better than none.

Some people get climbing right away. They know the sooner they get started, the sooner they will get to the top. Even if they don't get to the top, they'll still be above the flood waters. Consistent effort over time beats a desperate rush against time.

Which brings us to the last group. They don't start climbing until the water does. Then there's a desperate scramble up the steps. Their haste usually leads to falls and injuries that slow them down to where they drown. Such is the price of procrastination.

The heights of great men reached and kept
Were not attained by sudden flight,
But they, while their companions slept,
Were toiling upward in the night.

-Henry Wadsworth Longfellow

*These are actual results for these periods of time.
See chart at back of the book for the hard numbers.

BULLYING WITH BUCKS

He ranks sixth on the American Film Institute's list of greatest movie villains. He trails only Hannibal Lector, Norman Bates, Darth Vader, the Wicked Witch of the West, and Nurse Ratched. He ranks sixth despite being frail and old and confined to a wheelchair. He ranks sixth despite being a law-abiding citizen and a pillar of his community.

Our villain-in-question is Mr. Potter, from the Christmas classic *It's a Wonderful Life*. Mr. Potter's biggest fault is his uncontrolled greed. His greed made him the richest man in Bedford Falls. Yet, it isn't Potter's wealth or even his greed that makes him a classic villain. He ranks right up there with certifiable psychos because he used his wealth to bully an entire town into doing his will.

In recent years, bullying has received so much attention there is a government website to learn about and respond to bullying (www.stopbullying.gov). It states bullying behavior is typically aggressive, exploits an imbalance of power, and is repeated.

Adolescent bullying behavior usually disappears by adulthood. People usually grow up. Even if some adults wanted to behave like middle-school bullies, there's a higher price to be paid in adulthood.

Inequalities trigger bullying. In school, physical strength and popularity are the big inequalities. The quarterback is never bullied, but may be a bully. The scrawny introvert is rarely the bully, but is often bullied. These inequalities fade in adulthood and can even reverse. **In adulthood, brains rule over brawn, and**

"popular" doesn't exist. The quarterback may end up working for the scrawny introvert.

Adolescent bullying may fade in adulthood, but bullying behavior may not. Adults, like children, like to dominate – we just have different and, in many cases, more effective ways to dominate.

In elementary school, physical differences lead to a pecking order - big kids bully small ones. In middle and high school, social status is the big prize. Those who have it lord it over those who don't. What adults want more than physical or social dominance is *money*.

Adults gauge their position in the world through money more than anything else. Adults know physical strength and beauty fade. Adults know social status from a job can disappear if the job does. Yet, even if you're old and frail and ugly, even if you don't have a job and you're not well-liked; if you have enough money, you can exert influence and bully others. Just ask Mr. Potter.

There are countless ways to bully with money. An employer might require more output from employees, threatening wage and job cuts if they don't respond. A politician might withhold a contract unless an endorsement is given. A donor might demand a building be named after him in exchange for a donation.

Often, when people use money to compel others, they're bullying; often, but not always. Withholding a child's allowance until chores are done is not bullying with money. Offering workers a bonus for higher productivity is not bullying with money. **Bullying with money compels people to do something that's not in their best interests,** and that's often because the action is wrong.

Financial bullying occurs in marriages. If one partner dominates another through money, they're bullying with money. It may show up as a guilt trip over purchases, by controlling all credit cards and bank accounts, by limiting spending, or by belittling a partner's income.

One in ten couples claims a partner bullies with money, but it's double for couples under thirty-five. Many more men than women in this age group feel bullied. This imbalance may result from young women's increasing earning power and their demand for more control over their money.

Very few kids who are bullied in school ask for it. Adults living in poverty are like the smallest kids in the class. They're at the mercy of those with more, whether it's money or muscle. Adults, who through no fault of their own have little money, are easy targets for money bullies.

Some adults are innocent victims of money bullies, but some adults invite bullying by their own money weaknesses. They ask for it.

If you admire someone for their wealth alone, you set yourself up to be bullied with money. You judge them by how much money they have. How little character they may have doesn't matter. As long as they have money, you're a fan, and they can treat you as they wish. Your admiration of money alone also says something about *your* lack of character. If you admire someone for their wealth alone, you deserve the shabby treatment you'll get.

If you find yourself being bullied with money, you may have no one to blame but yourself. Going deep into debt, especially over vices like gambling, puts you in the position of slave to a master – the master being the one with money. Spending foolishly to maintain a high-status lifestyle is also an invitation to money bullies.

The more self-control you have over money, the less control you cede to others, especially money bullies.

In *It's a Wonderful Life*, George Bailey was the one person Mr. Potter couldn't bully with money. George wouldn't sell his integrity just to make more money working for Potter. George wouldn't let Potter's wealth blind him to the man's motives. And when Potter went all-out to ruin George, Potter's bullying with bucks proved no match for George's faith, family, and friends.

MEDIA, MOBS, AND MONEY

If you were asked to define *media*, you might give examples such as magazines, television, and the internet. *Media* is defined as "an intervening substance or agency through which something is transmitted, accomplished, conveyed, or transferred."

Media often has negative connotations, but media itself is not a problem; the content on media can be a problem. It's a software issue, not a hardware issue.

The term *Financial Pornography* was first coined in 1995. It referred to stories with titles such as "Top Ten Stocks to Own NOW!", "How to Double Your Money in a Year!", or "How to Retire Rich at 45!"

Financial pornography appeals to emotion. Emotion is dangerous to your financial health. **The media, including financial media, exploit the emotions of greed and fear.** They exploit whichever emotion dominates at that moment. That exploitation further increases the public's level of that emotion. Financial pornography is one of the reasons the stock market is more volatile and unpredictable than ever.

Financial pornography doesn't want to help you; it wants to sell to you. **All media is a business; it's not a public service. They exist to serve their interests, not yours.** When it comes to financial advice from mass media, you may think you are being informed when you are really being manipulated. Be skeptical.

Social media has been called word of mouth on digital steroids and the world's largest referral program. Social media has become the place for a business to be if they intend to stay in business. While it may be called social media, it is actually driven by market norms.

The real reason for the popularity of social media isn't the desire to keep up with friends; it's the almost endless opportunities for self-promotion.

Many people believe when you've got it, flaunt it. Social media is the perfect place to flaunt it. Social media doesn't have the self-imposed filters people use when face-to-face. **Social media is also an effective tool for peer pressure.** That peer pressure can include pressure to spend money you don't have for things you don't need.

Charles Revson, the founder of Revlon said, "In the factory we make cosmetics; in the store we sell hope." Revson understood that making a good product was no guarantee of success in the marketplace. Products need to be marketed as well as manufactured.

Manufacturing creates products. Advertising creates *desire* for products.

Advertising emerged in the twentieth century because of several factors. An industrial economy enabled more people to have disposable income. New media enabled advertising to reach more people. Finally, more people were concentrated in cities, making advertising more cost-effective by reaching larger numbers.

Reliable estimates say **Americans are exposed to 500 to 1,000 advertising exposures per day** – including TV commercials, billboards, print ads, internet ads, and logos on products from cereal to sandals. Studies have shown that the average American eight-year-old has a vocabulary of 4,000 words, of which 400 are brand names.

Constant advertising bombardment has two effects. Because of their sheer number, few messages have any impact. We become deaf to most of it. But there is a cumulative effect. Constant bombardment wears us down. Even if only 1% of the messages get through, that's 5 to 10 a day, every day.

As part of creating desire for a product, advertising attempts to make you feel dissatisfied with your present product. Most people are happy with a product until it is no longer state-of-the-art. **One way to get people to spend money is to make them believe they're regressing.**

While you may resist advertising's lure, your neighbors may not. If those around you are being seduced by advertising, you could become collateral damage. Seeing your neighbor's new car next to your old clunker every day might become too much to bear.

Consumer spending now accounts for two-thirds of our economy. Advertising drives a lot of consumer spending. Unfortunately, a lot of consumer spending is financed with debt for things that people merely want but don't need. Corporations borrow money for items that will make them richer. Consumers borrow money for items that will make them poorer.

Media, and the advertisers that finance it, see the public as a herd to be led. They see the public as a herd because they often act like a herd. **When things are going well, people act like a herd. When things go bad, they act like a mob.**

Part of this herd/mob mentality is instinctual. We are social animals; we want the acceptance of others. Many fear that taking a differing position will cause the group to doubt their intelligence, competence, or taste.

When submitting to a herd/mob mentality, it is easy to justify submission by deferring to the "collective wisdom" of the group. But collective wisdom is a myth.

Wisdom is created through personal experience. Unlike knowledge, wisdom cannot be effectively transmitted from one person to another. **Knowledge can be accumulated over time, and it can be shared over time and among people; wisdom can do neither.** To illustrate, while we have increased our ability to make weapons (cumulative/collective knowledge), we have not increased our ability to prevent war (wisdom).

In groups, people are more easily agitated. Every sentiment and act is more contagious and more likely to trigger action. A group regresses to its lowest common denominator, turning into a herd or a mob.

Stupidity proliferates faster than wisdom, especially in groups. The ability to quickly move money with a mouse click or a screen tap increases the danger that people will follow a herd/mob mentality and do really stupid things with their money.

There is one group in America that seems immune to media manipulation, including manipulation via social media. This group isn't manipulated by advertising to spend foolishly, either. They have no interest in competing with or comparing themselves to their neighbors through status symbols. This group seems impervious to media or mobs. This group is America's wealthy.

The wealthy believe that financial independence is more important than displaying social status. Their disinterest in status symbols liberates them from the influence of advertising and peer pressure. The wealthy have their own agenda, and they recognize that the media has a much different one. Finally, the wealthy know that a herd or a mob has many heads, but few brains.

THE MARCH TO AVERAGE

If there's one field where people are more statistics-crazy than finance, it's baseball. Major-league baseball has been around since 1876. There have been over 210,000 games played in its first 140 years. At least 2,400 games are played each year. Along with a rich history, major-league baseball has a huge database.

Despite a long and diverse history, here are some baseball stats that are predictable year after year:

- The best team will win around 100 games.
- The worst team will lose around 100 games.
- The best pitcher will win 20 to 24 games.
- The best hitter will have a .310 to .340 batting average.
- Your team won't win the World Series.

Because the baseball regular season has so many games (162 vs. 82 in basketball and hockey; 16 in football) statistics are more predictable. **As population size and time increase, the numbers move closer to their long-term averages. The technical terms for these moves are *progression/regression to the mean.***

The S&P 500 is the most-used measurement of the U.S. stock market. It has been around five years longer than major-league baseball. Its best year ever was 1933, when it gained 56.8%. Its worst year was 1931, when it lost 44.2%. Both are big swings, but the biggest gain came just two years after the biggest loss. Also, these years were during the Great Depression, when nothing in the financial world was normal.

The stock market can move a lot from year to year. It can even climb or fall for several years in a row. However, if you look at the S&P 500 over longer periods, such as 10 years, patterns become more predictable.

While the best one-year return for the S&P 500 was over 56%, its best ten-year average return was 21%. The worst one-year return was over minus-44%, but the worst ten-year average return was minus-5%. Just as in baseball, the longer the season, the more the results move toward their long-term averages. **Hot and cold streaks blend together over time and you end up with warm, cool, or tepid.**

Whenever something is running hot or cold, whether it's our favorite team or our investment portfolio, it feels like it will continue forever. **We take the recent past and extend it to infinity.** It's why a team gives a player a ten-year contract after one good year. It's also why they fire the manager after a ten-game losing streak. It's why individuals buy stocks when they've been soaring, despite high prices. It's also why they sell those same stocks at low prices when they've been sinking.

Streaks, hot or cold, hijack emotions. When our investments soar, we get greedy and want more. When they sink, we get fearful and sell at any price. We forget that our investments and our favorite team will regress or progress toward average, given time.

Understanding progression/regression to the mean may be consoling, but a long-term average can also mask a lot of short-term volatility. In 1987, the S&P 500 had a return of 5.7%. While that number would imply an average year, on one day alone, October 19th, the S&P 500 dropped by more than 20%! That year for investors was like standing in the kitchen with one hand on a hot stove and the other in the freezer. *On average*, the temperature is fine, but the extremes are a little hard to take.

If your investments are diversified, and if you understand progression/regression to the mean, you'll be less likely to let your emotions hijack you when the bulls and bears run amok on Wall Street. If you control your emotions and set realistic goals, the march to average will be good enough to get you there.

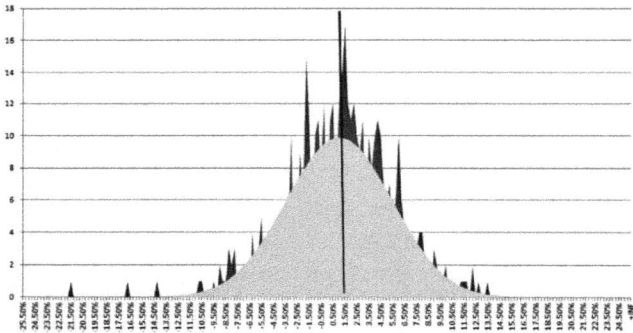

Distribution of monthly returns for the S&P 500

In prosperity, caution; in adversity, patience.

Dutch proverb

LET IT GROW

Most of us have heard the story of Peter Minuit and the Dutch purchasing Manhattan Island in 1626 for $24 worth of beads and trinkets. The story is told mostly to point out what a shrewd deal the Dutch made at the expense of the natives.

The shrewdness of this deal depends on your perspective. If you look at Manhattan in all its 21st century glory, Peter Minuit was a visionary genius. But the genius of the deal depends on several variables.

One variable is how much was actually paid for Manhattan in 1626. Payment was made in merchandise valued at 60 guilders, the Dutch coin. Guilders were made of silver, and 60 guilders weighed about 18 troy ounces (the measure for silver). At this writing, silver is worth about $15 per troy ounce, making the purchase price of Manhattan in 1626 closer to $270.

Another variable is Manhattan's worth today. At this writing, Manhattan real estate is valued at about $1,200 per square foot (really). Manhattan is 33.77 square miles or 941,453,568 square feet in size. At $1,200 per square foot, the land of Manhattan is worth about $1.13 trillion.

The final variable is the interest rate it would take to turn $270 into $1.13 trillion in 390 years (1626 to 2016). It would seem impossible to generate a high enough interest rate to turn *each dollar* into almost $4.2 billion in that period of time. The annual interest rate needed to turn $270 into $1.13 trillion in 390 years is - are you ready? - 5.85%. That's right - just 5.85%. Rounded to the nearest hundredth of a percent, that interest rate also leaves a surplus of $20.5 billion, enough to buy eight Empire State Buildings.

An interest rate of 5.85%, compounding for 390 years, turns $1 into more than $4.2 billion or $270 into $1.13 trillion. It may seem impossible, but it's really just math. (see appendix)

The trick to turning so little into so much is compounding. ***Compounding* means you let the interest payments stay with the rest of the money and continue to earn interest, too.** Over time, the amount of accumulated interest gets so big it dwarfs the original investment. Interest being left to earn more interest – that's all compounding is. The higher the interest rate and the longer the time, the bigger the pile of money becomes.

What if the original $270 in 1626 earned 5.85% annual interest, but the interest was taken out each year? How much would the interest payments amount to? An interest payment of 5.85% on $270 comes to $15.80 per year. Multiply $15.80 by 390 years and you get $6,162.

Which would you rather have – interest payments totaling $6,162, or a net worth of $1,130,000,000,000? Those numbers are the difference between taking the interest as income or leaving it to grow.

Since you won't live 390 years, you won't be able to turn $1 into $4.2 billion. But you're likely to live at least sixty years between your first paycheck and your last breath. One dollar invested for sixty years growing at an 8% compounded rate would become $101.26. One dollar became one-hundred more, but the original dollar bred less than five more dollars. The other ninety-five were bred by compound interest dollars that were reinvested to keep growing.

Both time and interest rates determine how much your money will grow. The dollar that was invested for sixty years grew more in the last ten than it did in the first fifty. If the interest rate had been only 6% instead of 8%, the total after sixty years would have been only $32.99 instead of $101.26. It would take twenty more years at 6% interest to get to $100.

If your only path to wealth is through work, you won't get there. If your path is through your money working, you have a much better chance. **The best way to put your money to work is find a productive place for it and then leave it to do its thing.**

Money doesn't grow on trees, but it grows like a tree. Finding a good place for it to grow is the first step. It will seem to grow slowly at first, but as it gets bigger, it adds size rapidly. It will also grow best when it isn't disturbed. And if you let it grow, it will eventually produce fruit even while the tree keeps growing.

"Compound interest is the eighth wonder of the world. He who understands it, earns it; he who doesn't, pays it."

-Albert Einstein

BLOWING UP YOUR MONEY

Imagine you buy a loaf of bread every two days at the corner bakery. The first day the bread costs $1. Two days later, it costs $2. Two days after that, it costs $4. The price doubles every two days. A loaf of bread that cost $1 at the beginning of the month costs almost $33,000 by the end of the month. Seems impossible, doesn't it?

This exact situation occurred in Germany in 1923. After losing World War I, Germany was forced to pay huge reparations to France and Great Britain. The German government began printing huge amounts of marks, the German currency, to meet all its obligations. All that money chasing a limited amount of things to buy sent prices soaring. In January 1923, a 5 million mark note was worth $714.29. By October of that year, it was worth $1/1,000^{th}$ of a cent.

What do people do when their money becomes worthless? For starters, they stop using it. They use more stable foreign currencies instead. They revert to a barter system. They also look for radical change in the government they blame for the problem. In the case of Germany, they eventually turned to the Nazi party and Adolf Hitler for a solution.

Inflation **is the term for money losing value over time.** You recognize inflation through rising prices. Germany in 1923 was a classic case of *hyper*inflation. The United States has never experienced anything so bad, though inflation frequently follows wars. Win or lose, wars cost a lot, and governments create more money to pay for wars.

Why would a government create more money if it will create more inflation? Many national governments, like the federal government of the United States, can create their own money. These governments also spend money – lots of it. Governments can pay for their spending in one of three ways. They can raise taxes, which is never popular. They can borrow, but that money has to be repaid with interest. They can also create new money, sometimes by printing it, but more frequently by creating it electronically. Creating money enables a government to spend freely now, but the cost is often paid later in the form of inflation.

Inflation is just another example of supply and demand at work. If everyone in your town suddenly saw their incomes double, you could expect prices of everything in your town to rise quickly, too. **If more money is chasing the same number of goods and services, the bidding for them will push prices higher.**

Prices can move in the other direction too, though it's rarer. During the Great Depression of the 1930's, the U.S. had *deflation*, where prices dropped. Millions were out of work, so there was little money in circulation and prices fell. Deflation may sound good (prices falling), but if people think something will be cheaper in the future, they won't buy today. If no one is spending, the economy grinds to a halt. In contrast, modest inflation can stimulate the economy because people know it's cheaper to buy something now than to wait.

If inflation is modest (under 5% per year) you won't pay much attention. But even modest inflation can hurt you financially over time.

If you got a 3% pay raise every year, but inflation averaged 3% every year too, in twenty years you would have made no progress. You would be making more money, but everything rose in price by the same amount. If your investments grew 3% per year during that time, you would have made no progress there, either. We work for pay raises and invest instead of spend with the hope that we will be able to buy more in the future. **If inflation eats up your pay raises and your investment gains, it's like walking up the down escalator.**

During your working years, pay raises can keep the effects of inflation from hurting you. Cost of living increases in wages are one way to reduce the effects of inflation. It's why these kinds of increases exist. As you progress in your career, promotions and the raises that go with them should keep you ahead of inflation. It's the years after you stop working that can be difficult.

Inflation, at various levels, goes on throughout your working life. Because of inflation, the amount you thought would be enough to live on in retirement may turn out to be far too little. For example, right now you may figure that $50,000 per year would be enough to live on when you retire. But that estimate is based on today's prices. If retirement is thirty years away, and if inflation averages just 3% per year between now and then, you won't need $50,000 per year in retirement; you'll need over $120,000. With 3% inflation per year over thirty years, what costs $50 today will cost $121 then. **You have to invest enough to allow for inflation. You also have to invest aggressively enough to outpace inflation.** If you don't, you may have far less to live on in retirement than you planned.

Inflation won't stop when you retire, either. Many retirees don't calculate for inflation in retirement, and many don't have incomes that can increase. If you were to live twenty years in retirement, and inflation averaged 3% per year during that time, what cost $1.00 at the beginning of your retirement would cost $1.80 at the end. On a fixed income, that would mean buying about half as much at the end of retirement as at the beginning.

When you listen to old people talk about the "good old days", one of their favorite topics is how much cheaper things were back then. In 1960, you could buy a new car for $2,000, a house for $10,000, and a year's tuition at a state university for $500. The price differences between then and today are the result of inflation over that time. Old people may think prices are high today, but one day you'll look back at today's prices and remember them fondly for being so low. The cycle of inflation also breeds a cycle of nostalgia.

Even though there's almost nothing you can do to affect the rate of inflation, the worst thing you can do about inflation is ignore it. **Your long-term financial plans should allow for inflation and resulting higher prices.** You may not enjoy paying $30 for a hamburger when you're eighty, but it would be nice to know you can.

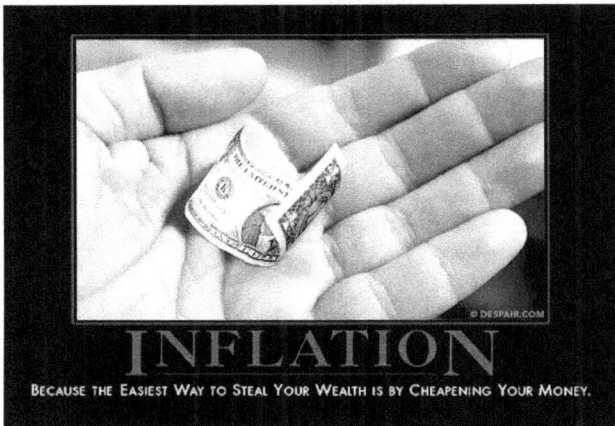

INFLATION
BECAUSE THE EASIEST WAY TO STEAL YOUR WEALTH IS BY CHEAPENING YOUR MONEY.

BALANCING ACT

If you want to know how you're doing financially, two statements will tell you. One is the *income statement* (more on that later). The other is the *balance sheet*. Your income statement shows how you did over a certain period. It's like the box score for a ball game. Your balance sheet shows how you stand at a certain point in time. It's like the league standings.

The balance sheet has two sides. One side lists *Assets*. Assets are anything you own that has value. For a business, it could be factories, offices, equipment, even their brand name. For an individual, it could be a home, cars, cash, retirement accounts, even a collection of vintage Star Wars action figures. If you own it and it has value, it goes on the asset side of your balance sheet. By now you realize **assets are good**.

The other side of the balance sheet lists *Liabilities*. Any duty to pay someone is a liability. Most liabilities are debts. Debts for an individual include mortgages, car loans, student loans, and credit cards. In addition to your own debts, if you co-signed a loan for someone, that's a liability. If you owe back taxes, that's a liability. If you injured someone in a car accident and didn't have insurance, that's a liability. By now you realize **liabilities are bad**, or at least too many of them are bad.

In businesses, the difference between the value of assets and liabilities is *Stockholder's Equity*. It's listed on the liabilities side of the balance sheet to get the balance sheet to balance. For you, the difference between the value of your assets and liabilities is *Net Worth*. If you want to be a millionaire, your net worth must be at least a million dollars; you need at least a million dollars more in assets than liabilities.

When we think about wealth, we usually think about income. Income is usually the main ingredient in creating wealth, but income alone doesn't create wealth. The income statement only tells you how you're using that main ingredient. The balance sheet tells you if you're actually wealthy. Income is what you make; wealth is what you keep. No matter how big your income, you won't become wealthy if you spend it all. **It isn't what you make, it's what you keep that matters.**

To increase wealth, you can increase the assets and/or reduce the liabilities. It takes time to increase assets or reduce liabilities. It doesn't take long to reduce assets or increase liabilities, though. Most people aren't wealthy because they forget that fact.

Think of your assets like a sponge, soft and squishy. The value of your assets can change, like the size and weight of a sponge. A stock portfolio, a house, a car, Star Wars figures - their values change all the time. And it's others, the buyers, who decide what your assets are worth. You try to own assets that will go up in value. You hope their value grows like a sponge filling with water; not shrink like a sponge getting wrung out.

Think of your liabilities like granite, hard and unbreakable. Almost all liabilities are created by contracts or laws. When you borrow money, you sign a contract written by the lender. It was designed to protect them, not you. There is only one way to reduce the liability – pay them back as promised in the contract. If a liability was created by a court decision, like child support, you can face jail if you don't pay. The only way to reduce liabilities is to chisel away at that granite until it's gone.

Sometimes the values of assets rise quickly, like real estate in the early 2000's, or the stock market every few years. When that happens, it's tempting to take on new liabilities. You can borrow money, buy some luxuries or take a vacation, and your balance sheet will still be OK. The problem is the asset values eventually shrink while the liabilities do not (sponges and granite).

If the liability side of your balance sheet became so large that your assets and income couldn't cover them, you might seek relief through *Bankruptcy*. Bankruptcy gives you a chance to get out from under that pile of granite, but at a price.

There are different types of bankruptcy. Under Chapter 7 bankruptcy, most of your debts would be cancelled; most, but not all. No bankruptcy gets rid of student loans, alimony, or child support. In exchange for debt relief, you may have to sell your "luxuries". You won't have credit cards, and you may not be able to get a loan for up to ten years.

Chapter 13 bankruptcy is less drastic than Chapter 7. Chapter 7 cancels most debts, but you have to qualify. Chapter 13 sets up a debt repayment schedule everyone can live with. If you have a steady income and the debts are under a certain amount, Chapter 13 is the lesser of two evils.

Bankruptcy is an act of desperation. It requires long-term pain for short-term gain. Trading long-term pain for short-term gain is always tempting if you're a short-term thinker. Unfortunately, the long-term arrives too soon and stays too long, long after the short-term gain is just a memory.

IN AND OUT

Are you someone who runs short of money between paychecks? Are you someone who can't explain where large chunks of income went? Do you feel like there's a leak in your checking account? If so, help is on the way.

You learned about balance sheets in the previous lesson. Your other important financial statement is the *income statement*. In a business, the income statement and balance sheet are two of the most important among many financial statements. For personal finance, a balance sheet and an income statement that includes cash flow information are sufficient.

The balance sheet shows your assets, liabilities, and net worth at a particular point in time. **The income statement shows the sources and uses of money over a certain period of time. Cash flow deals with the timing of money going in and out.**

An income statement can be for an individual or a household. If income is pooled and expenses are shared, a household income statement makes more sense.

For most, the income side of an income statement is simple. There are probably one or two incomes from jobs. There may be additional income from investments, but for most households, the income side of the statement is brief. Gross income before taxes can be listed on the income statement, but the figure you will compare against household expenses is the *net income*, the amount that comes home.

Since most of your expenses are paid monthly, a monthly income statement is the shortest period to cover. Personal balance sheets only need to be generated at year-end. You would also want to generate an annual income statement at year-end.

An income statement covering the period between balance sheets can show how your management of income and expenses created changes in your balance sheet. Early in your working life, your balance sheet will be affected more by your income statement. Early, you're building assets from a small base. During this time, your income will be the main source of assets added to your balance sheet. As assets grow over time, income adds a smaller proportion to assets each year.

In a business, the difference between gross income and expenses is labeled profit or loss. Your income statement will look at the difference between net income and expenses. Call that number what you want - profit, loss, victory, defeat, whatever. **Your goal is to have income exceed expenses; your financial stability depends on it.**

The hardest part of putting together an income statement is accurately recording expenses. Recurring expenses that leave a trail, like rent, mortgage payments, and insurance premiums are easy to track. Non-recurring expenses and ones that fluctuate from month to month like food, entertainment, and gas are harder to track.

Paying cash makes it harder to keep track of expenses, though paying with cash helps control overspending. Paying with a debit or credit card creates a record you can review to record expenses. Using a credit card is only recommended if you pay the credit card bill in full every month. Saving all receipts and keeping a log of all expenses will also help create a more accurate income statement. **The goal is to know where all of your money is going every month.**

If you know where your money has been going, you can redirect it to where you want it to go. It isn't the larger known expenses like a mortgage that create income-expense imbalances; it's things like dining out that don't seem like much but can really add up over a month or a year. You may be surprised at how much you actually spend on some expenses when you start keeping an accurate record.

Cash flow deals with the timing of income and expenses. For most households, cash flow isn't a major consideration because both income and expenses are consistent from month to month. If income is irregular, or if it comes less frequently than expenses, cash flow may be an issue. Also, if some expenses are large but infrequent, like an annual property tax bill, cash flow may suffer.

If income and/or expenses don't follow a regular pattern from month to month, **a reserve fund is needed to cover expenses that get ahead of income.** A reserve fund can get started when income exceeds expenses. The fund can then be used when expenses exceed income. Over the course of a year, income and expenses should smooth out. During shorter periods, cash flow may be uneven. If so, **a reserve fund will enable you to make all payments on time and protect your credit rating.**

Personal balance sheets and income statements are analytical tools to help you find where your money is going and how much is staying with you. **If you want more control over where your money is going and you want more of it to stay with you, creating these statements is one of the best ways to start.**

(Templates for balance sheet and income statement are in the appendix.)

TAKING CONTROL

One of the most effective psychological tools in breaking down a prisoner is creating the feeling in the prisoner's mind that he has no control. Everyone wants to control their lives; one of our greatest fears is the fear of losing control. At various times, we all experience feelings of loss of control and the psychological stress that goes with it. Some of the loss of control is caused by external forces; much of it is our own doing.

Mention the word *budget* to most people and they cringe. They cringe because they misunderstand a budget's purpose. A budget is often viewed as an indictment for reckless spending and as punishment for same. A budget shackles the individual to a program of austerity and denial that sucks all the joy out of life. Someone who has to "go on a budget" feels the resentment and humiliation of a chastised child. *Budget* is a dirty word because it's seen as a reaction to money mistakes, not as a proactive way to prevent mistakes.

A budget is not a loss of control of spending; it is gaining control of spending. A budget is you telling your money where to go; not asking where your money went. A budget is not present punishment; it is liberation from future punishment. A budget is not proof of financial incompetence; it is proof of good financial stewardship. If a budget causes a reduction of short-term pleasures, it more than offsets it by greatly increasing long-term financial security, opportunity, and success.

Someone may have an externally imposed budget if they fail to create their own budget. If their failure is big enough, an outside overseer like a bankruptcy judge takes control and imposes a budget. No one wants that.

One reason so many people cringe at the idea of a budget is they feel that a budget will constrain them. No budget can constrain you. A budget is nothing more than words and numbers on a spreadsheet. A budget by itself won't be able to constrain you if you see something at the mall and you "just have to have it."

The purpose of a budget is not to constrain, but to direct. A budget is a rudder, not an anchor. When people see their spending patterns and how those patterns hurt them in the long run, they will instinctively want to change those patterns on their own, without feeling constrained into doing it by a budget.

It's better to be drawn to do something than to be pushed to do it. A budget-as-constraint is like being pushed against your will. As soon as temptation presents itself, someone in the household will crack, and the budget will be busted. A budget-as-direction will draw everyone in the household to a better financial place. They will all be motivated for the right reasons, and success will be far more likely. Changing their spending patterns is something they will *want* to do, not something they feel they *need* to do.

Your budget should be created by you. You would decide how you want your income allocated. You would also create a record of where your money is currently going. A budget would show you the difference between where your money is going and where you want it to go.

Making the shift from your current situation to your new priorities should be evolutionary, not revolutionary. You would look at how much is currently going to each spending category. You would look at categories that are not getting enough funding, such as savings. You would develop a timetable to reduce the amount being wasted (such as credit card interest) and increase the amount to categories like savings. Each month you would shift a little more money from where it was misspent to the categories you determined are important.

Your finances should adapt to your budget. Your budget shouldn't beat your finances into submission.

Once a budget is established, the budget can actually be liberating, rather than constraining. In creating a budget, a family prioritizes their spending. Without a budget, money to be shared or saved will amount to whatever is left at the end of the month. Of course, without a budget, there is no money left at the end of the month. **A budget is the best way to put yourself at the head of the line to get your share of your money.**

A budget is also liberating because it can eliminate disputes about how much should be spent in what categories and which categories take priority. A budget sets priorities and limits, and it promotes self-control in spending. It also promotes team spirit and a shared vision for the household. A household budget developed with everyone involved (even children) can have positive effects for a family beyond the financial.

If you write down what you want, whether it's a plan to manage time or manage money, you begin to take control. You are saying "This is mine!" and that you, and only you, are going to decide how it is to be used. To create a budget is to take control. There's no better feeling.

HEAD OF THE LINE

Six months ago you went to work like any other day. At 10 o'clock, everyone was called into a meeting. The company was going through a rough period, so everyone was dreading this meeting. Layoffs were expected.

After giving a status report on the company's finances, the CEO announced that payroll reductions were necessary. Everyone was expecting layoffs, but the CEO gave the employees a choice.

Choice One: Five percent of the employees would be laid off. They would be chosen at random, so every employee had a one in twenty chance of becoming unemployed.

Choice Two: Every employee, from the CEO down, would take a 5% pay cut, effective immediately. Everyone would also keep their jobs.

That afternoon, the employees voted on which choice they preferred. By an overwhelming margin, they chose a 5% pay cut over 5% layoffs. The certainty of a 5% pay cut seemed better than the possibility of a 100% pay cut.

While you didn't like the idea of a pay cut, you were able to make the necessary adjustments to pay your bills. You became more careful with your spending, but your lifestyle was largely unchanged. After six months, you didn't even notice you'd taken a pay cut.

Six months before the company-wide meeting, you were in another meeting. It was a presentation on the company's 401(k) retirement plan. You were not participating in the plan. They talked about the importance of investing for retirement, about investment options, and about the company match on contributions.

It all sounded good, but you didn't think you could spare any income to participate at that time.

Looking back on it now, you realize you could have spared some income to begin investing in your 401(k) plan. You also realize something else.

When the take-home pay reduction was your choice and you were the beneficiary, you couldn't do it.

When the reduction wasn't your choice and you weren't the beneficiary, you discovered you could.

When we're tested by outside forces, we find we're capable of more than we thought. That's good. It also means we underestimate our capabilities. That's bad.

Many people don't save at all or don't save enough because they don't believe there's money to spare. Then some outside force comes along and they discover their true capabilities.

If those people recognized their capabilities and started saving earlier, they would have money to use in a financial emergency like a pay cut. They could also suspend saving until the emergency passed, freeing up money to help get through the emergency.

When it comes to putting money aside for their own benefit, the main reason so many don't isn't because they're incapable. **The main reason is they choose to stand at the end of the line.** By the time they get to the head of the line, the money is all gone.

If you're the one working and sacrificing for your money, shouldn't you be standing at the head of the line to benefit from it?

When asked this question, many people respond by saying they have all these other obligations to pay first. It's important to meet one's financial obligations. But many of those other obligations wouldn't exist or would be smaller if the obligation to oneself had been met first.

People who spend all they make and don't save might argue that money to pay themselves first can't be created out of thin air. True, but it could have been created by spending a little less on everything. If you resolved to save 5% of your income, you could come up with the money by spending 5% less on the things you spend money on now. You could also designate 100% of pay raises to go to savings.

It isn't a matter of income; it's a matter of priorities. There are people making a million dollars a year who don't save a dime. There are also people making 5% of that who manage to save 15% of their income. **No matter how much you make, unless you move to the head of the line, you won't be able to save anything.** There are an endless number of spending opportunities ready to cut in line ahead of you if you let them. Plant yourself at the head of the line and don't move!

One of the easiest ways to get to the head of the line and stay there is to pay yourself first – literally. Have money taken out of your paycheck – before you get it – and have it deposited directly into your 401(k) plan or a savings account where you won't touch it. If you look at your pay stub, you'll notice there's a deduction that's already made from your paycheck – taxes. If this system works for the government, it will work for you, too.

Beginning a savings program where you pay yourself first is a little like giving blood. It stings a little at the beginning, but very quickly you don't even feel it. It's also like giving blood in another way. What you give up is hardly missed and will get replaced in time. And what you give up serves a greater purpose where it's going.

IN THE HOLE

If you lived in Birmingham, England in 1816 and you couldn't pay a court-ordered judgment, you were likely to be sent to debtor's prison. You would have to pay for your keep through prison labor, and you would also have to work to pay off your debt before being released.

If you lived in Birmingham, Alabama in 2016 and you couldn't pay a court-ordered judgment, you were likely to be sent to prison. Miscellaneous court fees, fines, and charges would cause the amount you owed to triple. There would be no prison labor available to pay off the debt, and you weren't allowed to return to your job to earn money to pay off the debt.

The penalties for unpaid debt haven't changed much in two centuries. People can still be sent to jail for owing small amounts of money the court ordered them to pay. The difference between the nineteenth and twenty-first centuries is there is much, much more debt now.

If all personal and government debt were allocated to each American family, it would take those families more than five years to pay it off, using every penny they made. That debt doesn't include home mortgages, either.

Governments have been worse than households in adding debt. Even after adjusting for inflation, the per capita share of the federal debt is *fifty times* what it was a century ago.

The first modern credit card was issued by Bank of America in 1958. The average American household had more than $7,000 in credit card debt in 2016.

In 2010, total student loan debt surpassed total credit card debt for the first time. In 2016, the average student loan debt was over $33,000. **Student loan debt impedes** marriage, children, home-buying, and business start-ups, especially for graduates under thirty. Student loan debt impedes the entire economy.

Debt creates a financial hole. The first thing to do when you're in a hole is – stop digging. **The first step in reducing debt is to stop taking on more debt.** It may feel like going through drug withdrawal, but reducing debt first means getting rid of all credit cards. It also means declining all offers for new credit. If you've gotten into trouble with debt, you'll never get out of trouble unless you cut off all sources of debt.

The most common feeling expressed by people who report debt problems is a loss of control. This loss goes beyond the loss of financial control. People overrun by debt lose control over their bodies and minds. They suffer huge increases in physical and mental problems, relative to the general population. The emotional stress can break families apart. **Money problems, specifically overwhelming debt, are a leading cause of divorce.**

In 1956, William Fair and Earl Isaac began using mathematics and computers to analyze credit risk. They created the FICO (short for Fair Isaac Corp.) score. It's more common name is the credit score.

FICO scores range from 300 to 850. Most people score between 650 and 750. The score is based on ratings in five general categories:
- Payment History - 35%
- Amounts Owed - 30%
- Length of Credit History - 15%
- New Credit - 10%
- Types of Credit Used - 10%

You can improve your credit score with these steps:
- Pay your bills on time.
- If you missed payments, get current and stay current.

- Contact creditors or see a legitimate credit counselor if there's a problem.
- Keep balances low on credit cards.
- Pay off debt rather than moving it around.
- If you have a short credit history, don't open several new accounts too rapidly.
- Shop for a loan in a short period of time; it shows you're seeking a single loan and not multiple loans.
- Don't open new accounts you don't need.
- Don't co-sign loans for others.

The best way to reduce debt and raise your credit score is with a good-paying job. But high debt and a low credit score can be a major barrier to getting that job.

Part of the background check for job applicants now includes obtaining a copy of the applicant's credit report. There are reasons to check an applicant's credit history.

An employer runs a risk if an employee has financial problems. Theft from the employer is the most common risk. Theft of property is a risk, but the greater risk is the theft of money, primarily through fraud.

An employee with financial problems also presents the risk of a frivolous lawsuit. An employee with overwhelming debt may see a lawsuit as a source of cash and a way out of debt.

Your credit report can show a potential employer how you manage your affairs. If your personal financial management is a disaster, they will doubt your management of their business affairs will be any better.

A Chinese proverb is: *Luck is when preparedness meets opportunity.* Debt can leave you unable to take advantages of opportunities. A financial corollary to the Chinese proverb is: *Light Load + Liquidity = Luck.*

Keep your debt load as light as possible. Set money aside where it's accessible. You'll be amazed how many opportunities will cross your path. More important, you'll be able to take advantage of those opportunities.

Every person has an individual tolerance for risk; they also have an individual tolerance for debt. If you struggle to make debt payments and provide the necessities, you are past your tolerance for debt.

You may be financially capable of servicing more debt; you may not be psychologically capable. If the thought of borrowing more money troubles you, pay attention. **The benefit of a purchase made with borrowed money may be more than offset by anxiety from the extra financial burden.**

Too many people obsess about their credit score. They take great pains to keep the score as high as possible, including taking on new debt they don't need. Many of the actions that improve your credit score can hurt you financially in the long run.

Focus on your overall financial stability. **Keep debts to a minimum and honor the debts you make.** These two steps will give you a very good credit score. It will also put you in a position where you may not need credit at all.

175

RETIREMENT STARTS
AT GRADUATION

There are certain advantages to getting older. One advantage of age over youth is the young must imagine being old; the old must merely remember being young.

Remembering is easier than imagining, but it can still be tricky. When thinking across time, we remember the past better than it was, we view the present worse than it is, and we imagine a future better than it will be.

Old people may remember being young, but they have to imagine being young today. Being young today is different than in the past. A big difference is young people have to imagine being old while they're still young.

Today's young will live longer than any previous generation. They will also have a greater task of funding retirement than any previous generation. They may also be caring for aging parents, raising children, and saving for their retirement, all at the same time.

When Social Security began in 1935, half the workers never got to 65 and retirement. Those who made it lived an average of five more years. Most started working by age 15. They worked ten years to earn one year of retirement.

Workers in their twenties today may spend one year retired for every two years working. Twenty or thirty years of retirement won't come cheap. They will have to accumulate a lot of wealth while they're working.

You read about the price of procrastination earlier. That price was in dollars. Procrastination exacts a price in other ways, too. Retirement gets postponed because there isn't enough money. Retirement gets downscaled because income isn't enough to maintain the same lifestyle. Independence and dignity suffer.

In the past, lifespans were shorter and people had pensions that guaranteed lifetime incomes. Age determined when people retired. Most people retired when they could collect Social Security. Until the 1980's, mandatory retirement ages were common.

For a young worker today, age won't determine when retirement begins; health and wealth will.

Health will determine when retirement begins because poor health could make working impossible. Some jobs are too physically hard for older workers, even healthy ones. If mental health declines, so will productivity. If productivity declines, older workers may be forced into retirement.

Good health could be a mixed blessing. Good health may enable some to work longer. They may also live longer and need more money for retirement. Working three more years may be good. Living ten more years may be good. The extra years working won't pay for the extra years in retirement, though.

Maintaining good health and treating bad health both come at a price. While no one knows what health insurance will look like in forty or fifty years, it will be expensive. Getting, keeping, and paying for health insurance will help determine when and if retirement comes.

If health issues don't force someone to work longer or retire sooner than planned, wealth will determine when and how well someone can retire.

Social Security will be around for the foreseeable future. The retirement age and the tax rate may both increase, however. Social Security shouldn't be the main retirement income; it was meant to be a safety net, not a hammock. A decent retirement will require you to pay for most of it yourself.

People always want to know their "magic number" – how much money they will need to save before they can retire. That number is based on several factors: how long a retirement, income needed each year, other income, inflation during retirement, investment returns.

As a starting point and nothing more, a good "magic number" would be 20 to 25 times the income needed from investments in the first year of retirement. For example, if $50,000 were needed from investments in the first year, the magic number would be $1-1.25 million. This amount, properly invested, would likely be enough. It could provide steady income for life, enable increases to cover inflation, and continue income even when markets drop.

How does a young worker, just out of college and new to a job, start to save for retirement? Look to the employer for help.

Most employers offer a retirement plan, like a 401(k). Many employers do some matching contribution to boost employee participation. If a young worker begins saving 10% of income and if the money is properly invested, chances are excellent there will be enough money to retire at a reasonable age with a reasonable income.

Think of retirement funding as a wall to be scaled. The only way to avoid scaling the wall is to never retire. The only way to never retire is to work until you die. Since that may not be an option (even if you wanted it), assume you will have to scale a wall.

You have some say on the wall's height. The earlier you want to retire and the more money you want in retirement, the higher you make the wall.

You will use a board to scale the wall, putting one end on the ground and the other on the top of the wall. The length of the board is determined by two things - how early you start saving for retirement and how much you save each month. Saving earlier does more to lengthen the board than saving more (remember Jean and Sue). Saving early and a lot make a long board; saving late and a little make a short one.

If your wall isn't too high and you started saving early and save at least 10%, you can easily walk up the board like it's the gangplank on a cruise ship. However, if your wall is high and your board is short, you may not be able to scale the wall. You will have to lower the wall and lengthen the board. Both will require sacrifices.

The best way to finish at the top of your retirement class is to be first in your graduating class in planning for retirement.

ABOVE AVERAGE

As long as there's been a Wall Street, there have been people hatching plans to "beat the street". Some have been legitimate attempts to outperform the market. Most have been schemes to separate the gullible from their money.

If you're hoping to find a legitimate way to "beat the street", this lesson is as close as you'll get. For our purpose here, we will define "the street" as the S&P 500. The S&P 500 is a collection of 500 stocks of some of the largest and most well-known American companies. The lineup of companies changes about 5% each year, as companies move up or down in rankings.

The goal is to outperform the S&P 500, but without taking on any more risk than the S&P 500. To make sure we don't take on more risk than the S&P 500, we invest *only* in the S&P 500.

If we only invest in the S&P 500, and we're trying to outperform the S&P 500, the obvious way to do that is by market timing. Market timing attempts to move in and out of a market to capture more of the peaks and fewer of the valleys. **Market timing doesn't work; at least no one has made it work consistently.**

There is a method to buy more shares when the market is cheaper and buy fewer shares when the market is more expensive. This method requires no fortune-telling; it is brilliant in its simplicity and will lead to superior investment returns.

Here's how this method works. Take a percentage of your income this month and invest it in the S&P 500. Do the same thing next month. And the next month. And the next month. Keep doing it as long as you're earning an income. That's it.

You probably don't believe something so basic, so uncomplicated, so utterly simple could possibly yield above-average returns. It can, and it does.

This sure-fire method of superior returns is not new. You may already be using this method without realizing it. If you're investing money into your 401(k) plan every month, and you put the same amount every month into the same investment, you're following this method. Its formal name is ***Dollar-Cost Averaging.***

Here's how it works in its simplest form. If you invest $100 a month in a mutual fund, and the share price that month is $25, you'll buy four shares. If the share price the next month drops to $20, you'll buy 5 shares. **You automatically buy more shares when the price is lower and fewer shares when the price is higher.** In this simple example, you bought 9 shares for $200, or $22.22 per share, even though the average price during this period was $22.50.

There is a chart in the appendix showing a dollar-cost averaging plan with the S&P 500. The initial annual investment was $5,000 and increased 4% per year. It was a forty-year investment plan, representing the forty-year working life of most Americans. The share prices were the year-end values of the S&P 500 for each year from 1968-2007. This period included plenty of bull and bear markets, some of the best and worst times.

Some important observations from the chart:
- Annual investment increased with pay raises.
- In only 6 of 40 years did the account value decline.
- In those down years, more shares were bought than in the previous year.
- Total shares owned grew every year; only the rate of growth varied.

Over this 40-year period, the S&P 500's share price grew at an average annual rate of 6.9%. The average annual return of this portfolio was 8.5%.

The *investment* returned 6.9%. The *investor* received 8.5%. **The difference between the investment return and the investor's return is totally the result of dollar-cost averaging** – automatically buying more shares when the price drops and fewer shares when the price rises. The difference in dollars is significant. The 6.9% return would have a final amount of $1,769,097. The 8.5% return would have a final amount of $2,393,001. The difference was an additional $623,904, more than 35%.

Dollar-cost averaging does not guarantee a profit or prevent a loss. Continuously investing in the same investment regardless of price fluctuations magnifies gains; it doesn't guarantee them.

The S&P 500 makes an ideal investment for dollar-cost averaging. It won't go belly-up like an individual stock might. It gets tweaked slightly each year to keep it relevant. It doesn't rely on active management.

Making regular, continuous investments in the S&P 500 via mutual fund or exchange-traded fund (ETF) could be the simplest yet most effective way for you to build long-term wealth. It's set-it-and-forget-it. It does require you to stick with the method through thick and thin. You can't get greedy when the market is hot, or panic and sell when the market turns cold.

You don't need to be smart to become wealthy. You don't need to time markets or even understand markets. Let others knock themselves out trying to "beat the street." You will surely beat whatever they conjure up. Dollar-cost averaging is the most successful and the most democratic method of creating wealth ever devised.

PLAYING DEFENSE

In the movie, *The Blind Side*, a family takes in a young man who becomes a highly recruited offensive lineman. The mother explains why football offensive linemen are important and well-paid with this analogy.

Every housewife knows that, after you pay the mortgage, you next pay the insurance premiums. You don't risk losing your home by not paying the mortgage. You don't risk losing everything else by not paying for insurance to protect it. The offensive linemen are the quarterback's insurance.

Insurance is important, but it rarely gets the respect it deserves. In another movie, *Take the Money and Run*, Woody Allen is a bumbling criminal sentenced to a chain gang. For one punishment, he is forced to spend several days locked up in a sweatbox with an insurance salesman.

Some risks we can and should insure against are:
- Major medical bills (medical/health insurance)
- Income loss from illness/injury (disability insurance)
- Unintentional harm to others (liability insurance)
- Financial loss from death (life insurance)
- Loss to home or personal property (homeowners or renters insurance)
- Damage to your vehicle (collision/comprehensive insurance)
- Extended illness or injury (long-term care insurance)

The more you have to lose, the more you need insurance.

Financial strength begins with defense. Insurance is the foundation of that defense. It won't matter how large your assets are if those assets can all be lost due to events beyond your control.

183

Insurance doesn't protect you from a bad event; it protects you from the financial consequences of it. Your behavior is your best protection from bad events. But even careful people experience bad events. Insurance makes a bad event more bearable.

Uncertainty triggers stress. By defending against the financial consequences of a bad event, uncertainty is reduced, along with stress.

Many people equate insurance with gambling. They think insurance is betting on a potential loss. They may also think they've lost a bet with the insurance company if they don't have a loss. If you've had a loss that was covered by insurance, you were glad you had insurance. However, you would have probably preferred to have had no loss at all.

Insurance is the opposite of gambling. Gambling creates a risk of loss where none existed. When you buy insurance, you take an existing risk of loss and transfer it to the insurance company. To make this transfer, you take the sure loss of the insurance premium payment.

There are a couple of guidelines when deciding whether you need insurance and how much you need. First, **don't risk a lot to save a little.** Don't risk losing your home and its contents to avoid spending a thousand dollars a year to insure it all. Second, **don't spend a lot to reduce risk a little.** Extended warranties and low deductibles offer little coverage at high costs. **Insurance is for events that create a financial hardship.**

For decades, medical insurance was available mostly through employers. This benefit came about during World War II, when wage freezes were in place. Employers began offering medical insurance to combat wage freezes and labor shortages. For decades, people needed a job to get access to medical insurance.

Medical insurance is now available for everyone, so there is no longer an excuse to be uninsured. Medical insurance protects against expenses that can be frequent, severe, and unpredictable – the main things insurance protects against. **Uninsured medical expenses are the single biggest cause of personal bankruptcies. Every financial goal you have hinges on being insured against catastrophic medical expenses.** It really is that important.

Becoming disabled, even temporarily, takes a heavy toll. There is the physical trauma that created the disability. There is also the psychological toll of a disability, which may be worse than the physical toll.

People know about life insurance; they often ignore disability insurance. You are fifteen times more likely to become disabled than to die during your working life. Disabilities tend to be short or long; either less than four months or more than two years. Also, unlike with death, your expenses continue and often increase with a disability. **The risk of disability and the financial consequences are both too great to ignore.**

Next to a permanent total disability, the worst financial disaster for a family would be the death of the breadwinner. The term *life insurance* is really a misnomer; a more technically correct name would be *risk-of-premature-death insurance*, but that's a hard sell.

Life insurance is typically used to replace lost income for the financial dependents of the deceased. If no one depended on you for income, or if your death had no financial consequence for anyone, you wouldn't need life insurance. In calculating how much life insurance you need, you want your beneficiaries to maintain the lifestyle they had. The death of a loved one is hard enough; financial hardship should be avoided.

If you have a mortgage on your home, you're required to have homeowners insurance. **Homeowners insurance protects the dwelling, your personal property, and also insures you for liability in many situations, both at home and away.** Even if you don't have a mortgage, you need homeowners insurance. The cost is nothing compared to what you might lose.

If you're a renter, you need renters insurance. Renters insurance is similar to homeowners insurance, minus coverage on the building. Renters have risks from other renters that homeowners don't have, making renters insurance at least as important as homeowners insurance.

Your state sets auto insurance requirements. Their only requirement is for liability coverage, which protects other people if you cause an accident. **The minimum limits set by states for auto liability coverage aren't enough to properly protect you.** Most people find this out only after they get sued.

If you have a car loan, you need collision and comprehensive coverage. This coverage will repair or replace your car if it's damaged, regardless of fault. If you don't have a car loan, but you can't afford to replace your car out-of-pocket, you need this coverage.

There are other types of insurance, such as umbrella policies and long-term care, which become important as you get older and have greater wealth. If you're not there yet, **focus on medical, disability, liability, and life insurance needs first. They protect against your biggest threats.**

Legendary football coach Bear Bryant is credited with saying "Offense sells tickets, but defense wins championships." Insurance is your defense. It protects your blind side. Without the protection of insurance, you don't have a financial plan; you just have dreams.

JACKS AND MASTERS

If someone called you a "Jack-of-all-trades", how would you take it? You might take it as a compliment - a way of saying you are skilled in multiple areas. You might even equate the term with "Renaissance Man", a profound thinker on a variety of topics.

You might also stop to look up the definition of *jack*. One definition is a man who does odd or heavy jobs, like a lumber*jack*. Another is a male animal, especially an ass. Then you remember the rest of that saying: "and master of none." Now you feel more insulted than complimented.

During the Great Depression, most of the population was broke. They had to do most things for themselves because they couldn't afford to pay others to do them. Out of necessity, many became jacks-of-all-trades. While the individuals did learn some skills, they could never match the work of professionals. The overall quality of work suffered. The economy suffered too, as fewer people work for pay in a do-it-yourself world.

Some skills are easy to learn, and you may learn them out of necessity. You may cut your grass or change your car's oil yourself because you prefer not to pay someone to do it. Some skills, like woodworking, you may acquire just because you want to.

Competency in a variety of areas can be a good thing. It can be very handy to know how to unclog a toilet, change a tire, or make spaghetti sauce. A certain amount of that "rugged individualism" Americans admire is good. **But the more skills you acquire, the harder it is to become really good in any of them.**

There's another old term that's relevant here: "Penny-wise and pound-foolish." The term refers to someone who takes care in small matters but not in big ones. It can also refer to someone who sees the small picture but not the bigger one.

It can be penny-wise and pound-foolish to devote time and effort where the returns are small. **Many of our do-it-yourself efforts are penny-wise and pound-foolish.** The savings amount to pennies; the costs amount to pounds. We see the savings, but not the costs.

There is a well-accepted theory that 20% of our efforts yield 80% of our results. Richard Koch, author of *The 80/20 Principle*, recommends doing the following:

1. focus on exceptional productivity; ignore average efforts
2. look for short cuts
3. maximize control over your life with minimum effort
4. be selective, not exhaustive
5. become excellent in a few things, not just good in many
6. delegate and outsource as much as possible
7. choose careers with extraordinary care
8. become self-employed if possible
9. only do what you do best and enjoy most
10. seek ironies, oddities, and abnormalities to exploit
11. look at everything through the 80/20 lens

Note especially numbers 1, 5, 6, and 9. They are specific to the topics of a jack-of-all-trades and penny-wise and pound-foolish with your time and effort.

Even if you're the best person at a particular task, you may not be the best person to perform it.

In many small businesses, the CEO may be more skilled at several tasks than any employee. The CEO probably learned those skills in the process of building the business. The CEO may be tempted to personally do many of those tasks because of his/her higher skills. But that would be a mistake.

The CEO may be able to perform many of the tasks in the business, but the tasks the CEO should be doing are those that *only* the CEO can do. **The highest value tasks for anyone are not the many tasks that no one else can do better; the highest value tasks are the few tasks that no one else can do at all.**

For example, the CEO of a graphics firm may be better at laying out print advertising than any employee. But the CEO is also the only person at the firm who can negotiate contracts and bring in new customers. The CEO has to allocate his/her time and effort where it pays the biggest dividends.

A CEO doesn't have the luxury of being a jack-of-all-trades. A CEO can't afford to be penny-wise and pound-foolish. And a CEO must devote energies to the 20% of work that yields 80% of the results; in this case, negotiating contracts and bringing in customers, not laying out ads.

It pays to pay for good people. Very often when people try a do-it-yourself approach, they pay triple. First, there's payment of their own time and effort in doing the task themselves. When that doesn't work, they have to hire a professional to come in and undo the mess. Finally, the professional does the task the way it was supposed to be done in the first place.

Benjamin Franklin said, "The bitterness of poor quality remains long after the sweetness of low price is forgotten." Sir Henry Royce, the founder of Rolls-Royce Motors, said of his very expensive cars, "The quality is remembered long after the price is forgotten." Both statements are true, whether referring to products or services. Pay good people for good work, and you'll savor the sweetness of high quality. Try to do it yourself, and you may be gagging on the bitterness of poor quality.

It's estimated that it takes about 10,000 hours of practice to become an expert in most fields. Depending on the field and the individual's talent level, this figure may vary considerably. **It's also estimated that the top 20% in most fields earn more than the remaining 80%** - another variation of the 80/20 principle.

The time spent to become an expert is equivalent to five years of full-time employment. Over a 40-year working life, you could conceivably become an expert in eight different fields. Some 60-year-old CEOs have had comparable career paths. A CEO needs a broad range of skills to see unseen connections and position the organization for the future. The difference between such a CEO and the average jack-of-all-trades is the CEO has both a breadth and a depth of skills. **The jack-of-all-trades has breadth but no depth. And the 21st century job market values depth over breadth in most fields.**

There's nothing wrong in mastering multiple skills. You should strive for mastery. But trying to become a master of more than one trade at a time is likely to leave you no better than a jack-of-those-trades. **Focus your energy on becoming the best you can be in the field of greatest importance to you.** Once you achieve mastery, you're encouraged to take up a new challenge.

Two of the smartest investments you can make:
1) Develop mastery in your chosen profession.
2) Hire people who have mastery in their profession.

YOUR MARKET VALUE

What kind of skills – make that superpowers – would you have to possess to be worth 20,000 teachers?

No one without superpowers could be worth 20,000 teachers, at least when it comes to their positive effect on individuals. That doesn't mean someone's work couldn't have a similar market value as 20,000 teachers.

In 2014 (the most recent year for data), there were five hedge fund managers who each made more than 20,000 times the average teacher salary. The average *hourly* wage for *all* hedge fund managers was $211,538, even though the average return for their funds was ten percent *less* than the return for the S&P 500 in 2014.

There often seems to be little connection between the importance or difficulty of someone's work and what they get paid for it. But **the job market is no different than any other market.** Since everyone's pay comes from somewhere, that pay source is deciding the value of the work justifies the pay.

Pay varies widely among jobs. Brain surgeons make more than janitors for two reasons. Having a brain tumor removed has greater value than having your cubicle cleaned. Second, the difficult path to become a brain surgeon means there are few qualified to do it. Brain surgeons don't have a lot of competition. Becoming a janitor is far less difficult, so there are many potential janitors. Their wages only need to be high enough to attract enough people to meet the demand for janitors.

The professions that offer higher incomes and job security provide high value to the customer, and they don't easily attract competition.

191

The pay level for your work is controlled by the price for the product or service you produce. That price falls within a range. The cost to produce a product or service creates the price floor. The value of the product or service to the customer creates the ceiling. The space between the floor and the ceiling is profit.

Your pay is one of the costs that create the floor. Raising your pay raises the floor. If you raise the floor, you need to raise the ceiling, too. You raise the ceiling by raising the value to the customer. **Before you can get more, your customer needs to get more.**

Whether you become a brain surgeon, a business owner, or a janitor, **your success will depend on your customers' perception of the value you provide.** It's a loop, though. A happy employee produces work that creates satisfied customers. Satisfied customers produce feedback and sales that create happy employees.

Your parents may give you credit for your effort; your employer and the world at large will not. **In the workplace, only results matter.**

Results are measurable; effort is not. Results are also comparable; they're used to compare you to others. The world is a very bottom-line place. Effort that does not translate into results does not help the bottom line. **Your market value is determined by your results, not your effort.**

The purpose of a company's compensation system should be to get and keep the best people. It should not attempt to get right behavior from the wrong people.

Money is one way your employer shows appreciation of your work. But more money will not make you love a job any more than it would make you love a person.

You will never love a job you hate just because you are paid more. The rush of a raise will soon fade.

You will spend up to your new income level and then feel even more trapped in a job you now hate even more.

Most employees don't realize the hidden costs of keeping them on the payroll. For the average employee, **benefit costs as a percentage of total compensation run around 30%.** For example, if a company is paying an employee $35,000 a year, they are also paying another $15,000 for the benefits that employee receives.

There are required insurance and benefits a company must provide and pay for in whole or part. These requirements include workers' compensation, social security, and unemployment insurance. The most common optional employee benefits are:

- Paid Vacations
- Group Medical, Dental, Disability, Life Insurance
- Paid Sick Leave
- Parental Leave
- Education Reimbursement for Job
- Retirement Savings Plan

Some benefits, like paid vacations, are nice-to-have. Others, like medical insurance, are need-to-have. **When evaluating a job offer, consider the entire package, not just salary.** Generous benefits may more than offset a lower starting salary. It's also more important to get the need-to-have benefits than the nice-to-have ones.

The Myers-Briggs Type Indicator assesses four different aspects of personality and generates sixteen different personality types. One area of assessment is whether a person is an extravert or an introvert.

Income research shows that **extraverts outearn introverts in six of eight categories**, when other aspects are the same. This difference is likely due to extraverts' greater willingness to speak up for themselves.

The squeaky wheel gets the grease. **If you think you should be paid more, make your case with hard evidence. Then don't be shy about asking to get paid what you're worth.** Even if it doesn't come easily, it will be worth the effort.

Money deserves respect because money represents work, and all work deserves respect. Your employer shows respect and gratitude for the work you do through the paycheck you receive. **You show respect for your work by knowing the market value of your work and making sure you get it.**

If you believe your employer doesn't demonstrate sufficient respect for your work, as evidenced in your paycheck, you owe it to yourself to find an employer who does. If you do go looking, remember the employer you're looking for might just be you.

OF FUTURE VALUE

Regardless of their field of study, experts agree that the single biggest difference between humans and all other species is our imagination. We are the only creatures on earth that can form a mental picture of something that isn't there, that we've never experienced, or that has never existed.

Our imagination's greatest creation is the future.

At this moment, there are at least seven billion futures being imagined. Everyone imagines a future for themselves; many imagine multiple futures. Leaders and other visionaries imagine futures for entire societies, even for the entire planet. The number and types of futures are products of our imagination and are limited only by our imagination.

Humans can comprehend and measure time – past, present, and future. We can also measure future value, most specifically with money. These abilities enable us to calculate in hard numbers the future value of something that is only in our imagination.

Our abilities enable us to predict with reasonable accuracy what we will need in the future. We can also calculate what we have to do between now and then to meet our needs. **But predicting future needs and acting to meet them are two very separate endeavors.**

Even when an animal prepares for the future, it does not think about the future. When a squirrel stores nuts for the winter or a bird builds a nest to lay eggs, they're acting on instinct alone.

Humans have instincts, but our ability to think enables us to override our instincts. We may know instinctively that we have to prepare for the future. We can also think ourselves out of preparing. We can come up with plenty of reasons why we can't or don't need to prepare. **If you're going to override instinct, you have to replace it with wisdom and discipline – the wisdom to know what to do and the discipline to do it.**

We are very good at calculating future value, at least where money is concerned. There are formulas, tables, and software programs that can tell you precisely the future value of money for any period of time and any rate of return.

Theoretically, you could calculate to the dollar what you would need to retire at a certain date. Those calculations would only be theoretical because such calculations assume everything moves in a straight line.

Life does not move in a straight line. The biggest events in our lives typically come out of nowhere. **Your ability to adapt is even more important than your ability to predict in creating a future you want.**

The more specific the prediction, the more adjusting that prediction may require. If you predict next January 15th will be cold, you're more likely to be right than if you predict the high temperature that day will be 23 degrees.

As long as you're moving in the right direction, your predictions don't have to be overly specific. It's better to know you should save ten percent of your income to retire on schedule than to predict exactly how much you'll need to retire.

Future targets are moving targets. To reach them, you need to be going in the right general direction. Then you need to be able to adapt to their movement by making the necessary adjustments along the way. A ship's captain sets a heading, but then makes constant adjustments to account for wind and currents on the way.

How much thought have you given to your future where money is concerned? Reading this book indicates you are giving it serious thought. Hopefully, you're giving it serious thought without obsessing over it.

To think too much about future money might cause you to miss out on the present. It's sad to see someone who has more than enough money later in life, but who never enjoyed anything on the way there. You can't ignore the future, but you shouldn't sacrifice the present for it, either.

It's even sadder to see someone who only lived for the present and never prepared for the future. Their pleasures that are now in the past will be paid for by pain in their future.

Remember Aesop's fable of the ant and the grasshopper. You don't want to be the grasshopper in winter; you don't want to be the ant in summer, either. Imitate the bee instead. They work hard in summer. They build a hive and produce honey to get them through winter. They also take time to get out and enjoy the flowers.

As you work toward making the future you imagine a reality, don't forget the financial piece. The financial piece is often the make-or-break part of someone's future plans. Here are some final thoughts as you move toward your future.

Begin every financial transaction by asking "Why?" Asking why will make you think about the reasons for what you're doing. It will enable you to take actions for the right reasons and avoid taking actions for the wrong ones. And if you don't have a good answer to "Why?" it's a signal to do nothing until you do.

Spending on experiences is more rewarding than spending on things. At some point, almost everything you spent money on will be just a memory. You are more likely to look back fondly on a trip you took thirty years ago than a car you bought thirty years ago. Spending on experiences is also how you grow as a person. Such spending (within reason) is actually an investment in your growth.

Don't drain your soul to fill your wallet. Aim for proper prosperity. Wealth is good or bad based on the method used to obtain it. Cutting corners and compromising your integrity may seem acceptable on the way up, but once you're there you'll regret the price you paid.

Where your treasure is, there your heart will be also. Jesus spoke these words at the Sermon on the Mount. We tend to think we put our treasure where our heart is, and we do to an extent. We financially support what we emotionally support. Jesus points out that we do the opposite even more. What you invest in financially, you invest in emotionally, too. Make sure your money is going to places where your heart will also want to be.

Your best investment is you. Creating a better you creates greater future value. Education and self-improvement should not end with graduation, marriage, a promotion, or any other life event. Ideally, it should only end at death. Any investment in time, effort, and money to improve yourself will pay better returns than any stock you could ever own.

Make your future something of value. You'll be spending the rest of your life there.

ANNUAL RETURNS OF STANDARD & POORS 500

YEAR	S&P 500 RETURN	YEAR	S&P 500 RETURN	YEAR	S&P 500 RETURN	YEAR	S&P 500 RETURN
2015		1979	18.69	1943	23.6	1907	-24.21
2014	13.8	1978	6.41	1942	21.74	1906	0.64
2013	32.43	1977	-7.78	1941	-9.09	1905	21.29
2012	15.88	1976	24.2	1940	-8.91	1904	32.16
2011	2.07	1975	38.46	1939	2.98	1903	-17.09
2010	14.87	1974	-26.95	1938	17.5	1902	8.28
2009	27.11	1973	-15.03	1937	-32.11	1901	19.45
2008	-37.22	1972	19.15	1936	32.55	1900	20.84
2007	5.46	1971	14.54	1935	54.93	1899	3.66
2006	15.74	1970	3.6	1934	-8.01	1898	29.32
2005	4.79	1969	-8.63	1933	56.79	1897	20.37
2004	10.82	1968	11.03	1932	-5.81	1896	3.25
2003	28.72	1967	24.45	1931	-44.2	1895	5.01
2002	-22.27	1966	-10.36	1930	-22.72	1894	3.63
2001	-11.98	1965	12.45	1929	-9.46	1893	-18.79
2000	-9.11	1964	16.59	1928	47.57	1892	6.14
1999	21.11	1963	23.04	1927	37.1	1891	18.88
1998	28.73	1962	-9.2	1926	11.51	1890	-6.16
1997	33.67	1961	28.51	1925	25.83	1889	7.09
1996	23.06	1960	-0.74	1924	27.1	1888	3.34
1995	38.02	1959	11.59	1923	5.45	1887	-0.64
1994	1.19	1958	43.4	1922	29.07	1886	11.98
1993	10.17	1957	-9.3	1921	10.15	1885	30.06
1992	7.6	1956	6.38	1920	-13.95	1884	-12.32
1991	30.95	1955	28.22	1919	19.67	1883	-5.49
1990	-3.42	1954	55.99	1918	18.21	1882	3.61
1989	32	1953	-0.8	1917	-18.62	1881	0.27
1988	16.64	1952	18.35	1916	8.12	1880	26.63
1987	5.69	1951	23.1	1915	31.2	1879	49.37
1986	19.06	1950	34.28	1914	-5.39	1878	16.29
1985	32.24	1949	15.96	1913	-4.73	1877	-1.06
1984	5.96	1948	9.51	1912	7.18	1876	-14.15
1983	23.13	1947	2.56	1911	3.52	1875	5.44
1982	21.22	1946	-12.05	1910	-3.39	1874	4.72
1981	-5.33	1945	39.35	1909	16.15	1873	-2.49
1980	32.76	1944	19.67	1908	39.47	1872	11.16
						1871	15.64

Source: FactSet, as of October 31, 2013.

THE PRICE OF PROCRASTINATION FIGURES

YEAR	RETURN OF S&P 500	JEAN'S JAN. 1 BALANCE	JEAN'S 12/31 BALANCE	SUE'S JAN. 1 BALANCE	SUE'S 12/31 BALANCE
1954	55.99%	$600.00	$935.94	$0.00	$0.00
1955	28.22%	$1,535.94	$1,969.38	$0.00	$0.00
1956	6.38%	$2,569.38	$2,733.31	$0.00	$0.00
1957	-9.30%	$3,333.31	$3,023.31	$0.00	$0.00
1958	43.40%	$3,623.31	$5,195.83	$0.00	$0.00
1959	11.59%	$5,795.83	$6,467.56	$0.00	$0.00
1960	-0.74%	$7,067.56	$7,015.26	$0.00	$0.00
1961	28.51%	$7,615.26	$9,786.38	$0.00	$0.00
1962	-9.20%	$10,386.38	$9,430.83	$0.00	$0.00
1963	23.04%	$10,030.83	$12,341.93	$0.00	$0.00
1964	16.59%	$12,341.93	$14,389.46	$600.00	$699.54
1965	12.45%	$14,389.46	$16,180.95	$1,299.54	$1,461.33
1966	-10.36%	$16,180.94	$14,504.60	$2,061.33	$1,847.78
1967	24.45%	$14,504.60	$18,050.98	$2,447.78	$3,046.26
1968	11.03%	$18,050.97	$20,042.00	$3,646.26	$4,048.44
1969	-8.63%	$20,041.99	$18,312.37	$4,648.44	$4,247.28
1970	3.60%	$18,312.37	$18,971.62	$4,847.28	$5,021.78
1971	14.54%	$18,971.62	$21,730.09	$5,621.78	$6,439.19
1972	19.15%	$21,730.09	$25,891.41	$7,039.19	$8,387.20
1973	-15.03%	$25,891.40	$21,999.93	$8,987.20	$7,636.42
1974	-26.95%	$21,999.92	$16,070.95	$8,236.42	$6,016.71
1975	38.46%	$16,070.94	$22,251.83	$6,616.71	$9,161.49
1976	24.20%	$22,251.83	$27,636.78	$9,761.49	$12,123.77
1977	-7.78%	$27,636.77	$25,486.64	$12,723.77	$11,733.86
1978	6.41%	$25,486.63	$27,120.33	$12,333.86	$13,124.46
1979	18.69%	$27,120.32	$32,189.12	$13,724.46	$16,289.57
1980	32.76%	$32,189.11	$42,734.28	$16,889.57	$22,422.59
1981	-5.33%	$42,734.26	$40,456.54	$23,022.59	$21,795.48
1982	21.22%	$40,456.53	$49,041.42	$22,395.48	$27,147.80
1983	23.13%	$49,041.40	$60,384.70	$27,747.80	$34,165.87
1984	5.96%	$60,384.68	$63,983.62	$34,765.87	$36,837.92
1985	32.24%	$63,983.61	$84,611.94	$37,437.92	$49,507.90
1986	19.06%	$84,611.92	$100,738.98	$50,107.90	$59,658.47
1987	5.69%	$100,738.95	$106,471.03	$60,258.47	$63,687.18
1988	16.64%	$106,471.00	$124,187.81	$64,287.18	$74,984.56
1989	32.00%	$124,187.77	$163,927.91	$75,584.56	$99,771.62
1990	-3.42%	$163,927.86	$158,321.57	$100,371.62	$96,938.91
1991	30.95%	$158,321.53	$207,322.10	$97,538.91	$127,727.20
1992	7.60%	$207,322.04	$223,078.58	$128,327.20	$138,080.07
1993	10.17%	$223,078.52	$245,765.67	$138,680.07	$152,783.83
1994	1.19%	$245,765.60	$248,690.28	$153,383.83	$155,209.10
1995	38.02%	$248,690.21	$343,242.32	$155,809.10	$215,047.72
1996	23.06%	$343,242.23	$422,394.00	$215,647.72	$265,376.09
1997	33.67%	$422,393.89	$564,614.06	$265,976.09	$355,530.24
1998	28.73%	$564,613.92	$726,827.68	$356,130.24	$458,446.45

LET IT GROW — COMPOUND INTEREST CALCULATIONS

YEAR	AMOUNT	YEAR	AMOUNT
1626	$270	1663	$2,213
1627	$286	1664	$2,342
1628	$303	1665	$2,479
1629	$320	1666	$2,624
1630	$339	1667	$2,778
1631	$359	1668	$2,940
1632	$380	1669	$3,112
1633	$402	1670	$3,294
1634	$425	1671	$3,487
1635	$450	1672	$3,691
1636	$477	1673	$3,907
1637	$505	1674	$4,135
1638	$534	1675	$4,377
1639	$565	1676	$4,633
1640	$598	1677	$4,905
1641	$633	1678	$5,191
1642	$671	1679	$5,495
1643	$710	1680	$5,817
1644	$751	1681	$6,157
1645	$795	1682	$6,517
1646	$842	1683	$6,898
1647	$891	1684	$7,302
1648	$943	1685	$7,729
1649	$998	1686	$8,181
1650	$1,057	1687	$8,660
1651	$1,118	1688	$9,166
1652	$1,184	1689	$9,703
1653	$1,253	1690	$10,270
1654	$1,327	1691	$10,871
1655	$1,404	1692	$11,507
1656	$1,486	1693	$12,180
1657	$1,573	1694	$12,893
1658	$1,665	1695	$13,647
1659	$1,763	1696	$14,445
1660	$1,866	1697	$15,290
1661	$1,975	1698	$16,185
1662	$2,090	1699	$17,132

203

1700	$18,134	1740	$176,247
1701	$19,195	1741	$186,558
1702	$20,317	1742	$197,471
1703	$21,506	1743	$209,023
1704	$22,764	1744	$221,251
1705	$24,096	1745	$234,194
1706	$25,505	1746	$247,895
1707	$26,998	1747	$262,397
1708	$28,577	1748	$277,747
1709	$30,249	1749	$293,995
1710	$32,018	1750	$311,194
1711	$33,891	1751	$329,398
1712	$35,874	1752	$348,668
1713	$37,972	1753	$369,065
1714	$40,194	1754	$390,656
1715	$42,545	1755	$413,509
1716	$45,034	1756	$437,699
1717	$47,669	1757	$463,305
1718	$50,457	1758	$490,408
1719	$53,409	1759	$519,097
1720	$56,533	1760	$549,464
1721	$59,841	1761	$581,608
1722	$63,341	1762	$615,632
1723	$67,047	1763	$651,646
1724	$70,969	1764	$689,768
1725	$75,121	1765	$730,119
1726	$79,515	1766	$772,831
1727	$84,167	1767	$818,042
1728	$89,091	1768	$865,897
1729	$94,302	1769	$916,552
1730	$99,819	1770	$970,170
1731	$105,658	1771	$1,026,925
1732	$111,839	1772	$1,087,000
1733	$118,382	1773	$1,150,590
1734	$125,307	1774	$1,217,899
1735	$132,638	1775	$1,289,146
1736	$140,397	1776	$1,364,562
1737	$148,610	1777	$1,444,388
1738	$157,304	1778	$1,528,885
1739	$166,507	1779	$1,618,325

1780	$1,712,997	1820	$16,649,111
1781	$1,813,207	1821	$17,623,084
1782	$1,919,280	1822	$18,654,035
1783	$2,031,558	1823	$19,745,296
1784	$2,150,404	1824	$20,900,396
1785	$2,276,202	1825	$22,123,069
1786	$2,409,360	1826	$23,417,268
1787	$2,550,308	1827	$24,787,179
1788	$2,699,501	1828	$26,237,229
1789	$2,857,422	1829	$27,772,107
1790	$3,024,581	1830	$29,396,775
1791	$3,201,519	1831	$31,116,486
1792	$3,388,808	1832	$32,936,801
1793	$3,587,053	1833	$34,863,603
1794	$3,796,895	1834	$36,903,124
1795	$4,019,014	1835	$39,061,957
1796	$4,254,126	1836	$41,347,081
1797	$4,502,993	1837	$43,765,886
1798	$4,766,418	1838	$46,326,190
1799	$5,045,253	1839	$49,036,272
1800	$5,340,400	1840	$51,904,894
1801	$5,652,814	1841	$54,941,330
1802	$5,983,503	1842	$58,155,398
1803	$6,333,538	1843	$61,557,489
1804	$6,704,050	1844	$65,158,602
1805	$7,096,237	1845	$68,970,380
1806	$7,511,367	1846	$73,005,147
1807	$7,950,782	1847	$77,275,949
1808	$8,415,903	1848	$81,796,592
1809	$8,908,233	1849	$86,581,692
1810	$9,429,365	1850	$91,646,721
1811	$9,980,983	1851	$97,008,054
1812	$10,564,870	1852	$102,683,026
1813	$11,182,915	1853	$108,689,983
1814	$11,837,116	1854	$115,048,346
1815	$12,529,587	1855	$121,778,675
1816	$13,262,568	1856	$128,902,727
1817	$14,038,428	1857	$136,443,537
1818	$14,859,676	1858	$144,425,484
1819	$15,728,967	1859	$152,874,374

1860	$161,817,525	1900	$1,572,751,288
1861	$171,283,851	1901	$1,664,757,238
1862	$181,303,956	1902	$1,762,145,537
1863	$191,910,237	1903	$1,865,231,051
1864	$203,136,986	1904	$1,974,347,067
1865	$215,020,500	1905	$2,089,846,371
1866	$227,599,199	1906	$2,212,102,383
1867	$240,913,752	1907	$2,341,510,373
1868	$255,007,207	1908	$2,478,488,730
1869	$269,925,128	1909	$2,623,480,320
1870	$285,715,748	1910	$2,776,953,919
1871	$302,430,120	1911	$2,939,405,723
1872	$320,122,282	1912	$3,111,360,958
1873	$338,849,435	1913	$3,293,375,574
1874	$358,672,127	1914	$3,486,038,045
1875	$379,654,446	1915	$3,689,971,271
1876	$401,864,232	1916	$3,905,834,590
1877	$425,373,289	1917	$4,134,325,914
1878	$450,257,627	1918	$4,376,183,980
1879	$476,597,698	1919	$4,632,190,743
1880	$504,478,663	1920	$4,903,173,901
1881	$533,990,665	1921	$5,190,009,574
1882	$565,229,119	1922	$5,493,625,134
1883	$598,295,022	1923	$5,815,002,205
1884	$633,295,281	1924	$6,155,179,834
1885	$670,343,055	1925	$6,515,257,854
1886	$709,558,124	1926	$6,896,400,438
1887	$751,067,274	1927	$7,299,839,864
1888	$795,004,709	1928	$7,726,880,496
1889	$841,512,485	1929	$8,178,903,005
1890	$890,740,965	1930	$8,657,368,831
1891	$942,849,312	1931	$9,163,824,908
1892	$998,005,996	1932	$9,699,908,665
1893	$1,056,389,347	1933	$10,267,353,321
1894	$1,118,188,124	1934	$10,867,993,491
1895	$1,183,602,129	1935	$11,503,771,110
1896	$1,252,842,854	1936	$12,176,741,720
1897	$1,326,134,161	1937	$12,889,081,111
1898	$1,403,713,009	1938	$13,643,092,356
1899	$1,485,830,220	1939	$14,441,213,258

Year	Value	Year	Value
1940	$15,286,024,234	1979	$140,358,324,615
1941	$16,180,256,652	1980	$148,569,286,605
1942	$17,126,801,666	1981	$157,260,589,872
1943	$18,128,719,563	1982	$166,460,334,379
1944	$19,189,249,658	1983	$176,198,263,940
1945	$20,311,820,763	1984	$186,505,862,381
1946	$21,500,062,277	1985	$197,416,455,330
1947	$22,757,815,920	1986	$208,965,317,967
1948	$24,089,148,152	1987	$221,189,789,068
1949	$25,498,363,319	1988	$234,129,391,729
1950	$26,990,017,573	1989	$247,825,961,145
1951	$28,568,933,601	1990	$262,323,779,872
1952	$30,240,216,216	1991	$277,669,720,994
1953	$32,009,268,865	1992	$293,913,399,672
1954	$33,881,811,094	1993	$311,107,333,553
1955	$35,863,897,043	1994	$329,307,112,566
1956	$37,961,935,020	1995	$348,571,578,651
1957	$40,182,708,218	1996	$368,963,016,002
1958	$42,533,396,649	1997	$390,547,352,439
1959	$45,021,600,353	1998	$413,394,372,556
1960	$47,655,363,974	1999	$437,577,943,351
1961	$50,443,202,766	2000	$463,176,253,037
1962	$53,394,130,128	2001	$490,272,063,839
1963	$56,517,686,740	2002	$518,952,979,574
1964	$59,823,971,415	2003	$549,311,728,879
1965	$63,323,673,743	2004	$581,446,465,018
1966	$67,028,108,656	2005	$615,461,083,222
1967	$70,949,253,013	2006	$651,465,556,591
1968	$75,099,784,314	2007	$689,576,291,651
1969	$79,493,121,697	2008	$729,916,504,713
1970	$84,143,469,316	2009	$772,616,620,238
1971	$89,065,862,271	2010	$817,814,692,522
1972	$94,276,215,214	2011	$865,656,852,035
1973	$99,791,373,804	2012	$916,297,777,879
1974	$105,629,169,171	2013	$969,901,197,885
1975	$111,808,475,568	2014	$1,026,640,417,961
1976	$118,349,271,388	2015	$1,086,698,882,412
1977	$125,272,703,764	2016	$1,150,270,767,033
1978	$132,601,156,935		

EFFECTS OF INFLATION
WHAT IT TAKES TO BUY WHAT $1.00 BOUGHT
60 YEARS AT 3% ANNUAL INFLATION

YR.	AMOUNT	YR.	AMOUNT	YR.	AMOUNT
1	$1.00	21	$1.81	41	$3.26
2	$1.03	22	$1.86	42	$3.36
3	$1.06	23	$1.92	43	$3.46
4	$1.09	24	$1.97	44	$3.56
5	$1.13	25	$2.03	45	$3.67
6	$1.16	26	$2.09	46	$3.78
7	$1.19	27	$2.16	47	$3.90
8	$1.23	28	$2.22	48	$4.01
9	$1.27	29	$2.29	49	$4.13
10	$1.30	30	$2.36	50	$4.26
11	$1.34	31	$2.43	51	$4.38
12	$1.38	32	$2.50	52	$4.52
13	$1.43	33	$2.58	53	$4.65
14	$1.47	34	$2.65	54	$4.79
15	$1.51	35	$2.73	55	$4.93
16	$1.56	36	$2.81	56	$5.08
17	$1.60	37	$2.90	57	$5.23
18	$1.65	38	$2.99	58	$5.39
19	$1.70	39	$3.07	59	$5.55
20	$1.75	40	$3.17	60	$5.72

DOLLAR-COST AVERAGING WITH S&P 500   1968-2007

ANNUAL INVESTMENT	SHARE PRICE	SHARES BOUGHT	CUMULATIVE SHARES	CUMULATIVE INVESTMENT	ACCOUNT VALUE
$5,000	$103.01	48.54	48.54	$5,000	$5,000
$5,200	$85.02	61.16	109.70	$10,200	$9,327
$5,408	$95.88	56.40	166.10	$15,608	$15,926
$5,624	$103.94	54.11	220.22	$21,232	$22,889
$5,849	$116.03	50.41	270.63	$27,082	$31,401
$6,083	$96.57	62.99	333.62	$33,165	$32,218
$6,327	$76.98	82.18	415.81	$39,491	$32,009
$6,580	$100.86	65.24	481.04	$46,071	$48,518
$6,843	$102.03	67.07	548.11	$52,914	$55,924
$7,117	$89.25	79.74	627.85	$60,031	$56,035
$7,401	$99.93	74.06	701.91	$67,432	$70,142
$7,697	$114.16	67.43	769.34	$75,129	$87,827
$8,005	$129.55	61.79	831.13	$83,134	$107,673
$8,325	$120.40	69.15	900.28	$91,460	$108,393
$8,658	$145.30	59.59	959.86	$100,118	$139,468
$9,005	$163.41	55.11	1,014.97	$109,123	$165,856
$9,365	$179.63	52.13	1,067.10	$118,488	$191,684
$9,740	$211.78	45.99	1,113.09	$128,227	$235,731
$10,129	$274.08	36.96	1,150.05	$138,356	$315,206
$10,534	$257.07	40.98	1,191.03	$148,890	$306,178
$10,956	$297.47	36.83	1,227.86	$159,846	$365,251
$11,394	$329.08	34.62	1,262.48	$171,240	$415,457
$11,850	$343.93	34.45	1,296.93	$183,089	$446,055
$12,324	$408.78	30.15	1,327.08	$195,413	$542,484
$12,817	$438.78	29.21	1,356.29	$208,230	$595,113
$13,329	$481.61	27.68	1,383.97	$221,559	$666,532
$13,862	$470.42	29.47	1,413.43	$235,421	$664,908
$14,417	$636.02	22.67	1,436.10	$249,838	$913,390
$14,994	$786.19	19.07	1,455.17	$264,831	$1,144,043
$15,593	$980.28	15.91	1,471.08	$280,425	$1,442,071
$16,217	$1,279.64	12.67	1,483.75	$296,642	$1,898,670

$16,866	$1,394.46	12.09	1,495.85	$313,507	$2,085,900
$17,540	$1,366.01	12.84	1,508.69	$331,048	$2,060,884
$18,242	$1,130.20	16.14	1,524.83	$349,290	$1,723,362
$18,972	$855.70	22.17	1,547.00	$368,261	$1,323,768
$19,730	$1,131.13	17.44	1,564.44	$387,992	$1,769,588
$20,520	$1,181.27	17.37	1,581.81	$408,511	$1,868,549
$21,340	$1,280.08	16.67	1,598.49	$429,852	$2,046,189
$22,194	$1,418.30	15.65	1,614.13	$452,046	$2,289,325
$23,082	$1,468.23	15.72	1,629.85	$475,128	$2,393,001

PERSONAL BALANCE SHEET

Assets

Market Value of Home	$_____
Market Value of other Real Estate	$_____
Cash, Checking, Savings Accounts, CD's	$_____
Investments in retirement accounts (401k, IRA, etc.)	$_____
Other Investments (stocks, bonds, etc.)	$_____
Cash Value of Life Insurance	$_____
Other marketable assets	$_____

TOTAL ASSETS $_____

Liabilities

Mortgage Balance on Primary Residence	$_____
Other Outstanding Mortgages	$_____
Outstanding Balance - All Autos	$_____
Outstanding Balance - All Other Secured Loans	$_____
Outstanding Balance - All Credit Cards	$_____
Unpaid Taxes	$_____
All Other Liabilities	$_____

TOTAL LIABILITIES $_____

NET WORTH (total assets minus total liabilities) $_____

PERSONAL INCOME STATEMENT

Household Income

Gross Annual Salary/Bonus   You $_____   Spouse $_____

Monthly Take-Home Pay   You $_____   Spouse $_____

Monthly Soc. Sec. / Pension   You $_____   Spouse $_____

Other Monthly Income   You $_____   Spouse $_____

TOTAL MONTHLY <u>NET</u> INCOME $_____

Monthly Household Expenses

Mortgage/Rent	$_____	Church/Charity	$_____
Home Insurance	$_____	Medical/Dental (including insurance)	$_____
Auto #1 Loan	$_____		
Auto #2 Loan	$_____	Life Insurance	$_____
Auto Insurance	$_____	Disability Insurance	$_____
Gas/Auto maint.	$_____	Other Loans	$_____
Day Care	$_____	Entertainment	$_____
Utilities	$_____	Clothing	$_____
Food	$_____	Other Expenses	$_____
Clothing	$_____		

TOTAL MONTHLY EXPENSES $_____

PEARLS BEFORE SWINE

FINANCIAL WISDOM
FROM THE PAST
IGNORED IN THE PRESENT

Mark DiGiovanni

TABLE OF CONTENTS

FOREWORD

Swine? *Really?!?*

When selecting the title for this book, I knew I was running the risk of offending potential readers, which is typically not a good sales technique.

As a resident of the present, I'm not in a position to pass judgment on my contemporaries. I lack the proper perspective to compare current generations with those of the Age of Enlightenment or the Roman Empire. I am also guilty of many of the indictments that could be made of my fellow citizens. I have more house than I need (with a mortgage to match). I should save more than I do. I sometimes work too hard and other times I don't work hard enough. I don't practice delayed gratification very well. I want more than I'm willing to pay for. I have an inflated opinion of my own worth. I undervalue the opinions of others. I give money more thought than respect. My list of shortcomings is longer than this sampling.

As a lover of history, I am always interested in how past societies would view the way people behave in the twenty-first century. As a Financial Planner, I am especially interested in how people from the past might view our actions and attitudes about money, in all its aspects and mutations.

One reason for my interest is the many paradoxes that people in the twenty-first century have created for themselves when it comes to money. We think about money more than any previous culture, yet our knowledge about money is inadequate and our wisdom about money is pathetic.

We have the ability to save and invest in well-regulated markets and institutions, yet we don't take proper advantage of them.

We spend thousands upon thousands of dollars educating each of our children. Our children invest twelve to twenty years of their own lives in formal education. We sacrifice so our children can get good jobs, which is necessary to make good money. But nowhere along the way do we stop and teach them anything useful about money.

We have the freedom to choose almost any career we want, yet we gravitate to whatever pays the most and/or requires the least. Such compromises assure that we will never have great success in our careers and will want to retire from them as soon as possible.

We can pay for our basic needs (food, clothing, shelter, transportation, and medical) with fewer hours of work than at any time in history, yet we run up record amounts of personal debt pursuing what we merely want, not what we truly need.

We allow our governments to generate so much debt that their very integrity is at risk because we are as yet unwilling to receive less from and/or pay more to these governments to keep them solvent.

We spend more time planning a vacation to Disney World than we do planning our family's finances for the year.

We pay for the prestige of certain brands, even when we know there is no discernible difference in their quality compared to non-prestige brands. In the case of expensive items like cars, these purchases are usually made with borrowed funds.

We have the ability to be the healthiest creatures to ever walk the earth, but we choose to damage our health through poor diet, substance abuse, and inactivity. Then when we lose our health, we don't want to pay the high cost of getting well.

We can insure against most financial losses at a reasonable cost, yet we divert our capital to more pleasurable pursuits instead.

We have qualified advisers at our disposal through many media, plus the collective wisdom of centuries of mankind, yet we seek only what we want to hear, not what we need to hear.

It can be hard for us to recognize these self-made paradoxes because, when everyone is doing the same thing, we tend to think it is normal behavior. It takes the perspective of a different peer group to make us more fully aware of the folly of many of our financial habits.

What would Confucius, the Chinese philosopher who lived five hundred years before Christ, think about our inability to live within our means?

What would Virgil, the Roman poet from the time of Christ, think about our domination by fear and greed in the markets?

What would Benjamin Franklin, one of history's wisest and most prolific men on financial matters, think about our reluctance to plan for our future?

What would Abraham Lincoln, our 16th President, think of our attempts to receive more while working less?

What would Thoreau, Einstein, Socrates, Gandhi, Jesus, and others have to say about our misunderstandings about the role of money, wealth, possessions, and work in our lives?

The following pages contain the words of more than two-hundred individuals, spanning more than twenty-five centuries. Their purpose here is to give us a better sense of where we are today in a world that runs on money and to provide guidance and inspiration to help us become better stewards of what has been entrusted to us.

The average American today lives far better than the richest king of just a couple of centuries ago. Despite our material comfort, we do not seem happy with our lot. We worry constantly about money, even though we are the most comfortable humans in history. If these great figures from the past could reappear today and observe us firsthand, I do not think we would receive a glowing evaluation. They might view their words of wisdom as pearls cast before swine. It's not too late to prove them wrong.

THE OMNIPRESENT ABSTRACTION

To get an indication of just how deeply money is integrated into our lives, digest the following:

> *I, (Name), Take you, (Name),*
> *To be my (wife/husband);*
> *To have and to hold,*
> *From this day forward,*
> *For better, for worse,*
> *For richer, for poorer,*
> *In sickness and in health,*
> *To love and to cherish,*
> *Till death do us part.*

Traditional Wedding Vows

This wedding vow is the most solemn pledge that most people make in their lives, and some eighty-five percent of the population makes this pledge at least once in their lives.

Right there in the middle of these vows is the promise that we will remain married regardless of our financial condition in the future. We promise that we will remain together for better or worse, which is affected in no small part by our financial condition. We also promise to remain together in sickness and in health. There is a positive correlation between wealth and health, and comparatively few marriages break up because a spouse becomes ill.

These traditional wedding vows date back to at least 1549, when they were first published in the prayer book for the Church of England. Clearly, the danger to marriages posed by financial calamity or carelessness is not a new phenomenon.

Financial problems are often cited as a leading cause of divorce. Divorced couples cite financial problems as the cause of divorce more often than do professional counselors. This discrepancy is because, while most divorcing couples think that money problems are the cause, professional counselors can see that money problems are often a manifestation of other, more serious problems in a marriage.

For a man-made instrument with no intrinsic value, money sure kicks up a lot of dust.

That money is where most of us are tested says precisely as much about the weakness of man as it does about the power of money.

Jacob Needleman (1934-   )
Author, Philosopher

For better or worse, money has become our principal means of contact with the outside world. Think about all the contacts you have with people in a typical month. How many of them involve money as the main reason for the contact? Every business transaction would be included in this category. How many of these monthly contacts have some monetary aspect to them? Even organizations you belong to, such as a church or social club, have dues or financial pledges. Even such organizations that are not created for a business purpose will have a financial obligation as a condition for membership. There is a paid admission.

Even marriage, which should involve more love and less money than any other relationship, has a financial component from the beginning. The payment of a dowry is a four-thousand-year-old practice of the wife providing financial assets to begin the marriage. One of its main purposes is to protect the wife against ill treatment by the husband or his family. The dowry system is still practiced in parts of south Asia.

Modern western marriages begin with a major financial component, too - the engagement ring. The ring is supposed to symbolize the commitment of the partners, though it also has come to symbolize the financial strength of the groom-to-be. In the early twentieth century, DeBeers began suggesting that three months' wages was an appropriate amount to spend on an engagement ring. The average amount spent on an engagement ring today exceeds $2,000, which isn't close to three month's wages for the typical groom-to-be. While an engagement ring can be a major investment, at least it's encouraging that people aren't blindly following the guidelines set by the world's largest producer of diamonds.

> *Money is a new form of slavery, which differs from the old only in being impersonal, and in freeing people from all the human relations of the slave.*
>
> Leo Tolstoy (1828-1910)
> Russian Novelist

In this world, we have *social norms* and *market norms*. Social norms involve the interactions between humans. They are about helping each other and getting along. They are the glue that holds a society together. They are biological. Market norms involve a bottom line. They are transaction-based. They can be precisely measured. They are mechanical.

The first thing to realize is that when social norms collide with market norms, social norms lose. This collision almost always occurs when market norms invade the world of social norms. For example, many budding romantic relationships have come to a screeching halt because at some point the guy brought up how much he had spent on dates and that he wasn't "getting anything in return." That one comment shifted the relationship from social norms to market norms. In such a developing relationship, it also shifted the dynamic from pleasure to business. Nothing kills a relationship faster than shifting it from pleasure to business prematurely.

In business relationships, market norms should rule. In social relationships, social norms should rule. When you are invited to a friend's house for dinner, you bring a nice bottle of wine as a gift; you don't offer to "pay the tab" at the end of the evening. When your neighbor asks to borrow your chain saw, you lend it with the expectation he will return the favor in the future; you don't charge him rent.

If you introduce market norms where social norms prevail, market norms will win. But know that social norms may never return and that they never forget, either.

Riches should be admitted into our houses, but not into our hearts; we may take them into our possession, but not into our affections.

Pierre Charron (1541-1603)
French Philosopher

A wise man should have money in his head, but not in his heart.

Jonathan Swift (1667-1745)
English Novelist

You should always love people and use money, rather than the reverse.

> Bob Proctor (1940-   )
> Motivational Speaker

One of the primary reasons money seems to dominate so much of our lives is because we have allowed ourselves to become emotionally attached to it. We have allowed it to invade our hearts.

Our material and economic needs are important, but they were never meant to be more important than our spiritual needs. Ours is one of the first societies that have encouraged people to be self-sufficient and autonomous. We admire "rugged individualism." The problem with such autonomy, which is made possible with money more than anything else, is that it can lead to a disconnection between the individual and the rest of society, as well as a disconnection between the individual and that person's spiritual side.

Money is not required to buy one necessity of the soul.

> Henry David Thoreau (1817-1862)
> Author, Philosopher

There is a certain paradox to America. We have a very high standard of living, while at the same time we have a very high religious affiliation. No other country has a combined score in spirituality and materialism that is as high. Our collective faith, at least when measured by levels of participation in organized religious services, seems to keep us grounded enough that materialism doesn't totally consume us as a nation.

Prosperity is only an instrument to be used, not a deity to be worshipped.

> Calvin Coolidge (1872-1933)
> 30th U.S. President

Money is only a tool. It will take you wherever you wish, but it will not replace you as the driver.

> Ayn Rand (1905-1982)
> Novelist, Philosopher

When money becomes desired for what it is, rather than for what it can do, it is worse than someone who collects classic automobiles but never drives them. It seems a waste to just let a classic car sit, but it can still be admired for its styling. Money has no styling. You can't display it in a museum and charge admission. Unless money is serving some purpose, the possession of it and the effort made to acquire and possess it is a waste.

Money is like love; it kills slowly and painfully the one who withholds it, and enlivens the other who turns it upon his fellow man.

> Kahlil Gibran (1883-1931)
> Poet, Philosopher

Money is like manure. You have to spread it around or it smells.

> J. Paul Getty (1892-1976)
> Founder, Getty Oil Company

Money that is not in circulation is useless, just as your blood is useless if it isn't in circulation through your veins and arteries.

That's not to say that money that isn't being spent

isn't in circulation. Too many people and too many governments have been putting too much money into circulation, often borrowing the money from future generations. They have not saved and invested enough of the money that has crossed their palms.

Saving and investing does not take money out of circulation. It provides capital for the creation of more money in the future. Adequate savings and investments provide economic security for their owners, which is one of the most important tasks that money is asked to perform.

When the accumulation of money goes well past the point of what is necessary to maintain economic security, the efficient use of that money can become compromised. More important, the time and energy its owner expends in the accumulation of ever more money is inefficient. They trade ever-dwindling resources for a resource they don't need at all.

Riches are a good handmaid, but the worst mistress.
Sir Francis Bacon (1561-1626)
English Philosopher, Statesman

Money frees you from doing things you dislike. Since I dislike doing nearly everything, money is handy.
Groucho Marx (1890-1977)
Comedian

Money is history's greatest labor-saving device. Money enables work to be assigned to others who can do it more efficiently than you can. This process of assignment frees up your time to be used more efficiently.

When the accumulation and protection of money (and

those things that money can buy) begins to consume more and more of one's time and energy, money ceases to be a labor-saving device and becomes a labor-making device for its owner. In such circumstances, the owner of money becomes possessed by the possession.

Money is not exempt from the *law of marginal utility*, which states that the more we have of something, the less we value each additional unit. Individuals have to determine when they have reached a point where the effort to have more is not worth the more they will have.

> *The gratification of wealth is not found in mere possession or in lavish expenditure, but in its wise application.*
>
> Miguel de Cervantes (1547-1616)
> Spanish Novelist, Poet

> *A man who both spends and saves money is the happiest man, because he has both enjoyments.*
>
> Samuel Johnson (1709-1784)
> English Poet, Essayist

A true craftsman would much rather show you the products he has made than show you the tools with which he made them. It should be the same way with money.

We all have this same tendency, to varying degrees. Some people will use their money to buy items that clearly show how much money they spent, and by extension, how much money they have. Think about cars that cost upwards of six figures. There is no practical reason for someone to spend so much for a car. Certain makes and models of cars tell the world in no uncertain terms that its owner has some serious financial means.

There is a long list of items that we can buy whose primary, if not sole purpose, is to tell the world just how much we are worth in dollars and cents.

The true craftsman works his tools to create items that have both utility and beauty. A true craftsman with money should do the same thing. While there is nothing wrong with the occasional self-indulgent extravagance, if the majority of one's money is used for such a purpose, it can hardly be considered a wise application. A person's money should be allocated among sharing, saving, and spending. The amount allocated to each category will vary from person to person, but it is important that the stated order of priority be followed. When spending comes first, sharing and saving will always receive less than their due.

If your only goal is to become rich, you will never achieve it.

John D. Rockefeller (1839-1937)
Founder, Standard Oil Company

Becoming rich is a dream, if not a goal, for many of us. However, most people who become rich do so as a by-product of a different goal, which can be described generally as providing a needed product or service to as many people as possible. Becoming rich was the effect, not the cause.

"Becoming rich" is also a vague term. When we want to lose weight, we don't say we want to "become thin," because thin is a vague term that is subject to interpretation and is hard to measure. We will instead state a goal of reaching a target weight, then work toward that goal. Once we reach our target weight, we rarely continue losing weight just to see how thin we can

231

become.

Even if someone sets a wealth goal (a net worth of $1 million, $5 million, $100 million), that person is never satisfied once that goal is achieved. One of the characteristics of money is that it is addictive. The man who thought he would be happy with a net worth of $1 million will find himself working harder than ever when his net worth is $100 million. Making money can be like drinking sea water; it doesn't quench the thirst; it only increases it.

For the love of money is a root of all kinds of evil. Some people, eager for money, have wandered from the faith and pierced themselves with many griefs.

1 Timothy 6:7-10

So you think that money is the root of all evil? Have you ever asked what the root of money is? Money is made possible only by those who produce. Is this what you consider evil?

Ayn Rand (1905-1982)
Novelist, Philosopher

It's important to remember that the Biblical passage does not say that money is the root of all evil; it says that the *love* of money is the root of all evil.

It isn't money's fault that so many problems stem from its use, misuse, and abuse. Money is inert. It has no personality, no agenda, and it plays no favorites. The only problem with money is all the stupid things humans concoct to do with it. When people and money come together, it is important to remember that, of the two, only people are inherently flawed.

Any tool is subject to misuse. Anyone who has ever

232

been hit on the head with a frying pan or seen *The Texas Chainsaw Massacre* knows what I mean. Money, as we think of it, was started by King Croesus of Lydia over 2,500 years ago to facilitate trade. Croesus would be stunned to see how important money is in the modern world. He would also be stunned to see how creative we've become in finding new ways to abuse money.

If a man has money, it is usually a sign too, that he knows how to take care of it. Don't imagine his money is easy to get simply because he has plenty of it.
Edgar Watson Howe (1853-1937)
Novelist, Editor

Those who obtain riches by labor, care, and watching know their value. Those who impart them to sustain and extend knowledge, virtue, and religion know their use. Those who lose them by accident or fraud know their vanity. And those who experience the difficulties and dangers of preserving them know their perplexities.
Charles Simmons (1893-1975)
Member, British Parliament

Considering how much time we spend in the pursuit of money, we spend remarkably little time in trying to understand money. I'm not referring here to spending time learning how to make money. I'm talking about understanding the ways money affects individuals and societies.

Because we rarely take any serious time to look at how money can affect us, we end up unprepared for the changes that money can bring. If the people who play the lottery listened to the stories of past winners and the problems that sudden wealth caused them, many would reconsider spending good money on those tickets.

Money is not to be taken lightly because of the effects, both positive and negative, that it can have on all those who are touched by it. Only those who seriously attempt to understand money can hope to control it, rather than be controlled by it.

Men, such as they are, very naturally seek money or power; and power because it is as good as money.
Ralph Waldo Emerson (1803-1882)
Philosopher, Essayist

The men who can manage men manage the men who manage only things.
The men who can manage money manage all.
Will Durant (1885-1981)
Historian, Philosopher

Between money and power, I believe money is the more desirable. Power is only power, but money can buy power and almost everything else, too. The Colt revolver was called the Great Equalizer in the Wild West. Money has similar powers in the modern world. Money has the ability to make unequals seem equal and to make equals seem unequal.

Almost everyone gives greater deference and latitude to someone if we think that person has money. We can see it even in the halls of justice, where everyone is presumed to be equal. Recall the revised definition of capital punishment - those who have the capital don't get the punishment.

Money buys preferred treatment in the more mundane tasks of life, too. Those of us who fly coach must suffer the indignity of walking past our fellow travelers who are already comfortably ensconced in first class. Studies have shown that drivers wait longer to honk at someone who fails to proceed at a green light if that person is driving an expensive car.

> *I am opposed to millionaires, but it would be dangerous to offer me the position.*
>
> Mark Twain (1835-1910)
> Author, Humorist

> *To suppose as we all suppose, that we could be rich and not behave as the rich behave, is like supposing that we could drink all day and stay sober.*
>
> Logan Pearsall Smith (1865-1946)
> Essayist

> *A rich man is nothing but a poor man with money.*
>
> W.C. Fields (1880-1946)
> Comedian, Actor

One luxury the rich don't have that the rest of the population enjoys is the opportunity to mock the rich. Many a movie and television show has poked fun at the supposed ways of the rich, from the inanity of Thurston Howell III on *Gilligan's Island* to the sadistic greediness of Carter Pewterschmidt on *Family Guy*.

Part of the reason for such negative stereotypes is ignorance on who the rich really are. The best-selling book *The Millionaire Next Door* revealed that most millionaires are little different from the general population. Most are first-generation rich and earned their fortunes by starting businesses that the author refers to as "dull-normal."

The best way to realize the pleasure of feeling rich is to live in a smaller house than your means would entitle you to have.

Edward Clarke (1841-1931)
British Solicitor-General

One of the most important factors cited in how millionaires become millionaires is their belief that financial independence is more important than displaying high social status. That core principle is the inspiration for the book's title. That principle also means there are two truths about millionaires that most people have wrong. The first truth is that most of the millionaires out there are camouflaged, living well below their means in modest, but comfortable, homes and driving sensible cars.

The second truth is that many of the people we think are millionaires are probably faking it. The social status that is to be gained by appearing to be rich is so tempting that many people put themselves into financial ruin by trying to maintain such appearances. The more opulent the lifestyle, the greater the chance that it will all collapse like a house of credit cards.

Poor men seek meat for their stomachs.
Rich men seek stomachs for their meat.

English Proverb

If any man is rich and powerful he comes under the law of God by which the higher branches must take the burning of the sun, and shade those that are lower; the tall trees must protect the weak plants beneath them.

Henry Ward Beecher (1813-1887)
Clergyman, Abolitionist

No one would remember the Good Samaritan if he'd only had good intentions. He had money, too.

> Margaret Thatcher (1925-   )
> British Prime Minister

Wealth is created by producing more than you consume. Poverty is created by consuming more than you produce. This axiom is true for both nations and individuals.

Before rich men seek stomachs for their meat, they first make sure their own stomachs are full. They recognize that the best way to keep their own stomachs full is to fill other stomachs, for a price.

Wealth is created by creating something of value to others, something for which others are willing to pay. It is certainly easier to create something of value to others, and to create wealth in the process, when you are well-fed, well-educated, and well-capitalized. When you are spending most of your waking hours seeking meat for your stomach, creating something of value to others doesn't even enter into your head.

When thinking about creating something of value for others, the most valuable creation is the opportunity for others to create value for others, and thus, in time, create wealth for themselves.

There is only one class in the community that thinks more about money than the rich, and that is the poor. The poor can think of nothing else. That is the misery of being poor.

> Oscar Wilde (1854-1900)
> Irish Writer, Poet

This is one of the bitter curses of poverty:
it leaves no right to be generous.

George Gissing (1857-1903)
English Novelist

When the rich think about becoming richer, they tend to think in terms of new products or services they can provide, as well as more efficient ways of providing current goods or services. When the poor think of becoming rich, they do not tend to think in terms of new products or services they can provide. For most of them, they do not possess the skills or the capital to provide products or services of value to others. The poor think of becoming rich through long shots, like winning the lottery, which does not create wealth, but merely transfers it. Counting on a long shot to end one's poverty merely deepens the poverty with every scheme that fails.

In a country well governed, poverty is something to be
ashamed of. In a country badly governed, wealth is
something to be ashamed of.

Confucius (551-479 BC)
Chinese Philosopher

A decent provision for the poor is the true test of
civilization.

Samuel Johnson (1709-1784)
English Poet, Essayist

The worst country to be poor in is America.

Arnold Toynbee (1889-1975)
English Historian

Because we in America believe our form of government to be the best that mankind has yet devised,

238

we feel the need to act when we see poverty in our midst. However, poverty is a *result* of a lack of money; it is not a *symptom* of a lack of money. Poverty is a symptom of a lack of production. A person in poverty is not producing anything anyone wants to buy, at least not in sufficient quantities to provide an adequate income. The reasons for a person's lack of production can run the gamut from severe birth defects to just plain laziness.

I'm not convinced that there are a lot of lazy people in poverty for the simple reason that poverty has a way of beating the laziness out of all but the worst sloths. The worst sloths are the ones who simply won't be productive, regardless of the consequences.

I'm also not convinced that there are huge numbers of Americans who can't be productive. The percentage of people in poverty who, because of a physical or mental handicap, can't do anything is fairly small. (I consider the elderly in a separate category, as most were productive when they were younger.) These people are the poor that Jesus said would always be with us. These people are the poor that have no hope of lifting themselves out of poverty. These people are the poor that should cause us shame should we choose to ignore them.

A lean purse is easier to cure than endure.
George Clason (1874-1957)
Businessman

The majority of those in poverty have the desire and the ability to work their way out of poverty, if they are given the opportunity. They actually prefer a hand up to a handout. The challenge is to teach them how to create wealth for themselves.

We respect most the money we earn through our own hard labors. The respect for that money is merely an extension of the respect we have for ourselves for earning that money through our own hard labors. When people are not given the opportunity to be self-supporting, the opportunity to earn that self-respect is denied. Well-intentioned programs that bestow what can and should be earned disserve those it means to serve.

The Ten Cannots:
- *You cannot bring about prosperity by discouraging thrift.*
- *You cannot strengthen the weak by weakening the strong.*
- *You cannot help little men by tearing down big men.*
- *You cannot lift the wage earner by pulling down the wage payer.*
- *You cannot help the poor by destroying the rich.*
- *You cannot establish sound security on borrowed money.*
- *You cannot further the brotherhood of man by inciting class hatred.*
- *You cannot keep out of trouble by spending more than you earn.*
- *You cannot build character and courage by destroying men's initiative & independence.*
- *And you cannot help men permanently by doing for them what they can and should do for themselves.*

William Boetcker (1873-1962)
Presbyterian Minister

When the rich and the poor think about each other,

240

two stereotypes seem to emerge. The rich give in to the stereotype that the poor **will not** work to obtain wealth. The poor give in to the stereotype that the rich **did not** work to obtain wealth. While there are examples of the stereotype in both groups, the vast majority in both groups do not fit the stereotype at all.

> *That some should be rich shows that others may become rich and, hence, is just encouragement to industry and enterprise. Let not him who is houseless pull down the house of another, but let him labor diligently and build one for himself, thus, by example, assuring that his own shall be safe from violence when built.*
> Abraham Lincoln (1809-1965)
> 16th U.S. President

> *Those who condemn wealth are those who have none and see no chance of getting it.*
> William Penn Patrick (1930-1973)
> Entrepreneur

As long as someone without money sees the possibility of obtaining money, that person is not likely to favor radical redistribution of wealth. Such redistribution serves as a disincentive for wealth creation, to those who are currently producing wealth, and also to those who hope to be producing it in the future. No one wants to learn new disciplines and make new sacrifices if the gains to be made from those sacrifices can't be retained.

Wealth is not a pizza. If I have too many slices, you don't have to eat the Domino's box.

P.J. O'Rourke (1947-   )
Satirist, Journalist

Wealth is a resource. When we think about resources, we tend to think about natural resources, like gold or oil. Those kinds of resources are finite. When we consume a unit of that resource, it is gone forever. If a finite resource is hoarded or wasted, others can be adversely affected. When it comes to a finite resource that everyone wants, disputes over ownership and fairness of distribution can lead to wars, between classes as well as countries.

Wealth is a resource, but it is hardly finite. The people who create wealth are at least as valuable a resource as the wealth they create. Wealth as a resource is like knowledge, not oil. An increase in my knowledge doesn't make everyone else dumber, and an increase in my wealth doesn't make everyone else poorer.

In 1950, the economies of Afghanistan and South Korea were approximately the same size. Today the economy of South Korea is fifty times the size of Afghanistan's. South Korea's only natural resource is its people. They have created wealth by creating knowledge among its people. They maintain that wealth through hard work and thrift. South Korea has created wealth as a nation in the same way individuals create wealth, by understanding that wealth is created primarily with an unlimited resource that all humans possess to some degree.

A great fortune is a great slavery.

Seneca (54 BC - 39 AD)
Roman Statesman

God must love the rich or he wouldn't divide so much among so few of them.

H.L. Mencken (1880-1956)
Essayist, Satirist

While no one aspires to be poor, it's important to remember that there are drawbacks to being wealthy, too. Even those who are not rich know that the more you possess, the more your possessions may possess you. Think about something as simple as owning a second car. The utility and/or pleasure of owning that second car may be more than offset by the effort required to maintain it. Everything we own makes demands of us, and when we own a lot of something, even money, what we get in return may not be worth what we sacrifice to own it.

Worldly riches are like nuts; many clothes are torn getting them, many a tooth broke in cracking them, but never a belly full in eating them.

Ralph Venning (1621-1674)
English Clergyman

Anyone who works with tools for a living knows that it's important to keep the tools of one's trade in good working condition. These tools enable the job to be done, and to be done in a more efficient manner. However, a tool must be used often enough and efficiently enough to justify its cost and its upkeep. It makes no sense to have tools that don't offset the cost in time, effort, and money to own them by generating wealth through the production of goods or services.

Money is a tool, too. Because money is precise, we know when the monetary cost exceeds the monetary benefit. We rarely know with any accuracy when the intangible costs of maintaining wealth exceed the benefits of that wealth. We usually become aware of these "hidden costs" only after they exact an exorbitant price.

No amount of money is worth the sacrifice of one's better instincts, of one's self-respect – of one's soul, if you wish. Riches not gained legitimately and decently are not worth having.

B.C. Forbes (1880-1954)
Founder, Forbes Magazine

Like any tool, money in the right hands used for the right purpose can greatly benefit all whom it touches. And, like any tool, money in the wrong hands used for the wrong purpose can bring great destruction.

Once someone has had money for a time, money's limitations become evident. Also, as we get older and realize our own limitations (especially the limitation of time), we begin to think less of how our money might benefit us and more of how it might benefit others. It is at this point in one's life that a philanthropist is born.

Today, the world knows the poetry of Shakespeare, the music of Wagner, the art of Rembrandt; but who knows even the names of the money barons of their day – or cares to know? If you want your name to live after you, you'll not give all your thought to money.

Edwin Baird (1886-1957)
Publisher

Too many people spend too many years working too hard to get money. They expend their health to obtain wealth, only to then spend their wealth to regain their health. It isn't just the time and effort we sacrifice that is the price of wealth. The bigger price comes in the long-term damage to our physical, mental, and spiritual health.

The first wealth is health.
> Ralph Waldo Emerson (1803-1882)
> Philosopher, Essayist

I don't like money actually, but it quiets my nerves.
> Joe Louis (1914-1981)
> World Boxing Champion

The great majority of the workforce takes jobs that offer little more than the biggest paycheck. People work such jobs like they're a prison sentence, counting the days until they can retire. Often, the stress of working a job that's a misfit causes health problems that force a premature retirement or damages the quality of retirement. Working a job that is fun and fulfilling is much healthier, even if it pays less and requires a few more years in the workforce. I would personally rather work forty years at a job I love than thirty years at one I hate.

Despite the fact that a large number of people stress themselves out in the pursuit of wealth, it is better for your health to be rich than poor. Like everything else in life, the trick is to find a proper balance between what you want and what you are willing to sacrifice to get it.

I am indeed rich, since my income is superior to my expense, and my expense is equal to my wishes.

Edward Gibson (1837-1913)
Lord Chancellor of Ireland

You are financially secure when you can afford anything you want and you don't want anything.

Art Buchwald (1925-2007)
Author, Journalist

Most of the money problems people have are less the result of too little money and more the result of too much desire. Few of us have the ability to control our incomes - we all have the ability to control our desires. As such, it makes sense to control what we have the ability to control.

Controlling the desire for material goods is not easy in a country where credit is easy to obtain and we also receive nearly three-thousand marketing messages every day. Both the credit pitch and the marketing pitch are designed to create desire, and desire involves things we want, not things we need.

When we first attend to the financial items we need (savings, insurance, 401k, etc.), we greatly reduce the risk that we will run into financial problems. People who live at a poverty level are unlikely to be able to fund all their financial needs. If they can't afford health insurance, it isn't usually because they bought a new car instead. Placing wants over needs and putting one at financial risk is more common in the middle class, where credit is easier to obtain, where the pressure to keep up with the neighbors is stronger, and where there is greater optimism that earnings will increase and that everything will work out in the end.

*Goods can serve many other purposes besides
purchasing money, but money can serve no other
purpose besides purchasing goods.*

Adam Smith (1723-1790)
Scottish Philosopher, Economist

There is a paradox to money, in that it is an instrument of precision that creates great distortions. We judge the importance and worth of other human beings based on how much money they earn. Because money is our most common denominator, we use it as the default measure of a person's worth.

There are hedge fund managers that have made as much in a year as twenty-thousand teachers combined. We want to think that we would treat the hedge fund manager and the teacher equally, but we know which one will get the media attention and the preferential treatment.

What's worse than judging others by their wealth and income is judging ourselves by that standard. We beat ourselves up because we don't have a bigger income, because we don't have a bigger stock portfolio, because we don't have a nicer home, a nicer car, or a nicer (fill-in-the-blank).

We all know someone who makes more money than we do, who is also a person of inferior character. We know that we are the better person in every human quality that matters. We have integrity that other person can't touch. And yet, we will still feel a sense of inferiority when we remember that we are the one with less money. We feel this way because the other person is using money to make everyone else feel inferior, and it's easy to submit to that mindset. Also, we defer to whatever method of comparison we can quantify. We can't measure one's integrity, but we can measure their net worth, so that becomes the basis of comparison.

If you want to know how rich you really are, find out what would be left of you tomorrow if you should lose every dollar you own tonight.

William Boetcker (1873-1962)
Presbyterian Minister

Money is always with us - motivating us, goading us, measuring us, judging us. Money can wield great power over us, but only to the extent we let it.

INTERNAL IMPERFECTIONS

In 1974, the Doobie Brothers released an album titled *What Were Once Vices Are Now Habits*. The album's title succinctly and accurately described what had been transpiring over the previous decade.

The period from the mid-sixties to the mid-seventies may have been the most socially upheaving period in American history. There were certainly many positive changes during that period, such as the passage of the Civil Rights Act and the moon landing. We also had assassinations, the Vietnam War, Watergate, urban riots, and the hippie movement, to name a few of the less stellar events of the period.

Behavior that was condemned by society in the early sixties was tolerated, condoned, and sometimes celebrated by the mid-seventies. Consider the aforementioned Doobie Brothers. *Doobie* is slang for marijuana joint. Can you imagine a group naming themselves the Doobie Brothers, getting signed by a record label and getting songs played on the radio in the early sixties, when the charts were dominated by artists like the Shirelles, Chubby Checker, Brenda Lee, and Fabian? What Were Once Pariahs Are Now Rock Stars.

Many without punishment; none without sin.
                                  John Ray (1627-1705)
                                  English Naturalist

In 1969, Diana Ross and the Supremes recorded a song titled "Love Child." The song was controversial at the time because it dealt directly with the subject of a potential unplanned and unwanted pregnancy. The singer urges her boyfriend to be patient about having sex. She was herself a "love child," born out of wedlock with no father around. She did not want her child to suffer the way she had suffered by growing up without a mother and father raising her together.

Fast forward to 1997, a generation later. B-Rock and the Bizz have their only hit, a song titled "My Baby Daddy." In the song, when the girl's current boyfriend asks about the man she has been seen with, her dismissive reply (repeated some fifty times) is "That's just my baby daddy."

It is a wise father that knows his own child.
William Shakespeare (1564-1616)
English Playwright

In 1940, just 3.8% of U.S. births were to unmarried women. Today that figure is around 40%, a ten-fold increase over three generations. When "Love Child" was released, less than 25% of black children were born to unmarried mothers. When "My Baby Daddy" was released, that figure had climbed to nearly 70%. It is unlikely that either song had a measurable effect on the out-of-wedlock birthrate. Their importance is as an indicator of the change in attitude over a generation.

The out-of-wedlock birthrate has also climbed in most of the industrialized world, with the exception of Japan, where the rate is only about 2%. Japan is a homogeneous population, where an individual's rights do not extend to the point where the individual can act in a way that creates a burden on the larger society. The social pressure not to create a child that the state may have to support is much greater in Japan than in the U.S.

One of the misfortunes of our time is that in getting rid of false shame we have killed off so much real shame as well.

Louis Kronenberger (1904-1980)
Author, Drama Critic

Over the last four or five decades, we have become much less judgmental toward others. Such change is good when we have been judgmental about what a person is. Unfortunately, in our desire to be less judgmental about what a person **is**, we have abdicated our responsibility to be judgmental about what a person **does**.

When a society is no longer willing to do the difficult and sometimes unpleasant task of passing judgment on the actions of others, that society often justifies such inaction by reclassifying vices as habits.

Both vices and habits are what a person does; they are not what a person is. As such, they are subject to the judgment of society. A society has both the right and the responsibility to pass judgment on the actions of a person, when those actions have an adverse effect on the larger society.

The chains of habit are too weak to be felt until they are too strong to be broken.

Samuel Johnson (1709-1784)
English Poet, Essayist

As a free society, we should pass judgment on vices, but not on habits. Most habits, such as poor hygiene, may not be applauded by society, but they do not offend to the point where taking action to curtail such a habit is warranted. Upgrading a vice to a habit relieves society of

251

their responsibility to act in any meaningful way.

While we have become less judgmental about some actions that affect society, we have become more judgmental about some areas that affect society less. We no longer feel it is our right to pass judgment on someone producing children that will require state support, yet we are perfectly comfortable telling that same person that they may not smoke. Just as we have upgraded vices to habits to remove responsibility to judge them, we have downgraded some habits to vices to justify passing judgment on others.

What maintains one vice would bring up two children.
Benjamin Franklin (1706-1790)
Founding Father

Whether someone's personal behavior is labeled a vice or a habit, the responsibility of society to pass judgment on that behavior begins when the society as a whole is adversely affected by it. A society can and should debate the moral and cultural effects of a vast array of human behavior, from smoking pot to viewing pornography.

When individual rights get measured against unquantifiable damages to society, the courts are likely to decide in favor of individual rights. To enable society to justify limiting individual rights, society must prove that a behavior causes a quantifiable damage to society. And the best way to quantify anything in society is with our old friend, money.

Prohibition was not repealed because it impinged on individual freedoms or because studies on alcohol consumption proved it wasn't harmful. Prohibition was repealed because it did not reduce alcohol consumption,

252

and the money that used to go to legitimate businesses and to tax coffers was going instead to tax-evading criminal organizations.

The War on Drugs is now more than forty years old, and drug use in the U.S. is higher now than when that war began. This war is being re-evaluated, not because anyone thinks that drugs are good for society, but because after spending approximately one trillion dollars, there has been no discernible progress.

Prohibition and the War on Drugs are examples of efforts to restrict bad behavior that have failed by any financial measure. There are examples of efforts to restrict bad behavior that have succeeded, too. Stricter drunk driving and seat belt laws have reduced deaths and injuries from auto accidents. Such laws are defensible because the economic cost of injuries and death are not borne solely or even primarily by the person who drinks and drives or who doesn't wear a seat belt. Society is required to build more hospitals, hire more EMTs, increase the court docket, and pay higher insurance premiums.

If we don't discipline ourselves, the world will do it for us.

William Feather (1889-1981)
Publisher, Author

Whether we are talking about an individual or a nation, they follow the same pattern when it comes to how their behavior is affected by their support system. For both, the larger and more anonymous the safety net, the more careless is their behavior.

Before the creation of the European Union and a common currency, individual countries in Europe bore the full brunt of their own fiscal mismanagement. When these countries decided to tie their economic fates together, it was inevitable that some of them would behave more recklessly, knowing they could count on their partners to rescue them. That rescue was assured because their ties meant that if one country drowned, they were all in danger of drowning.

The same behavior can be found all the way down to the family level. When there are parents, siblings, and other kin there to back up and bail out a member, there is a greater chance that someone in that family will behave in a manner that necessitates the backup or the bailout.

When the backup/bailout comes in the form of thousands or millions of anonymous taxpayers, the temptation to give in to one's vices increases dramatically. This behavior is hardly limited to the person who has a child out of wedlock, knowing that there will be public assistance to cover most of the expense of raising that child.

The financial meltdown of 2008 was largely precipitated by firms that knew they could privatize the profit but socialize the risk because they were "too big to fail." If their reckless behavior caused a problem, no matter how catastrophic, anyone and everyone who would be adversely affected would come to the rescue, if only to protect their own interests. The larger the parties to be adversely affected and the more numerous they were, the larger and stronger the safety net was for these firms. They were playing with house money.

If you do what you should not,
you must bear what you would not.

Benjamin Franklin (1706-1790)
Founding Father

We have become a society of enablers. An enabler is a third party that takes responsibility for, and makes accommodations for and assumes liabilities of another party's harmful conduct. The enabler's actions are intended to help, but only tend to perpetuate the problem. Addicts never seek treatment as long as there are enablers shielding them from the full force of the damage they are causing. Drugs and alcohol are not the only addictions, and they may be some of the milder ones. Individuals are addicted to entitlements paid for by others. Corporations are addicted to risk for a quick stock boost. Governments are addicted to debt to keep themselves in power. Only when individuals, corporations, and governments are required to bear the full brunt of their actions will they act responsibly.

Discipline without freedom is tyranny.
Freedom without discipline is chaos.
Cullen Hightower (1923-2008)
Writer

A refusal to accept responsibility for one's actions is an invitation to regulation by others. Chaos is too often solved through tyranny. Take something as common as driving your car. Your state requires you to have liability insurance to protect others before you can even drive your car. When you get in your car, you are required by law to buckle up. These regulations were put in place because too many people did not have insurance or wear their seat belts when it was voluntary, even though they were aware of the potential harm their actions could cause to themselves and others.

There are at least two problems with increased regulation. First, for every new regulation that is put in place, resources have to be devoted to enforcing that regulation. Those resources are siphoned from other areas that are almost always more productive. Second, the people the regulations are trying to control most are also the ones most likely to ignore the regulations. If a regulation is put in place because 10% of the population is engaging in a harmful behavior, that 10% will usually continue to engage in that same behavior. Meanwhile, the 90% who already behave appropriately will be burdened with proving their compliance.

It takes 20 years to build a reputation and 5 minutes to ruin it. Think about that - you'll do things differently.
Warren Buffett (1930-   )
Investor, Philanthropist

A person's reputation is the collective opinion of everyone who has an opinion of that person. Only people who are independently wealthy and have no need for human interaction can be unconcerned about their reputation. For leaders in business and government, their reputation is their most valuable asset. Your reputation determines the quality and quantity of your interactions with others, especially people who can be of help. The people who give the least thought to their own reputations are the ones most likely to become parasites. Their reputation becomes their own worst enemy.

Probably the greatest harm done by vast wealth is the harm that we of moderate means do to ourselves when we let the vices of envy and hatred enter deep into our own natures.
Theodore Roosevelt (1858-1919)
26th U.S. President

256

If we evaluate our financial position in absolute terms, most of us would see that we are in pretty good shape. The great majority have adequate food, clothing, and shelter, plus many luxuries and conveniences that didn't even exist a generation ago. The average American today lives better than 99% of humans throughout history, including the average American of a generation or two ago.

We don't evaluate our financial position in absolute terms, though; we judge it in relative terms. We don't look to see if we have what we need; we look to see what others have. Our satisfaction is based on how we feel when we compare ourselves financially to others we observe.

Studies have shown that people have increased dissatisfaction when they lose financial position relative to others, even when their absolute financial position improves. For example, a man is in the 50th percentile in income; half make more; half make less. He gets a 10% raise and feels better about his financial position. Then he finds out that he is now in the 55th percentile in income. Despite his raise, the number of people making more than he does has increased from 50 to 55%. That one additional piece of information took that man from feeling better about his situation to feeling worse, even though he still has a 10% increase in income.

The darkest hour of any man's life is when he sits down to plan how to get money without earning it.
                                        Horace Greeley (1811-1872)
                                        Newspaper Editor

We have progressed as a society to the point where it is extremely rare that someone must resort to crime to provide the necessities of life. We don't have to suffer the guilt of living in a society that creates characters like Oliver Twist or Jean Valjean. Today when people attempt to get money without earning it, they are motivated not by hunger, but usually by greed, sloth, or envy.

Nothing breeds envy and promotes criminal behavior like comparisons. Modern communications make comparisons not only easier, but inevitable. We can't avoid seeing what others earn and how they spend it; unfortunately, the ones who flaunt it seem to make the most for doing the least, which only increases the temptation to take shortcuts to wealth.

He that maketh haste to be rich shall not be innocent.
Proverbs 28:20

He who wishes to be rich in a day will be hanged in a year.
Leonardo da Vinci (1452-1519)
Italian Artist, Inventor

Most of the imperfections we are saddled with don't rise to the level of vice. Most don't even meet the definition of habit. Most of our imperfections are simply part of our human nature, and they only reveal themselves in out-of-the-ordinary situations. Most of our behaviors do not merit any punishment, which is not to say that such behaviors do not have consequences. Sometimes the consequences of merely being human are more severe than the punishment of actually doing something bad.

In recent years a new field of study known as Behavioral Economics has emerged. Behavioral

Economics developed as a legitimate field of study in large part because the way people should behave with money (according to traditional economists) is not the way they behave at all.

Traditional economists base their analyses and expectations of the economy on what people should logically do in given situations, which is the fatal flaw in their thinking. People rarely behave logically, especially when there is money involved.

Happy the man who has learned the cause of things and has put under his feet all fear, inexorable fate, and the noisy strife of the hell of greed.

Virgil (70-21 BC)
Roman Poet

As a rule, human beings make decisions emotionally, then use whatever logic enables them to rationalize their decision. Even when we are aware we are making decisions in this manner, we are unlikely to admit to it. When it comes to irrational decisions about money, the two emotions that cause the most harm are greed and fear.

Greed is an emotion that has been most in evidence on Wall Street in recent years. The financial crisis that reached its nadir in 2008-2009 was triggered in large part by Wall Street firms taking huge risks with other peoples' money to maximize profits.

Then there is the greed of the individual stewards of others' assets. Such greed may be rather benign, as when a broker recommends an investment, not because it will benefit the client, but because the commission will benefit the broker.

There is the more malignant greed of the steward who

overtly steals from clients to finance a certain lifestyle. There have been too many stories in recent years about corrupt financial advisers. They plundered the accounts of elderly clients to buy items like yachts, exotic cars, and Faberge' eggs.

Earth provides enough to satisfy every man's need, but not every man's greed.

Mohandas K. Gandhi (1869-1948)
Indian Statesman

Even the little guy gets caught up in the emotion of greed. Something as simple as buying near the top of the market is a symptom of greed. That person is hoping that recent outstanding returns will continue indefinitely. Emotion overrules reason when people overpay for anything.

Using credit to purchase investments, whether stock, real estate, gold, whatever, is also a symptom of greed. The use of credit greatly increases the risks, but the desire for greater rewards, a symptom of greed in such cases, clouds one's judgment.

You try to be greedy when others are fearful and you try to be very fearful when others are greedy.

Warren Buffett (1930-   )
Investor, Philanthropist

The average person's approach to investing doesn't seem dysfunctional to that person, unless it is compared to buying and selling a different, more tangible item.

If you were in the market for a pair of shoes that has a typical price of $100, you would not likely buy them if the price rose to $200. On the other hand, if the price dropped to $50, you would probably buy as many pairs as you could afford to take advantage of the sale.

Do average people buy stocks that way? No - they tend to do just the opposite. When the market is in full bull mode and stock prices are well above their historic averages, people can't buy them fast enough. When we are in a severe bear market, and prices may be half of their historic average price, you can't give the darn things away.

In prosperity, caution; in adversity, patience.
Dutch Proverb

We have similar dysfunctions when it comes to holding on to investments in bad times. Because we can get daily, if not hourly, updates on our investment portfolios, we know exactly what someone else will pay for it at any given moment. If the amount they are willing to pay keeps going down, we panic and sell out of fear that the trend will continue and eventually our investments will be worthless.

Imagine if, every few days, you received an email telling you what others were willing to pay for your house on that day. Now suppose that for several weeks on end, the price that others were willing to pay kept dropping. Would you panic and sell out of fear that your house might soon become worthless? It's doubtful. You would likely become offended that these idiots keep annoying you with these emails on a subject about which they clearly know nothing. You would label them as spam and get on with your life.

By developing your discipline and courage, you can refuse to let other people's mood swings govern your financial destiny.

Ben Graham (1894-1976)
Economist, Investor

If the previous scenario makes perfect sense when talking about your home, why do people not act the same way when it comes to their investments?

Because your home is a very visible, tangible asset, it is easier to determine its value to you, even if that value differs from what others think. Your home has value as your home, not just as an investment in real estate. You may not like it if others denigrate your home by making low-ball offers, but it isn't likely to goad you into selling your house because you feel you know its worth better than they do.

When it comes to a basket of intangibles, like a stock portfolio, we are much less certain about what the true value is. We defer to the experts, in this case, "the market." If the market is down, it is because there are more sellers than buyers. If you join the ones who are panicking and selling, you are only contributing to the downslide.

The key to making money in stocks is not to get scared out of them.

Peter Lynch (1944-   )
Investor

If everyone knows that the key to making money with any investment is to buy low and sell high, why do people consistently do the opposite? The biggest reason why people tend to buy high and sell low is because that

262

is what most of the other people are doing. When prices get too high, it's because more people are buying than selling, and when they get too low, it's because the majority is doing just the opposite.

Even though it is easier to march along with the herd, it is the few who are willing to run counter to the herd who reap the profits. The average investor reaps about one-third of the actual gains of his/her investments, which is the result of buying high and selling low. Where do the other two-thirds go? It goes to the person on the other end of the trade who is willing to buy from others' fears and sell to their greed. Those people are being richly rewarded for being different.

The desire for safety stands against every great and noble enterprise.

Tacitus (56-117)
Roman Senator

Mankind's ability to adapt to changes in our environment is one of the reasons we have become the dominant species on the planet. Adaptation is a good thing - mostly.

No one likes to be taken for granted, although there isn't a human being alive that doesn't take someone for granted occasionally. Taking someone or something for granted is a manifestation of adaptation. We adapt to those closest to us and come to expect that they will continue to do what they have always done for us. We adapt to our surroundings, especially if those surroundings are comfortable. If something or someone is to our liking, it takes no effort to get used to it.

*Mankind, by the perverse depravity of their nature,
esteem that which they have most desired as of no
value the moment it is possessed, and torment
themselves with fruitless wishes for that which is
beyond their reach.*

Francois Fenelon (1651-1715)
French Archbishop

We adapt quickly to improvements in our material condition. A pay raise will be absorbed so quickly in increased spending we soon wonder how we ever got along with our old income. Our new, improved car, TV, smartphone, or job quickly becomes the new minimum acceptable standard, even when it was just a dream a few months before.

Adaptation causes us to shortchange ourselves on the pleasure of having something new and better. Since improvements in technology come at an ever-faster rate, we barely get used to a new gadget before an improved version is introduced.

Apple has been a great innovator with products like iPods, iPads, and iPhones. But even as their customers camp out to be the first to get the latest product, their enjoyment is already being tempered by the knowledge that Apple will soon introduce a newer, better version that will ruin their enjoyment of a product they don't even yet possess.

*Is not dread of thirst when your well is full, the thirst
that is unquenchable?*

Kahlil Gibran (1883-1931)
Poet, Philosopher

The younger and/or wealthier someone is, the more

susceptible they are to the downsides of adaptation. You never see old people camping out to be the first one to get the new iPhone. When you grew up before the advent of television, not only do you not clamor for a phone that has internet, a camera, music, email, plus thousands of apps, such a device probably intimidates the hell out of you. The status quo is the friend of the old, but not the young.

Our unceasing desire to make things better and to make more of them is part of the human makeup, and America has turned that desire into an art form and has created the largest economy in history. And yet, how often do we take a break from our quest for something new to appreciate anew what we already have? When was the last time you went through a drawer, a trunk, or a closet, found some item that was once near and dear to your heart, and rediscovered the pleasure that it gave you all those years ago?

> *Every gain made by individuals or societies is almost instantly taken for granted. The luminous ceiling toward which we raise our longing eyes becomes, when we have climbed to the next floor, a stretch of disregarded linoleum beneath our feet.*
> Aldous Huxley (1894-1963)
> English Writer

The law of marginal utility states that the more we have of something, the less we value each additional unit. For example, if you have a million dollars, an extra ten dollars doesn't do much for you. On the other hand, if all you have is ten dollars, an extra ten makes a huge difference. Because even the poor in America have more possessions than most of the rest of the world, we don't fully appreciate all that we have.

He who gains a victory over other men is strong;
but he who gains a victory over himself is all powerful.
Lao Tzu (5th Century BC)
Chinese Philosopher

I count him braver who overcomes his desires than him
who conquers his enemies; for the hardest victory is the
victory over self.
Aristotle (384-322 BC)
Greek Philosopher

Lao-Tzu and Aristotle never knew each other. No one in either part of those worlds even knew of the existence of that other part of the world. Yet both men, more than four hundred years before Christ, expressed the same thought in almost the exact same words.

Perhaps no part of ourselves is harder to control than our emotions. Victory over our emotions is victory over self.

We are not talking here about the ability to express emotions. One of the hallmarks of the present time is that people are encouraged to express their emotions. Expressing emotions is generally healthy, healthier than repressing them and letting the stress of repression lead to ulcers, migraines, and strokes.

There is a difference, however, between expressing emotions and surrendering to emotions. It is perfectly alright, even healthy, to express your fears about a declining stock market threatening your retirement portfolio. However, expressing those fears sometimes makes it easier to act on those fears. When that happens, expression of that emotion goes from being healthy to unhealthy to your physical and psychological well-being, as well as to your retirement portfolio.

The plans of the diligent lead surely to advantage, but everyone who is hasty comes surely to poverty.

Proverbs 21:5

Emotions prompt us to action, but acting on our emotions is almost always bad in the long run. When we act on our emotions, we are usually trying to accomplish one of two things - create pleasure or avoid pain. Either of these powerful drives can lead us to hasty actions that have adverse consequences.

Many people buy or lease cars they know they can't afford. They find themselves in such a situation because they ignored the previous quote. They were not diligent in determining just how much car they could afford. They did not do adequate research into finding out what cars would fall within their budget. Finally, they let their emotions get the best of them when they saw a new car in the showroom, smelled that new car smell, sat in those heated leather seats, cranked up the 300 watt stereo, and felt the surge of that powerful engine. The problem was that they were seduced by the upscale car that was out of their price range, and they were too hasty to close the deal.

A man who has committed a mistake and doesn't correct it is committing another mistake.

Confucius (551-479 BC)
Chinese Philosopher

Once we find ourselves in such a situation, we are often reluctant to take steps to correct our mistake because before we can correct our mistake, we must admit our mistake. Admitting mistakes is not easy for anyone because the emotion of pride gets in the way.

Admitting a mistake to ourselves is bad enough, but admitting it to others, whether to parents, children, spouses, or others is a humbling experience. Often, the people to whom we have to admit a mistake have been harmed by our mistake and may have advised us against the action we took. All of which makes it that much harder to admit our mistake and take steps to undo the damage.

All problems become smaller if you don't dodge them but confront them. Touch a thistle timidly and it pricks you; grasp it boldly and its spines crumble.
William F. Halsey (1882-1959)
Admiral, U.S. Navy

Because we are reluctant to first admit and then correct our financial mistakes, they continue to prick us. The person who spends too much for a car gets pricked monthly for four, five, six, even seven years. Every car payment that is in excess of what should have been spent reduces funding for items that truly need funding, like retirement, home maintenance, or emergency savings. It may be a blow to one's pride to sell a car that should never have been bought in the first place, but that single blow to one's pride is preferable to the death by a thousand cuts to one's financial security by a never-ending stream of car payments.

The idea that God would take his attention away from the universe in order to give me a bicycle is just so unlikely I can't go along with it.

Quentin Crisp (1908-1999)
English Raconteur

When we want something badly enough, we can delude ourselves in a variety of ways to justify obtaining the object of our desire.

One of the more amusing and potentially dangerous rationalizations invoke God. The rationalizations are along the lines of, "We prayed about it, and we know God wants us to have this (object of our desire)." If God wants you to have something, God will provide you with the means of acquiring it **first**. The creator of the universe does not put the cart before the horse. Only people make that kind of mistake.

The more we pay for something we desire, whether in money, time, work, or a combination of sacrifices, the more we are likely to suffer the emotion of regret later. We are not very good at calculating future happiness. We are also not very good at judging past happiness, either.

One sees the past better than it was;
one finds the present worse than it is;
one hopes for a future happier than it will be.

Madame d'Epinay (1726-1783)
French Writer

The emotion of nostalgia clouds our judgment of both the past and the present. The human memory does an incredible amount of filtering in order to retain a lifetime of information. In our recollection of the past, we tend to filter out negative aspects from the past. That's only natural because we can only remember so many details, we want our memories to be pleasant, and filtering out the "impurities" enables us to remember more things the way we want to remember them.

Remembering the past through the gauze of our memory can affect our actions in the present, as well as our appreciation of the present. A distorted view of the past leads to a distorted view of the present, which can only suffer in comparison to an idealized view of the past. If we can remember that the good old days were not really as good as we remember them, today begins to look a whole lot better.

An optimist sees an opportunity in every calamity;
a pessimist sees a calamity in every opportunity.
Winston Churchill (1874-1965)
British Prime Minister

Idealizing the past leads to underestimating the quality of the present, which leads one toward pessimism. There are good and bad aspects to every era. If I remember the seventies with any affection, it is because I remember it as the decade I graduated high school and college, moved to a new state, started a career, and met my wife. I don't dwell on our defeat in Vietnam, Watergate, oil embargoes, stagflation, or disco. If I did, I would remember that Doonesbury referred to the seventies as "a kidney stone of a decade."

If a distorted view of the past affects our appreciation of the present, it also cripples our ability to be optimistic about the future. If we think the past was better than it was and, as a result, we think the present is worse than it is, we will extrapolate that train of thought and assume that the future will be worse than the present, which we already hold in low esteem.

There is no security on this earth – only opportunity.
Douglas MacArthur (1880-1964)
General, U.S. Army

When we become pessimistic, we focus on security instead of opportunity. We think of the future as something to survive instead of enjoy. We stop connecting with others through organizations like churches and Rotary Clubs. We buy gold and guns instead of stocks and bonds.

Pessimism is a self-fulfilling prophecy in that pessimists create a future in which no one wants to live. Only optimists are willing to do the work that is necessary to create a future that is better than the present. Only optimists are willing to take risks now that are necessary to earn rewards in the future.

Far better it is to dare mighty things, to win glorious triumphs, even though checkered by failure, than to take rank with those poor spirits who neither enjoy much nor suffer much, for they live in the gray twilight that knows not victory nor defeat.
Theodore Roosevelt (1858-1919)
26th U.S. President

Everything worth having has its price. I'm not referring to material possessions in this context. Material possessions have a price, but that price is in dollars, and it is easy to determine if that price is one you are willing to pay. I refer here to those intangibles that should not have a dollar value placed upon them.

A successful marriage requires giving up some individuality for the sake of the partnership. Being a good parent does not guarantee your children will turn out like you expect. Being a good son or daughter does not guarantee the approval of your parents. Friendship is not always reciprocated. Rewards will not always be commensurate with the risks taken and the effort given.

Those things most worth having do come at a price, but it is not a firm, fixed price for everyone. One couple may glide through a half-century of marriage with hardly a ripple, while another couple may be on the brink of divorce every other year. One person may barely crack a book while making the dean's list at college, while another studies constantly to keep off academic probation. One person's business may practically hemorrhage profits, while another wilts from a lack of customers.

What is a cynic? A man who knows the price of everything and the value of nothing.
>> Oscar Wilde (1854-1900)
>> Irish Writer, Poet

Those things most worth having are only available to those who are willing to pay the price, while having no certainty of what that price will ultimately be. Only an optimist is willing to pay an uncertain price for something of inestimable value.

We live in an era of unbridled emotions, and we have paid a price for it. We get too high, then we get too low, and our finances get whipsawed in the process. We could use some of the stoicism of the ancient Spartans or the stiff-upper-lip attitude of the British during the Blitzkrieg.

Our unbridled emotions do more to hurt us financially, individually, and nationally than any other single factor. The good news is our emotions are the one factor affecting our finances that we have the ability to control. As long as our emotions continue to control us, we will have good reason to be pessimistic.

Hell is the state in which we are barred from receiving what we truly need because of the value we give to what we merely want.

Virgil (70-21 BC)
Roman Poet

Americans define a need as a 48-hour old want.

George Will (1941-   )
Journalist, Author

We put ourselves through Hell getting things we think we need, only to find out after a while that not only didn't we need them, we didn't really want them much, either. Such mistakes wouldn't be a major problem except that in satisfying our short-term wants, we sacrifice our ability to satisfy our long-term needs.

When someone "needs" a new car and buys or leases twice as much car as is needed and, at the same time, is not adequately funding his/her retirement account, that person is putting short-term wants above long-term needs. When someone "needs" a vacation, but the money spent on a vacation means that person no longer has the money to pay for an adequate life insurance policy to protect his/her children, that person is putting short-term wants above long-term needs.

Need is not measured by someone's level of desire for something. Need is measured by the negative effects on a person that are beyond that person's control if what is needed is withheld. We need, air, food, water, and sleep. If we do not receive a sufficient amount of all of these requirements, we will die.

As a species, we need sex to continue the species. As individuals, we don't need sex to survive. Nature has designed sex to be something we want badly enough that we think of it as something we need, thus insuring the survival of the species. Sex is merely the strongest and most prevalent example of how strong desires can cause us to confuse wants with needs.

Semper inops quicumque cupit.
(Whoever desires is always poor.)

> Claudius (10 BC-54 AD)
> Roman Emperor

The inability to control one's desires leads inevitably to an inability to control one's spending. Most of our desires can be satisfied through some financial transaction, which can lead to financial problems in the present and the future. The inability to control one's desires is also a habit that gets worse over time, guaranteeing that one's financial problems will also get worse over time.

Ill-luck is almost always the result of taking pleasure first and duty second, instead of duty first and pleasure second.
> Theodore T. Munger (1830-1910)
> Clergyman

It is our duty to take care of our needs and the needs of those who depend on us. It is our pleasure to take care of our wants and the wants of those we love. Duty involves making a sacrifice now for something better in the future. Pleasure involves living for the moment, with no thought to the future.

The true way to gain much is never desire to gain too much. He is not rich that possesses much, but he that covets no more; and he is not poor that enjoys little, but he that wants too much.

Francis Beaumont (1584-1616)
English Dramatist

Misfortunes always come in by the door that has been left open for them.

Czech Proverb

When we are constantly in pursuit, we are not in a position to receive. Good things come to those who wait, but good things also come to those who aren't running around chasing after whatever has just lit the spark of desire. We associate action with progress, but, very often, the best way to attract what you want is to be still and at peace and let the object of your desire come to you.

One great difference between a wise man and a fool is the former only wishes for what he may possibly obtain; the latter desires impossibilities.

Democritus (460-370 BC)
Greek Philosopher

All the money in the world is no use to a man or his country if he spends it as fast as he makes it. All he has left is his bills and the reputation for being a fool.

Rudyard Kipling (1865-1935)
English Poet, Novelist

275

The wisest man is the one who controls his desires, rather than letting his desires control him. Such men and women are scarce, and they not only control their lives, but come in time to control others' lives as well. Next in line is the man who has desires within his ability to attain, which can be a mixed blessing, as obtaining one's desires provides positive reinforcement to a behavior that may be harmful in the long run. Finally, there's the fool who chases after impossibilities. The fool sees zero return for his investment of time, effort, and money.

You can tell the difference between these three types with the following example. The first man doesn't play the lottery because he knows the odds are ridiculously long, and both his time and his money are too valuable to waste on it. The second man invests in his retirement plan, but buys a lottery ticket every week because "you never know." The last man buys a hundred lottery tickets a week because that is his retirement plan.

We have been descending into a culture of victimization for at least two decades now. People are quite willing to accept risks when they consider the upside, but when a negative outcome occurs, those same people are looking for someone other than themselves to take the blame (and pay for their financial loss, as well as their pain and suffering).

Consider smokers in the U.S. Since 1965, cigarette makers have been required to print warnings on every pack of cigarettes. The date of this requirement means that anyone one who started smoking after 1965 (which means almost everyone born after 1950) knew the risks the first time they lit up. Still, you hear of lawsuits and multi-million dollar awards being given to people who chose to smoke, despite being warned of the dangers before they ever started, with the warnings coming directly from the manufacturer of the product.

It is impossible to protect people from themselves if they don't first accept the responsibility to protect themselves. Pleasure-seeking often involves risky behavior. One way to reduce risky behavior is to reduce submission to desires. Unfortunately, the same people who are the weakest when it comes to controlling themselves are also the first ones to look for someone else to blame when the chickens come home to roost.

For even when we were with you, we used to give you this order: if anyone is not willing to work, then he is not to eat, either. For we hear that some among you are leading an undisciplined life, doing no work at all.

2 Thessalonians 3:10-11

Poverty is not dishonorable in itself, but only when it comes from idleness, intemperance, extravagance, and folly.

Plutarch (46-120)
Greek Historian

You can divide a population into four different types of people. The first, and best, are those rare few who are looking for nothing-for-something. These are the people who only think of giving, never taking. Anonymous philanthropists and saints fall into this category.

Next we have those who are looking for something-for-something. This is the group that includes most of us. These people believe in paying their own way, in free and fair markets, and in the principle that first you give, and then you receive.

Third is a group as rare as the first one. These are the people who are looking for nothing-for-nothing. They are rare because, in order to be looking for nothing, you have to be totally self-sufficient and independent. Our lives have become too complex and intertwined to enable someone to live in such isolation. We have also become so specialized in our skill sets that trade with other people is more necessary than ever in order to survive. This group may not take anything from the rest of humanity, but they don't add anything, either.

Finally, we have the bottom of the barrel - those who are looking for something-for-nothing, or at least something-for-less-than-something. It's not easy being a something-for-nothing person. If you give nothing for something, you don't get repeat business, which requires you to constantly find new hosts to continue your parasitic ways. Something-for-nothings offset their small numbers by creating big disasters wherever they go.

There is hardly anything in the world that some man can't make a little worse and sell a little cheaper, and the people who consider price only are this man's lawful prey.

John Ruskin (1819-1900)
English Art Critic

Did you get your money by fraud? By pandering to men's vices or men's stupidity? By catering to fools, in the hope of getting more than your ability deserves? By lowering your standards? By doing work you despise for purchasers you scorn? If so, then your money will not give you a moment's or a penny's worth of joy. Then all the things you buy will become, not a tribute to you, but a reproach; not an achievement, but a reminder of shame.

Ayn Rand (1905-1982)
Novelist, Philosopher

The person whose aim is to give less than what is equitable or to take more than is earned is the one who is potentially the most damaging to society. Such people are dangerous for two reasons. First, they can be hard to detect and they can take advantage of others for years, even decades, before their reputation finally destroys them. Second, and perhaps more important, this person dwells inside all of us, at least from time to time.

Even the most upright, honest, hardworking person has taken advantage of the occasional opportunity to cut a corner, thumb the scale, or shirk a duty at work. It's impossible to work thirty or forty years and never give in to such opportunities. The danger from the person who behaves this way all the time is serious. Even more serious is the danger posed when good people in the something-for-something group give in to the lure of something-for-less-than-something. That kind of decay from within can be hard to stop once it takes hold.

Doing for people what they can and ought to do for themselves is a dangerous experiment. In the last analysis, the welfare of the workers depends upon their own initiative. Whatever is done under the guise of philanthropy or social morality which in any way lessens initiative is the greatest crime that can be committed against the toilers.

Samuel Gompers (1850-1924)
Labor Union Leader

Just as it is in our nature to try to get more than we give in a transaction, it is also in our nature to try to avoid unpleasant tasks. For many people, one of life's unpleasant tasks is earning a living. It would be nice if everyone could love their job and could look forward to going out and earning a living every day. However, there will always be low-paying, unpleasant jobs that will need to be done. There will always be people who never find the right career, who spend their lives as a square peg in a round hole. There will always be people who prefer not to work, no matter the job. And so, there will always be people whose only reason for doing a job is the paycheck.

Initiative is one of the greatest human attributes, and anything that stifles a person's initiative is detrimental to the individual and to society as a whole. Nothing stifles initiative like removing the necessity of performing a task. People don't have to rely on their initiative to do the things they want to do; they rely on their initiative to do the things they need to do.

When the necessity of doing something, such as earning an income or caring for one's children, is transferred from the individual to others or to the state, that individual's initiative is depleted.

Initiative is not something we compartmentalize. If our initiative to perform one duty is depleted, our initiative to perform our other duties is depleted, too. Well-intended but misguided efforts to do the duties of others have a corrosive effect on the intended beneficiary. Like corrosion, the effects are slow and subtle, but the damage is incessant and, if not stopped early on, will render the person useless.

A proud man is seldom a grateful man, for he never thinks he gets as much as he deserves.

Henry Ward Beecher (1813-1887)
Clergyman, Abolitionist

A gift much expected is paid, not given.

George Herbert (1593-1633)
English Poet, Priest

My pride fell with my fortunes.

William Shakespeare (1564-1616)
English Playwright

If you've done much charity work in your life, at some point you have probably been surprised at an apparent lack of gratitude by some recipients of that charity. If it happens often enough, it can diminish your desire to be charitable in the future.

Some of the apparent lack of gratitude by some can be explained by our ever-increasing entitlement mentality. If someone is entitled to something, there should be no need to express gratitude to anyone. Viewing charity as an entitlement removes the stigma of being someone who has to rely on charity. One problem with such a perception is if the charity ceases, the recipient becomes angry, not that charity ceased, but that an entitlement has been stolen.

You can think about such behavior in another context. You would expect that the French and the Iraqi peoples would both be grateful to America - after all, we liberated both of them from the yoke of oppression. We're not particularly loved in either country, though the reason isn't ingratitude, it's pride. In both countries, Americans did what, from the perspective of the French and the Iraqis, should have been done by themselves. To be saved from one's helplessness is a reminder of that helplessness, and the more helpless one feels, the less initiative one demonstrates in the future.

*Don't expect to be paid a dollar an hour for your
working hours when you then use your leisure hours as
though they were not worth five cents a dozen.*

Henry L. Doherty (1870-1939)
Financier, Oilman

With the flood of new technology in the last couple of decades, the line between work and leisure is more blurred than ever. In many jobs, people can work from anywhere at any time. Leisure has invaded the workplace, but mostly in superficial ways like casual dress. Work has invaded leisure much more, simply because you're always connected to your work if you have nothing more than a smartphone.

Social media has also given everyone the chance to put their leisure activities out there for all the world, including current and potential employers, to see. Everyone has the right to use their leisure time as they wish, though leisure time is a valuable resource and shouldn't be squandered, either by debauchery or by more work. Knowing that your leisure life may now be scrutinized as closely as your work life by an employer, workers need to be sure that their leisure activities are not going to create a problem at work, and workers need to be ever more discreet about what leisure activities they make available through social media.

*The common idea that success spoils people by making
them vain, egotistic and self-complacent is erroneous;
on the contrary, it makes them for the most part,
humble, tolerant and kind. Failure makes people cruel
and bitter.*

W. Somerset Maugham (1874-1965)
English Playwright, Novelist

*There must be a reason why some people can afford to
live well. They must have worked for it. I only feel
angry when I see waste; when I see people throwing
away things we could use.*

Mother Teresa (1910-1997)
Catholic Missionary

An abundance of money is unlikely to change one's character unless the money was not earned by the person who has it. If a man accumulates a million dollars over a decade of hard work and delayed gratification, that man will have the same character at the end of the decade that he had at the beginning. If another man wins a million dollars in the lottery, that person's character is more likely to be affected by the windfall, especially if he were not wealthy before. By the end of another decade, the man who earned a million dollars will likely have accumulated two or three million more. The man who won the lottery is likely to be broke, the money lost to frivolous spending, scams, and parasitic friends and relatives.

*Ever wonder about those people who spend $2 apiece
on those little bottles of Evian water? Try spelling
Evian backward.*

George Carlin (1937-2008)
Comedian

In order to have a proper understanding of money when it comes to disbursing it, people first need a proper understanding of money when it comes to creating it. The harder and longer someone works to become wealthy, the less naïve they are likely to be when it comes to spending money. When money is given to someone and they didn't have to work for it, a lot of that money is likely to be spent wastefully. Even if someone earns money, but they earn a disproportionately large amount (athletes, movie stars, and CEOs, for example), a lot of that money may be spent frivolously, too. The more you put into getting your money, the more you expect to get from your money.

EXTERNAL EXCITATIONS

Are you part of a typical American household? Probably not, since there is no typical American household, which could be defined as one where the major characteristics of that household are shared by a majority of the population. While there is no typical American household, allow me to create a hypothetical one for our purpose here.

Our American household in 2016 has two adults and two children. One adult works full-time, the other part-time. Their combined annual income is $65,000. They own a house valued at $150,000. They also owe $120,000 on their mortgage, $12,000 on one of their two cars, and a $2,000 average balance on their credit cards. Their total debt to income ratio is a fairly consistent 2:1.

Or is it? We have not factored in their share of the federal debt, which comes to $50,000 per person, or $200,000 for their four-person household (Kids have an equal piece of the debt in this hypothetical.) In addition to this current debt load, the federal government is currently adding $1.5 trillion to the total every year, which means that our hypothetical household's total share of the federal debt is increasing by $1,600 *per month.*

The budget should be balanced, the Treasury should be refilled, public debt should be reduced, the arrogance of officialdom should be tempered and controlled, and the assistance to foreign lands should be curtailed, lest Rome become bankrupt.

Cicero (106-43 BC)
Roman Statesman

I need to provide a couple of definitions at this point. The federal debt is the total of all the money the federal government owes at a given moment. The federal deficit is the difference between federal revenues and expenditures for the current year. Every year, the deficit for that year is added to the federal debt. Deficit spending causes debt.

When media pundits and policy wonks begin discussing the federal debt and deficit, it's easy for most of us to disconnect. It's hard to get your mind around a figure like $15 trillion when a ten-dollar increase in the cable bill gives you a headache. If they would break these numbers down into what the average family's share is, a lot more people would appreciate the magnitude of the problem.

I believe a lot more people would also be driven to action if they fully understood their personal stake in government spending. Our hypothetical household works hard to pay their bills every month and to make a dent in their outstanding debt. If, after all their efforts, they still find themselves $1,600 deeper in debt every month because of someone else's spending, that is cause for action.

There are 10^{11} stars in the galaxy. That used to be a huge number. But it's only a hundred billion. It's less than the national deficit! We used to call them astronomical numbers. Now we should call them economical numbers.

Richard Feynman (1918-1988)
Physicist

A billion dollars here, a billion dollars there, and pretty soon you're talking about real money.

> Everett Dirksen (1896-1969)
> Member, U.S. Senate

The federal debt is roughly equal to all the outstanding mortgage debt in the U.S. To put it one way, if there were no federal debt, everyone who owns a home could own another one of similar value without increasing their debt load. To put it yet another way, the federal government has saddled every homeowner in the U.S. with a debt equal to their outstanding mortgage without giving them a second home to enjoy.

The American Republic will endure until the day Congress discovers that it can bribe the public with the public's money.

> Alexis de Tocqueville (1805-1859)
> French Historian

Why is our government in such dire financial straits? There are many reasons, but we need to boil it down to the most basic reasons that no one can refute. First, the population as a whole has demanded more from their government than they are willing to pay. Second, our elected officials will not say no to these demands if it means they will no longer be our elected officials.

Obviously, not everyone in our country is receiving a dollar's worth from the federal government while only paying in fifty-eight cents. In fact, hardly a soul would land right on the average input/outgo ratio for the government as a whole. Many pay a great deal and receive little, while many receive a great deal and pay nothing.

In general, the art of government consists in taking as much money as possible from one party of the citizens to give to the other.

Voltaire (1694-1778)
French Writer, Philosopher

Any society that takes away from those most capable and gives to the least will perish.

Abraham Lincoln (1809-1965)
16th U.S. President

A government which robs Peter to pay Paul can always count on Paul's support.

George Bernard Shaw (1856-1950)
Irish Playwright

Every popularly elected government struggles to find a proper balance between helping the poorest without decimating the richest. In a country as large and diverse as the U.S., there will always be people who need help from their government, just as there will always be people who are able and willing to provide that help. A properly run government will try to help the poor, but not so much that it stifles personal initiative. They will also ask the rich to fund that help, but not so much that it stifles the incentive to create wealth.

Taxes are paid in the sweat of every man who labors. If those taxes are excessive, they are reflected in idle factories, tax-sold farms and in hordes of hungry people, tramping the streets and seeking jobs in vain.

Franklin D. Roosevelt (1882-1945)
32nd U.S. President

The methods in which a government collects and

distributes money are akin to the way the human organism keeps itself healthy. If the organism takes in too much food and doesn't use it, it goes to waste and makes the organism unhealthy. If it takes in too little food, the organism becomes weak in a variety of ways, since it cannot support its essential functions.

For the organism to grow healthily, the growth must be equitably distributed. Organs develop simultaneously with muscles, bones, and nerves. Delaying development in one area in order to speed up development of another area leads to a weakening of the entire organism.

When injury or disease harms part of the organism, resources are focused on healing the parts of the organism most injured or most essential to the life of the organism. When the crisis passes, the organism returns to its normal pattern of collection and distribution of nutrients.

Every new tax is immediately felt more or less by the people. It occasions always some murmur, and meets with some opposition... Debt is not immediately felt by the people, and occasions neither murmur nor complaint.

Adam Smith (1723-1790)
Scottish Philosopher, Economist

The big difference between an organism and a government is that an organism must live in the present only. If an organism is hungry, it cannot borrow food from tomorrow in order to eat today. If it is suffocating at the moment, it cannot breathe next week's air. An organism must take care of itself every single day, because it cannot count on anything but the resources it can acquire today to keep it alive.

Governments, on the other hand, can borrow from the future to finance whatever they want to do today. This ability to tap into future resources can be essential to survival, as when our government borrowed billions to finance victory in World War II.

The ability to easily borrow from the future can also create great temptations. When you are a politician elected by the people, you can garner votes by promising to give them what they want without asking them to pay for it - now. Eventually, inevitably, such methods create problems, chaos, even disaster if unattended. When our hypothetical family's share of the federal debt is $200,000 and climbing $1,600 a month, we have definitely reached disaster stage if it continues unattended.

No government can guarantee security. It can only tax, production, distribution and service and gradually crush the power to pay taxes. That settles nothing. It only uses up the gains of the past and postpones the developments of the future.

Henry Ford (1863-1947)
Founder, Ford Motor Company

Taxes are money that has been earned in the past. Debt is money that is expected (but not guaranteed) to be earned in the future. Which do you spend more carefully - money that has already been earned by labor you've already done or money that you will earn by labor you will do in the future? Studies show that people pay, on average, 17% more when they buy on credit than when they buy the same item for cash. If we discount the value of our own future labor by such an amount, imagine how much we discount the future labor of someone else. And we have been assuming for decades that the debt our government has been accumulating will be paid by "someone else." We expect that when the day of reckoning comes, we will either be dead or retired with our guaranteed social security and the power of our senior voting bloc.

Inflation is taxation without legislation.
Milton Friedman (1912-2006)
Economist

You have to go back to the late 70's and early 80's to find a period of serious inflation in the U.S. Even during that period, annual inflation was never more than 15%, which is uncomfortably high, but not catastrophic.

Between the end of World War I in 1918 and 1923, the value of the German paper Mark to the German gold Mark went from 1:1 to 1 trillion:1; meaning the German paper Mark was worthless. Germany had chosen to finance the war through debt rather than taxes, and the additional debt they incurred from the payment of war reparations paved the way for the rise of Adolf Hitler in the coming decade.

In recent years, Zimbabwe has had official annual inflation rates as high as 11 million percent. This hyperinflation was caused by the government printing money as needed, with nothing to back it up. Printing more money does not create wealth, it only devalues the currency. Zimbabwe's attempt to create wealth where none existed only served to destroy what wealth had existed in the form of their currency.

In order to increase the money supply and stimulate the economy, the federal government has implemented a program called quantitative easing. A central bank initiates quantitative easing by purchasing financial assets with money that it creates electronically. They don't even bother to print the paper money; they create it with a few keystrokes. In a slow economy, the risks of inflation caused by quantitative easing are small. However, if quantitative easing has the desired results, that additional money created from thin air will create a higher rate of inflation in the future.

> *There is far more danger in a public monopoly than there is in a private monopoly, for when the government goes into business it can always shift its losses to the taxpayer. The government never really goes into business, for it never makes ends meet, and that is the first requisite of business. It just mixes a little business with a lot of politics, and no one ever gets a chance to find out what is actually going on.*
>
> Thomas A. Edison (1847-1931)
> Inventor, Businessman

> *When everybody has got money they cut taxes, and when they're broke they raise taxes. That's statesmanship of the highest order.*
>
> Will Rogers (1879-1935)
> Humorist, Actor

We've all seen pie charts used for financial illustration purposes. Let's take it a step further and think of an actual pizza pie. When the economy is doing well, the pizza is large, and the government doesn't need a big slice of a large pizza. When the economy is doing poorly, the government needs a bigger slice of that smaller pizza in order to get the same amount of pizza they had before. They could just take less pizza, but entitlements force them to take a minimum amount of pizza, even if that means that others receive far less. Of course, they can also borrow someone else's pizza, which they have been doing more and more in recent years. When it's time to pay that pizza back, we will be going hungry for quite a long time to come.

Creative Destruction was a term coined by Joseph Schumpeter in his 1942 book, *Capitalism, Socialism, and Democracy*. Creative destruction occurs when something newer and better comes along and kills its predecessor. Free markets let creative destruction occur because it is best for everyone in the long run. Digital picture-taking almost killed Kodak, but limitless high-quality photography is now available to everyone who can afford a digital camera or cell phone.

No one but a government official would consider impeding that kind of progress in order to keep a few thousand employed in an antiquated industry. Creative destruction isn't always pretty, especially if it's your job and your employer that are being destroyed, but the process is as necessary to a healthy economy as the replacement of old cells with new ones is to an organism.

Those who look to government to generate prosperity believe that, in our economic engine, private enterprises are the moving parts and government is the gasoline. In truth, private enterprise is the gasoline, and the workers and the customers are the moving parts. What is government's role? Government is the oil in the economic engine. Oil is not fuel; it is a lubricant. Oil does not power the engine, but without oil the engine will seize up and be rendered useless. Oil has a vital role to play in an engine's performance, but oil is confined to certain parts of the engine, and is not allowed to mix with gasoline. When they invade each other's space, both oil and gasoline's ability to do their jobs are compromised.

A multitude of laws in a country is like a great number of physicians, a sign of weakness and malady.
Voltaire (1694-1778)
French Writer, Philosopher

If you have ten thousand regulations you destroy all respect for the law.
Winston Churchill (1874-1965)
British Prime Minister

Why do we have fifty different titles in the Code of Federal Regulations (with thousands of regulations under each title),but we only have Ten Commandments?

Government intrusion most often takes the form of burdensome regulations. These regulations may have a noble purpose, but often their effect is to suffocate the economic engine. There is the time and expense of trying to meet several, and often conflicting, regulations. The difficulty in meeting these regulations often leads to a disregard of the regulations, either by intent or ignorance.

God limited his Commandments to ten for a reason. He knows we aren't very bright, and ten is about our limit when it comes to remembering something. (Can you recite all Ten Commandments right now?) Also, when there are only ten rules to follow, no one can claim ignorance of the law. The greater the number of rules and regulations, the greater the percentage of rules and regulations that will be overlooked, ignored, or intentionally disobeyed. A profusion of little rules makes it that much harder to enforce the big rules.

I firmly believe that the army of persons who urge greater and greater centralization of authority and greater and greater dependence upon the Federal Treasury are really more dangerous to our form of government than any external threat that can possibly be arrayed against us.

Dwight D. Eisenhower (1890-1969)
34th U.S. President

Like Ancient Rome at its peak, the U.S. today has little to fear from outside attackers. That is not to say we are immune from attack. Like Ancient Rome, we can defeat anyone who might attack us, which discourages attack from without.

Our danger lies, not in attack from without, but in decay from within. The Roman Empire became more decadent over the centuries, which enabled its enemies to take advantage of weaknesses the Romans did not previously have. The more dependent the individual becomes on the government, the more the government and the individual are weakened. These weaknesses will then be exploited. There will be real enemies who will try to exploit our weaknesses to destroy us. There will also be those who are not our enemies, but merely our competitors. They will exploit our weaknesses to defeat us, not in military conflict, but in economic competition.

There is nothing like competition to sharpen one's game, and we have not had stiff competition in the marketplace for quite some time. We have certainly lost thousands of jobs to foreign competition, but we have also created new jobs and more skilled jobs to replace them. We've been secure in our position as the world's leading economic power. However, as our debt rises, our capital investment shrinks, and our productivity lags, our competitors can sense the tide turning.

If ever this free people, if this government itself is ever utterly demoralized, it will come from this incessant human wriggle and struggle for office, which is but a way to live without work.
                                                    Abraham Lincoln (1809-1965)
                                                    16th U.S. President

If we are going to demand that government spend less, we will also have to expect less from government. When nearly half the money the government spends is borrowed, it is safe to say that hardly a soul in the country is receiving less than he or she is paying. That hypothetical family we looked at earlier is no exception. They pay taxes, but they are likely receiving government benefits, either directly or indirectly, that exceed the value of their payments.

For example, if defense spending this year is $550 billion, and the U.S. population is 310 million, the per capita bill to finance defense spending is $1,775 per person, or $7,100 for a family of four. Our hypothetical family likely paid less than that in income taxes, so they did not even cover their portion of being protected from attack. Someone had to pay the difference on that, not to mention the cost of all the other benefits the family received, from education for the kids to roads to take them to work and school.

When we begin to realize that all of us are getting more than we are currently paying, we are prompted to do two things. First, we demand greater care in the spending of our tax dollars. We will take on the responsibility to ask questions such as, do we really need to spend $1,775 per person per year to be safe? Second, we will recognize and accept that, even as we demand that the government spend less and provide more value for what they spend, it will also be necessary for everyone to pay more if these deficits are going to be reduced enough to make a difference.

Our federal debt now equals our annual national GDP, which means that it would take every dollar earned by every man, woman, and child over the next year to pay off what we owe. That could only be done if we all went on a year-long fast, didn't pay any of our bills, and simply turned over every cent to the U.S. Treasury. Since we can't do anything remotely close to that, it will be a long time getting our debt down to a manageable level, even with painful steps taken.

When we live our personal lives with ever-increasing debt, we are at least aware that such a pattern cannot go on forever. We can remain in denial for only so long because every month the bills come in and we are reminded of just how deep a hole we have dug for ourselves. We know on some level that it must all end, and end badly, unless we take serious action to reverse the trend. We may contemplate bankruptcy, which is often only a temporary fix, as the real problem is a habit of spending more than we earn, and until that cycle is broken, financial peace will never come.

Government debt is more destructive for several reasons. First, bankruptcy is not an option. It might be tempting to think that the U.S. could just walk away from several trillions of dollars in debt obligations, but if that ever happened, the collapse of the world economy would make the Depression Thirties look like the Roaring Twenties.

Second, government debt is an orphan - no one wants to accept that they have contributed to the problem. Even those who pay in nothing and receive much feel no responsibility because what they receive is labeled "entitlements." Such labeling removes the stigma of charity, but also makes it far more difficult to reduce what is being given.

No single raindrop believes it is to blame for the flood.
Popular Poster
Despair.com

Finally, government debt is worse than personal debt because we can delude ourselves longer about the day of reckoning. Imagine how you would feel if, every month, along with your regular bills, you also received a statement from the U.S. Treasury, stating your household's liability for the federal debt. For our hypothetical household, that liability is currently about $200,000 and goes up about $1,600 per month. There might be no minimum payment due, but the huge balance due and the never-ending accumulation of principal and interest would be enough to make most people sick, and then galvanize them to take action. The one thing that a monthly statement wouldn't do is allow anyone the continued luxury of remaining ignorant on just how serious the nation's and, by extension, their personal situations really are.

They that will not be counseled cannot be helped.
If you do not hear reason she will rap you on the
knuckles.

Benjamin Franklin (1706-1790)
Founding Father

We ask advice, but we seek approbation.
Charles Caleb Colton (1780-1832)
English Cleric, Writer

I have not yet determined whether the increasing political polarization in the U.S. is a symptom or a cause of something larger. There is no doubt that we have become more polarized in our politics over the last couple of decades.

The media have either caused or at least capitalized on this polarization, depending on your point of view. In either case, there is no shortage of media outlets that cater to either a liberal or a conservative viewpoint.

The trend in providing news that caters to a particular point of view is the result of the tendency people have for *Confirmation Bias*. Confirmation Bias is a tendency to search for or interpret information in a way that confirms one's preconceptions. If we hold a particular viewpoint, we seek out, consciously or unconsciously, sources that confirm that we are correct in our thinking. We want to think we are seeking illumination when, in fact, we are seeking only validation.

Because validation is easier to obtain than illumination, people rarely become wiser; they merely become more entrenched in their ways of thinking and acting. Such behavior occurs in our financial, as well as our political, lives. Books on how to make a killing in various markets greatly outsell books on how to become thriftier because our bias has always been toward getting more, not needing less. Books that don't confirm what you already believe are a tough sell, which is why those books on how to make a killing with some investment aren't going to tell you that any investment that enables you to make a killing is equally capable of killing you.

299

Most men believe that it would benefit them if they could get a little from those who have more. How much more it would benefit them if they would learn a little from those who know more.

William Boetcker (1873-1962)
Presbyterian Minister

People are no different when it comes to seeking financial advice from a person. There are approximately 63,000 Certified Financial Planners in the U.S., which is one for every five-thousand Americans. CFPs should be completely overwhelmed by the sheer number of people seeking their advice; that is not the case.

Certified Financial Planners have an ethical obligation to tell their clients what they need to hear, which is very often not what they want to hear. As a result, people will gravitate to a "financial adviser" who will tell them that they don't need to spend less and save more; they merely need to buy this particular financial product that will solve all their financial problems. The difference between the two is like the difference between a doctor who tells you to lose weight by eating healthier and exercising more and a salesman who says you can lose that weight by just taking this little pill he's selling. We know to whom people prefer to listen, and we know who has a solution that might actually work.

One reason people look for a miracle financial cure is that we have been sold an idealized view of retirement, usually by firms that are trying to sell us something. Most of us have seen marketing material for a financial product aimed at those at or near retirement. There are pictures of a grey-haired (but still attractive) couple golfing, sailing, walking on the beach, etc. The implication is here you see what successful people do in retirement, and you can do these things too, if you only purchase their product.

Such a retirement has appeal if you loathe your current job, which probably feels more like serving time than merely marking time. The contrast between where you are and where the people in the brochure are is so stark that you will naturally want what they have and will pay for it. That idealized view of retirement also has the effect of increasing anyone's unhappiness on the job, simply by making such a comparison.

If you think about retirement a week at a time, you can see through the imagery. There are three periods a day (morning, afternoon, and evening) and seven days a week. That's twenty-one squares a week that have to be filled with something. Even if you fill five of them with golf, you still have sixteen left. Most of the activities with which we expect to fill those squares cost money, too. The people who can afford to live such a retirement are likely to be so successful they don't want to retire from what they do, and they are in the position they can do those things on a regular basis without having to retire.

Advice after injury is like medicine after death.
Danish Proverb

Advice is what we ask for when we already know the answer but wish we didn't.
Erica Jong (1942-)
Author

Receiving unsolicited advice after something bad has occurred can be annoying. Soliciting advice after you've done something bad can be frustrating to whomever you're soliciting. The best advice is that which is solicited before you take any action and that you are willing to follow because you trust the advisor to give you advice which will lead to the outcome that is best for you in the long run.

There is nothing more frustrating in my profession than to be contacted by someone who is now seeking advice on how to extricate themselves from a situation they wouldn't be in if they had solicited advice before they took an action. The main reason they didn't solicit advice beforehand is they knew they would be advised against doing whatever it is they were determined to do. When the unpleasant yet totally foreseeable result happens, the adviser can usually help only to the extent that he or she can turn back the hands of time.

The wise man sees in the misfortune of others what he should avoid.

Publilius Syrus (1st Century BC)
Latin Writer

There's no education in the second kick of a mule.

Ernest F. Hollings (1922-   )
Member, U.S. Senate

At the very least, we should learn from our mistakes. At the very best, we should learn from the mistakes of others and avoid altogether the behavior that creates problems. At the very worst, we keep making the same mistakes, somehow thinking that this time it will be different. Those who fall into the first category comprise the majority of us. Those who fall in the second category are the most successful among us. Those who fall in the last category literally fall to the bottom. The only thing that keeps the last group from making the same mistake in perpetuity is the evaporation of funding.

Few people at the beginning of the nineteenth century needed an adman to tell them what they wanted.
> J. K. Galbraith (1908-2006)
> Economist

Advertising is basically the creation of desire where it didn't previously exist. Advertising became effective in the twentieth century because of several factors. The Industrial Revolution created a large class of people with disposable income. New forms of communication enabled more people to be reached by advertising. Finally, more people were concentrated in cities, which made advertising more effective and which reduced distribution costs.

Studies have shown that the average American eight-year-old has a vocabulary of four-thousand words, of which four-hundred are brand names. While estimates vary widely, the most reliable data suggests that the average American is subjected to almost a thousand marketing messages a day. These messages would include overt advertising like billboards and TV commercials, but also include more subtle messages like seeing a logo on clothes, cars, or computers. With that much constant pounding, you tune out most of what we see and hear, but you don't get a thousand times a day without some of those punches getting through.

As part of the goal of creating desire for a product, advertising attempts to make you feel dissatisfied with your present situation. Most people are very happy with their state-of-the-art gadget right up to the moment that it is no longer state-of-the-art. The functionality of their gadget has not changed, only the reference point has. The way to get people to spend money they normally wouldn't spend is to make them feel that they are regressing.

In the factory we make cosmetics;
in the drugstore we sell hope.

Charles Revson (1906-1975)
Founder, Revlon

I think American salesmanship can be a weapon more powerful than the atomic bomb.

Henry J. Kaiser (1882-1967)
Industrialist

If others are buying something that is newer and better than what you have, you will be losing ground to them if you don't upgrade, too. Your abandonment of a perfectly good item for the sake of competing with others becomes irrelevant. Because we are a very competitive culture, it is easy to sell people on the basis of comparison to others.

Consumer spending now accounts for two-thirds of our economy, which is good in the sense that a healthy level of consumer spending leads to a growing economy. Unfortunately, a lot of consumer spending is financed with debt for things that people merely want but don't need. When a corporation borrows money, it is typically to improve production and distribution or for other efficiencies that will increase revenues by more than enough to pay off the debt. Corporations borrow money for items that will make them richer; consumers borrow money for items that will make them poorer.

Even if advertising isn't stimulating you to make

unnecessary purchases, the same can't be said for your neighbors. If the people around you are buying items because they are being persuaded by advertising, you may become a peripheral casualty. The commercials for a new car may not have much of an impact on you, but that new car in your neighbor's driveway might just do the trick. The car may not appeal to you in a commercial, but looking at your neighbor's new car and then looking at that comparative hunk-o'-junk in your driveway might just become too much to bear after a while.

Thousands upon thousands are yearly brought into a state of real poverty by their great anxiety not to be thought poor.

William Corbett (1942-   )
Poet, Essayist

Never keep up with Joneses: drag them down to your level. It's cheaper.

Quentin Crisp (1908-1999)
English Raconteur

When you ask people who grew up during the Great Depression what it was like to be poor, a typical response is, "We were poor, but since everyone else was poor, we really didn't think of ourselves as poor." Such a response demonstrates that we judge our financial condition in relative terms. Our financial condition should be judged in absolute terms. One is either rich or poor, regardless of what others have.

Status, unlike financial condition, is judged totally relative to others. Our problem is that we have intertwined financial condition and status to the point where we cannot distinguish between the two. People in the Great Depression were poor, but they didn't feel they were because everyone else was poor, too. People today are rich, at least compared to the people in the Great Depression and to much of the world today. We don't feel rich because we see that most people have as much as we do, and many have a lot more. Our financial condition is good, but our status is low, so we believe that our financial condition is low, too. Such beliefs trigger dissatisfaction and a desire to climb the status ladder, which too often leads to financial trouble.

If there is a need to compare one's financial position, such comparisons should be made to one's own previous financial position, rather than making comparisons to someone else. The best way to make such a comparison is to look at one's personal balance sheet. The balance sheet totals all the assets and subtracts all the liabilities to determine a person's net worth. If the net worth is climbing over time, that's all that matters. An effective, albeit unglamorous, way to improve one's balance sheet is to pay down debt, which reduces liabilities. The balance sheet is the most important status symbol to those millionaires next door. They know that a solid balance sheet provides true status, not the bogus kind that comes from a Mercedes in the garage.

Too many people spend money they haven't earned, to buy things they don't want, to impress people they don't like.

Will Smith (1968-   )
Actor, Musician

When people focus on external status instead of internal security, they end up with neither status nor security. The money that is devoted to impressing others

306

is no longer available to strengthen the personal balance sheet.

There are consequences beyond the financial, too. The people who are impressed by cars, jewelry, or clothes are not worth anyone's time or attention, and they certainly aren't worth blowing good money in an effort to impress. What is worse, when someone blows good money in that manner, that person becomes someone impressive in an unintended manner. To impress means to affect or influence deeply, which can mean in a positive or a negative way. Anyone worth impressing in a positive way would only be impressed in a negative way by someone seeking status through spending. The people worth impressing are impressed by what others gave, not by what they got.

> *Wall Street is the only place that people ride to in a Rolls Royce to get advice from those who take the subway.*
>
> Warren Buffett (1930-   )
> Investor, Philanthropist

The more someone is the real deal about anything, the less it is necessary to publicize their authenticity. Let's compare two well-known billionaires, Warren Buffett and Donald Trump. Buffett is known for his wealth, but in recent years he has become known for giving his wealth away. His net worth in 2016 is estimated at $56 billion, and he has already given approximately $20 billion to charity. Warren Buffett lives in a 6,000 square-foot house in Omaha that he bought in 1958 for $31,500.

Donald Trump is known for... being Donald Trump. Trump's net worth is estimated to be $2.8 billion -

307

considerably less than Buffett, though still a healthy sum. Trump's two main residences are his 30,000 square-foot apartment atop the Trump Tower in Manhattan and Mar-a-Lago, a 110,000 square-foot estate home in Florida.

As for his charitable nature, over the last twenty years, Trump's charitable contributions total approximately $4 million, all provided through the Donald J. Trump Foundation. Donald Trump's net worth is $1/20^{th}$ of Warren Buffett's; his charitable contributions are $1/5000^{th}$ of Buffett's.

Both men are very smart and very successful. Buffett has never been obsessed with wealth and certainly not with the trappings of wealth. The same cannot be said for Trump. In 1991, Buffett spoke of Donald Trump and the perils of leverage. At that time, Tump had an estimated $2.5 billion in assets and $3.5 billion in liabilities. (Trump has filed three corporate bankruptcies since 1991.) Buffett said, "I would suggest that the big successes I've met had a fair amount of Ben Franklin in them. And Donald Trump did not." Not coincidentally, Ben Franklin and Warren Buffett are quoted in this book more than anyone else; there are no quotes from Trump.

Unfortunately, the image most people have of the super-wealthy is closer to Donald Trump than Warren Buffett, though Buffett more accurately personifies that group. Such misperceptions are understandable based simply on the difference in the way each man interacts with the media. Warren Buffett may want people to emulate him, especially regarding charitable giving, but he doesn't promote himself in any way. Donald Trump seeks media exposure to promote himself because he wants people to envy him. Such envy is the basis for class warfare and the desire to see the rich brought low.

People who have little thought of the relations of the rich to the poor generally assume that all that is necessary is for the rich to give to the poor, or that they should be compelled to give part of their wealth, and all would be well. But this is a great mistake.

Leo Tolstoy (1828-1910)
Russian Novelist

It has been speculated that if the wealth of the richest five percent of Americans was given to the poorest five percent, within five years the richest would have all the wealth back. Such speculation does not mean that the wealthy are clever crooks or that the poor are incompetent dolts. What it is does mean is that the wealthy got that way because they know how to make and preserve wealth; the poor do not. What the poor don't know about money is the main reason they remain poor. Giving them money will not make them smarter about money, which is the first and most necessary step in fighting poverty.

Nothing is crueler than giving someone a taste of something they crave, then denying it to them. Transfers of money from rich to poor in large amounts do not teach the poor how to use money wisely; it actually only encourages misuse of money. The best way to alleviate poverty on a large scale is to make sure that everyone in the society, starting in grade school, learns how wealth is really created and preserved and learns how people go about creating their own wealth, rather than looking to transfer it from someone else.

*We should be careful to get out of an experience all the
wisdom that is in it — not like the cat that sits down
on a hot stove lid. She will never sit down on a hot
stove lid again — and that is well; but also she will
never sit down on a cold one anymore.*

Mark Twain (1835-1910)
Author, Humorist

How many times do we get burned by our
investments? More important, why do we get burned
more than once? Are we not learning from our own
experiences? Are there forces at work conspiring to
continuously trick us into making mistakes with our
money?

If someone is getting burned on investments more
than once, it isn't likely a vast conspiracy; it's more
likely an inability to tell what is hot and cold.

Let's use Twain's cat analogy. The cat gets burned on
a hot stove lid and avoids all stove lids in the future.
Such an overreaction is like getting burned by investing
in certain stocks and then forsaking all stocks
forevermore. Stocks run hot and cold, just like stove lids.
The trick is to test to see if they are hot or cold before
you pick them up. Testing can be done with some simple
analytical tools and an absence of emotion.

Getting burned more than once also involves another
blind spot. This blind spot is not recognizing that stove
lids aren't the only things that can burn you. There are
people out there who got burned on tech stocks because
everyone was buying them. They then moved into real
estate because everyone was buying it. They then moved
into gold because... well, you know. These people keep
getting burned because they are following others who
have already heated up that investment before it ever

310

gets into their hands.

It isn't just the investments that can run hot and cold. The heat of the investment is actually directly related to the heat of the investors. Investments are inert - they do not generate their own heat. That heat comes from the people who keep touching and rubbing them. One of the best ways to keep from being burned on an investment is to see how hot the people who are touting it are. If they are unusually hot about something, the chances are extremely high you will get burned if you touch it.

We all know the investment axiom of buy low and sell high. We don't always know what constitutes high and low, however. Perhaps a better axiom, and one in line with our analogy here is - buy cold and sell hot. If you pick up an investment that is cold, it means that others haven't been rubbing and touching it much lately, and you won't get burned by lifting it. You can also then detect when that investment goes from cold to warm to hot, and you will unload it when it gets too hot to hold. You will know this in large part because you picked it up when it was cold, so you know how cold it can become again.

I find television very educational. Every time somebody turns on the set, I go into another room and read a book.

Groucho Marx (1890-1977)
Comedian

If television encouraged us to work as much as it encourages us to do everything else, we could better afford to buy more of everything it advertises.

Cullen Hightower (1923-2008)
Writer

311

Television, the hardware, may be the greatest invention of all time. Television, the software, is another story. The ability to have a device in your home that enables you to watch hundreds of different programs at any time and to watch events unfold in real time from around the world is truly amazing.

Because you can choose among hundreds of shows to watch at any given time, you know there is a lot of crap on at any given time, too. People may say that this was not a problem in the Golden Age of Television; although, when there were only three channels and three hours of prime time television each night, shows like *My Mother the Car* and *The Flying Nun* still managed to slip past the net.

> *The one function that TV news performs very well is that when there is no news we give it to you with the same emphasis as if there were.*
>
> David Brinkley (1920-2003)
> Newscaster

> *Television has a real problem. They have no page two. Consequently every big story gets the same play and comes across to the viewer as a really big, scary one.*
>
> Art Buchwald (1925-2007)
> Author, Journalist

There are certainly bad movies, music, and books, too. Many of these end up in one form or another as bad television. It is easier to avoid bad books, movies, and even music than it is to avoid bad television. When you arrange the main room in your house around the television, and you then spend several hours a day staring at it, you are going to be affected by what you are watching, for better or worse.

Forty years ago, the only financial information you got from television was a brief report on the local news about what the local stocks had done that day and Walter or David or Chet telling you on the network news what the Dow did, right before going to commercial break. With limited air time for news, financial news had to qualify as real news to get on the air.

Today there are at least four channels that broadcast financial and business news 24/7. Even if you have no interest in watching those channels, the regular news channels, of which there are even more, keep a running tab on the stock market throughout the day. There are also regular stories on those networks about what is going on in the financial world. CNN gives more air time in an hour to financial news than CBS gave to it in a week in the 1960's.

Assuming you still read a newspaper, the financial news in the paper is usually in the back of the paper and is simple and straightforward. You can see how the markets did and which companies made news, but everything is quite low key. The purpose of this news is to inform, not to excite.

The same cannot be said for financial news on TV. The cable news channels, as well as the financial news channels, are in a fight-to-the-death for ratings, which translates into advertising dollars. They know that informing their audience isn't enough to get them watching and keep them there. As a result, every bit of news is broadcast as though the fate of the world hangs in the balance. Bright colors, high definition, multiple boxes, and crawlers on the screen only add to the illusion that whatever they are telling you is vitally important to you and your portfolio.

What is good for these purveyors of news is bad for the consumers of that news. The ever-increasing volatility of markets has nothing to do with world events and everything to do with how those events (and non-events) are being reported. When an event is reported in such a sensationalistic way that action on the viewer's part is strongly implied, if not overtly stated, viewers will frequently swallow the bait and take some action that will have damaging effects on their long-term financial security. When it comes to creating long-term financial success, you might, in certain circumstances, respond to events; you don't react to them. TV prompts its viewers into reacting, rather than responding (or not), which disserves the audience it purports to serve.

Beware lest you lose the substance by grasping at the shadow.

Aesop (620-564 BC)
Greek Writer

All media exist to invest our lives with artificial perceptions and arbitrary values.

Marshall McLuhan (1911-1980)
Canadian Scholar

Television news can be so impactful that it can be hard to remember that what we are shown and told may not be how it is. As long as humans provide the programming, that programming will have some biases and will serve the interests of the media over the interests of its audience. If we get all our news and information from television, and especially if we get it from just one channel, we risk becoming parrots

314

spouting another's point of view, rather than well-informed discerning observers of events.

Men are not against you; they're merely for themselves.
Gene Fowler (1890-1960)
Journalist, Author

It's fairly easy to spot someone who is against you. Subtlety is not a trait most Americans possess. We can also assume that people are acting in their own self-interest, even when they are acting in a way that benefits others.

Selfishness and self-interest are not the same thing. Everyone who acts selfishly is acting in self- interest, but not everyone who acts in self-interest is acting selfishly. For example, people go to work every day to earn money, which is acting in their self-interest. Work becomes selfish only when rules or norms get violated, such as when an employee steals or takes credit for the work of another.

Just because people act in their own self-interest, it doesn't mean that their actions can't benefit others. Human interactions mimic biology in that they can be classified similarly. *Mutualism* is a relationship that benefits both parties. Most people seek such relationships because they form the best foundation for long-term benefits. *Commensalism* is a relationship where one party benefits while the other party is unaffected. In biology, this relationship is fine with both parties. In human relationships, commensalism can lead to resentment by the "unaffected" party, who can begin to feel exploited.

Commensalism can be confused with *parasitism*, which is a relationship where one party benefits while

315

the other party is harmed. Such relationships are initiated by the parasite, and these are the relationships we need to fear. When it comes to parasites, it's OK to be a little paranoid.

Finally, there is *amensalism*, where one party is harmed while the other party is unaffected. The laws of unintended consequences come into play here. For example, the push to convert corn into ethanol had little effect on our consumption of foreign oil. However, the shifting of corn from food to fuel has led to increases in the price of many different types of food all over the world, especially in the poorer nations. In amensalism, one party is harmed by a party that does not benefit and is oblivious to the harm they are causing.

The goal in relationships should always be mutualism. Mutualism always provides the most benefits to either party over time. Commensalism is acceptable in small doses, but only if there is reciprocity, and soon. Parasitism is to be avoided, but it has to be avoided by the host; the parasite has every incentive to have such a relationship. Amensalism occurs when the unaffected party doesn't pay enough attention to the condition of the affected party, and the affected party doesn't speak up. When someone is standing on your foot, it doesn't benefit either of you if you keep quiet about it.

Sometimes one pays most for the things that one gets for nothing.

Albert Einstein (1879-1955)
Theoretical physicist

Everyone is tempted by the free lunch. Seniors are invited to a free meal if they are willing to listen to someone talk about protecting their nest egg in retirement. Before they can get out of the room, those seniors get pummeled with a sales pitch about investing in annuities, gold, or whatever the "host" is peddling that day. Even the mosquito that's looking for a quick snack often finds itself on the receiving end of a fatal swat if it takes too much or takes too long.

It's never something for nothing; it's only something for nothing now. When you buy something on credit, you are getting something for nothing now, but at least you know that you will pay later and how much you will pay. The something-for-nothing ploy has you paying later, but the terms are unknown. The payment may be in money, but it can also be in time and aggravation.

If you remember that people always act in self-interest, it is easier to be more alert to something-for-nothing deals. If someone can make parasitism look like altruism, it becomes a lot easier to establish a relationship. If someone can make it look like they are giving rather than taking, the victim will invite the relationship and will remain unaware of the parasitism far longer than otherwise. The best cons work that way. By doing the mark a favor - giving something for nothing - they can then bleed the victim dry.

We should aim rather at leveling down our desires than leveling up our means.

Aristotle (384-322 BC)
Greek Philosopher

Lord, grant that I may always desire more than I can accomplish.

Michelangelo (1475-1564)
Italian Artist

317

Humans desire many things, but at or near the top of any list would be material wealth and personal accomplishment. The two are often interrelated. Some people strive for accomplishment as a way to material wealth. Some people believe that material wealth is an accomplishment in itself, regardless of how it is acquired. Some people use material wealth to enable personal accomplishments that might otherwise be unattainable. Some seek personal accomplishment without any regard to the material cost or reward that their pursuit might entail.

The noblest personal accomplishments are those that have no connection to material wealth and are not motivated by the desire to be recognized by others. People who work in anonymity to achieve a goal, typically a goal that will benefit others, would fall into this category. Examples might include volunteers working to eradicate a disease or someone training to complete a marathon for the first time. In this category, you are only trying to impress yourself, even if your accomplishment will benefit others.

Some people accomplish great things for less than great reasons. Actors, musicians, and athletes who perform their craft well, but are motivated by the desire for fame and fortune would be examples. For these people, fame and fortune are the cause and expertise in their profession is the effect. Ideally, expertise in one's profession should be the cause, with fame and fortune the effect.

Some people see material wealth as an accomplishment worthy of whatever sacrifices are necessary to achieve it. Many of the CEOs responsible for creating the financial crisis in recent years would fall into this category, as would Mafia kingpins and everyone else who doesn't care about the damage they inflict in the course of reaching their goal.

Some people will use material wealth to accomplish goals that were previously unattainable. Bill Gates is using his wealth to lead the final push to eradicate polio in the world. His vast wealth makes it possible for him to make such an accomplishment possible. Such an accomplishment never entered Gates' head until he had accumulated the financial resources to make it happen.

Almost everyone desires fame and fortune because they symbolize personal accomplishment. That desire can motivate people to accomplish some great things. The problem with that kind of external motivation is that once the fame and fortune are achieved, there can be hollowness to them. The accomplishments that a person pursues because it will help others and/or because it will make that individual a better person are the accomplishments that are most rewarding when they are finally accomplished.

There is a vast difference between success at twenty-five and success at sixty. At sixty, nobody envies you. Instead, everybody rejoices generously, sincerely, in your good fortune.

Marie Dressler (1868-1934)
Canadian Actress

How others react to our success can greatly affect our reaction to that success. There will always be people who are envious of others' success, and we have to ignore them if we are going to accomplish anything in life. People applaud success they feel is deserved, which is one reason why success at sixty is applauded more than success at twenty-five. Every year at graduation

319

time, there will be a story about someone in their eighties or nineties who is finally graduating high school. It's the kind of story that makes everyone feel good because no one believes an octogenarian didn't earn that diploma. An eighteen-year-old who accomplishes the same thing with six decades less experience doesn't get recognized for the same accomplishment, largely because if someone accomplishes something at a young age, we tend to think it is the result of luck or God-given talent. Success at an early age can be difficult to deal with under the best of circumstances. When others question the validity of that success, merely because it came early in life, the individual can begin to question their own worthiness.

Too many people overvalue what they are not and undervalue what they are.

Malcolm Forbes (1919-1990)
Publisher, Forbes Magazine

To expand on the preceding quote, we also overvalue what we don't have and undervalue what we do. We see what others have, and we become envious, while not caring for and appreciating what we already have. We let others dictate our feelings about our own station in life. We cede control of our well-being to strangers.

Before we let others manipulate us that way, it might help to remember that most of them have become misguided by our culture, and a lot of them are just plain morons. Give yourself credit for knowing what is really important in life, and it will be easier to tune out the droning from the herd.

A LIVING & A LIFETIME

Have you ever wondered how much thought you were given? I'm referring to how much thought your parents gave to you before they created you. Some parents plan for years before they have a child. For some, it comes as a pleasant surprise. For some, sadly, it comes as an unpleasant surprise.

Before having a child, there are many thoughts to be thought. Are the parents ready to take on that responsibility? Are there health risks to having a baby? In what kind of world will that child grow up? Who else can be depended on to help when needed? What are the costs involved?

That last question, if it could be accurately answered prior to conception, would cause many prospective parents to reconsider. The USDA provides data on costs to raise a child from birth to age eighteen. For a low-income family, the annual cost for one child is about $11,000; for a middle-income family, about $15,000; for an upper-income family, about $25,000. The cost-per-child drops as more children are added, due to economies of scale and less money to spend per child.

As sobering as those figures are, they do not take into effect two other expenses - inflation and higher education. The above figures are from 2013. Even if inflation averages less than 3% during the eighteen years of a child's minority, the total cost to get a child through high school is over $200,000 for a low-income family, almost $300,000 for a middle-income family, and nearly $500,000 for an upper-income family.

The above figures only go as far as high school graduation. If the child goes on to earn a Bachelor's

Degree, the cost is currently in the $100,000 to $200,000 range. For a child born today, that figure will double or triple by the time he/she gets to college.

For a lower-income family, a child can cost more than $200,000, even if they are just getting by now. For an upper-income family (over $100,000 per year), they could be looking at expenses totaling nearly a million dollars by the time the parental obligation ceases. Unless the potential parents are serious about wanting to become parents, their best investment would be in contraceptives.

My hair stands on end at the cost and charges of these boys. Why was I ever a father! Why was my father ever a father!

Charles Dickens (1812-1870)
English Novelist

For thousands of years, the only security people could hope for in their old age (assuming they even lived that long) was their children. There were no methods to accumulate wealth, save for retirement, or insure proper care at the onset of old age. Since it was impossible for all but lords and such to finance their own care in old age, the next best thing was to have several children, with the expectation that at least one of them would live long enough to provide the necessary care in old age. Until the last hundred years or so, one's social security was in the form of one's progeny.

With the advent of Social Security, pensions, 401(k)'s, and long-term care insurance, people no longer need children to be assured of support when they can no longer earn a living. One reason for declining birth rates in all the developed countries is that the motivation for having children has shifted from need to want. In these countries, people want children for the sake of having children. In the less developed countries, children are still the source of old age security, and birth rates in those countries remain high.

It is a testament to the instinctive drive to keep our species going that we keep having children. We certainly have the means to easily prevent conception. There is generally no financial incentive to have children. They may be a tax deduction, but if a couple making $150,000 per year raises two children, the money they would spend on those children could have grown into $7-10 million if it were invested at 7% and withdrawals began at age 70. It is unlikely that any child, no matter how successful, could support Mom and Dad in the same style that $7-10 million could. These figures do not include any lost income that might occur if a parent should leave the workforce to care for the children.

In Japan and many European countries, people are looking at such numbers and deciding that the cost of parenthood is too high. As a result, the populations in these countries are in decline or, at best, they are being propped up by immigrants from developing countries. Declining populations have negative long-term ramifications, as both the labor force and domestic markets will also shrink in the future.

Children sweeten labours, but they make misfortunes more bitter.

Sir Francis Bacon (1561-1626)
English Philosopher, Statesman

Fortunately, the U.S. has maintained a healthy population growth, fueled by both immigration and a healthy birth rate among the citizenry. Even though Americans are aware of the high cost of raising children, we also recognize the long-term benefits to our nation to maintain a balance in our population. More important, we also know that the joy of raising children is worth all the sacrifices, including sizeable financial ones.

Money is becoming a larger factor in our lives before our lives even begin. Paradoxically, the people who can most afford children are the ones looking closest at the numbers and having the fewest children. Birth rates are still higher at the lower income levels, even though it is a greater struggle to meet the financial demands of parenthood. Money not only determines the quality of life, but also whether a life will even be created in many cases.

It is the mind that makes the body rich.
William Shakespeare (1564-1616)
English Playwright

The first glimpse of what life is like for adults occurs the day a child first goes to school. For the first time, a child's routine mimics the parents' - they have to get up, get ready, and be at a specific place at a specific time to spend the day completing tasks that are set by others. Those others will also evaluate the child's performance; and promotions, praise and punishments will be meted out based on the quality of the effort and the performance.

The national average spending per-student per-year is currently around $10,000. The U.S. ranks in the top five in per-student spending; the only ones who spend more are a handful of small developed countries in northern Europe. The figures vary widely by state, though. New

York is at or near the top, spending 70% above the national average. Utah is at or near the bottom, spending less than 60% of the national average, or less than one-third the per-pupil spending of New York. Despite the disparity in per-student spending, Utah has a higher high school graduation rate than New York.

The lesson to be learned from these numbers is that, while money is a vital ingredient in a good education, it is only one of many factors that determine how well our children are learning.

If a man empties his purse into his head, no one can take it from him. An investment in knowledge pays the best interest.

Benjamin Franklin (1706-1790)
Founding Father

By the time a student graduates from high school, his/her education will have already cost from $60,000 to $200,000. These figures are for public schools; private schools can run much higher. If a student plans to go to college, the numbers really start to climb. The average state college costs about $8,000 per year in tuition and fees. The average private college averages about $28,000, so a Bachelor's Degree can cost from $32,000 to over $100,000 in most cases. The final tab for all this education ranges from about $100,000 to over $300,000.

Is it worth it? According the U.S. Census Bureau, it probably is. On average, high school graduates can expect over their lifetime to earn $1.2 million; those with a Bachelor's Degree, $2.1 million; a Master's Degree, $2.5 million; a Ph.D., $3.4 million; and those with a professional degree, $4.4 million. Annual salary differentials may be even greater, as more years in school mean fewer years at work.

Formal education will make you a living.
Self-education will make you a fortune.

Jim Rohn (1930-2009)
Motivational Speaker

Although the data support formal education as a source of greater income potential, our formal education system cannot claim credit for making Americans wealthier. Almost nowhere in America's formal education system is there any instruction on financial planning, money management, wealth creation, or any other topic related to what we should do with money once we possess some of it.

There are some theories as to the reasons for our reluctance to teach our children about money in school. One major reason has to do with the mindset of educators. People who go into education do not do so for the money. As a group, they are not motivated by money, but by what they believe are higher ideals. There can be a tendency to think of any financial education as submission to the powers of capitalism, materialism, and the almighty dollar. The result of this collective mindset is that financial education is considered less worthy of attention compared to traditional subjects like math or social studies.

There is a contradiction in such thinking. The main reason people spend hundreds of thousands of dollars to educate their children is to enable them to get good jobs. What is the definition of a good job? There are many factors to consider, but the most universally agreed upon feature of a good job is a high income. What is the purpose of a high income? One purpose is to live well in the present, but the most important purpose of a high income is to build wealth for the future. In summation, the most important reason people have to spend great sums on formal education is to increase their ability to create wealth. Wouldn't it be more effective to actually teach people the proper ways to create wealth, rather than merely teaching them how to get a job that will pay more and hoping that when they get that money they might somehow figure out how to keep some of it?

Nothing is really work unless you would rather be doing something else.

James M. Barrie (1860-1937)
Scottish Author

Once students graduate, other issues surface. First, it is likely if they have graduated college that they are in debt, and the meter begins running to pay back college loans right after graduation. It doesn't matter if they are unemployed, either. The ease of obtaining loans of all kinds in college (due in large part to the safety net of the parents) now comes back to haunt these graduates when they discover how much and for how long they will be paying every month to clear these debts. In 2016, the average student loan debt was $32,000. As tuitions continue to rise faster than the inflation rate, the average debt will rise even faster.

Another issue that new graduates face is the lack of training to quickly assume the duties of most of the jobs they will acquire. Most jobs have specific skills that are often taught after a person is hired. The need to begin an intense training program right out of college can be depressing for recent graduates. They can begin to question the value of their education and why they needed a four-year degree simply to be eligible to get a job that requires still more intense learning.

While new graduates dream of beginning a successful and fulfilling career, most of them have to settle for getting a job, at least right out of school. Many people spend their twenties finding out the careers they don't want to have. There is a lot of trial and error in the early stages of one's working life, but that is usually necessary to find out what that person can do and wants to do.

The test of a vocation is the love of the drudgery it involves.

Logan Pearsall Smith (1865-1946)
Essayist

In the early years of a working life, it's hard to plan for the future. Wages are low; debts can be high; households are being established, and the future consists of getting set up for a promotion or investigating a better job elsewhere. As a result, valuable time gets lost in planning for the future, and the longed-for promotion that can offset the procrastination rarely happens as planned.

Many careers have long apprenticeships that follow many years of formal education. Fewer doctors and lawyers would endure the grueling early years of their careers if they hadn't already put so much time and expense into it. Such a high expense in time and money can force people to remain in careers for which they are not suited.

The early years of one's career are the high effort/low reward years. Those who change careers frequently may find they never reach the low effort/high reward years. When people talk about paying one's dues, they typically refer to paying those dues within a specific career. Getting transfer credits in a career can be like getting transfer credits in college; the place a person is transferring into decides what credits will be accepted from prior places.

Profit is a byproduct of work;
happiness is its chief product.

Henry Ford (1863-1947)
Founder, Ford Motor Company

The best augury of a man's success in his profession is
that he thinks it is the finest in the world.

George Eliot (1819-1880)
English Novelist

Few of us have any choice of whether or not we will work. Even those who have the option not to work choose to work when they enjoy what they do. Since few of us have the option not to work, we should at least attempt to find the type of work that can fill our spirits as well as our wallets.

Many people end up gravitating into careers they don't particularly like because, at certain points in their careers, they took a job that paid more without giving equal consideration to their affinity for the job. This short-term desire for higher pay very often ends up costing more in the long run. To be among the best in any profession requires skill, experience, and also a love of the work. In a great many career fields, the top 10% make 50% of the money. The top 10% don't get there without having a love for the work they do. It can be more lucrative to forego short-term raises in a job you dislike to pursue long-term success in a job you love.

Working at a job you dislike is still preferable to unemployment, which many people don't believe when they are working at such jobs. However, the people who dislike their jobs are typically the first ones to be let go, in part because their attitude affects their performance in a negative way. Once they become unemployed, they soon realize how important their old job was to them. Like the song says, you don't know what you got 'til it's gone, and that's especially true of a job that provides you with, not just a paycheck, but also stability, security, and the pride of contributing to, rather than taking from, society. During times of high unemployment, job dissatisfaction may actually increase, as everyone is working harder. However, complaints are fewer because alternatives are, too.

Work banishes those three great evils, boredom, vice and poverty.

Voltaire (1694-1778)
French Writer, Philosopher

He that never labors may know the pains of idleness, but not the pleasures.

Samuel Johnson (1709-1784)
English Poet, Essayist

Because there is so much emphasis on formal education today, and by formal I mean a Bachelor's Degree and higher, too many young people are finding themselves unemployed or underemployed. The reasons go beyond a slow economy.

As our economy has moved from manufacturing into services, we have stopped encouraging young people to get into "the trades." We have been led to believe that only those with a Bachelor's Degree (or more) can earn a decent living. While the statistics presented earlier bear that out for the population as a whole, it does not mean that it applies on an individual basis.

How many parents in the U.S. who have the ability to send their children to a four-year college have encouraged them to look at alternatives? Very few, probably. Many more parents have given their children no option but to go to college, even when those children show little interest in higher education.

These children go off and earn degrees in art history or political science or philosophy, then end up working the next five years stacking slacks at The Gap. Meanwhile, a high school classmate who didn't have the same options went to trade school and became a plumber, where he now charges $75 an hour and will soon be starting his own business. At their twentieth high school reunion, the college graduate is stuck in a lower-management position that isn't fulfilling spiritually or financially, while the plumber has two-hundred employees and a second home at the lake.

The best investment is in the tools of one's own trade.
Benjamin Franklin (1706-1790)
Founding Father

Higher education has become too expensive to ignore the cost-benefit relationship. The census figures regarding lifetime earnings at various education levels assume that everyone in those groups is otherwise equal in areas like intelligence and initiative. If someone has the intelligence and discipline to earn a Master's Degree, it is unlikely that same person, if only limited to a high school diploma, would only earn the average lifetime income for high school graduates. That person would likely need to be self-employed to make a good living without higher education, but it is entirely possible that such a person could make even more money without a degree than with one. The biggest factor in determining career success is not education, but the innate talents and work ethic of the individual.

Before spending six figures on a college degree, it's important to assess how that degree will affect that individual's earning potential. Going to college has become too expensive to think of it in terms of a "life experience." Whether someone goes to college needs to be analyzed from the perspective of return on investment. If the case can be made that such an investment in time and money will generate a sufficient return, then go for it. Otherwise, for an investment of four years and a hundred grand, there are far more rewarding "life experiences" to be had.

It is not the employer who pays the wages.
Employers only handle the money.
It is the customer who pays the wages.

Henry Ford (1863-1947)
Founder, Ford Motor Company

If you mean to profit, learn to please.

Winston Churchill (1874-1965)
British Prime Minister

Regardless of whether you become a doctor, a business owner, or a fry cook at McDonalds, your success will ultimately be measured by how your customers perceive the quality of your work. Talent, degrees, and even celebrity will not protect you from the

332

judgment of the people who are served by your work. The best businesses recognize that shareholder satisfaction and employee satisfaction are the direct result of customer satisfaction.

Many people work in jobs where they don't have direct contact with customers; that is irrelevant. The assembly line worker is far from the customer, but if the quality of that person's work is substandard, it will show up in the product. Customer complaints and lost sales will be noticed by management, who will seek the source of the problem. They will find it soon enough, and if the worker is at fault, the worker will soon be out of work.

Unless the job means more than the pay, it will never pay more.
H. Bertram Lewis (1867-1944)
Businessman

Men who do things without being told draw the most wages.
Edwin H. Stuart (1890-1968)
Businessman

Everyone who has ever uttered the phrase, "It's not my job" to a boss has probably done more harm to his/her career than they realize. Those words can be like fingernails on a blackboard to an employer, and they never forget those who utter them.

Part of the blame for such an employee attitude can be placed on the job description. Employers create job descriptions so that employees can be held accountable for performing the duties listed in that job description. The implication, though, is that the stated duties are the only duties for which the employee is responsible. When the employer set a floor of expectations regarding what an employee is to do, they unknowingly also set a ceiling on what they could expect an employee to do. Unions will codify this ceiling into labor contracts, which don't merely discourage, but may expressly forbid, an employee doing work outside of specified duties.

When employers get too specific on job duties, they stifle initiative. When employees assume that a task is not their job, they demonstrate a lack of initiative. Initiative is the hormones of any enterprise. Initiative is more abundant in smaller, newer enterprises because there are many things to be done and too few people to do them. Saying "It's not my job." in these organizations doesn't work because everyone is doing everything that needs to be done to make the business successful. When organizations become large and bureaucratic, job duties get more specific; every task is expected to be assigned in a job description, and employees are less likely to show initiative by performing additional duties.

They copied all they could copy,
But they couldn't copy my mind;
And I left them sweatin' and stealin',
A year and a half behind.

Rudyard Kipling (1865-1935)
English Poet, Novelist

Every organization needs to make sure they have a culture in place that encourages employees to make suggestions, to offer improvements, to improve efficiencies and customer service without fear that they will be criticized for overstepping their responsibilities.

Employees, for their part, need to look for ways to do all the above, even if management isn't initially receptive. Any organization that stifles employee initiative is not a place that any employee with initiative should want to remain. The employee is better off using that initiative to find a workplace where its use is encouraged and rewarded.

Any use of a human being in which less is demanded of him and less is attributed to him than his full status is a degradation and a waste.

Norbert Wiener (1894-1964)
Mathematician

If people truly believe in the mission of the organization that employs them, they should want to do everything within their power to help that organization accomplish that mission. If that means doing work that falls outside the normal day-to-day duties of their job, they should be willing to do them. Of course, no employer should ask any employee to do anything that violates an individual's ethics or the law. Employees should also know the difference between a good employer that is asking everyone for their best effort and an employer that exploits and abuses its employees.

If you are a boss and if you lost a good employee over a five percent pay raise from a new employer, you need to face a fact. The reason the employee left was not the raise - it was you.

Research has shown that it typically takes only a five percent raise to compel an unhappy employee to change employers, but it takes a twenty percent raise to compel a happy employee to change. When someone is happy in their work environment, their preference is to stay there, rather than take a risk by changing jobs. When workers aren't happy, they will assume that almost anyplace is better than where they are now, so it takes very little financial incentive to get the unhappy employee to move.

A good man likes a hard boss. I don't mean a nagging boss or a grouchy boss. I mean a boss who insists on things being done right and on time; a boss who is watching things closely enough so that he knows a good job from a poor one. Nothing is more discouraging to a good man than a boss who is not on the job, and who does not know whether things are going well or badly.
William Feather (1889-1981)
Publisher, Author

When people talk about bosses they held in high regard, a common description of them is "firm but fair." If a boss isn't firm, the slackers will slack, and the good workers will have to pick up that slack. If they aren't fair, anyone who isn't getting favored treatment is resentful.

The firm-but-fair boss is able to balance the concern for results (firm) and the concern for people (fair). It is more art than science, which is why truly great bosses can be rare. Great bosses can still be unappreciated by some workers. Those workers often end up losing their jobs and realize how good they had it only after they discover the flaws in their new boss.

To be firm but fair requires constant reassessing and recalibration. Both the needs of the employees and the needs of the organization are constantly changing. In tough economic times, it can be easy to assume that less attention should be given to the employees to focus more attention on the health of the organization. The attention a boss gives to the organization and the employees is not a fixed total, though. Greater attention to one should not come at the expense of the other. In fact, during tough economic times, a good boss ramps up attention to both the organization and the employees, who feel vulnerable during this period and need to know the boss has them covered. Great bosses are actually made during the tough times because they have to carry extra-heavy loads of firmness and fairness, while keeping them both balanced.

When we were in school, the one adjective we hoped would be ascribed to us was "popular." There was often recognition of the most popular students at the prom or in the yearbook; but something happened during the transition from school to work. Evaluations of popularity ceased. Instead of being lauded for being popular, we now had a new accolade to strive for - "competent."

There's a man in the world who is never turned down,
Wherever he chances to stray;
He gets the glad hand in the populous town,
Or out where the farmers make hay;
He's greeted with pleasure on deserts of sand,
And deep in the aisles of the woods;
Wherever he goes there's a welcoming hand —
He's the man who delivers the goods.

Walt Whitman (1819-1892)
Poet

In the workplace, the only person who might be classified as popular is likely a perky-but-competent low-level individual who isn't considered a threat to anyone. The popular person in the office may be universally liked, but no one aspires to be that person, at least not within the office environment. To be popular as we think about it generally requires that someone has no real responsibilities to others.

In the workplace, the only thing that matters is results. The only ones who will give you credit for your efforts are God and your parents. They care enough about you to look at your effort as well as your results; your employer and the world at large do not. Results are measurable, while effort is not. Results are also comparable, and the world uses them to see how you compare to your competition. The world is a very bottom-line place, and effort that does not translate into results does not help the bottom line. When your parents said that life isn't fair, this is one reality to which they were referring.

Every man should make up his mind that if he expects to succeed, he must give an honest return for the other man's dollar.

E.H. Harriman (1848-1909)
Railroad Executive

A day's pay for a day's work is more than adequate when both the work and the pay are appreciated as much as they are expected.

Cullen Hightower (1923-2008)
Writer

Whenever there is exchange between people, there is the possibility that one or even both parties will feel they have been exploited. As long as the market for exchanges is as free as possible, that possibility is lessened. If both parties are free to accept or decline an offer, the odds increase that the parties will eventually reach a deal that is satisfactory to both. When one party is compelled to accept a deal, you end up with a win-lose, rather than a win-win proposition.

When the auto unions held great power and foreign competition was insignificant, the auto companies agreed to compensation and benefit packages that became unsustainable with increased competition. The high labor costs compromised the ability to make a competitive car at a competitive price, and the result was bankruptcy for two of the big three U.S. automakers. The workers paid a high price, in that there are now far fewer auto workers making far less money than in the past.

The worst crime against working people is a company which fails to operate at a profit.
Samuel Gompers (1850-1924)
Labor Union Leader

Profit is not about taking advantage of workers, which will cause a company to soon fail. Profit is not about enriching shareholders; although, shareholders are entitled to a reward commensurate with their risk. Profit is about supplying the company with the lifeblood to keep going. Without profit, a company cannot adapt and grow to successfully compete. Without profit, shareholders will find a better use for their money. Without profit, wages stagnate, and the best employees leave for greener pastures. Without profit, there is no point to it all.

If there is an adversarial relationship between employer and employees, that organization is doomed to fail. There are too many enemies from without for people to spend their resources fighting enemies from within. External forces often prompt organizations to resolve some internal disputes, but such solutions are rarely permanent.

Competition within an organization is good, unless it creates an adversarial relationship. There is always a certain adversarial relationship between labor and management. Competition occurs between similar individuals or groups working toward a particular goal. If there is competition to improve efficiency or increase sales, everyone benefits, as long as the efforts made are toward the goal. When competition becomes about beating the other guys, it can deteriorate into trying to make the others fail, rather than focusing on self-improvement.

Some see private enterprise as a predatory target to be shot, others as a cow to be milked, but few are those who see it as a sturdy horse pulling the wagon.

Winston Churchill (1874-1965)
British Prime Minister

In 2015, federal government spending was more than 21% of GDP. In extraordinary times, as in World War II and the Great Depression, the government spends more to stimulate the economy or to defend the nation. Even during the New Deal of the 1930's, federal spending rarely exceeded 10% of GDP. During normal periods since World War II, that percentage has hovered around 20%. Total government spending, which includes state and local governments, exceeded 40% of GDP in 2015.

Why is this level of spending a problem? For starters, some 40% of government spending is in the form of borrowed funds. That level is simply not sustainable.

Also, government spending is less efficient than business spending, because there is no profit motive. Less efficient spending results in fewer benefits to the economy from each dollar spent. Private enterprises spending money also generates more tax revenues than government spending of the same amount generates. When government takes money from private enterprise to spend, they actually hurt their own revenue stream in the future.

Never stand begging for that which you have the power to earn.

Miguel de Cervantes (1547-1616)
Spanish Novelist, Poet

A person who can acquire no property, can have no other interest but to eat as much, and to labor as little as possible.

Adam Smith (1723-1790)
Scottish Philosopher, Economist

Private enterprise is the best means yet devised to enable people to earn a living and acquire property. Only private enterprises create property, which is synonymous with wealth. That wealth also enables wages to be paid, creating future wealth.

It is not from the benevolence of the butcher, the brewer, or the baker, that we expect our dinner, but from their regard to their own interest.

Adam Smith (1723-1790)
Scottish Philosopher, Economist

Quid pro quo is a Latin phrase we often hear used in legal references. Its translation is *what for what*, which

341

we further translate to mean a favor for a favor, give and take, and even tit for tat.

Quid pro quo is one manifestation of how people act in their own self-interest. Our economic system is based on the concept of quid pro quo. Every business that sells a product or service does so because they expect to be compensated financially. When customers are no longer able to pay, they are no longer customers. Quid pro quo and our entire economic system are based on the biological concept of mutualism that was discussed previously.

No one willingly makes a deal when they feel they are giving up more than they are getting. Since it is rare that both parties in any transaction feel that they traded exactly evenly, how do any deals ever get done?

Take the example of the butcher in the previous quote. The butcher has meat, but meat's usefulness as meat to the butcher diminishes as his belly gets full. Money is far more useful than meat, at least to the butcher, so he will gladly exchange meat he won't personally consume for a price. The customer is hungry, and since money is inedible, the customer is willing to exchange money for meat. The only thing left to be worked out is how much money for how much meat. The cost is determined by many factors, including the desperation of each party to make the exchange. The older the meat, the more desperate the butcher is to sell it and the less desperate the customer is to buy it.

It is in everyone's self-interest to have money, because money is the best tool to supply people with what they need and want. It is in everyone's interest to obtain that money by legitimate means because the consequences of getting money by illegitimate means are too serious for most of us to risk. It is, therefore, in everyone's interest to work in some way to legally provide goods or services for which others will pay a fair price.

But this I say. He which soweth sparingly shall reap also sparingly, and he which soweth bountifully shall reap also bountifully.

II Corinthians 9:6

We have no more right to consume happiness without producing it than to consume wealth without producing it.

George Bernard Shaw (1856-1950)
Irish Playwright

If you go to a pastry shop in many parts of Louisiana and order a dozen donuts, you will get your dozen. The proprietor will typically add a thirteenth donut and say, "Lagniappe." Lagniappe is a little extra something that a merchant gives a customer, as a way of generating goodwill.

If you've ever eaten at a restaurant where they bring a mint or a chocolate with your check, you may have gotten a couple of extras from your server, who will make a point to mention that they aren't supposed to do that, but you were really nice people! Naturally, you leave a nice tip and look forward to going back.

Giving more than expected, more than is your contractual obligation, is the best way to guarantee return business and long-term success. I doubt any pastry shop ever went bust because they offered an extra donut. Even if the server at the restaurant had to pay for the extra candies out of pocket, the extra tips and goodwill would more than cover it.

The more men, generally speaking, will do for a dollar when they make it, the more that dollar will do for them when they spend it.

William Boetcker (1873-1962)
Presbyterian Minister

We think of money as something to invest, but we don't often think about our investment in money. Older people are often less willing to pay as much for certain items as younger people. Part of this reluctance may stem from different financial situations and different maturity levels regarding money. Part of it is also the perspective of the older person. If a seventy-year old can remember when a new Chevy cost $1,600, there will be a reluctance to spend ten to fifteen times that amount for a new Chevy today. The seventy-year old remembers how many hours' wages it took to save up the $1,600 back in 1960, and that person is mentally paying for a 2016 car with 1960 dollars.

Even when we become successful and make a lot of money, it's hard not to think back to the days when we were doing hard work for the minimum wage. Knowing how hard we had to work to make $100 back in the day makes it harder to spend $100 today, even if we only had to work an hour or less today to earn it. Such prudence can be a good thing, provided it doesn't keep us from enjoying any of the fruits of our labors.

He who will not economize will have to agonize.

Confucius (551-479 BC)
Chinese Philosopher

Ask thy purse what thou should spend.

Scottish Proverb

Far worse than old people who don't spend money they could spend are young people who spend money they shouldn't spend. Generally speaking, if an old person has money, it was likely accumulated through a lifetime of prudent spending. Decades of habit can't just be turned off, especially when that person no longer earns an income and worries about the cost of living in old age.

Habits of thrift are uncommon in younger people, for several reasons. Most grew up in relative affluence, and thrift was never instilled at an early age. If such habits aren't learned in one's youth, they aren't likely to be acquired once that person is working and earning a decent income for the first time. Younger people are also more susceptible to marketing messages, so the temptations to spend frivolously are greater. Finally, younger people don't picture themselves ever getting old, disabled, or even unemployed for an extended period. They see no compelling reason to be careful with money now because they can't picture a time when money won't be readily available.

One cannot both feast and become rich.

Ashanti Proverb

When prosperity comes, do not use all of it.

Confucius (551-479 BC)
Chinese Philosopher

By sowing frugality we reap liberty, a golden harvest.

Agesilaus (444-360 BC)
King of Sparta

There was a time when being called frugal was a compliment. Since World War II it has become something of an insult. One synonym for frugal is *parsimonious*. Some synonyms for parsimonious are *stingy, ungenerous, miserly, mean and tightfisted.*

Frugality simply means avoiding unnecessary expenditures. It does not mean avoiding necessary expenditures or any expenditure where the benefit outweighs the cost. To be frugal means to take your money seriously. More people choose to do the opposite, to be frivolous with money, because it is more fun and less work to do so.

> *Economy is a distributive virtue, and consists not in saving but in selection. Parsimony requires no providence, no sagacity, no powers of combination, no comparison, no judgment.*
>
> Edmund Burke (1729-1797)
> Member, British Parliament

Frivolity involves a default answer of Yes to a purchase. Parsimony involves a default answer of No to a purchase. Frugality involves a default answer of "I'll think about it" to a purchase. A blanket Yes or No answer to a question is the easy way out. Thinking about it involves work, and as we know, work is the essential ingredient to creating wealth. Therefore, one of the surest ways to wealth is the practice of frugality.

> *Frugality includes all the other virtues.*
>
> Cicero (106-43 BC)
> Roman Statesman

There is nothing like a shortage to spur frugality. You may have had the experience of flying down the highway and discovering two things simultaneously: you

346

were almost out of gas, and you were uncertain if you had enough to reach the next gas station. At that point you slowed down, turned off the A/C, and did everything you could to coax the maximum mileage to avoid having to walk the last few miles to the gas station. Of course, once your tank was full again, you resumed your spendthrift driving habits.

Frugality is founded on the principle that all riches have limits.

Edmund Burke (1729-1797)
Member, British Parliament

If you are young, if you have a good job with a bright future, if the economy is strong and you have few obligations, your income potential seems unlimited. During these times it would be easy to develop the habits of thrift because income is high and obligations are low, so one can be thrifty and still have an enjoyable lifestyle. Of course, in such a position, maybe one person in a hundred might show such self-control.

The Great Recession of recent years is the first time most American workers have experienced a true financial crisis, both nationally and personally. They have realized for the first time that their income and wealth potential are limited. They have also become aware that valuable time has been lost in their efforts to increase income and accumulate wealth needed for retirement. Because many people did not internally impose frugality during the good times, they have had it imposed externally during the bad times.

For a great many Americans, they will never again live the lifestyle they had before the Great Recession. Even if their incomes rebound completely, they will have to save more and spend less if they hope to have even a semblance of the retirement they thought was a certainty just a few years ago.

Psychologically, many have had their spendthrift ways kicked out of them, which is actually a good thing. The more severe the impact of the Great Recession is on a person or a family, the more likely they are to retain the lessons of frugality they've learned, even when the crisis has passed.

Economy does not consist in saving the coal, but in using the time while it burns.
Ralph Waldo Emerson (1803-1882)
Philosopher, Essayist

No gain is as certain as that which proceeds from the economical use of what you already have.
Latin Proverb

There is always the risk that hard times will create a population that becomes averse to any spending, even spending that is beneficial. Just as wasteful spending hinders the ability to build real wealth, hoarding money can also have the same effect. If you don't perform necessary maintenance on your home, you may not be spending money, but the value of your home may decline by far more than the cost of maintenance. If you don't replace a bad car in order to avoid buying a newer one, you may lose income or even your job because you couldn't make it into work because of breakdowns. If you don't invest in the tools of your trade (the most important being your brain), you run the risk of losing promotions or even losing your job to those better equipped to do it.

The key to financial success and security is in the wise use of resources, not in their mere retention.

Waste is worse than loss. The time is coming when every person who lays claim to ability will keep the question of waste before him constantly.

Thomas A. Edison (1847-1931)
Inventor, Businessman

Economy is too late at the bottom of the purse.

Seneca (54 BC-39 AD)
Roman Statesman

Doing more with less is the mantra of both businesses and individuals today. Competition within the business world forces organizations to constantly look at the way they do business and look for ways to increase outputs and/or reduce inputs. Households don't face such competition, but they don't have the same ability to increase revenues that businesses do. Increasing revenues in a household is a long-term proposition that requires more education, relocation, or other steps that don't happen overnight. Decreasing and prioritizing expenses is one of the few short-term tools available to a household to improve efficiency.

The single biggest reason why so many people fail to reach their financial goals is because they never set any. The first step to any financial success is to set a goal that can be measured. Any such goal needs to be measurable in both time and dollars. For example, people often set a target date for retirement, but don't complete the goal by setting an amount. You may say you want to retire at sixty-two, but unless you know how much money it will take to retire at that age, you can't begin to take the steps necessary to reach that goal.

Plan ahead: it wasn't raining when Noah built the ark.
> Richard Cushing (1895-1970)
> Archbishop of Boston

A goal without a plan is just a wish.
> Antoine de Saint-Exupery (1900-1944)
> French Writer

Once a goal has been quantified with a date and an amount, it is necessary to create a plan to get from here to there. Most people can set a date for such goals, but determining an amount is more difficult, and formulating a plan to get there is beyond the skill set of all but a few. Certified Financial Planners are trained to help people formulate realistic goals and devise and implement a plan to get them where they want to go.

The man who is prepared has his battle half fought.
> Miguel de Cervantes (1547-1616)
> Spanish Novelist, Poet

By failing to prepare you are preparing to fail.
> Benjamin Franklin (1706-1790)
> Founding Father

Most of our financial goals are long-term goals. Short of winning a lottery or receiving an unexpected inheritance, there is no way to seriously compress the time frame needed to reach those long-term goals. If someone needs to save for twenty years to fund ten years of retirement, they can't start at fifty and retire at sixty, unless they are certain they will be dead by sixty-five. If they start at fifty and they are expected to live to eighty-five (a reasonable assumption), they would have to work until seventy-four in order to save enough to retire. Every day of delay in starting a plan creates a day of delay in meeting a goal.

Plans should not be static, either. In the 1990's, when the stock market was climbing 20% year in and year out, people were planning for retirement assuming similar returns would continue indefinitely. The first decade of the twenty-first century blew a serious hole in those plans, and those who haven't adapted by increasing savings or delaying the starting date for retirement will find retirement something to be dreaded instead of anticipated.

There will always be external forces that will affect your financial plans, and very few of those forces will affect them positively. It is a common trait to be overly optimistic when considering possible outcomes. We think this way because we want the best outcome to prevail, and so we make the best outcome the most likely outcome in our calculations. Unfortunately, the world doesn't often cooperate - inflation spikes, markets crash, pensions disappear, promotions evaporate, and Junior is still living at home when he's in his thirties.

Few people even bother to calculate how much they will need to save for retirement, even though that is the most critical financial obligation they will have in their lifetimes. Retirement planning involves some calculation of your income needs in retirement, which is based on expected number of years in retirement, expected income needs, plus a calculation for inflation both prior to and during retirement. It's a daunting task, and one reason most people don't do this type of planning is they know on some level that what they are currently doing is inadequate. Denial may be comforting now, but the discomfort later isn't worth it.

A man with a surplus can control circumstances, but a man without a surplus is controlled by them, and often he has no opportunity to exercise judgment.
Harvey Firestone (1868-1938)
Founder, Firestone Tire Company

If you've ever tried selling a car on your own, you have probably encountered the prospect who makes a lowball offer and has cash to buy the car on the spot. If you were not pressed financially at that moment, you could afford to decline the offer. However, if you needed cash right away to avoid some financial calamity, you may have had no choice but to sell your property for far less than its true value. The cause of this one-sided deal was a surplus of cash by one party and a dearth of it by the other. The party with the ready cash controlled the circumstances and, therefore, the terms of the deal. The buyer could walk away more easily than the seller could.

Annual income twenty pounds, annual expenditure nineteen six, result happiness.
Annual income twenty pounds, annual expenditure twenty pounds ought and six, result misery.
Charles Dickens (1812-1870)
English Novelist

The man least indebted to tomorrow meets tomorrow most cheerfully.
Epicurus (341-270 BC)
Greek Philosopher

The difference between surplus and deficit may not be big, but it will always be significant. The difference between a five percent surplus and a five percent deficit is only ten percent of income. In many cases a ten percent change in income may not cause major changes. However, if it turns a deficit into a surplus, or vice versa, it can be the difference between prosperity and insolvency. The distance between the windward and leeward side of a mountain may only be a few yards, but which side a seed lands on determines if it will dissolve into soil or become a mighty tree.

The rich rule over the poor and the borrower becomes the lender's slave.

Proverbs 22:7

Debt is the worst poverty.

Thomas Fuller (1608-1661)
English Writer, Historian

Until the sixteenth century, the church forbade the charging of interest on a loan. Previously, the charging of any interest was considered usury, which we define today as the charging of excessive interest (the definition of excessive varies). The reason for the ban on charging interest was the belief that only a person in dire financial straits would seek out a loan; further, to take advantage of a person in that situation for personal profit was considered a sin. Naturally, if interest could not be charged, loans were made for altruistic reasons only, which meant there was little borrowing or lending before the sixteenth century.

As our understanding of finance increased, we realized that there could be profit in borrowing money, so it was only right that there should be profit in lending money, too. Borrowing was almost always limited to the financing of a business enterprise, whether it was a loan for a farmer to buy seed or a blacksmith getting a loan to build a new forge.

The profit incentive also greatly increased the funds available to be loaned. Once it became possible to make money with money alone, banking soon developed. Banks brought borrowers and lenders together in an orderly manner.

Only in the last century has borrowing occurred at the consumer level. A combination of new products for the home and the individual, plus demand generated by advertising, combined with more sophisticated techniques by retailers, including the financing of purchases, created the debt-fueled consumer culture we take for granted today.

Back in the first half of the twentieth century, credit was given by individual businesses to customers, without any third parties. The creation of the Diner's Club Card in 1951 enabled a single charge account to buy items from many different businesses. Diner's Club was a charge card, not a credit card, which meant the balance had to be paid in full at the end of each month. Credit cards, as we know them today, were introduced in 1958. With a credit card, the balance did not have to be paid in full, although interest charges would accrue.

The ability to accumulate large amounts of unsecured debt has led to financial disaster for millions of households over the last fifty years. As credit card debt became more acceptable, so did greater debt on secured loans, like cars and homes. Large loan amounts were often limited because of the size of the monthly payment. Lenders overcame that obstacle by increasing the period of time to repay the loan. In the 1950's, the maximum repayment period on a car loan was twenty-four months; today it is eighty-four. Back then, the maximum repayment period on a home loan was twenty years; today it is thirty.

Longer repayment periods have increased the debt load of households because consumers focus on the monthly payment, not on the amount borrowed. The creation of interest-only loans with adjustable rates has enabled borrowers to borrow more while paying less each month. Such loans seem like a good deal until interest rates rise and the time comes to begin repaying principal. Then it all begins to fall apart for the consumer.

The largest single item of debt for most households is their home, which is nothing new. However, the process by which many homeowners obtained their mortgage is very different from times past.

To preserve our independence, we must not let our rules load us with perpetual debt. We must make our election between economy and liberty, or profusion and servitude.

Thomas Jefferson (1743-1826)
3rd U.S. President

It is difficult to set bounds to the price unless you first set bounds to the wish.

Cicero (106-43 BC)
Roman Statesman

In the twentieth century, mortgages originated from, and were held by, the local banks. There were strict underwriting standards because the bank was loaning the money of its depositors, and any default had to be absorbed by that bank alone. Naturally, they were cautious in their lending.

More recently, mortgages were not held by the people who originated them. They were sold, resold, bundled together with similar mortgages, cut into pieces called tranches, and sold to investors who were looking for high-yielding "safe" investments. The demand for these investments brought in a flood of money for lenders to lend. As a result, lenders were more than eager to lend almost any amount to almost anybody. There were large fees to be made, and the loan originators assumed no risk in the event of default - that had been shifted to those investors who bought these new investments, known as collateralized debt obligations (CDOs).

Naturally, many of the loans that were made were not being repaid as agreed. When the defaults began to mount up, the value of all of these CDOs began to crash. The total value of these CDOs was in the trillions, and Wall Street firms, major banks, insurance companies, pension funds, even governments were holding huge amounts of these things. It was the collapse in value of these allegedly safe investments that led to the near total collapse of the world economy in 2008.

It seems crazy that the entire world economy could have imploded because people, mostly in America, were buying more home than they could afford. However, what happens on a macro level is simply a magnification of what is happening on a micro level. If an abnormally high percentage of American households were defaulting on their mortgages, the damage should be limited to those households. Because of the increasingly complex and interconnected financial markets, people all over the world can pay the price for bad financial decisions made in just a small percentage of American homes. Bad decisions and risky behavior can infect even those who pay their debts on time and who never knowingly take undue risks.

Good times are when people make debts to pay in bad times.

Robert Quillen (1887-1948)
Journalist, Humorist

When all this money was being pumped into the mortgage market by investors looking for higher yields with low risk, it naturally created a bubble in housing prices. Prices are based on supply and demand, and demand is based on how much money is available to pursue the supply. Because housing prices were on a steady climb, people were refinancing their homes to pull out the equity to spend on cars, vacations, college tuition, even second homes.

Many borrowers used interest-only, adjustable-rate mortgages to get into their dream home. Even though they knew that there would be an interest rate increase in the future and that there would be a balloon payment as well, they looked at the price appreciation statistics and calculated that by the time those events occurred, the value of their home would have increased enough that they could tap the increased equity and just keep going.

Statistics are no substitute for judgment.

Henry Clay (1777-1852)
Member, U.S. Senate

All these new homes needed to be furnished, so other debt, especially credit card debt, also soared during this period. The one thing that wasn't soaring during this period was household income, which was keeping up with inflation, but nothing more. The monthly debt service was creating a cash flow crisis in households across America.

The final straw occurred when housing prices not only stopped increasing, but began a steep decline. For those people who had bought at the top of the market, made no down payment, had an interest rate hike and/or a balloon payment coming up, and who also owed twenty or thirty percent more than the house was now worth, the solution was simple - walk away.

The sound of your hammer at five in the morning, or eight at night, heard by a creditor, makes him easy six months longer.

Benjamin Franklin (1706-1790)
Founding Father

The relative ease with which so many people defaulted on their mortgages was a shock to the financial system and nearly destroyed it. Looking back at the situation though, the reaction of these homeowners was about the only logical act in the whole tragedy.

If someone has none of his/her own hard-earned money in an investment, if the monthly debt service has increased to the point where it is impossible to cover it, and if the penalty for defaulting is nothing more than a damaged credit history (no more debtor's prisons), it is perfectly logical to default. Personal bankruptcies also shot up during this period. The stigma of bankruptcy has largely disappeared, and even if it were still there, for many it was preferable to drowning under a tsunami of debt.

Neither a borrower nor a lender be
For loan oft loses both itself and friend,
And borrowing dulls the edge of husbandry.
William Shakespeare (1564-1616)
English Playwright

The personal debt accumulated by Americans in recent years, and their inability to pay back much of it, has rocked financial markets. What has gone largely unseen is what the borrowing has done to families and friends who were lenders. Many of the homes that were foreclosed on were purchased with money borrowed from relatives to cover down payments or closing costs. When people began feeling the full weight of their debt, and the usual lenders were no longer amenable, they turned to friends and relatives to bail them out. Whether the requests were granted or not, the request itself was sure to put a strain on the relationship. At a time when family and friends were needed for moral support, the relationship was suffering because of financial support either given or denied.

Do not be among those who give pledges, who become
guarantors for debts. If you have nothing with which
to pay, why should he take your bed from under you?
Proverbs 22:26-27

An acquaintance is someone we know well enough to
borrow from, but not well enough to lend to.
Ambrose Bierce (1842-1913)
Journalist, Satirist

Personal loans were one thing, but many friends and relatives cosigned for loans during this period. When the cosigner became responsible for the debt and they didn't have the resources to pay, they saw their own good credit ruined. If someone makes a personal loan, all that is at risk is the amount of the loan. Cosigning a loan can be far more costly than simply lending that person the money directly, though that's quite risky, too.

> *If you owe the bank $100, that's your problem. If you owe the bank $100 million, that's the bank's problem.*
>
> J. Paul Getty (1892-1976)
> Founder, Getty Oil Company

If average American borrowers had been aware of how lending had changed in recent years, they would not have been so willing to defer to the judgment of the lenders as to their own credit-worthiness. Many borrowers assumed that, if the banks were willing to loan them the money, then they shouldn't worry about their own ability to repay it. What the borrowers didn't realize was that the banks 'interest was in making the loan and selling it, not in making sure it was a good loan to make. Had the average borrower recognized that the bankers were operating like car salesmen, they might have been a more skeptical about accepting the banker's word that repaying this loan would be easy.

> *For which of you, intending to build a tower, does not sit down first and count the cost, whether he may have enough to finish it; lest perhaps, after he has laid the foundation and is not able to finish, all those seeing begin to mock him, saying, This man began to build and was not able to finish.*
>
> Luke 14:28-30

One of the tragedies of the debt-fueled housing bubble and bust of the 2000's was the long-term damage that so many families have incurred. Part of the American dream is to own your own home. The government, along with organizations like Fannie Mae, attempted to increase homeownership. While their intentions may have been noble, they ended up doing a great disservice to those they intended to serve. Homeownership is a big responsibility. First, there is a mortgage that is likely the single biggest monthly expense, and it continues in most cases for thirty years. Then there are property taxes and homeowners insurance to be paid. There is also the obligation to maintain the property. There are financial costs to maintenance that can be both high and unpredictable. There is the unstated requirement that the homeowner devote personal time and effort in the home's upkeep. Maintenance is necessary to protect the investment, but also to protect the integrity of the neighborhood and good relations with the neighbors. Many people who bought homes during the boom years saw only the upside; by the time they fully saw the downside, it was too late.

There is no dignity quite so impressive
and no independence quite so important
as living within your means.

Calvin Coolidge (1872-1933)
30th U.S. President

More people should learn to tell their dollars where to
go instead of asking them where they went.

Roger W. Babson (1875-1967)
Founder, Babson College

If wisdom is learned through suffering, then Americans and much of the world should be much wiser now than they were at the beginning of the millennium. For those who still have time to rebuild their assets, they are likely to take a more disciplined approach, recognizing that the behavior of the investor is more important than the behavior of the investment.

Human behavior tends to swing like a pendulum, though. Those who assumed too much risk and got burned in recent years are likely to become too risk averse. They may become so conservative that they will be unable to reach their long-term goals. They are like the golfer who, after slicing the first tee shot off to the right, overcompensates by hooking the next one off to the left.

Here is an example of how being too conservative can be costly. A new college graduate begins work and starts saving for retirement. If that person is conservative and earns only a 4% return on contributions over the next forty years, the contributions will grow by about 140%. If the return is 7%, the same contributions will grow by almost 400%.

All man's gains are the fruit of venturing.
Herodotus (484-425 BC)
Greek Historian

There is no way to skate around the economic axiom that risk and reward move in the same direction. The shenanigans of Wall Street in recent years were due in large part to attempts to socialize the risk while privatizing the profit. There will always be people trying to game the system, which is why strong regulation and enforcement will always be needed.

For the average citizen-investor, the reward they get will be commensurate with the risk they are willing to assume. After recognizing this fact, the first mistake that often gets made is misjudging one's own tolerance for risk. When everything is going well, we don't tend to see risk when it exists, and we become too risk tolerant. When everything is going badly, we swing like a pendulum in the other direction, becoming too risk averse and over-estimating the real dangers out there.

Many, if not most people get the risk-reward relationship wrong. They think that the risk they need to assume is based on the reward they are seeking. They see the reward as fixed and their tolerance for risk as flexible. In truth, the reward you get is based on the risk you can tolerate; the risk you tolerate isn't based on the reward you seek.

Consider the self-employed business owner. Most of the millionaires in the U.S. are members of this class. Most people look at the income, wealth, and freedom that this class of people has, and everyone would like the same for themselves. What doesn't get taken into account is the enormous risks that these successful businessmen and women took to create a successful business. What also isn't seen are the corpses of all the businesses that failed while the successful ones were fighting for survival. People want the rewards of owning a successful business; they just don't want the risks. If people could adjust their risk tolerance to match their desired reward, there would be millions more small businesses being created every year.

Big shots are only little shots who keep shooting.
Christopher Morley (1890-1957)
Novelist, Journalist

Whenever you see a successful business, someone once made a courageous decision.

Peter Drucker (1909-2005)
Management Consultant

Relatively few people venture out and start their own business, and fewer still ever reach a level of success that makes the rest of us jealous. The traits that make someone successful in creating a business are also needed for someone successful in the world of investing - courage, faith, patience, knowledge.

Nothing tells in the long run like a good judgment, and no sound judgment can remain with the man whose mind is disturbed by the mercurial changes of the stock exchange. It places him under an influence akin to intoxication. What is not, he sees, and what he sees, is not.

Andrew Carnegie (1835-1919)
Founder, U.S. Steel Corporation

With the exception of a few celebrities, no one can expect to get rich from one's own labors. Wealth is created when you enable some of your money to go out into the world and reproduce with abandon. Money, like people, cannot reproduce without taking on a certain amount of risk.

Investments that are truly risk-free will earn, at most, enough interest to keep even with inflation. In other words, if you invested $1,000 in something that merely kept up with inflation, you could buy the same item in forty years that you could have bought for $1,000 today, with nothing left over. You would have gained nothing; you would have postponed the use of that item for forty years, however.

Most people will work for about forty years. Hopefully, during that entire time they will be contributing to a retirement plan. If they will be retired for twenty years (a modest expectation) and if their "safe" investments only return enough to offset inflation, those people would need to save *one-half* of their incomes over their forty year working life to adequately fund retirement; no one can be expected to do that.

Over the last forty years the S&P 500 has increased thirteen-fold (excluding dividends), despite all the economic and political turmoil during that period. If the S&P 500 outpaces the inflation rate by 4% per year on average, investing in the S&P 500 would require saving only *one-fifth* of one's income over a forty-year working life. Since employers typically make some contribution as well, the worker's required savings rate would be reduced by the employer's contributions.

Anyone can hold the helm when the sea is calm.
Publilius Syrus (1st Century BC)
Latin Writer

No one would have crossed the ocean if he could have gotten off the ship in the storm.
Charles F. Kettering (1876-1958)
Inventor, Businessman

When it comes to investing, the seas will never be as calm as they were in the past. The reason is we keep churning them up.

In the old days, a person's retirement fund was managed by professional money managers, who made the investment decisions regarding the pension fund. The employee had neither responsibility nor input as to the management of the fund. Because the management was left in the hands of people who were not emotionally attached to the money, they could behave rationally regarding investment decisions. As a result, performance was adequate to fund the company's pension obligations.

When the traditional pension was replaced with the 401(k) plan, the investment decisions were shifted to the employee. This shift was bad for two reasons. First, the average employee could not hope to know a fraction of what professionals knew about investment management. Second, even with adequate knowledge, the emotional attachment to the money being managed meant that the employee would react to short-term market movements, rather than remain focused on the long-term. It also didn't help that they could check on their 401(k)'s every morning when they logged on to their computers.

People have a tendency to take what has happened in the recent past and extrapolate it out into the indefinite future. If the last three months have been bad in the stock market, many people think the trend will continue for the next three decades and pull their money out of stocks. For these people, they find themselves sitting on the sidelines when the inevitable rebound occurs. Once they are certain the bear market is over, they get back in, which is usually somewhere close to the end of the bull market. They then manage to ride the next down cycle before panicking again and selling. They are participating in the market, but only during bad times.

The stock market is a giant distraction from the business of investing.

John C. Bogle (1929-   )
Founder, Vanguard Group

In the short run, the market is a voting machine.
But in the long run, it is a weighing machine.

Ben Graham (1894-1976)
Economist, Investor

Because information is available to everyone instantly at little or no cost now, there is no advantage to frequent trading, or even moves in and out of the market altogether. If everyone has access to the same information, the price of any investment will already have that piece of information factored in before you or anyone else can act to take advantage of it.

We believe that according the name 'investors' to
institutions that trade actively is like calling someone
who repeatedly engages in one-night stands a
'romantic.'

Warren Buffett (1930-   )
Investor, Philanthropist

It is certainly possible to "beat the market," though that phrase is something of a misnomer. In order to beat the market, you merely have to be more disciplined than the herd. On good news, most people will buy; on bad news, they will sell. The person who is really making money is the person on the other end of those trades.

Going back to a variation on the pendulum analogy, if someone is swerving from pessimism to optimism with every market gyration, they are swerving to the right and then the left, when their destination is straight ahead. If your destination is ten, twenty, thirty, or forty years into the future, will the movements of the market in a single day, week, or even a month have any impact on arriving at your destination on time? Unless you can travel forward in time to know with certainty what the markets will do in the near-term, focusing on the near-term is a waste of time.

> *The big money is not in the buying or the selling, but in the waiting.*
>
> Jesse Livermore (1877-1940)
> Stock Speculator

> *The intelligent investor is a realist who sells to optimists and buys from pessimists.*
>
> Ben Graham (1894-1976)
> Economist, Investor

When events are unfolding rapidly, and especially when markets are being affected, the natural instinct is to want to "do something." There is a bias toward action. However, time and time again it has been proven that, when everything and everyone seem to be going crazy, maintaining self-discipline and, if action is warranted, responding rather than reacting, are the keys to winning. Whatever the majority is doing is almost always the least profitable course of action.

> *One of the funny things about the stock market is that every time one man buys, another sells, and they both think they are astute.*
>
> William Feather (1889-1981)
> Publisher, Author

> *The market, like the Lord, helps those who help themselves. But unlike the Lord, the market does not forgive those who know not what they do.*
>
> Warren Buffett (1930-   )
> Investor, Philanthropist

Part of the frustration of investing is the knowledge that you could have always done something better. It doesn't matter if you have beaten the market and all of your peers in the investment arena. As long as some money was left on the table, it is hard to be completely satisfied. Also, as long as we are not completely satisfied, there will be the temptation to do something more. Giving in to that temptation, however, is likely to leave us even less satisfied when our actions work against us.

Speaking of the investment arena, it isn't one. An arena is a place where competition takes place and where there are winners and losers. Investing is not a competitive sport. Your job is to focus on meeting your goals, which do not include beating anyone else. If your brother-in-law is bragging about his great investment returns, ignore him. His results have no effect on your results, and besides, he's probably lying.

In order to understand the stock market, we have to realize that, like anything enormous and inert, it's fundamentally stable, and like anything emotion-driven, it's volatile as hell.

P.J. O'Rourke (1947-   )
Satirist, Journalist

As long as we remember that investment markets were designed by and exist to serve human beings, it is easier to accept all the human quirks and faults that manifest themselves in those markets. In the short-term, people may drive us crazy, but we don't give up on the whole lot and become hermits. We accept them with all their faults and recognize that we're better off with them than without them. So it is with the markets as well.

*I distrust men or concerns that rise up with the speed
of rockets. Sudden rises are sometimes followed by
equally sudden falls. I have most faith in the
individual or enterprise that advances step by step.
A mushroom can spring up in a day; an oak takes fifty
years to mature. Mushrooms don't last; oaks do.*
B.C. Forbes (1880-1954)
Founder, Forbes Magazine

*Time is the friend of the wonderful company, the enemy
of the mediocre.*
Warren Buffett (1930-   )
Investor, Philanthropist

*Never invest your money in anything that eats or needs
repairing.*
Billy Rose (1899-1966)
Showman, Lyricist

The three determinants of investment success are investment selection, asset allocation, and investor behavior. Investment selection involves picking the specific stocks, bonds, etc. that make up the investment portfolio. Asset allocation involves deciding what percentage of a portfolio will be in stocks, bonds, etc. Asset allocation is where the risk in a portfolio is measured.

Investor behavior is everything the investor does in setting up a portfolio and managing it afterward. Investment selection can be affected by the investor's proclivity to trade versus buy-and-hold. Asset allocation can be affected by whether the investor is aggressive or conservative.

Studies that looked at how these three pieces

contribute to investment success had some surprising results. Investment selection had an effect of about 5%; asset allocation had an effect of about 15%; investor behavior had an effect of about 80%.

What do these findings mean? The specific stocks, bonds, etc. that you select has only a minimal impact on your returns. Much more important is the asset allocation. Over the long run, it's less important what stocks you own than to simply own stocks.

By far, the single most important factor in investment success is the human factor, aka, investor behavior. If you sell a stock when it's temporarily down, you hurt yourself. If you buy and sell frequently, you hurt yourself. If you are too aggressive for your tolerance or too conservative for your goals, you hurt yourself. If you get too hot when things are hot and too cold when things are cold, you hurt yourself. If you follow the herd instead of marching steadily to your own destination, you hurt yourself. When it comes to investing, we are usually our own worst enemy.

Retirement at sixty-five is ridiculous.
When I was sixty-five I still had pimples.
>   George Burns (1896-1996)
>   Comedian

When the Social Security Act was passed in 1935, the retirement date was set at age sixty-five. At that time, half the workers eligible for Social Security never lived to sixty-five, and the other half lived an average of only five years after retirement. In the early years of Social Security, ten workers paid into the system for every person who collected benefits.

Today, there are five workers paying into the system

for every two people collecting benefits. The earliest age to begin receiving benefits has dropped from sixty-five to sixty-two. These changes have occurred over a period when the average life expectancy of Americans has increased by nearly twenty years.

Social Security was created to be a safety net for the elderly in the midst of the Great Depression. It was also created to entice older workers into retirement, which would enable younger workers to find jobs and thus lower the unemployment rate. Social Security was never meant to be the primary source of retirement income.

If sixty is the new forty, then why are people clamoring to retire at ever earlier ages? If sixty is the new forty, it is due largely to the extra years that medical advances have provided to us. If the average American worker now lives at least fifteen years longer than his/her counterpart from the 1930's, is it unrealistic to expect that worker to spend at least half of those bonus years at work?

How old would you be if you didn't know how old you are?

Satchel Paige (1906-1982)
Baseball Player

The question isn't at what age I want to retire, it's at what income.

George Foreman (1949-   )
World Boxing Champion

Retirement is not an entitlement, at least not a retirement that encompasses a quarter or more of one's life and is funded largely by others. Everyone who lives to a normal life expectancy and retires at the normal retirement age will collect more in Social Security benefits than they ever paid in, even after accounting for inflation.

The failure of Social Security to increase the qualifying age for benefits as our lifespans have increased not only jeopardizes the integrity of the entire system, it also sends the wrong message to millions of Americans. Because we have been told from the day we first went to work that it is normal to retire at or around sixty-five, we have spent our entire adult lives aiming to do just that. As a result, people have focused more on getting to retirement age than finding a career from which they would never want to retire. Additionally, some of the best workers leave the workforce prematurely, simply because they've been trained to believe that's what they are supposed to do at a certain age.

There are certainly jobs that become difficult, if not impossible, to do beyond a certain age. Those jobs, however, make up a much smaller percentage of the economy than they did in 1935. Our current retirement system makes no consideration for the ease or difficulty of certain jobs for older workers. An insurance actuary can collect Social Security benefits at the same age as a construction worker, even though one job is clearly much easier for a sixty-year-old to do than the other.

The few jobs that still offer traditional pensions have also not changed with the times. Many jobs with pensions are in the public service sector, as businesses have moved from defined benefit to defined contribution retirement plans. To qualify for these pensions, one typically has to work for thirty years or have a combination of age and years on the job that totals eighty-five. These requirements mean that a person who begins a job at age twenty-five can retire with full benefits at age fifty-five. Most of these jobs offer some cost-of-living increases, too. Since these workers may live another thirty years in many cases, they stand to collect more in pension payments than they ever received in pay.

Most people retire while they are still productive workers. Many go into retirement unsure about what they will do, as well as having doubts about the financial viability of retirement. Leaving a job that provides a sense of purpose as well as financial stability for the uncertainties of retirement is often the result of societal pressure, not choice.

Retirement kills more people than hard work ever did.
Malcolm Forbes (1919-1990)
Publisher, Forbes Magazine

Many retirees, especially those who retire artificially early, often find themselves struggling financially after a few years. By then though, they may not be in good enough health to return to work. They may also not have the up-to-date skills that would be needed to return to work. It would be better to retire with security at sixty-seven than to retire at sixty-two, only to find yourself struggling at seventy-two with another decade or more to live.

More people are transitioning into retirement, rather than going from full-time work to full-time nothing in one step. They typically retire from a full-time job, but then work part-time doing something of interest to them. This intermediate stage helps them make their two most difficult adjustments: they begin living on a smaller income, and they begin to fill hours that were previously spent on the job.

Don't think of retiring from the world until the world will be sorry that you retire.

Samuel Johnson (1709-1784)
English Poet, Essayist

Current retirees generally have three sources of income: Social Security, pensions, and personal savings. The luckiest have all three. Future retirees should count on only one source of retirement income - their own personal savings.

Social Security is likely to be around in some form for the foreseeable future, but demographics and economics will force it to provide an ever-smaller percentage of a retiree's income. Even those jobs that currently provide a traditional pension at retirement can't be counted on to provide that pension when the time comes. Such plans have no ceiling on costs for the employer, which means that employers will continue to do away with them and replace them with defined contribution plans, which we know as the 401(k).

The problem with saving for retirement with a 401(k) plan is that the best time to invest in the plan is when you are so young that retirement is almost unimaginable. If you are twenty-five, you can't picture yourself at sixty-five. If you can't picture yourself at sixty-five, you aren't going to defer current spending to fund a 401(k). With retirement plans that mandatorily deducted contributions from the employee's paycheck, or that were funded totally by the employer, funding was not a problem. Today, the employee has to make the decision to defer income now to be invested into the 401(k).

Cessation of work is not accompanied by cessation of expenses.

Cato the Elder (234-149 BC)
Roman Statesman

The shifting of retirement funding from the employer (pension) to the employee (401(k)) has meant that the determining factor of when a worker retires is no longer age or years of service; it is the balance in the 401(k).

As much as someone may want to retire at sixty-five (or sixty-two or fifty-five), age and years of service will not be a factor. In order to retire today, people will need to have a sufficient amount in their retirement and other accounts.

What is a sufficient amount? It varies with the individual, but here is a general guideline. If someone retires around age sixty-five, he/she should plan to be around for at least twenty years. For a withdrawal period of that length, it is prudent not to withdraw more than five percent of the balance in the first year. That guideline means that you would need twenty times your first year's withdrawal in your 401(k) on the day you retire. If someone anticipated needing $50,000 from the account the first year, they should have a starting balance of $1 million.

This situation assumes a "normal" retirement age and an investment portfolio that isn't overly conservative. If someone wants to retire at sixty and if he/she only wants "safe" investments, at least thirty times the first year withdrawal will be needed to maintain solvency through a normal retirement.

A man is not old until regrets take the place of dreams.
John Barrymore (1882-1942)
Actor

Growing old is not for sissies.
Bette Davis (1908-1989)
Actress

Most people working today, even those close to retirement, are unaware of what it will take to live with some semblance of dignity and independence in retirement. If they did, many might just give up and not even bother saving for retirement, thinking that it was a lost cause. Living in denial does not change the facts, though. Even if these people think that they will just keep on working, almost everyone reaches the stage in life where they can no longer work, regardless of whether they need the income.

Hopefully, those who choose to live in denial would make up a small minority of the population. For the rest, the solution is two-fold: invest more now and expect to work longer. Increasing contributions to the 401(k) plan works best for younger workers - the older we are, the less time there is for the contributions to grow. Working longer helps in two ways - every year of working enables more contributions to be made to the 401(k). In addition, every year of work is a year that is not spent in retirement, drawing down precious capital.

Even if most of us have to work into our seventies, our working lives are better than those of our grandparents. Even our retirement is likely to be both longer and better than that of our grandparents, if we each accept our responsibility to make it so.

BRIGHTER REFLECTIONS

When people look for labels to describe our many good and bad behaviors, they will often refer to our "lower natures" or our "higher natures." When considering human behavior as it relates to money, greed would epitomize our lower nature, while generosity epitomizes our higher nature.

These labels are more accurate than one might think. The *nucleus accumbens* is one of the oldest and most primitive parts of the human brain. It is sometimes referred to as the pleasure center. The highs that are experienced from sex, drugs, gambling, and other addictions all originate in the nucleus accumbens. The highs that come from acquisition and accumulation, the manifestations of greed, also originate there. The nucleus accumbens is the biological source of some our worst behavior when it comes to money.

There is a different part of our brain that can take credit for our best behavior regarding money. The *posterior superior temporal sulcus* (PSTC for short) resides at the top of our brain. The PSTC takes care of our social calendar and all our human relationships. All development as a human society is the result of the PSTC. It is the part of the brain that most separates human beings from animals. The PSTC is also where our generosity resides.

And He sat down opposite the treasury, and began observing how the people were putting money into the treasury; and many rich people were putting in large sums. A poor widow came and put in two small copper coins, which amounts to a cent. Calling His disciples

379

to Him, He said to them, "Truly I say to you, this poor widow put in more than all the contributors to the treasury; for they all put in out of their surplus, but she, out of her poverty, put in all she owned, all she had to live on."

Mark 12:41-44

Brain studies have shown that the nucleus accumbens and the posterior superior temporal sulcus cannot function simultaneously; when one is active, the other goes dormant. We can be greedy or we can be generous, but we cannot be both, at least not simultaneously.

The nucleus accumbens has an unfair advantage in this competition. It produces dopamine, the chemical that can make anything and everything feel good to us. Addictive behavior is the result of dopamine being released when we engage in certain activities. Greed can be an addictive behavior if it produces large amounts of dopamine. In truth, what humans become addicted to is dopamine, and we will undertake any activity that will produce it in sufficient quantities, even harmful and antisocial behavior.

Money giving is a very good criterion, in a way, of a person's mental health. Generous people are rarely mentally ill people.

Dr. Karl Menninger (1893-1990)
Psychiatrist

Our impulse to be generous operates on a much higher level. We possess no instinctive desire to be generous. Small children provide evidence that generosity must be taught, but that selfishness is inherent. Despite the unfair competition, how does generosity manage to manifest itself in a sizable portion of mankind?

Sigmund Freud defined three main parts of our psychiatric apparatus - the id, the ego, and the superego. The id is all about seeking pleasure and avoiding pain. The id is about I-me-mine. Freud called the id, "the dark inaccessible part of our personality…a cauldron full of seething excitations."

The nucleus accumbens is the physical address for greed and selfishness; the id is their psychological address.

The ego represents our common sense, and it spends its days trying to find a happy medium between the id and the superego.

The superego is where our conscience resides. The superego is the psychological manifestation of the PSTC. If the id represents our lower nature, the superego represents our higher nature. If we are generous, it is because the superego has gained the upper hand over the id and has given the PSTC a chance to show that it can provide experiences that, if not exactly pleasurable, are certainly rewarding.

We make a living by what we get;
we make a life by what we give.
                              Winston Churchill (1874-1965)
                              British Prime Minister

Leave the woodpile higher than you found it.
                              Paul Harvey (1918-2009)
                              Broadcaster

Because of money's versatility, how people deal with money may be the best indicator of whether the id or the superego is in control.

People have been saying that time is money ever since money was first invented over 2,500 years ago. When it comes to generosity, giving money has been used as a substitute for giving time for just as long. For many givers, time is a more precious resource than money, so giving money is the easier sacrifice. For many receivers, money provides the flexibility to buy the time of others to meet their needs. If you cannot provide your time directly to help others, your money may prove just as useful to them.

People have also been saying that money can't buy love for at least 2,500 years. Money can actually be one of the best tools ever invented for the *expression* of love. However, it is one of the worst tools ever as a *substitute* for love.

There are times when only your time and only your love are acceptable to others. The most obvious example is in your relationship with your children. Children need the time and love of their parents, and no amount of wealth can substitute for them. The closer your relationship is with any individual or group, the less you can use a gift of money as a proxy for the gift of yourself.

We do not quite forgive a giver. The hand that feeds us is in some danger of being bitten.
Ralph Waldo Emerson (1803-1882)
Philosopher, Essayist

When you are generous, whether it is with your time or your money, there is always the chance that your generosity will not be appreciated. One reason that people may bite the hand that feeds them is that they resent the need to be fed. If you need to rely on others to be fed, you may feel like a failure, or at least inferior to someone who has a surplus to offer to you. Their resentment may be at themselves or at the circumstances that created their current situation, but the convenient target of that resentment is often the person who is trying to help.

When there is a lack of appreciation by the recipients of generosity, there is a natural tendency to want to withdraw support and find more "worthy" recipients. Before making such a move, it may help to try to view things from the perspective of the "ungrateful" recipient. Everyone needs his/her dignity and self-respect and charity can strip those away. For those who seem unreceptive to a handout, what they may really need is a hand up. A hand up may require more than a handout, but the results will almost always be better. The recipient can maintain his/her dignity and will be less likely to require a handout in the future.

For where your treasure is, there your heart will be also.
Luke 12:34

We can tell our values by looking at our checkbook stubs.
Gloria Steinem (1934-   )
Feminist, Journalist

Which comes first, the money or the commitment? Most people would say that the money follows the commitment, which makes sense on first review. If you believe in a cause, you are more willing to devote time and money to it. It certainly makes it easier to write a check if you agree with the goals of an organization.

Jesus took a different approach. He believed that if

you committed your money to something, you would then commit yourself, too. Two examples will serve to illustrate.

Children are sent to private schools with the expectation that they will receive a superior education than they would receive at public school. To insure that they get what they are paying for, the parents of children in private school devote much more time and effort (as well as money) in supporting the mission of the school. If their children are receiving a superior education at private school, it is due primarily to the level of involvement of the parents, rather than the quality of the teachers.

The housing collapse that led to the financial crisis has been studied in depth. Many causes have been considered, and much data has been collected. There is one statistic that stands out, though. Regardless of geography, demography, or any other classification, there was one constant - the lower the down payment on a house, the higher the incidence of default. When people had their own money sunk into their home, they were much more likely to do everything in their power to keep it their home. In both of these examples, the financial commitment created an emotional bond, not the reverse.

Never measure your generosity by what you give, but rather by what you have left.

Fulton J. Sheen (1895-1975)
Archbishop of New York

Make all you can, save all you can, give all you can.
John Wesley (1703-1791)
English Cleric

Altruistic intentions can be a great motivator to create wealth. When personal wealth reaches the point where a person can fulfill every material desire, the only motivation to continue creating wealth is to give it away. The motivation may be as personal as funding a college education for grandchildren, or it may be as grand as creating an endowment that provides scholarships in perpetuity. In addition to motivating wealth creators to continue creating wealth, altruism helps assure that the methods used to create wealth meet the highest ethical standards. Few people want to help one group of people with money that was obtained by harming another group of people.

Work for your future as if you are going to live forever, for your afterlife as if you are going to die tomorrow.
Arabian Proverb

One of the great motivations for philanthropy, altruism, charity, generosity, whatever you label it, is the desire to leave a legacy of some sort. Older people give at higher levels than younger people. This tendency prevails even when incomes and expenses favor the younger group. The older we get, the more we recognize our own mortality. As we realize that our time is becoming more and more limited, the desire to do something that will live beyond us becomes stronger.

We can give in one of three ways - time, talent, or treasure. Not everyone has talents that translate into benefits for others in need. Time always seems to be in short supply, and even if there is the time, there is usually the need for some talent to go along with the time.

Treasure can be the most useful gift for several

reasons. First, money is fungible - it can be mixed with other money without changing any of the money's characteristics. Second, money has an indefinite useful life. Time that is given to a cause is gone immediately. Talent may produce something of more permanence, but even cathedrals decay over time. Finally, money is flexible. Money that is given to a good cause today might not be spent for fifty years. In fifty years' time, that money might be used to supply a product or fill a need that the donor could not have imagined a half-century before.

Someone is sitting in the shade today because someone planted a tree a long time ago.
> Warren Buffett (1930-   )
> Investor, Philanthropist

Despite money's many qualities, including its ability to be transported to the future, one quality it does not possess is the ability to be taken with us when we die. When people realize they can't take it with them, they begin to think of ways to maintain some control of their money from the beyond. The less they trust their beneficiaries to do the right thing with an inheritance, the more restrictive and ironclad the trusts will be that control the estate.

Estate laws are so complex that attorneys can spend their entire careers in that one specialty. As long as wealth can be accumulated, but can't be taken into the next world, and as long as those who remain behind may fight over and squander an inheritance, there will be a need for trusts to carry out the wishes of the person who created the wealth.

Study the past if you would divine the future.
> Confucius (551-479 BC)
> Chinese Philosopher

When beneficiaries of a trust complain about the restrictions of the trust, they probably don't stop to think that there was a reason those restrictions were put in place. If the deceased had simply wanted to be mean, the best thing would have been to leave the beneficiary nothing at all. A person who is the beneficiary of a restrictive trust must face two facts - the dear departed cared enough to make that person a beneficiary, and the beneficiary had not behaved in a manner to earn complete trust.

The excesses of our youth are drafts upon our old age.
> Charles Caleb Colton (1780-1832)
> English Cleric, Writer

Many people take no care of their money till they come nearly to the end of it, and others do just the same with their time.
> Johann Wolfgang von Goethe (1749-1832)
> German Writer, Philosopher

When most people hear the word *stewardship*, they think of the annual pledge drive at their church. Stewardship is actually the careful and responsible management of something entrusted to one's care. To accept the role of steward is to first accept that, although we might possess something, it doesn't mean we own it.

In a country like the United States, with our emphasis on individual property rights, it can be difficult to accept that we are merely stewards of what we legally own. However, we have all known people who lost what they

387

legally owned through neglect or carelessness or abuse. Whether you consider it a law of economics, of nature, or of God, a prerequisite to getting more is taking care of that which is already possessed.

Those who make the worst use of their time most complain of its shortness.
Jean de la Bruyere (1645-1696)
French Essayist, Moralist

Time is the most valuable resource because the proper use of time is the source of all wealth. Unless a person is a good steward of his/her time, it is impossible to be a good steward of anything else. Considering the amount of time the average American spends watching TV and surfing the internet, a strong case can be made that, as a nation, we are not good stewards of our time.

In addition to wasting the present time, too many of us are depleting our reserves of time. Medical advances may be adding years to our lives, but we reduce both the quality and quantity of our future time by not taking proper care of ourselves.

Some believe that we have only so many heartbeats in our lifetime and don't want to waste them exercising. However, if an hour of exercise each day lowered a person's resting heart rate from seventy-two to sixty, that person would gain four hours of heartbeats per day, even after allowing for the extra beats used exercising. The essence of good stewardship is taking care of what you have today to enable having more in the future.

The future is purchased by the present.
Samuel Johnson (1709-1784)
English Poet, Essayist

It is better to have a hen tomorrow than an egg today.

Thomas Fuller (1608-1661)
English Author, Historian

Just as we should allocate our money between sharing, saving, and spending, we should do the same with our time. Even if we are good at making such allocations with money, we often avoid doing so with our time. This avoidance may result from a feeling of no control over our time. It may also result from the uncertainty of how much time we have. Money, which is measurable with great accuracy, does not suffer such uncertainties.

We don't need to know how much time we have left to begin allocating it. We all have twenty-four hours each day. Those twenty-four hours should be allocated between sharing (doing something to help others), saving (doing something to make your future better), and spending (living in the moment). If we take care of each day in this manner, the future, no matter how much of it we have, will become better.

The cost of a thing is that amount of life which must be exchanged for it.

Henry David Thoreau (1817-1862)
Author, Philosopher

There is a difference between living *in* the moment and living *for* the moment. Living in the moment means you get everything the present has to offer. Living for the moment means you see nothing but the present. Living in the moment makes the future better without compromising the present. Living for the moment sacrifices the future for the pleasures of the present.

389

By the street of By-and-By, one arrives at the house of Never.

Miguel de Cervantes (1547-1616)
Spanish Novelist, Poet

You can't escape the responsibility of tomorrow by evading it today.

Abraham Lincoln (1809-1965)
16th U.S. President

We know about the price of procrastination when it comes to saving for retirement, but we don't often think about how procrastination affects our future in less measurable ways. Procrastination is defined as needless delay. The definition should be broadened to say that procrastination is needed action needlessly delayed. It is only the delay of needed action that has consequences. If you don't get a haircut this week, neither you nor the world is likely to suffer. If you don't have needed surgery this week, you and the world are likely to suffer as a result.

Most of us are aware, on some level, of the consequences of our procrastination. Even if we can't fully comprehend the consequences on our own, there is rarely a shortage of family and friends who are imploring us to take needed action now to avoid some future disaster. Procrastination does not occur unintentionally; it involves knowingly doing nothing with full knowledge that the price to be paid in the future is higher than the price to be paid today.

Cause and effect, means and ends, seed and fruit cannot be severed; for the effect already blooms in the cause, the end preexists in the means, the fruit in the seed.

Ralph Waldo Emerson (1803-1882)
Philosopher, Essayist

While no one can predict the future, we all have a power even more awesome - the ability to affect the future. Because we can each affect our future, for better or worse, there is no need for predictive powers. In exchange for these powers, we are charged with accepting responsibility for that which we can change for the better, but choose not to. For example, none of us knows when we will die, and few of us would really want to know. We do have the power to affect that date by lifestyle choices we make every day. On this matter, most would prefer the ability to affect the outcome than to predict it.

The afternoon knows what the morning never suspected.
Swedish Proverb

We will never be able to affect everything to the extent we would like. Part of unpredictability is not knowing how much of an effect our efforts will have on a future outcome. In addition, many of the major events in our life come at us out of deep left field. There is nothing to be done about them. We can only deal with what we know might happen. If we focus on those matters of higher probability, we will be in a better position to deal with the occasional matter that blindsides us.

391

Don't worry 'bout the mule goin' blind;
just keep loadin' the wagon.

Appalachian Proverb

When a large part of the world was freed from the yoke of communism toward the end of the last century, they were faced with a new problem. In their longing for greater opportunities, average people never realized that they would now become more responsible for their own fates. Communism had provided a cradle-to-grave floor and ceiling for these people. Unfortunately, the ceiling was just inches above the floor. They were glad to be rid of the ceiling, but they had to lose the floor as well. Some soared, but many crashed.

When one door closes another door opens; but we often
look so long and so regretfully upon the closed door
that we do not see the ones which open for us.

Alexander Graham Bell (1847-1922)
Scientist, Inventor

It is amazing how focused and productive people can become when they are under the pressure of a deadline. Part of this productivity can be explained in relative terms; they are productive near the deadline in comparison to their procrastination when the deadline was in the distant future. Even people who are consistently productive manage to find another gear when it becomes necessary. If everyone were consistently as productive at work as they are right before they leave on vacation, there would be no economic problems in this country.

It is not half as important to burn the midnight oil as
it is to be awake in the daytime.

E. W. Elmore

Many people argue that they "work best under pressure." The pressure of a deadline may kick start them into working harder, but "working best" is hardly the same thing as doing one's best work. Ask any college professor who has ever graded term papers. The papers that have been assembled consistently throughout the semester always outshine the ones that were assembled in a panicked state in the last forty-eight hours before the deadline. The only point of pride the procrastinating student can claim is that they were very productive for the small amount of time and effort they expended on the project, which is not really something to brag about.

Forty is the old age of youth.
Fifty is the youth of old age.

Victor Hugo (1802-1885)
French Poet, Novelist

If it is sensible for the child to make an effort to learn
how to be an adult, then it is essential for the adult to
learn how to be aged.

Alfred Stieglitz (1864-1946)
Photographer

There is a reason why advertisers prefer to sponsor TV shows that have high ratings in the 18-34 age bracket. They prefer this age group over the 50-and-older age group even though the second group has much more disposable income. Why do advertisers go after the younger audience? Simply put, the younger the audience, the more gullible they are.

Most of us get wiser with age. We may decline in most other aspects once we pass fifty, but if we've been paying attention to the world at all, we should be accumulating no small amount of wisdom by that age. Wisdom is the combination of experiences and the willingness to learn from those experiences. Both ingredients are essential, which is why there are few wise young people and why there can still be foolish old people.

Old people who have cultivated and harvested wisdom throughout their lives rarely regret getting old. They see their physical decline as a small price to pay for their increased insight. Those who have learned little over the decades, but have merely grown old, are those seniors you see who can find no comfort in their advancing years. A wise senior is a happy senior. We should appreciate the wisdom of this group and try to learn all we can from them.

> *If all our misfortunes were laid in one common heap, whence everyone must take an equal portion, most people would be content to take their own and depart.*
> Socrates (469-399 BC)
> Greek Philosopher

All of us have uttered the idiom, "Better the devil you know" at some point. Invoking that phrase is an admission that, while we may not always be treated fairly, we also realize we could be treated even more unfairly, and it is risky to tempt the fates.

One manifestation of wisdom is the ability to recognize that we rarely have control over outcomes. We do, however, have control over inputs, which are the main determinants of outcomes. Too many people go through life under the delusion that their inputs will have no effect on outcomes, that it is all controlled by others, the fates, or the stars.

> *Life is like a game of cards. The hand that is dealt you represents determinism; the way you play it is free will.*
> Jawaharlal Nehru (1889-1964)
> Indian Prime Minister

How is it that some people are born into poverty and become captains of industry, while others are born into wealth and privilege and become broken and destitute? While such cases often involve some lucky and unlucky breaks, the real determinant is how the characters played the cards they were dealt.

If you've ever ridden a ten-speed bicycle, you know that you work very hard and don't go very fast when you are in the lower gears. That situation is similar to people who are born with no inherent advantages and have to struggle to cover any ground. You also know that once you work your way up to tenth gear, you cover ground quickly with relatively little effort. That situation is similar to people who are born to great advantage, who are in effect placed at birth on a bicycle that is already moving at a high speed. Someone who is placed on a bicycle travelling at speed may have an initial advantage, but they also haven't worked their way through the gears, and that lack of experience and perspective can make them a greater risk to crash.

Good and bad luck is a synonym, in the great majority of instances, for good and bad judgment.
John Chatfield (1826-1863)
Colonel, Union Army

Lots of folks confuse bad management with destiny.
Elbert Hubbard (1856-1915)
Writer, Philosopher

"I'm a victim of coicumstance!" When Curly of The Three Stooges uttered that phrase, it was hilarious. It's not hilarious today, when so many people say it in total seriousness. Victim mentality has become rampant in recent years. Every misfortune must have an accountable party, yet that party is never the recipient of misfortune.

The most successful people are those who recognize that misfortune is a part of life and that there are some misfortunes that are unavoidable. These people also recognize that it makes no sense to try to control uncontrollable circumstances. They devote their energy to responding positively to events and looking to turn a disadvantage into an advantage. They look for ways to make the best of a bad situation, rather than looking for someone to blame for the bad situation.

It never occurs to fools that merit and good fortune are closely united.
Johann Wolfgang von Goethe (1749-1832)
German Writer, Philosopher

Where no plan is laid, where the disposal of time is surrendered merely to the chance of incident, chaos will soon reign.
Victor Hugo (1802-1885)
French Poet, Novelist

Successful people have an obsession about moving forward. Progress, more than profits, are their driving force. To that end, they do not leave the course of their journey to chance. They plan meticulously, while maintaining flexibility to adapt to changing conditions along the way. They also see any misfortune as a learning opportunity. They do not adopt a victim mentality; quite the opposite. They will look closely at any misfortune to see what **they** did wrong, in order to learn from the experience and avoid similar mistakes in the future.

'Tis known by perseverance in a good cause, and obstinacy in a bad one.

Laurence Sterne (1713-1768)
Anglo-Irish Clergyman

Successful people also have the ability to discern when effort reaches a point of diminishing returns. They are known as *satisficers*, rather than *maximizers*. Maximizers will stick with something until it is perfected which, if it ever occurs, may take so much effort to get there that it isn't worth it. Satisficers work until they are satisfied, and then move on to another project. They are typically satisfied when they recognize their time and efforts can yield more progress if spent elsewhere. While the quest for perfection may seem noble, it is almost never practical. Successful people are nothing if not practical.

Failure can be bought on easy terms.
Success must be paid for in advance.

Cullen Hightower (1923-2008)
Writer

Successful people not only know when to stop working on a project, they know when to start, too. All success is the result of initiative, the willingness to get started on something without being forced to. Those with initiative are successful because they understand that, until they get on the bike and start pedaling, they will never be able to cruise in high gear.

Failures are divided into two classes – those who thought and never did, and those who did and never thought.

John Charles Salak (1880-1959)
Journalist

Have you ever seriously considered the command "Ready, Aim, Fire!"? They are three simple instructions, all of which must be followed in the proper sequence to offer any chance for success. Some people never even bother to get ready. Some people will get ready and aim, but never muster the courage to fire. Worst of all are those who amend the sequence to "Ready, Fire, Aim!" They are the worst because they expend energy and resources wastefully and, because they fire before they aim, they risk doing more harm than good by their actions. Their haste makes waste and sometimes worse.

Everyone who has ever played golf knows the agony of flubbing a shot because, in the rush to look up and see a great shot, the head came up too soon, guaranteeing the duffer wouldn't like the results. Nothing hurts the chances for a good result like being in too big a rush to see that result. There will always be time to admire a great result, but it will come only by remaining focused on the task while the task is still being performed.

It is the mark of a good action that it appears inevitable in retrospect.

Robert Louis Stevenson (1850-1894)
Scottish Novelist

Successful people are less likely to lose focus while working on a task because they are good at visualizing the results. They know what a good result looks like, and they know how to create that result. Because they remain "in the moment" when they are working on something, they can look back with pride when they finish. Rare is the person who can combine a sense of vision with the discipline and ability to successfully execute that vision.

Manners often make fortunes.

John Ray (1627-1705)
English Naturalist

Civility costs nothing and buys everything.

Mary Wortley Montagu (1689-1762)
English Aristocrat, Writer

When we think of people who are disciplined and successful, there is also a tendency to think of them as domineering, overbearing, even bullies. While some certainly fit that description, the most successful do not. They understand that you do not get the best work from people by employing such tactics. They also understand that such tactics create enemies, not allies.

One look at popular culture will confirm that we are far less civil than in the past. This decline in civility is actually an advantage for those who can show consideration for others. The bar is now set so low for personal behavior that it is easy to stand out as someone who knows how to treat others properly. Such a person never lacks for business opportunities.

Wealth, like happiness, is never attained when sought after directly. It comes as a by-product of providing a useful service.

Henry Ford (1863-1947)
Founder, Ford Motor Company

Success is not the key to happiness.
Happiness is the key to success.

Albert Schweitzer (1875-1965)
German Theologian, Physician

Of all the great accomplishments of our Founding Fathers, perhaps none is greater than the inclusion of our right to "the pursuit of happiness" in the Declaration of Independence. No government had ever been founded on such a vague concept, and there were certainly guffaws in the Parliament when that passage was first read. The British must have thought us mad to risk annihilation over such a trivial desire. Still, there were some there who marveled at the audacity of it all, and they knew that a people who believed that happiness was a right would not be easy to defeat.

Although we value our right to pursue happiness, we often don't have a good understanding of what happiness is or how to achieve it. One of the most common mistakes we make is confusing pleasure with happiness. Pleasure is typically sensual in nature and involves receiving rather than giving. Happiness is more emotional and involves giving more than receiving. Pleasures can be bought, but they do not last, and the pursuit of them often impedes the opportunities for happiness in the future.

All earthly delights are sweeter in expectation than enjoyment; but all spiritual pleasures more in fruition than expectation.

Owen Feltham (1602-1668)
English Essayist

Because money can buy things that can give us pleasure and because we tend to confuse pleasure with happiness, we then believe that money will make us happy or that it can buy happiness.

Studies have shown that there is only a slight correlation between wealth and happiness. People at low income levels are less happy, which is due in large part to the daily struggle to meet basic needs. However, disparities in income do not translate to similar disparities in happiness. The middle class is only slightly happier than the lower class, and the upper class is barely any happier than the middle class. A severe lack of money can make someone unhappy, but an abundance of money will not make someone happy.

Not everything that can be counted counts.
And not everything that counts can be counted.

Albert Einstein (1879-1955)
Theoretical physicist

Each of us has our own idea and interpretation of happiness. Because we can choose what makes us happy, we do not have to get extravagant in what we do to become happy. Most people agree that true happiness comes from actions that lead to self-fulfillment or in actions that help others. Happiness can come from learning a new skill or from teaching someone else a new skill. Money may be a useful tool in the creation of happiness, but it is hardly an essential ingredient.

For what does it profit a man to gain the whole world, and forfeit his soul?

Mark 8:36

The trouble with the rat race is, even if you win, you're still a rat.

Lily Tomlin (1939-   )
Actress, Comedian

Misunderstanding the relationship between success and happiness, as well as misunderstanding the difference between the two, has led to a lot of disappointment over the centuries. To begin with, many people think that, if they become successful, happiness will follow, just as night follows day. They never stop to define what happiness means to them, so they never know what they are seeking. They expect that happiness will simply appear and that they will know instinctively when it has arrived.

While these people don't define what happiness means to them, they usually create some definition of success for themselves. Success is typically defined by them through position or money, with the main purpose of position being to provide a lot of money. Because money is the primary measurement of success, it also is expected to bring happiness in proportion to its amount. As studies have shown, more money does not lead to more happiness, so the people who thought that more money leads to more happiness inevitably find themselves disappointed and still looking for a source of happiness.

The tragedy for many of these people is the extent to

which they compromised their principles to achieve financial success. Many merely allowed relationships to suffer because their attention was elsewhere. Many hurt their own physical and emotional health by obsessing over money. Some went to the extreme of breaking the law to get what they wanted. When their goals were achieved, they realized too late that the prize was not worth the price.

To be without some of the things you want is an indispensable part of happiness.
>   Bertrand Russell (1872-1970)
>   English Philosopher

There are three ingredients in the good life: learning, earning and yearning.
>   Christopher Morley (1890-1957)
>   Novelist, Journalist

We should all take time to carefully calculate the cost-benefit balance before we undertake any attempt at success and happiness. Such analysis can be difficult, however, because it is too easy to miscalculate the benefit side of the equation. If the cost becomes higher than we originally estimated, we will compensate by increasing our perception of the benefit. One of the biggest problems with this type of cost-benefit analysis is the inability to know the true value of the benefit until it has been obtained. By then, all the costs have been incurred and if the benefit doesn't live up to expectations, there can be a lot of disappointment.

Despite the difficulties in accurately estimating the level of happiness one can expect from various endeavors, we should never stop looking for new challenges. Once people achieve financial success and find it to be less rewarding than expected, they can begin to look for new challenges that don't involve material gain for personal benefit. They may look to challenges of a physical, mental, or spiritual nature, such as running a marathon, earning a degree, or studying a new religion. They may also continue with financial challenges, but with a different twist. They may become fundraisers or philanthropists for causes close to their heart. Achieving a goal in any of these categories is likely to bring greater happiness than any personal financial accomplishment they may have achieved.

Hope itself is a species of happiness, and, perhaps, the chief happiness which this world affords; but, like all other pleasures immoderately enjoyed, the excesses of hope must be expiated by pain.

Samuel Johnson (1709-1784)
English Poet, Essayist

An optimist is a product of faith combined with hope. Pessimists can be a necessary counterweight to a world full of optimists, but the optimists keep the world moving forward. Even though optimists are the drivers of progress and even though hope is a key ingredient to optimism, there needs to be an element of realism as well. Realism can make the optimists more flexible, allowing them to maintain their optimistic nature even when events turn out badly.

Hope is a good breakfast, but it is a bad supper.

Francis Bacon (1561-1626)
English Philosopher, Statesman

He that lives upon hope will die fasting.
> Benjamin Franklin (1706-1790)
> Founding Father

One of the great characteristics of America and Americans is our optimistic nature, even during hard times. We have this personality as a nation because we are a place where hope continues to spring anew. Because opportunities for the individual are more unlimited here than anywhere else, there is always a high measure of hope among the population. As long as our citizens feel confident that they have a reasonable chance of realizing their dreams, hope will remain high.

America is like spring training in baseball. The slate has been wiped clean, and every team feels they have a shot at the championship this year. By August your team may be out of it, but even then you can console yourself that there is always next year. However, if the team owner and managers never take steps to convert hope into victories, the fans will eventually run out of hope. Hope cannot be refilled unless it is at least occasionally fulfilled.

Everything that is done in the world is done by hope.
No merchant or tradesman would set himself to work
if he did not hope to reap benefit thereby.
> Martin Luther (1483-1546)
> Founder, Protestant Reformation

A pessimist is, by nature, someone devoid of hope. No enterprise, much less a successful one, was ever started by a pessimist. Even those who bet against the market hope their predictions will be correct. They are optimistic that they can profit from the pessimism of others during such periods. No one ever started a business with the slogan, "This isn't gonna work." If anyone did, they were proven right in short order.

As previously stated, risk and reward move in the same direction. To generate greater rewards requires the assumption of greater risks. No one takes on risk, especially higher levels of risk, unless there is the hope that the risks will be managed and the rewards will be reaped.

We must dream of an aristocracy of achievement arising out of a democracy of opportunity.
Thomas Jefferson (1743-1826)
3rd U.S. President

It shouldn't be surprising that America is a nation of (mostly) optimists. As a nation of immigrants, we were populated by people who came to the U.S. with the hope of building a better life. If there were any pessimists on the boat coming over, they either became optimists once they got settled, or they eventually became discouraged and returned to the old country.

There is no sadder sight than a young pessimist.
Mark Twain (1835-1910)
Author, Humorist

Young people are similar to immigrants in that they are new to the workforce and have a long future ahead of them. Like most immigrants, they are starting at the bottom of the ladder and will have to work their way up.

If young people lose hope for their future, America's future is in serious jeopardy. If they feel that their inheritance will be nothing more than trillions of dollars of debt, they will lose hope, and we will quickly become a nation of pessimists. A nation of pessimists is a doomed nation. Perhaps the most important duty of any citizen is the building of a foundation of hope for the next generation. Each generation has the responsibility to make their own achievements, but each generation also has the responsibility to create for the next generation as many opportunities as they themselves enjoy.

Hope is independent of the apparatus of logic.
> Norman Cousins (1915-1990)
> Journalist, Author

It can be tempting to think that honesty and integrity impede profitability. Unfortunately, in the short term, that is often the case. One of the problems of the current system of compensation for corporate executives is the emphasis on bonuses for short term results. Those who think only in the short term will be more likely to compromise their principles to improve their financial position. As a result, unethical and often illegal methods are used to boost profitability and generate executive bonuses. Such methods may work for a brief period, but eventually the truth comes out when the schemes collapse under their own weight.

The superior man seeks what is right;
the inferior man, what is profitable.
> Confucius (551-479 BC)
> Chinese Philosopher

If honesty did not exist, we ought to invent it as the best means of getting rich.

Honore De Mirabeau (1749-1791)
French Revolutionary

The overwhelming majority of businesses are run by honest, ethical, hardworking people. In the short run, they will be at a disadvantage to competitors who are not honest and ethical. Eventually, the unethical are discovered for what they are, if not by the law then by their customers. Once the discovery is made, it is only a matter of time before they are put out of business. Unfortunately, there will always be some new competitor looking to cut corners.

He who is faithful in a very little thing is faithful also in much; and he who is unrighteous in a very little thing is unrighteous also in much.

Luke 16:10

Integrity cannot be compartmentalized. When evaluating the behavior of leaders, whether they are in the public or the private sector, it is tempting to claim that their private behavior should not affect our opinion of their job performance. That attitude might be appropriate for someone who has no position of leadership. However, leading isn't what someone *does*; a leader is who someone *is*. A leader is always a leader, even when not executing the duties of leadership. Leaders aren't allowed the luxury of compartmentalizing their lives. Any unethical behavior affects every aspect of their lives, most especially their ability to lead.

I would rather have people laugh at my economies than weep for my extravagance.

Oscar II (1829-1907)
King of Sweden

Inevitably, when someone with questionable ethics moves into a leadership position, those ethics surface in the execution of duties. It is folly to think that a person with a poor history of personal financial management will do any better with the company's finances. It is folly to think that a person who has been unfaithful to a spouse will be faithful to the shareholders and employees. It is folly to think that a person who has always put his/her interests above those of others would act any differently when put in a position to act in even greater self-interest.

Few men have virtue to withstand the highest bidder.

George Washington (1732-1799)
1st U.S. President

No one worth possessing can be quite possessed.

Sara Teasdale (1884-1933)
Poet

Personal integrity and technical competence are not mutually exclusive. In fact, integrity is the foundation upon which competence is built. Personal integrity involves setting standards of behavior that are not subject to negotiation. People who unilaterally set high expectations for their personal behavior will also set similarly high expectations for their job performance. Conversely, people who do not hold themselves accountable for their personal behavior cannot be expected to act any differently on the job.

The best way to become a respected leader and reap financial rewards is to first demand a standard of behavior of yourself that makes you worthy of such position and wealth.

COUNTERPOINT

When we were young, at some point, we all had to endure some old geezer complaining, "When I was your age…," followed by some rant about how his/her generation endured more/complained less, worked harder/played less, gave more/took less, and especially about how they were so much better behaved than our present generation.

Every generation is shaped by the circumstances of their times. If the people who grew up in the Great Depression were exceptionally frugal, it was because they had no money. The armies that won World War II knew that living under Nazi rule would be worse than death itself. History shows that the human race responds to circumstances as it needs to in order to survive.

Our relative physical comfort today is not the result of laziness; it is actually the result of hard work and imagination. Air conditioning, microwaves, automobiles, and countless other inventions have enabled us to channel our energies into new and more productive efforts. One of the main reasons that women are now the majority of the workforce is because inventions of the twentieth century greatly reduced the amount of time and effort it took to perform the tasks of maintaining a home. Women work as hard as they ever did; they have simply been relieved of some of the hard work their predecessors performed.

We have become too fat in recent years, which is the first time in history where widespread obesity has even been possible. The poorest state in the U.S., Mississippi, also has the highest obesity rate, which would have been an unimaginable phenomenon just a few decades ago.

Hunger around the world today is largely the result of political conflicts, not food shortages.

Dr. Norman Borlaug died in 2009 at the age of ninety-five. He was a recipient of the Nobel Peace Prize, the Congressional Gold Medal, and the Presidential Medal of Freedom. You probably never heard of him, even though he is credited with saving over *one billion* people to date.

Dr. Borlaug is considered the founder of the Green Revolution, which refers to the series of scientific advances in agriculture that greatly increased crop yields. Dr. Borlaug's work over a period of more than sixty years enabled the number of hungry people in the world to decline even as the population of the world was tripling.

In 1968, Dr. Paul Ehrlich wrote *The Population Bomb*, which predicted wars and other devastation over the fight for food to feed an ever-increasing population. The book speculated that we might not even make it to the twenty-first century. Dr. Ehrlich's work has been discredited because of the work of Dr. Borlaug and others. The Green Revolution is an example of how the human race rises to meet challenges when they must be met. If obesity is our major health problem, there isn't a person from the past who wouldn't exchange obesity for the major health problem of his/her own era: pneumonia, typhus, smallpox, tuberculosis, polio, cholera, diarrhea, bronchitis, influenza, malnutrition - the list of candidates was quite long. Most of these killers aren't even on our radar screen anymore.

There is one factor that determines the economic success or failure of a people more than anything else, and it is a factor we don't often consider. The single greatest determinant of economic success is the type of government a society establishes.

One need only look at the difference between North and South Korea or the difference between East and West Germany before reunification to see that places that initially differ only in their form of government can end up with very different economic conditions. These differences are evident even within a single country. China has become an economic power because its government, while still very controlling, has scrapped the old communist model for a more free market approach to growth.

Free countries are rich countries. In 1950, only about 43% of the world's population lived in democracies. Today that figure is approaching 70%, despite the fact that population growth is still highest in countries that are not democracies. The Middle East, one of the last bastions of totalitarianism, is currently undergoing enlightenment by the people that they will continue to fall behind if they allow these dictators and monarchs to remain in power. They are using democracies as inspiration for their demands for change. Such reforms can rarely be imposed from the outside, but they can be very successful if they are produced by the citizenry of a nation.

Democracy has spread to many nations; it has also spread more evenly within nations. We have been a democracy for nearly a quarter of a millennium, but only in the last half-century have many of our citizens become more fully enfranchised. In less than a lifetime, African-Americans, women, gays, and many other groups who were previously denied a full share of the American dream are now part of the mainstream. This progress required the majority of Americans to think differently than their parents and grandparents thought.

As much as any generation before, Americans today want to do what is right, even if it isn't easy.

The furor over global warming has obscured an important fact - the environment is in better shape today than it has been since the early days of the Industrial Revolution. There will be challenges going forward as more of the world enjoys more material prosperity, but the environment has never been as protected as it is today.

The automobile of today emits less than 5% of the pollutants of its 1970 counterpart. That figure will continue to improve as hybrids and electric cars become more common. Fuel economy has vastly improved, even as engines have become more powerful. Cars are safer than ever before. Even though the total miles driven have more than tripled since 1950, the number of annual auto fatalities in the U.S. is lower today. We go farther, faster, on less fuel, and with less pollution than ever before.

If electric power were the great invention that enabled the growth of the twentieth century, the microchip is the great invention for the twenty-first century. The microchip and the powerful computers it has spawned will change the way we live more than any invention since the wheel. We have only begun to scratch the surface of what we can do with this still-young technology. Most of the solutions to the problems we face today will involve computer technology in some way. The existence of the microchip and the solutions it can provide also means that we will be able to solve more of our problems in the future than we ever could in the past. It is no longer a question of if we can solve our biggest problems; it is only a question of when.

The average American household annually donates

about five percent of its income to charities. While this percentage has held fairly steady over time, it can be somewhat deceptive. Over the years, the percentage of tax revenues that are allocated to help the disadvantaged has increased significantly. As a result, the average American family today gives more to help others than previous generations did. Despite the fact that much of that giving is non-discretionary in the form of taxes, discretionary giving has held steady as a percentage of income. Instantaneous communication has also enabled the population as a whole to be more informed about people in need, as well as being able to contribute immediately through online giving and electronic transfers.

We operate in a closed system. When I say "we," I am referring to Planet Earth. A closed system means there is nothing that comes from, or goes to, anything outside the system. Because we operate in a closed system, we are responsible for everything that happens within that system. If we damage the environment, we can't blame anyone but ourselves. If we declare war on each other, we can't blame anyone but ourselves. If we spend ourselves into financial ruin, we can't blame anyone but ourselves.

Many of the illustrious figures I've quoted in this book would disparage us for our alleged financial malfeasance. Much of their criticism would be justified. Never in history has a population had such abundance, and yet were willing to risk destroying the financial system that made this abundance possible, merely to have more sooner, rather than later.

Some of these illustrious figures would recognize that we are as human today as they and their peers were. We suffer the same temptations, weaknesses, and stupidity that have plagued mankind since our inception. They might lament our lack of progress, but they would understand that, if their peers were placed in our position, they would have probably gotten into the same predicaments.

I believe that virtually all of these great minds would reserve final judgment to see how we address the problems we have made for ourselves. They would be most impressed if we can recognize our folly for what it is and take steps to change before we create a full-blown crisis. They would be significantly less impressed if it took a full-blown crisis of our own making to galvanize us into actions that would have been less painful if we had been more proactive and less reactive.

Finally, I believe that every one of these founts of financial wisdom would justifiably condemn us, should we neglect our responsibilities to ourselves and our posterity and allow our financial recklessness to destroy a system that created wealth that they could have never imagined. If we choose such a course of action, "swine" is too good a word for us.

INDEX OF QUOTATIONS
(Add 214 to page number in this edition)

6,000,000 MINUTES ON THE CLOCK

WORKING FOR MEANS AND MEANING

Mark DiGiovanni

To Beth

For Mara

TABLE OF CONTENTS

FIRST OF ALL - WHY?

Why Do You Need This?

Let's do the math first. In America, according to a Gallup poll in 2014, the average work day is 9 hours and 20 minutes, or 560 minutes. According to the U.S. Census Bureau, the average round-trip commute to work is 51 minutes. The average American works 240 days a year. So far, that's (560 + 51) x 240 = 146,640 minutes per year devoted to work.

Most people get on the clock right after high school. It doesn't matter whether you get a job or go to college; it's still work. College merely delays the financial benefit of the work. So, you begin this odyssey around age 18. How long you have to work is a function of several variables, which include your ability to save money and live below your means, your preference between security and opportunity, and your life expectancy and lifestyle after retirement. Since the life expectancy of an 18 year-old today is about 75 *additional* years, and since even good savers can expect to work 2 years to afford 1 year in retirement, it is reasonable to expect to spend *50 years* in the workforce. Multiply the 146,640 minutes per year by 50 years and you get 7,332,000 minutes. Even if your workday, including commute, were only 8 hours per day, at the end of 50 years you would have racked up 5,760,000 minutes. Close enough.

The staggering amount of time Americans spend at work (we lead all developed nations in this category) is reason enough to read this book. Even a minor improvement on such a large investment can pay huge dividends, emotionally and financially.

A great deal of our self-worth is connected to the work we do. We aspire to jobs that not only pay well, but that also earn the admiration (even envy) of others and that might even make us famous.

When you meet someone for the first time, one of the very first questions you're asked is what you do for a living. Even the phrasing of the question is interesting. They don't ask what you do to earn money; they ask what you do for a living. You are what you do, or so it is assumed. You may place other roles such as spouse, parent, or American above your role at work, but that last role is the one that most identifies you in the eyes of others.

When something contributes so much to your identity and self-concept, it is very important that you find a good fit for who you are and who you want to be. Your job can pay psychological as well as financial benefits. Your job can also exact a huge psychological toll if it's the wrong job for you. At the very least, you don't want to spend half a century, when asked what you do for a living, responding with something like "I'm a claims adjuster (but I really wanted to be an astrophysicist)."

Half of the money earned in most private sector fields is earned by the top 10% in that field. This is something financial advisors, realtors, and brain surgeons have in common with NFL quarterbacks. In terms of earnings, the top 10% in many fields earn as much as the remaining 90%. The free market pays for performance, and the free market says that the top 10% accomplish as much as the other 90%.

That's the private sector. Jobs in the public sector and jobs where compensation is determined separately from one's productivity (such as union jobs) do not have as strong a correlation between pay and performance. As a result, those with the most talent and ambition have historically gravitated to the private sector. Such people do not worry about having a floor of income; they just don't want a ceiling on their income.

Money is how the world tells you how much they value the work you do. When one job pays more than another, the implication is that the higher paying job is more valued by the world; therefore, the person who performs it is more valued. Being paid more is rewarding in that you have greater buying power. More pay gives our egos a boost, and it increases our status in the eyes of others.

The discrepancies in incomes in various occupations can often seem ridiculous. On its face, it is hard to defend a quarterback making $10,000,000 a year, while a special education teacher makes $40,000. The teacher's work is critical; the quarterback merely provides entertainment. The reason the quarterback makes so much more is that, while he provides a discretionary service in the form of entertainment, he provides it to millions of fans. The teacher provides a critical service, but only to a very few. **If making large sums of money is your goal, it is better to make a few dollars from the masses than to try to get large sums from a few.**

No matter how much you love your work, you would be unlikely to continue doing it if you weren't paid. More money is the major motivator in most job changes. It may be difficult to compare job-related factors like satisfaction or stress, but you always know which job pays more.

For better or worse, most of our contact points with the outside world are through money. Our work and the pay we receive for doing it are just the most obvious example. Because money is easy to measure, people often assume that a move to a higher-paying job is always the right thing to do. Everything else being the same, that logic would be correct. However, there are many other factors to consider that have nothing to do with money. When people choose or change jobs or careers based on the pay alone, they are very likely to regret the change down the road.

The right career is one where you go to work every day and think, "I would want to do this work *even if* they didn't pay me." The wrong career is one where you go to work every day and think, "I don't want to do this work *despite* the fact that they pay me."

To sum it up, here's why you need this book:

- You're likely to spend more hours at work than at any other waking activity in your life. It's a big investment.
- Your work will define you to the outside world more than anything else you do. It may also be the main way you define yourself. For better or worse, you are what you do.
- Money is the most indispensable tool in co-existing with the outside world, and for almost all of us, our only source of money is our work. You want to get the maximum return on your investment.

Why Does an Organization Exist?

The mission statement of any organization should state clearly and succinctly why that organization exists. An organization that doesn't have a mission statement may not know why it exists. An organization that has the kind of mission statement includes nonsense like "increase shareholder value" doesn't know why they exist, either.

The goal of an organization should not be to do business with anyone who simply wants what you have. It should be to focus on the people who believe what you believe. When we are selective about doing business only with those people who believe in our WHY, trust emerges. My clients tell me that trust is the single most important factor in our relationship. They can't trust me unless they have a clear understanding of why I do what I do. They don't buy what I do – they buy why I do it.

In your relationship with any employer, you should clearly understand:
- **Why that organization exists**
- **Why they want you to be part of that organization**
- **Why you want to be part of that organization**
- **How you can help the organization fulfill its mission**

Whysdom for You

Think back to your own experiences as a student. The most boring and uninspiring classes you took were probably ones that only asked "who?", "what?", "when?", and "where?" questions. You memorized data, regurgitated it back to the teacher, and were rewarded or punished based on your ability to perform that task.

431

Even if you were good at that task, you probably received little intrinsic reward for what you had memorized.

The most inspiring, mind-altering classes you took probably asked a very different question - "why?" The difference between the first group of questions and the second is the difference between the left and right brain. The left brain is the analytical, computer-like part of the brain. The right brain is where our curiosity, our creativity, even our humanity reside. Asking "why?" engages the right brain. Asking "why?" lights a fire. Those other questions are merely filling buckets.

When you understand why you need to know something, the who-what-when-where questions become interesting to answer, which means the answers also become easier to retain. If students in a history class can learn why a war was fought several centuries ago, they are much more likely to remember who the combatants were, where the war was fought, and when it took place. And if they don't first learn why a war was fought, what's the point of even learning the other facts?

Don't just seek wisdom; **seek WHYSDOM – becoming wise by asking why.** Millennials are naturally good at this. Knowing why you are doing something is essential if you are to keep doing it when obstacles get in the way. A good boss should be able to tell you why your job is important or why a particular task needs to be performed in a particular manner. A good boss is not one who responds to a why question with "Because I said so!" As long as you are not acting like an over-inquisitive child, you should not be treated like one.

HOW DID WE GET HERE?

Imagine living in a society where two-thirds of the adult population must work full-time in an effort to keep a killer under control. Because of the tremendous manpower (and womanpower) needed to fight this killer, progress in a multitude of areas, from science to civics, is stymied. Yet, despite the back-breaking efforts of millions, this killer succeeds hundreds, even thousands of times each year.

Better Things to Do

In 1840, when steam engines, trains, and the whole Industrial Revolution were heating up, 70% of the American workforce was engaged in agriculture to feed our population of 17,000,000. There were over 6,000,000 farmers. Even at that ratio, malnutrition was common, and starvation was not unknown. Even when adequate food supplies could be raised, preserving and transporting it to the people in cities were logistical nightmares.

Today, barely 2% of the workforce is in agriculture, which comes to about 2,000,000 farmers. Yet, they feed our nation's population of over 300,000,000, with plenty left over to export to other countries.

Food production has become so efficient that a single farmer today produces enough food for 150 people, compared to just 3 people in 1840. The cost of food, as a percentage of income, is the lowest in the history of the world. As a result, much of the world has stopped worrying about starvation and started worrying about obesity. Some may say we've gone from being killed

433

from too little food to killing ourselves from too much food.

Agriculture is an example of the one constant in the ever-changing world of work - tasks continue to be done more and more efficiently. This constancy is to be expected. **In the ever-changing world of work, two aspects never change - knowledge is cumulative, and competition is relentless.** If we don't use what we already know to learn more and to become more productive and efficient, we will lose out to our competitors.

Many people look at the changes in agriculture and see only the loss of jobs and the breakup of the family farm. While such change may be sad, if agriculture were as efficient today as it was in 1840, we would need 100,000,000 more farmers than we have. Those 100,000,000 would not be available to work in other areas like:

- Finding a cure for AIDS
- Developing a pollution-free automobile
- Building a new hospital
- Taking care of elderly in a nursing home
- Creating software
- Writing books
- Teaching preschoolers

…and thousands of other jobs, all of which improve our quality of life and also create new and better jobs for a growing population. Also, if all those jobs in agriculture still existed, food would be so expensive, few of life's luxuries would be affordable, and many of what we consider to be necessities would be unaffordable, too.

They Wanted It More

General Motors in the 1950's was almost broken up by the federal government because they had over two-thirds of the U.S. auto market; they were being called a monopoly. Today their market share is closer to 20%, and they are a little more than a shell of their former self.

Until the 1970's, the Japanese automakers' share of the U.S. market was very small, less than 5%. The American automakers did not see them as a threat. The Japanese made small cars that were not as profitable as the big cars Americans had been buying for years.

Then in 1973 came the Yom Kippur war between Israel and its Arab neighbors. Gas prices doubled almost overnight, and there were shortages and long lines at the gas pumps. People started looking for alternatives to the gas hogs they currently owned.

Nineteen-seventy-three was also the first year for a new car, the Honda Civic. What Americans discovered when they test drove a Honda or Nissan or Toyota was that, in addition to being fuel-efficient, these cars were well-made and vastly superior to their American competitors, like the Ford Pinto, Chevrolet Vega, and AMC Gremlin. A trend toward foreign cars began that continues to this day.

Back then, the American automakers had a virtual monopoly on the American market. Their only competition was among themselves, and none of them were going to make a great effort to increase market share as long as profits for all of them were good.

The Japanese automakers forced a change in the auto business. They were hungry for a share of the U.S. market, and they were willing to offer a better car at a lower price to get it. To succeed, the Japanese carmakers

435

had to get their employees to think harder and to work harder.

For the U.S. automakers, it was time to discard old habits. Complacency was dead. Competition now came from all over the world. Workers and management now had to cooperate with each other, not confront each other. They had to start making better cars, more fuel-efficient cars, and they had to produce these more efficient cars more efficiently. Everyone's job was on the line. It was hang together, or hang separately.

Copyright 2003 by Randy Glasbergen.
www.glasbergen.com

GLASBERGEN

"We found someone overseas who can drink coffee and talk about sports all day for a fraction of what we're paying you."

Job security became less a function of how big your employer was and more a function of how well you did your job. Costs were constantly being cut to remain competitive. Greater productivity from everyone was required. The unproductive employee (deadwood) was no longer tolerated. As would happen with almost every other sector of American business, employment with a large corporation no longer meant lifetime job security.

To fully understand the potential consequences of underestimating a competitor and believing that the status quo is good enough, one need only look at the once-great city of Detroit today.

Hit Any Key to Continue

The typical desktop computer of today has more computing power than existed in the entire world in 1950.

In 1971, I took a graphic arts class. One of the first required projects required using a platen printing press. This process involves arranging individual metal letters and spaces backwards to print something. The process was slow and painstaking, and the quality of the product was inconsistent. The platen printing process was still in use in 1971, essentially unchanged from the time Johannes Gutenberg invented it around over 500 years earlier.

Barely four decades later, this book is being written on a PC. I can choose between hundreds of fonts and sizes; spacing is automatic; I can add graphics, and I can print everything out in full color. Within a week of completing the final proof-reading, hard copies and electronic versions of the finished product will be available online to almost everyone around the world.

The equipment that enables me to accomplish this feat costs about 9 days' wages for the average worker. The book retails for about 2 hours' wages for the lowest-paid worker in the nation. When they were published in 1455, Gutenberg's Bibles sold for the equivalent of 3 years' wages for the average worker. They were still only a fraction of the cost of the hand-printed Bibles that preceded them, which could take 20 years to complete.

The technology on your lap or in your pocket is amazing, especially compared to what existed barely two decades ago. It's exciting to think how much more this technology will advance in the next twenty years. It's also a little scary.

The learning never ends. There will always be new discoveries, new inventions, and new technologies. If you are going to be gainfully employed in the future, you will have to learn about these new creations, and learn how to use them to be better at what you do for a living. For those of you unwilling to even learn how to program your DVR, here is your wake-up call.

Anyone who thinks education ends with a diploma or a degree is grossly misinformed. **A college degree tells a potential employer that you are trainable on a higher level.** You should not assume that your degree has taught you all you need to know to perform a job properly. Your new employer certainly understands this. They will prove it to you starting on day one of your employment. Once you earn your degree and enter the workforce, your *real* education can now begin.

It Worked for Darwin

Every job is in one of four phases:
1. Creation
2. Evolution
3. Reduction
4. Extinction

Let's start with jobs that already exist.

Most jobs will continue but will be constantly evolving. People won't gravitate to jobs that are being reduced or are becoming extinct. They will seek the ones that seem to have a future. Competition will be strong for the better positions. **One of your greatest assets in an evolving job will be your ability to learn and adapt quickly.**

There are likely to be two divergent trends in job evolution. The first will involve the breaking up of jobs into smaller and smaller tasks. The tasks will be assigned to the lowest cost producer. In the future, a job of today could have part of it done by a computer and part of it done by an Indonesian. The tasks that will stay are the ones that are done most efficiently by the person currently doing it. All tasks will be constantly reviewed to see if they are being done as efficiently as possible.

At the same time, many new jobs will be created that coordinate many tasks. The people doing these jobs won't *perform* many tasks; their job will be to *coordinate* many tasks.

For example, in the past, people have used a stockbroker, an insurance agent, an accountant, an attorney and others to plan and protect their financial future. There was rarely any coordination among these people. They often worked at cross purposes, to the detriment of the client. The Certified Financial Planner developed to fill a need to oversee and coordinate these functions.

The more complicated systems become, individuals who see the bigger picture and bring the pieces together to run more smoothly will be in demand. They will have the jobs of power, prestige, and pay in the future.

Many jobs will continue, but with a reduced number of workers doing them. An example would be TV repair. As long as we have TVs, there will always be some need for people to fix them. More often, people will replace, rather than repair a TV.

A job being reduced still evolves for the people still doing it. TVs continue to evolve; so will the job of the TV repair people, even while there are fewer of them. Jobs in this category can be doubly stressful – you have the pressure of upgrading your skills and becoming more efficient, while at the same time wondering if you will survive the next big shakeout.

Jobs will become extinct for one of two reasons:

- There's no market for the goods or services produced, or
- A machine is more efficient at producing it.

Some jobs get totally eliminated by newer technologies. Eastman Kodak, which once employed nearly 150,000, now employs less than 20,000. The development of digital imaging virtually killed the film business, Kodak's bread and butter for over a century. In 1979, General Motors employed 680,000 people in North America. They produced 6.4 million vehicles, an average of 9.4 per employee. In 2009, General Motors filed for bankruptcy protection. During that year, their 112,000 North American employees produced 3.3 million vehicles, an average of 29.5 per employee. Kodak's workforce shrunk by 85% because there was no longer a market for their biggest product, film. GM's workforce shrunk by a similar percentage, partly because sales declined by nearly half. However, over 250,000 GM jobs vanished because robots and computers enabled vehicles to be built by fewer people. Over the last three decades, machines have replaced a quarter-million humans at GM's North American plants alone.

The following is a direct copy from a web site home page, www.thefutureofwork.net :

Future of Work is an active global community of

organizations and individuals who believe in the power and importance of collective intelligence in creating the future. Our focus is on the changing nature of work, the workforce, the workplace, and management practice. We help organizations **reduce their cost of operations and workforce support by 30% or more** while creating work environments that attract and retain the best and brightest talent - by providing strategic guidance, change readiness assessments, executive learning, and program management. (The emphasis in the above paragraph is theirs, not mine.)

To know what jobs will exist in the future requires imaginative thinking. As you look at any current job and wonder what future there is in it, ask yourself:

- How can this job be done more efficiently?
- Can someone in another country do this job as well and cheaper than it is currently being done?
- Can technology, especially new technology, come along and change or eliminate this job?
- Is the type of business the job is part of growing, changing, or dying?

What requires more imagination is to look at where we are now and figure out how a situation can be made better. A basic axiom of economics is "Find a need and fill it." With so many of our needs already filled, that axiom could be expanded to include "Find a want and fill it." Wants fulfilled have a habit of becoming needs, which improves job security. Columnist George Will says that Americans define a need as a 48-hour old want, so there is security in finding wants and filling them.

Basic necessities like food, clothing, and shelter are not likely to provide many new jobs, even if the population increases. Those jobs will become more efficient at the same time. New jobs in older industries are likely to center on improving efficiencies. Those jobs will focus on reducing the number of workers in that industry.

Fortunately for job growth, new inventions become new necessities. Examples include automobiles, television, the internet, microwaves, and cell phones. Five generations ago, the automobile didn't exist. Three generations ago, television didn't exist. Microwaves, cell phones, and the internet are all less than forty years old. They are as necessary to our daily routine as the automobile, the electric light, or the toilet.

What Have You Got for Me?

What you can offer the world comes down to three categories: your physical skills, your left-brain skills, and your right-brain skills.

Your physical skills may be highly developed, or very basic. Some examples of high-skills jobs would be those of a professional athlete or musician. If you are born with a certain physical ability and if you develop it and it is marketable, you can make a living. The professional athlete or musician is well paid because of a rare, highly developed skill that can be mass-marketed to a large audience. The ability to make money with a highly developed skill is one of the main reasons people will spend years developing that skill, with no guarantee of a financial payoff for the sacrifice. The potential payoff is one reason you see so many young men working for a chance to play in the NFL. The lack of a potential payoff is one reason you see so few young men working to become a great mime.

Basic Physical Skills (BPS) jobs may be along the lines of framing a house or cooking a meal. The level of

pay depends on:
- the number of people who can and will do the same work (the competition)
- the number of people who will pay for the service
- the amount they are willing to pay (the market).

Since BPS jobs can be done by a large number of people, the pay scale never gets too high. The skills required to do the job are basic, so there are few barriers to entry. As the pay rises for a particular job, more people start to do it. Many of these jobs get filled by new immigrants to the U.S. and increasingly by people in other countries, if the job can be moved overseas. People gravitate to the highest paying job for which they are qualified. The job gravitates to whoever can adequately do the job for the lowest wage. These two factors, taken together, keep any basic skills job from becoming a high-paying job.

In addition to competition from other people, someone in a BPS job faces competition from machines. The Japanese automakers got a jump on their American counterparts in the 1970's and 80's by automating much of the assembly process. The robots replaced human labor and were more reliable and less expensive. The quarter-million jobs that General Motors shed over the last thirty years were due to the ability of machines to perform the same tasks as the workers; only to do it better, faster, and cheaper.

Some jobs aren't eliminated, but are changed by automation. The job of the house framer (the one who puts up the 2 by 4 and plywood framing of a house) was transformed by the invention of the air-powered nail gun. Not only could one person now do the work faster and better, he no longer needed as much strength to do it. Fewer framers were needed, and the pool of potential framers was increased because the physical requirements were relaxed.

Your left brain is the logical, analytical part. It consumes and analyzes data, much like a computer. Unfortunately, as computers improve, more and more of our left brain functions can be done by computers. It's almost impossible now for even the best chess players to beat a computer at chess. Supercomputers can analyze 200,000,000 positions per second. Even a chess app for a mobile phone can analyze 20,000 positions per second. How can a human brain compete with that?

Jobs utilizing left brain skills generally have better working conditions and pay more than BPS jobs. They are also at risk of being eliminated. These are usually good paying jobs. There is incentive for employers to eliminate unnecessary workers to reduce costs.

For example, eliminating a framer's job paying $10 per hour saves an employer $20,000 a year in wages. If more is spent in a year on a substitute, money is lost. The employer is better off keeping the framer at $10 per hour.

A different employer has a data analyst on the payroll at $50,000 a year. That employer could spend up to $50,000 a year to replace the data analyst through automation and come out ahead. The automated replacement can also work 24/7/365, doesn't need health insurance, and won't gossip about the boss behind his/her back. The higher the salary, the more motivated the employer is to find a substitute. High union wages at General Motors were a great incentive to replace workers with robots whenever possible.

In addition to automation, left brain jobs are vulnerable to outsourcing. Left brain jobs involve data.

Data can be transported instantly from anywhere to anywhere. There aren't physical limitations to where the work can be done. If a data analyst in India can do the job of a data analyst in Indiana for half the wage, that job is likely to end up in India.

Left brain skills are a prerequisite for most future jobs. You will have to prove you can perform certain functions just to gain entry to most jobs. You will most frequently demonstrate this ability with a piece of paper - a college degree being the most common requirement.

It is important to understand what the college degree tells a potential employer. With few exceptions, it does not tell any potential employer that you have the training to tackle that new job right away. **Your college degree tells a potential employer that:**

- **You are willing to delay gratification for a more worthwhile long-term goal.**
- **You are willing to jump through many hoops on command to reach your goals.**
- **You have the basic intelligence and skills to be trained at the higher level the employer needs you to reach to become a true asset to the organization.**

Your left brain probably did most of the work that got you the job. Once ensconced in that job however, you better get your right brain working if you want to keep it.

The right brain performs all the functions that make humans unique and irreplaceable. It is the emotional side – love, hope, faith, and fear all dwell there. From the right side come perception, intuition, creativity, concepts, hunches, fantasies, humor, curiosity, analogies, and relationships. **The jobs that can't be eliminated are the jobs that utilize the unique talents of the right brain.** The jobs that utilize the right brain can't be eliminated because, at this time, there is nothing on earth that can replicate what the right brain of a human being does.

The irreplaceable jobs not only utilize the right brain, they are also a product of the right brain. Utilizing your right brain in your current job makes you that much more likely to create your own next job. It takes someone with imagination (a product of the right brain) to think outside the box and come up with a new way to use one's skills. Your dream job may exist right now, but in no place but your right brain. It's up to you to extract it.

Love It or Leave It

The single most important feature of your next (and every future) job is that you love it. Nothing stimulates the right brain like doing something you love to do, something for which you have a passion. There is a direct correlation between doing what you love and gaining economic advantage. It's hard to be good at something to which you're indifferent. In addition, if you're not good at your job, it won't be your job for long. As Albert Schweitzer, winner of the Nobel Prize said, "Success does not lead to happiness; happiness leads to success." If you find something you love to do, you will be happy. If you are happy, you are much more likely to be successful in that work.

Some younger people may be feeling pressured by others (parents, advisors, other well-meaning adults) to go into a particular career field. Their reasons might include some of the following:
- It's a growing field in the future.
- There's job security.

- You can make a nice living.
- It's a prestigious career.
- It's a lot better than what *you're* thinking of doing!

All of these claims may be valid. They can be plusses in choosing a career, but they ignore the most important ingredients – a talent and a passion for your chosen line of work. Later, we'll look at determining your areas of talent. Let's talk about your passions now.

Passion is a right brain function. Your love of what you do is right brain – the talent to perform it is left brain and/or physical in origin. It's thought-provoking that you can find accountants and lawyers writing novels and painting pictures in their spare time, but you rarely find an artist working on a tax return or brushing up on the penal code for fun. No six-year-old boy in the history of the planet, when asked what he wanted to be when he grew up, replied "Insurance Underwriter".

Passion means you love doing your job so much that the pay you get is like icing on the cake. Your passion is your cause – the money is just the effect. Mondays don't scare you; you might actually look forward to them.

Passion means you willingly put up with all the downsides to a particular job in order to work in that field. A passionate veterinarian accepts that getting bitten, scratched, kicked, and urinated on by patients comes with the turf.

Find what you are passionate about and make it your life's work. There is no more important prerequisite to success. Speaking on behalf of the world, we don't need any more ambivalent attorneys who are only doing it to make their mothers happy.

Free Agents All

This section is dedicated to Curt Flood. He's the reason you can't invest too much emotionally in your favorite sports team any more. He's the reason you can't invest too much emotionally (or anything else) in your employer any more. Maybe that's dumping too much on Curt. Some background is in order here.

Curtis Charles Flood was a baseball player – a good one. He was a three-time All-Star and won the Gold Glove seven straight times (1963-69). He hit over .300 six times in his fifteen-year major league career. From 1964 through 1968, his St. Louis Cardinals won two World Series championships in three appearances.

At the end of the 1969 season, the Cardinals attempted to trade Flood to the Philadelphia Phillies. At that time, baseball had the Reserve Clause. It bound a player in perpetuity to the club who owned his contract.

Flood objected to the restrictions on offering his services to others. He challenged the legality of the Reserve Clause. The case made it to the U.S. Supreme Court, which ruled against Flood in 1972. Though he lost the case, Curt Flood's lawsuit was a catalyst for change. By 1975, free agency was becoming the standard in baseball, and eventually in other sports.

Flood Brings Sea Change

Curt Flood's pioneering of free agency in

professional sports carried over into the corporate world in the coming years. There was one major difference, though. In professional sports, the free agency was initiated by the employees. A competitive bidding process for their services would increase their salaries. In 1975, the average major league baseball salary was $45,000. In 2015, the average salary was over $4,000,000. It worked.

In the corporate world, free agency was initiated by employers as a way to reduce staff and payrolls. After employers started moving away from the concept of lifelong employment, employees started to test the waters to see what they were worth on the open market.

The changes initiated by Curt Flood reverberate in the workplace today. Even employment in a stable Fortune 500 company is no guarantee of a job for life. While such changes may create more stress for the average employee, it has also created opportunity. With the mindset of a free agent and with tools like the internet, anyone can regularly check out other opportunities in the job market. You no longer just assume there is or isn't something better out there. You have the ability to know for sure. If there is something better, you can go after it. If there isn't, you stay put, content in the knowledge that you are in the best place to be for the present.

In many countries in Europe, labor contracts and other regulations limit an employer's ability to discharge unneeded workers. By handcuffing an employer's ability to fire, it also has the effect of handcuffing their ability to hire. Employers don't want to hire someone if they can't fire them if the situation requires it. They make do with whoever is already on the payroll. Unfortunately, productivity suffers, and they lose the ability to compete.

With companies not hiring, employees are unable to take advantage of one of the great benefits of free agency - rising wages as a result of open bidding for them. Such restrictions help explain why unemployment rates in many countries in Europe run two to three times the unemployment rate in the U.S.

In the U.S., the increased ability and willingness of employers and employees to seek their most efficient use is one reason the U.S. economy has remained strong. Even during down cycles, the U.S. economy has suffered less than most of Europe.

Free agency has led people into their most productive occupations. It has enabled employers to adjust payroll to reflect their competitive situation. Free agency has enabled the U.S. to lead the developed nations in economic growth and productivity. Even during periods of recession, the ability to adjust employment levels quickly enables employers to respond to conditions. They can keep the company solvent and quickly rehire people when the situation improves. This flexibility will help us remain competitive with developing nations like China and India, who will compete more and more for the higher-paying jobs in the global economy.

Destigmatized

For the generation that grew up in the Great Depression and won World War II, employment was a very different animal than it is today. There was less individuality and more *esprit de corps* then. This was due in no small part to the historic events these people had experienced.

When 25% of the population was out of work, as was the case during the depths of the Great Depression, you took a job, said thank you, kept your mouth shut, kept your shoulder to the wheel, and forgot about self-fulfillment. If your stomach was full, you were better off than most. If you felt like complaining, there were 20 guys waiting to take your place.

World War II required a team thinking we hadn't needed before and haven't seen since. The millions serving in the military certainly had it. They couldn't defeat two powerful enemies on two different fronts unless they put the needs of the country ahead of their own. Those on the home front made sacrifices as well. There was rationing of almost everything. The entire economy was skewed to produce war materiel. There were wage and price freezes in effect, plus many other limitations that would not be tolerated in peacetime.

When this generation went to work after the war, they carried those values and habits into the workplace. They tended to dress alike. They were disciplined. They put the good of the company above their own self-interest. And they stayed loyal to their employer. Leaving one job for another was not a common practice. A person needed a compelling reason (more compelling than a modest raise) to leave a company. Frequent job hoppers were looked at like someone with a disfiguring social disease.

They put in their time, worked their way up the corporate ladder, and retired with a nice pension. Pension is something some of you under 30 may not know. Back in the old days, there were no 401(k) plans. In exchange for years of loyal service, your employer would provide a lifetime of financial support for you and your spouse upon your retirement. It was known as a pension. You couldn't outlive it. It didn't fluctuate with the stock market. In exchange for the best years of your life (25 years was usually the minimum service time to earn one of these pensions), your employer promised an income for you and your spouse for the rest of your lives.

The immobility of the pension also tended to make the worker immobile, too. After a decade or two with an employer, workers would question the wisdom of tossing away a nice retirement income to start again somewhere else. Few situations could justify such a move from a financial standpoint.

Long-time employees were comfortably nestled in their jobs. They would mark time until they hit their magic number, collected their gold watches, and headed off for unlimited fishing. Their productivity might sag in those last years as they set it on cruise control. But an employer was unlikely to fire a long-timer without substantial cause.

The children of these loyalists were the Baby Boomers. They took a different approach. They grew up in an age of affluence and economic security. Because they had never known economic insecurity, they didn't place as high a value on such security as their parents. Baby boomers sought opportunity more than security when they entered the workforce.

When opportunity knocks, you answer. Baby boomers changed jobs, even careers, more than any previous generation had. Part of this practice was a response to the increasing speed of change in the workplace. In addition to sweeping changes brought on by technology, there were also legislated changes such as new anti-discrimination policies. There was also an entry of women into the workplace on an unprecedented scale in history.

At the same time, the corporate perspective of employees was changing. As the economy struggled in the late 1970's and early 80's, companies had to reassess the old notion of lifetime employment. Technology was rendering many jobs obsolete. Competition from outside the U.S. was growing. Pressure from stockholders to improve the bottom line was intense.

Layoffs were becoming commonplace. And it wasn't just the last-hired-first-fired routine. Companies were looking at productivity as the main measure of who got to stay and who had to go. With every round of layoffs, the survivors got more nervous. All the old rules of the workplace seemed to be falling away.

Internal Revenue Code Section 401(k) was introduced by the Revenue Act of 1978. The basics of a 401(k) retirement plan are:

- The employee makes contributions to the plan, which are tax deductible.
- The employer typically matches employee contributions in some ratio.
- The contributions can be invested in stocks, bonds, and mutual funds that provide long-term growth.
- No income tax is due until money comes out of the 401(k).
- The cost is less for the employer, compared to a traditional pension plan.
- The employee can take the money in the 401(k) plan with him/her upon departure from that employer.

Read those last two items again. *The cost is less for the employer.* How long do you think it took for practically every company in America to establish a 401(k) plan for its employees? Corporations hate traditional pension plans because they can't get a good handle on what the cost will be to fund them. Just when the number-crunchers think they have the average life-expectancy and cost-of-living increase numbers figured out, there's a spike in inflation or some medical breakthrough increases life spans and throws all their calculations out the window. With a 401(k) plan, the employer can gauge how much they will have to contribute each year, based on employee contributions. They can even make the employer contributions contingent on corporate profitability; they are not on the hook unless the company makes money.

Such a contingency eases the financial pressure on the company. It also provides an incentive for the employees to keep the old noses to the grindstone. In short, **a traditional pension defines the *benefit* the employer must provide, regardless of the cost. With a 401(k), the *contribution* is defined by the employer.** The cost of the 401(k) is controllable and predictable. The pension isn't, which is why the pension in the private sector is now almost extinct.

The second item is *The employee can take the money in the 401(k) plan with him/her upon departure from that employer.* You are no longer tethered to a company in a dead-end job just because you have so much time invested toward a pension that you can't afford to start over somewhere else.

Everything you put into a 401(k) plan is yours right away. Typically, the company contributions have a vesting schedule. Step-vesting is common. You get to keep 20% more of the company contributions each year until you are completely vested.

When you leave the company, you can roll over the proceeds from the 401(k) plan into an IRA. There it will keep doing the same thing it was doing before – growing the funds you will need for retirement. In the meantime, you get yourself enrolled in the 401(k) plan at your new job and keep the ball rolling.

Today, someone with decades of service at one company is often viewed in the same manner as the job hopper of fifty years ago. Unless they are in the upper echelons of corporate management, the unspoken question seems to be, "What's wrong with that person?"

There's probably nothing wrong with that person. The corporate world needs both types. It needs the long-timers. They provide stability and a sense of corporate culture to all the new, wet-behind-the-ears types. The corporate world also needs the free agents. They need those who are willing to consider making a change under the right circumstances. Those people make a company keep its compensation and work environment up to date and enticing to current and potential employees. The one thing no one needs is a hummingbird.

There's no one less enticing to an employer than someone who is constantly flitting from one job to another. When someone has a pattern of changing jobs like the changing of the seasons, the problem lies with that person, not the mosaic of former employers. If you've had ten different employers in the last five years, the one common factor in all ten cases is you.

Once the pattern is established, the only organizations who hire hummingbirds are the desperate ones. Desperate organizations are not good places to work, so the hummingbird soon leaves, and the downward spiral continues.

Freedom Isn't Free

There is one big difference between professional athletes and the rest of us when it comes to putting ourselves on the open market. It's called a guaranteed contract.

455

Part of the negotiation for an athlete, in addition to salary, is the length of the contract. The older the athlete, the less they worry about opportunities and the more they worry about security. (Come to think of it, we all tend to be that way.) The athlete wants to know that if he is injured, or just can't perform at peak level any more, he will still draw a nice paycheck.

The Average Joe gets no such arrangement. Teachers typically sign a one-year contract, but that is done primarily to lock the teacher into a school system, not to guarantee a paycheck despite performance. It's hard to have any leverage when you're an Average Joe.

Increased freedom to move around to find your best place is mostly a good thing. You have a better chance of working in a field for which you have a passion. You have a better chance of getting paid more than if there weren't such freedom of movement. People respect your time more when you're a free agent because they can't control you. You can self-define success. You aren't stigmatized if you change jobs, as long as you don't become a hummingbird. But there's a price to be paid for such opportunity. You are at the mercy of the market. When the economy starts to sputter, you can feel like you're in a rowboat in the middle of the ocean in a hurricane.

Even if the general economy is OK, if your employer is struggling, the first thing they will look to do is "trim the fat." Very often lean muscle is trimmed from the payroll as well. It doesn't much matter which you are if you've been trimmed. You still have to go find another job.

Sometimes the economy is good, your company is doing fine, but they keep pushing the employees harder anyway. While it has become easier for an employee to leave for other opportunities, it has also become easier for employers to dismiss workers. They typically have to show just cause, but that interpretation is fairly liberal most times. It's to be expected that an employer will try to wring as much productivity out of employees as possible. You just need to know when it's gone too far and what to do at that point.

The main thing to remember in the era of free agency is **you must constantly prove your worth to your employer, just as they must prove their worth to you.**

WHO DO YOU THINK YOU ARE?

Question: Who is responsible for the Beatles, night baseball, *The Godfather*, and the "crawler" at the bottom of the screen on CNN? Answer: Thomas Edison

Four of Edison's most well-known inventions are the phonograph, the electric light, the movie projector, and the stock ticker. Without those inventions, the above list doesn't happen.

Perhaps more than anyone else in history, Thomas Edison seems the perfect fit for the work he did. He held 1,093 patents on his inventions. He had so many things going on at once, he had to start a company to keep everything running smoothly. We know it as General Electric.

Thomas Edison was known for his work habits. Twenty-hour workdays and hundred-hour workweeks were common. Edison worked an estimated 14,000,000 minutes in his life. (12 hour days; 6 day weeks; 50 weeks/year; 65 years).

Edison famously said, "Genius is 1% inspiration, and 99% perspiration." He recognized the sweat of the brain and the brow were necessary for success.

How could someone work like that for more than sixty years without burning out? Edison loved his work so much he didn't *want* to do anything else. Edison spent the better part of two years creating a practical light bulb. He tested thousands of filaments (over six thousand plant filaments alone) before finding one that would last. It may seem obsessive-compulsive to most of us, but look at the results. Turn on a light first; you'll see better.

Edison is the poster boy for what kind of success is possible when the right person is in the right job. Edison points out in his biography that it isn't hard work that kills someone (he died at 84); it's stress and worry. Few things are more worrisome than wondering if you're wasting your life doing the wrong work.

There are countless ways that people define work. Most of them involve an exchange of time and talent for treasure. For the moment, exclude money from the following definition: work is doing what you *have* to do; play is doing what you *want* to do.

If work is defined as doing what you have to do, then many of the things we have to do qualify as work even though we don't get paid to do them. On the other hand, if we get paid for doing things we want to do, it's like getting paid to play. Given the choice, would you rather be like Edison and spend 14,000,000 minutes of your life getting paid to do things you want to do? Or would you rather spend 6,000,000 minutes doing things you have to do? The second choice is shorter; it only feels longer.

Edison invented many things, but his first and most important invention was his career. Then as now, there were no colleges where one could learn to become an inventor. Edison learned at an early age what he loved to do and what he was good at. One of the reasons he loved what he did was he could see the benefits to mankind that his work produced. He invented a career that enabled him to do what he did best and that gave people many ways to make their lives better.

People who are doing work that's ill-suited for them are easy to spot – they look like a square peg in a round hole. It's no fun feeling like that square peg, getting pounded into that round hole day after day. It's no fun for the hole, either. When someone is in the wrong job, the employee, the employer, and the customers all suffer. It's a lose-lose-lose proposition.

For better or worse, much of our identity is connected to our work. When you meet someone for the first time, one of the first questions people ask is "What do you do for a living?" Many of us strive to have an impressive answer to that question, even if the most correct answer might be, "I'm a square peg in a round hole." If you based your career choice on impressing others or money (often the same thing), then being a square peg in a round hole is on you.

Here's a little test to see how well your job fits you. Just answer the questions honestly; there are no right or wrong answers.

- As you are getting ready for work, what are you feeling – anticipation, dread, or just apathy?
- Is your work a source of your energy or a consumer of your energy?
- Do you feel you are making a contribution to your organization and to the world at large?
- Do you feel that your contribution is recognized, at least within your organization, if not by the world at large?
- Is there a sense of pride when you describe what you do for a living?
- Is your level of happiness in your job as high as your level of success in your job?
- Do you support and respect your employer and believe in their mission statement?
- Can you see yourself in this same line of work in ten years? In twenty? If not, why not?
- Ignoring your immediate financial situation, would a 15% pay cut make you leave your current line of

work?

- If you-in-the-present went back to visit you-as-a-ten-year-old and described what you do for a living, how would you-as-a-ten-year-old react?
- Would you want your child to be in your line of work when he/she grows up?

Before we go any further, the purpose of this book is not to create dissatisfaction for anyone with his/her job or career choices. That would do a disservice to the reader and would be counterproductive.

For those who are already dissatisfied with their current work, you want to recognize *why* you are dissatisfied and take steps to find satisfaction. (By the way, satisfaction is what *you*, not someone else, define it to be.) The steps may involve a change of employers or even careers, but not necessarily.

Many of you may be quite satisfied with your work, but for some reason you can't see it. Maybe peers keep telling you that you should be doing something else. Maybe you think you should go where the pay is the highest. Maybe your parents haven't quite embraced your chosen calling. Maybe you're just in a spot right now where the cons are more obvious than the pros. This book may help you recognize that you are in the right place. As a result, you may become happier and more successful. If so, this book is useful to you, too.

Remember most of all, **you change careers to fit you; you don't change who you are to fit a career.** Careers are like clothes. You may have to try several on until you find the right size and style that's a perfect fit. Also, your clothes change as your style and size change; your career should, too. With clothes and careers, we work within what works for us.

The Sweet 16

I am an ENFJ, along with people like Pope John Paul II, Abraham Lincoln, Ronald Reagan, Barack Obama, and Oprah Winfrey. My kinship to these people is based on the Jung Typology Test. Carl Jung (1875-1961) was an eminent Swiss psychiatrist and the founder of analytical psychology. Among other things, Jung gave us the concept of the introvert and the extrovert.

According to Jung's typology, every individual can be classified using these three criteria:
- Extroversion – Introversion
- Sensing – Intuition
- Thinking – Feeling

Isabel Briggs-Myers (1897-1980), a noted American psychiatrist, added a fourth criterion:
- Judging – Perceiving

Isabel, along with her mother, Katharine Briggs, developed the Myers-Briggs Type Indicator (MBTI). The MBTI is not a test, in that tests have right and wrong answers. The MBTI is a personality inventory in which there are no right or wrong answers, and it is designed to measure how people perceive the world and make decisions.

Taking any personality evaluation online can help assess your personality traits, but the results of such evaluations should not be the basis for making changes in careers, relationships, or even investments. Further evaluation by trained professionals would be necessary before making any major life changes.

Humanmetrics.com definition of the four criteria follows:
- "The first criterion, **Extroversion - Introversion** defines the source and direction of energy expression

for a person. The extrovert has a source and direction of energy expression mainly in the external world while the introvert has a source of energy mainly in the internal world.

- The second criterion, **Se**nsing - i**N**tuition defines the method of information perception by a person. Sensing means that a person believes mainly information he or she receives directly from the external world. Intuition means that a person believes mainly information he/she receives from the internal or imaginative world.
- The third criterion, **Thinking - Feeling** defines how the person processes information. Thinking means that a person makes a decision mainly through logic. Feeling means that, as a rule, he/she makes a decision based on emotion.
- The fourth criterion, **Judging - Perceiving** defines how a person implements the information he/she has processed. Judging means that a person organizes all his/her life events and acts strictly according to his/her plans. Perceiving means that he/she is inclined to improvise and seek alternatives."

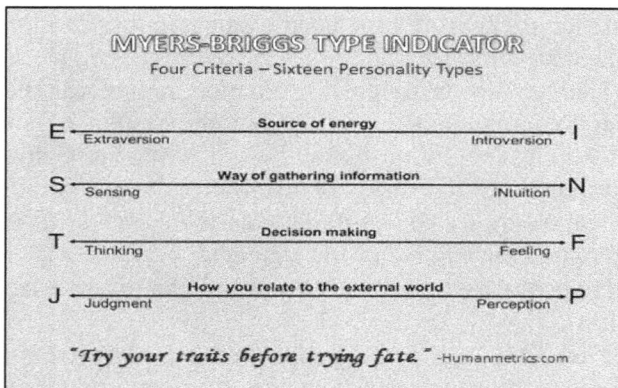

MYERS-BRIGGS TYPE INDICATOR
Four Criteria — Sixteen Personality Types

| E | Source of energy | I |
| Extraversion | | Introversion |

| S | Way of gathering information | N |
| Sensing | | iNtuition |

| T | Decision making | F |
| Thinking | | Feeling |

| J | How you relate to the external world | P |
| Judgment | | Perception |

"Try your traits before trying fate." -Humanmetrics.com

Different combinations of these criteria determine a personality type. There are sixteen types. Every type has a name, based on the combination of criteria. The sixteen types are listed below, with the percentage of the U.S. population that falls into each type:

ISTJ-11.6%	ISFJ-13.8%	INFJ-1.5%	INTJ-2.1%
ISTP-5.4%	ISFP-8.8%	INFP-4.3%	INTP-3.3%
ESTP-4.3%	ESFP-8.5%	ENFP-8.1%	ENTP-3.2%
ESTJ-8.7%	ESFJ-12.3%	ENFJ-2.4%	ENTJ-1.8%

Here is more detailed information about these eight different personality traits and the people who possess them:

EXTROVERTS:
- Are energized by being with other people
- Like being the center of attention
- Act, then think
- Tend to think out loud
- Are easier to read and know, share personal information freely
- Talk more than listen
- Communicate with enthusiasm
- Respond quickly, enjoy a fast pace
- Prefer breadth to depth

INTROVERTS:
- Are energized by spending time alone
- Avoid being the center of attention
- Think, then act
- Think things through inside their head
- Are more private, prefer to share personal information with a select few
- Listen more than talk

- Keep their enthusiasm to themselves;
- Respond after taking the time to think things through, enjoy a slower pace
- Prefer depth to breadth

SENSORS:
- Trust what is certain and concrete
- Like new ideas only if they have practical application
- Value realism and common sense
- Like to use and hone established skills
- Tend to be specific and literal, give detailed descriptions
- Present information in a step-by-step manner
- Are oriented to the present

INTUITIVES:
- Trust inspiration and inference
- Like new ideas and concepts for their own sake
- Value imagination and innovation
- Like to learn new skills, get bored easily after mastering skills
- Tend to be general and figurative, use metaphors and analogies
- Present information through leaps, in a roundabout manner
- Are oriented toward the future

THINKERS:
- Step back and apply impersonal analysis to problems
- Value logic, justice, and fairness; one standard for all
- Naturally see flaws and tend to be critical
- May be seen as heartless, insensitive and uncaring
- Consider it more important to be truthful than tactful

FEELERS:
- Step forward, consider the effect of actions on others
- Value empathy and harmony
- Naturally like to please others, show appreciation easily
- May be seen as overemotional, illogical, and weak
- Consider it important to be tactful as well as truthful

JUDGERS:
- Are happiest after decisions have been made
- Have a work ethic - work first, play later
- Set goals and work toward achieving them on time
- Prefer knowing what they are getting into
- Emphasize completion of the task
- Derive satisfaction from finishing projects
- See time as a finite resource and take deadlines seriously

PERCEIVERS:
- Are happiest leaving their options open
- Have a play ethic - play now, work later
- Change goals as new information becomes available
- Like adapting to new situations
- Emphasize how a task is completed
- Derive satisfaction from starting projects
- See time as a renewable resource

The following synopsis of each of the sixteen personality types is excerpted from Introduction to Type by Isabel Briggs Myers, published by CPP. Inc.:

ISTJ
Quiet, serious, earn success by thoroughness and dependability. Practical, matter-of-fact, realistic, and

responsible. Decide logically what should be done and work toward it steadily, regardless of distractions. Take pleasure in making everything orderly and organized – their work, their home, their life. Value traditions and loyalty.

ISFJ
Quiet, friendly, responsible, and conscientious. Committed and steady in meeting their obligations. Thorough, painstaking, and accurate. Loyal, considerate, notice and remember specifics about people who are important to them, concerned with how others feel. Strive to create an orderly and harmonious environment at work and at home.

INFJ
Seek meaning and connection in ideas, relationships, and material possessions. Want to understand what motivates people and are insightful about others. Conscientious and committed to their firm values. Develop a clear vision about how best to serve the common good. Organized and decisive in implementing their vision.

INTJ
Have original minds and great drive for implementing their ideas and achieving their goals. Quickly see patterns in external events and develop long-range explanatory perspectives. When committed, organize a job and carry it through. Skeptical and independent, have high standards of competence and performance – for themselves and others.

ISTP
Tolerant and flexible, quiet observers until a problem

appears, then act quickly to find workable solutions. Analyze what makes things work and readily get through large amounts of data to isolate the core of practical problems. Interested in cause and effect, organize facts using logical principles, value efficiency.

ISFP
Quiet, friendly, sensitive, and kind. Enjoy the present moment, what's going on around them. Like to have their own space and to work within their own time frame. Loyal and committed to their values and to people who are important to them. Dislike disagreements and conflicts, do not force their opinions or values on others.

INFP
Idealistic, loyal to their values and to people who are important to them. Want an external life that is congruent with their values. Curious, quick to see possibilities, can be catalysts for implementing ideas. Seek to understand people and to help them fulfill their potential. Adaptable, flexible, and accepting unless a value is threatened.

INTP
Seek to develop logical explanations for everything that interests them. Theoretical and abstract, interested more in ideas than in social interaction. Quiet, contained, flexible, and adaptable. Have unusual ability to focus in depth to solve problems in their area of interest. Skeptical, sometimes critical, always analytical.

ESTP
Flexible and tolerant, they take a pragmatic approach

focused on immediate results. Theories and conceptual explanations bore them – they want to act energetically to solve the problem. Focus on the here-and-now, spontaneous, enjoy each moment that they can be active with others. Enjoy material comforts and style. Learn best through doing.

ESFP
Outgoing, friendly, and accepting. Exuberant lovers of life, people, and material comforts. Enjoy working with others to make things happen. Bring common sense and a realistic approach to their work, and make work fun. Flexible and spontaneous, adapt readily to new people and environments. Learn best by trying a new skill with other people.

ENFP
Warmly enthusiastic and imaginative. See life as full of possibilities. Make connections between events and information very quickly, and confidently proceed based on the patterns they see. Want a lot of affirmation from others, and readily give appreciation and support. Spontaneous and flexible, often rely on their ability to improvise and their verbal fluency.

ENTP
Quick, ingenious, stimulating, alert, and outspoken. Resourceful in solving new and challenging problems. Adept at generating conceptual possibilities and then analyzing them strategically. Good at reading other people. Bored by routine, will seldom do the same thing the same way, apt to turn to one new interest after another.

ESTJ

Practical, realistic, matter-of-fact. Decisive, quickly move to implement decisions. Organize projects and people to get things done, focus on getting results in the most efficient way possible. Take care of routine details. Have a clear set of logical standards, systematically follow them and want others to also. Forceful in implementing their plans.

ESFJ

Warmhearted, conscientious, and cooperative. Want harmony in their environment, work with determination to establish it. Like to work with others to complete tasks accurately and on time. Loyal, follow through even in small matters. Notice what others need in their day-by-day lives and try to provide it. Want to be appreciated for who they are and for what they contribute.

ENFJ

Warm, empathetic, responsive, and responsible. Highly attuned to the emotions, needs, and motivations of others. Find potential in everyone, want to help others fulfill their potential. May act as catalysts for individual and group growth. Loyal, responsive to praise and criticism. Sociable, facilitate others in a group, and provide inspiring leadership.

ENTJ

Frank, decisive, assume leadership readily. Quickly see illogical and inefficient procedures and policies, develop and implement comprehensive systems to solve organizational problems. Enjoy long-term planning and goal setting. Usually well informed, well read, enjoy expanding their knowledge and passing it on to others. Forceful in presenting their ideas.

Keep in mind that your answers may vary depending on your situation or mood when you take the test, so don't feel like you are locked into a personality type based on a single taking of the test. Below are the questions. They all require either a Yes or No answer:

- You are almost never late for your appointments.
- You like to be engaged in an active and fast-paced job.
- You enjoy having a wide circle of acquaintances.
- You feel involved when watching TV soaps.
- You are usually the first to react to a sudden event: the telephone ringing or unexpected question
- You are more interested in a general idea than in the details of its realization.
- You tend to be unbiased even if this might endanger your good relations with people.
- Strict observance of the established rules is likely to prevent a good outcome.
- It's difficult to get you excited.
- It is in your nature to assume responsibility.
- You often think about humankind and its destiny.
- You believe the best decision is one that can be easily changed.
- Objective criticism is always useful in any activity.
- You prefer to act immediately rather than speculate about various options.
- You trust reason rather than feelings.
- You are inclined to rely more on improvisation than on careful planning.
- You spend your leisure time actively socializing with a group of people, attending parties, shopping, etc.

- You usually plan your actions in advance.
- Your actions are frequently influenced by emotions.
- You are a person somewhat reserved and distant in communication.
- You know how to put every minute of your time to good purpose.
- You readily help people while asking nothing in return.
- You often contemplate about the complexity of life.
- After prolonged socializing you feel you need to get away and be alone.
- You often do jobs in a hurry.
- You easily see the general principle behind specific occurrences.
- You frequently and easily express your feelings and emotions.
- You find it difficult to speak loudly.
- You get bored if you have to read theoretical books.
- You tend to sympathize with other people.
- You value justice higher than mercy.
- You rapidly get involved in social life at a new workplace.
- The more people with whom you speak, the better you feel.
- You tend to rely on your experience rather than on theoretical alternatives.
- You like to keep a check on how things are progressing.
- You easily empathize with the concerns of other people.
- Often you prefer to read a book than go to a party.
- You enjoy being at the center of events in which other people are directly involved.

- You are more inclined to experiment than to follow familiar approaches.
- You avoid being bound by obligations.
- You are strongly touched by the stories about people's troubles.
- Deadlines seem to you to be of relative, rather than absolute importance.
- You prefer to isolate yourself from outside noises.
- It's essential for you to try things with your own hands.
- You think that almost everything can be analyzed.
- You do your best to complete a task on time.
- You take pleasure in putting things in order.
- You feel at ease in a crowd.
- You have good control over your desires and temptations.
- You easily understand new theoretical principles.
- The process of searching for a solution is more important to you than the solution itself.
- You usually place yourself nearer to the side than in the center of the room.
- When solving a problem you would rather follow a familiar approach than seek a new one.
- You try to stand firmly by your principles.
- A thirst for adventure is close to your heart.
- You prefer meeting in small groups to interaction with lots of people.
- When considering a situation you pay more attention to the current situation and less to a possible sequence of events.
- You consider the scientific approach to be the best.
- You find it difficult to talk about your feelings.
- You often spend time thinking of how things could be improved.

- Your decisions are based more on the feelings of a moment than on the careful planning.
- You prefer to spend your leisure time alone or relaxing in a tranquil family atmosphere.
- You feel more comfortable sticking to conventional ways.
- You are easily affected by strong emotions.
- You are always looking for opportunities.
- Your desk, workbench etc. is usually neat and orderly.
- As a rule, current preoccupations worry you more than future plans.
- You get pleasure from solitary walks.
- It is easy for you to communicate in social situations.
- You are consistent in your habits.
- You willingly involve yourself in matters which engage your sympathies.
- You easily perceive various ways in which events could develop.

Because everyone ends up in one of only sixteen types, people within a type can still vary widely in terms of their overall personalities. There are some 42 million ISFJs in the U.S. alone, and they will hardly be clones of each other. We can, however, look at the eight personality traits to get an indication of how someone who possesses those traits is likely to act in various situations

It can be easy to look at these personality traits and stereotype people who possess them, usually in a negative way. It can be easy to assume that extroverts are loudmouths, that feelers are bleeding hearts, or that perceivers are slackers. Of course, we will not have negative stereotypes of the traits *we* possess. Since fifteen of sixteen personality types are *not* you, you do yourself a disservice to create too many negative stereotypes of such a large group of others.

Extroverts tend to act before thinking, which can lead to some regrettable decisions regarding their health and wealth. Their bias for action also puts them in the lead in many new ventures. Extroverts are more likely to be in on the ground floor of some game-changing new products and services. Extroverts are like the baseball player who leads the league in home runs *and* strikeouts.

Extroverts talk more than they listen, so they may be deaf to warnings issued by others. They can also turn a deaf ear to the naysayers who say nay to some very good ideas. Their filters are often less discerning between good and bad ideas than the extrovert imagines them to be.

Extroverts enjoy a fast pace and are quick responders. Extroverts prefer breadth to depth and are likely to have their thumbs in many pies and many irons in the fire. Extroverts are likely to buy investments on the high-risk-high-return end of the spectrum.

Because they seek out social relationships more than introverts, extroverts are more likely to reap the benefits of those relationships, such as a greater sense of well-being and lower levels of stress.

When you think of introverts, you may picture an economics professor with a bow tie and sweater vest, working on a new method to calculate standard deviation or something. Such an introvert would be more interested in developing a new economic theory than in discussing it on CNN. Introverts think first and then act. They are slow and deliberate. It is more important for them to get it right than to get it right now.

Introverts listen more than they talk. They will gather as much information as possible in order to make the most informed decision possible. This trait can cause them to develop information overload, which can lead to decision paralysis.

Introverts prefer depth to breadth. They are likely to hold fewer stocks in their portfolio than extroverts, but they will have more in-depth knowledge of the companies they own.

Introverts won't hit a lot of home runs; they won't strike out much, either. They will not get rich overnight; they may get rich over time. Introverts do not necessarily favor security over opportunity, nor do extroverts necessarily favor the opposite.

Research shows that the brains of introverts are more active than the brains of extroverts. Introverts prefer to exercise their minds while extroverts prefer to exercise their jaws. There is a bias in professional and lay circles that extroverts are happier than introverts. Studies have led to this conclusion, though the testing methods may favor the way extroverts choose to express happiness.

The worst aspect of introversion is that the introvert may feel pressure to become an extrovert. There is nothing wrong with preferring to read a book than to go to a party. Introverts try to become extroverts far more than extroverts try to become introverts. This disparity may explain in part the lower stress levels of extroverts; they're not trying to be something they aren't.

Introverts tend to favor quality over quantity and specialization over generalization, as compared to extroverts. Introverts are more likely to practice moderation in their habits, which can serve them well. Introverts prefer to do a few things and to do them well, which can lead to a greater sense of accomplishment. Introverts are less likely to need the approval of others to boost their self-esteem.

Sensors trust what is certain and concrete, though they may eventually find little to trust in a world filled with uncertainty. Once sensors lose trust in something, it may never return.

Sensors are not likely to be on the vanguard of something new, due to their preference for using established skills and ideas that have an immediate practical application. They will be more conservative in most life choices, including how they save, spend, and invest their money. Sensors are specific and literal, which means you are not likely to convince them of something by appealing to their imagination.

Sensors are oriented to the present, which is not to say that they don't plan for the future. Their vision of the future is grounded in the present, so they plan for the future based on what they are certain of in the present. One drawback to this strategy is that the constant change of modern life means that what is certain today may not be at all certain in the future. During stable times, sensors fare quite well. Rapid change requires adaptability, with which sensors often need help.

Because sensors are more oriented to the present, it can be difficult to get them to imagine themselves as old when they are young. A forty-year-old sensor may have difficulty imagining how the habits of today will affect him/her in three decades. Aging well is a process of adaptation, which is not a strong suit of the sensor.

Intuitives make up the great majority of entrepreneurs. An entrepreneur is not someone looking to make a quick buck in a business; it's someone who loves to take an idea and make it a reality. True entrepreneurs are more missionary than mercenary. Being intuitive is a great asset in that line of work.

Intuitives like new ideas for their own sake, so they may find themselves investing in concepts that turn out to have no economic benefit. Because they are open to new ideas and concepts, they are also more likely to see the potential in an idea before everyone else does, causing them to be the leaders in new fields. Imagination and innovation are highly valued, so the best and brightest are drawn to work with intuitives.

Intuitives are oriented to the future, which is why so many of their ventures pay off. They see now what becomes obvious to the rest of us only much later. The downside to such a future orientation is a lack of attention to the present. More often than not, the Intuitive is derailed not by a bad idea, but by inattention to present realities, which can upset the best-laid plans.

Although intuitives are oriented to the future, that doesn't mean they are taking good care of themselves in the present. The focus on the future often means the drudgery of the present is avoided, and a good future does require a certain measure of drudgery in the present.

Thinkers are very left-brain people. Their minds are like high-powered computers. There are some paradoxes with Thinkers. They value justice and fairness, but are viewed as heartless and insensitive. They view themselves as holding on to principles; others view them as rigid and unfeeling.

Thinkers are capable of stepping back and applying impersonal analysis to problems. This trait makes them very good at getting to the unvarnished truth. When something is going wrong in a business, Thinkers are the ones who will roll up their sleeves and figure out what needs to be done. Because they value truth more than tact, when they report their findings to management, they may do so in a way that actually gets in the way of needed reform.

Because Thinkers are more accurately *critical* thinkers, they are good at finding flaws. This perspective also tends to make Thinkers more pessimistic than the general population; they will see the glass as half-empty, as well as dirty and chipped. A pessimistic outlook combined with a frustration over the imperfections of life can inhibit Thinkers from taking long-term risks for long-term rewards.

Thinkers are good at putting the brakes on activities that are going too fast. Brakes alone don't go anywhere, though. Thinkers need relationships with those who move forward to avoid stagnation.

Thinkers will take care of themselves if it is logical to do so. They will be motivated by statistics on heart disease, not by a commercial for an energy drink. The natural pessimism of thinkers can be more than a liability in the present (pessimism is far more stressful than optimism). That pessimism can make it harder to imagine a future that is worth making any sacrifices for in the present.

Feelers are team players. They value empathy and harmony and are always considerate of the feelings of others. They will not gain at the expense of others and may be more inclined to be taken advantage of by others. In a competitive environment, Feelers will have a problem, and they will not choose a tournament-style conflict if there are alternatives.

Because they understand the human aspect in any situation better than most, Feelers are better equipped to motivate people to action. Thinkers may be great at knowing which direction people should go, but it usually takes Feelers to actually get the people moving in that direction.

Feelers are cooperative, not competitive. Because of this nature, Feelers may not fare as well in the short term. However, in the long term, Feelers will fare better than most others because the more long-term the goals are, the more cooperation, rather than competition, is needed to achieve them. Feelers are not combative, and they might lose many battles. They are more likely to end up winning a war, though.

Judgers are not likely to end up being supported by their children in their old age. They are very good at setting goals and working toward achieving them by the deadline. Judgers are motivated by the satisfaction they get from completing a project. Nothing makes them happier than setting a goal of being financially independent by a certain date and actually achieving that independence.

Judgers believe in business before pleasure. They will make sure that all financial obligations (including obligations to themselves) are met before they spend money on items like vacations or luxury cars. They also are likely to succeed in starting their own businesses because they are more likely to make the sacrifices necessary in the early years to enable a business to succeed in the long run.

Judgers are deadline-conscious and so value time as a finite, exhaustible resource. This trait is mostly useful because it encourages careful use of time. Judgers can also put unnecessary pressure on themselves to complete a task on time, which can sometimes result in compromises in quality, or even major errors in judgment. Strict adherence to deadlines can confine Judgers when flexibility may be the more valuable trait.

Perceivers are recognized for their flexibility and adaptability, but they can sometimes resemble a boat with a sail and no rudder. The desire to keep their options open can cause them to avoid setting goals.

Perceivers enjoy the mechanics of completing a task more than the accomplishment of the task itself. They are good at developing the tactics necessary to implement the strategy that was created by others. They can adapt as new information becomes available, though they are not likely to be the ones generating that new information.

Perceivers see time as a renewable resource, so they are prone to find themselves out of time. For them, it's pleasure before business. Perceivers may be more inclined to work to a much older age, in part because they still see themselves as young and vital, but also because they may have procrastinated in taking concrete steps to enable them to afford to retire. In the Aesop's fable, the ants would have been Judgers; the grasshopper, a perceiver.

Personality evaluations like the MBTI can be helpful in assessing your strengths and weaknesses. Because it is impossible for us to be objective about our own strengths and weaknesses, the MBTI can make us aware of such traits. Awareness can help you better utilize your strengths, while enabling you to get help from others who are strong where you may be weak.

There is no ideal personality type. When you read the characteristics of the eight different personality traits, it can be tempting to think that a certain combination is the magic formula for career success. Because every human is unique, no one possesses these personality traits in the exact same combination as anyone else. We are like snowflakes in that respect; the ingredients may be simple, but the product is endlessly varied.

The MBTI can be very helpful in assessing your strengths and weaknesses to help you align your career path with your personality. If you are in a job that doesn't mesh with your personality, you aren't going to be very good at it. If you aren't very good at your job, you aren't likely to be happy or healthy, and you aren't likely to be well paid for it, either.

Personality evaluations can help you find a career that better suits your personality and your strengths, which should enable you to do a better job and make more money. More importantly, getting into a career that fits your personality will greatly increase your chances for happiness on the job, as well as success on the job. You may have spent years trying to make yourself fit a job. Finding out your personality type can enable you to find a job that fits you instead. Since you will spend some 100,000 hours of your life on work-related activities, you should do everything you can to make sure you spend that time in the right place, not as a square peg in a round hole.

Finally, if you are going to take an MBTI or similar evaluation, wait several days after reading this chapter. The information here may influence your answers and turn you into someone you're not. Also, take the evaluation when you are in a good frame of mind, without stress or distractions. You will get a more accurate result, which is what you want.

A Little Temperamental

Keirsey Temperament Sorter is in the same vein as MBTI/Jung. This "personality instrument" classifies people into one of four temperaments – artisan, guardian, rational, or idealist. KTS-II, as it's called, can help clarify and reinforce results from the MBTI. It can be taken at www.keirsey.com, which provides the following details.

Temperament is a configuration of observable personality traits, such as habits of communication, patterns of action, and sets of characteristic attitudes, values, and talents. It also encompasses personal needs, the kinds of contributions that individuals make in the workplace, and the roles they play in society. Dr. David Keirsey has identified mankind's four basic temperaments as the Artisan, the Guardian, the Rational, and the Idealist.

Each temperament has its own unique qualities and shortcomings, strengths and challenges. What accounts for these differences? To use the idea of Temperament most effectively, it is important to understand that the four temperaments are not simply arbitrary collections of characteristics, but spring from an interaction of the two basic dimensions of human behavior: our communication and our action, our words and our deeds, or, simply, ***what we say*** and ***what we do***.

Communication: Concrete vs. Abstract

First, people naturally think and talk about what they are interested in, and if you listen carefully to people's conversations, you find two broad but distinct areas of subject matter.

Some people talk primarily about the external, concrete world of everyday reality: facts and figures, work and play, home and family, news, sports and weather -- all the who-what-when-where-and how much's of life.

Other people talk primarily about the internal, abstract world of ideas: theories and conjectures, dreams and philosophies, beliefs and fantasies --all the why's, if's, and what-might-be's of life.

At times, of course, everyone addresses both sorts of topics, but in their daily lives, and for the most part, **Concrete** people talk about *reality*, while **Abstract** people talk about *ideas*.

Action: Utilitarian vs. Cooperative

Second, at every turn people are trying to accomplish their goals, and if you watch closely how people go about their business, you see that there are two fundamentally opposite types of action.

Some people act primarily in a utilitarian or pragmatic manner, that is, they do what gets results, what achieves their objectives as effectively or efficiently as possible, and only afterwards do they check to see if they are observing the rules or going through proper channels.

485

Other people act primarily in a cooperative or socially acceptable manner, that is, they try to do the right thing, in keeping with agreed upon social rules, conventions, and codes of conduct, and only later do they concern themselves with the effectiveness of their actions.

These two ways of acting can overlap, but as they lead their lives, **Utilitarian** people instinctively, and for the most part do what *works*, while **Cooperative** people do what's *right*.

The Four Temperaments

- As *Concrete Cooperators*, **Guardians** speak mostly of their duties and responsibilities, of what they can keep an eye on and take good care of, and they're careful to obey the laws, follow the rules, and respect the rights of others.

- As *Abstract Cooperators*, **Idealists** speak mostly of what they hope for and imagine might be possible for people, and they want to act in good conscience, always trying to reach their goals without compromising their personal code of ethics.

- As *Concrete Utilitarians*, **Artisans** speak mostly about what they see right in front of them, about what they can get their hands on, and they will do whatever works, whatever gives them a quick, effective payoff, even if they have to bend the rules.

- As *Abstract Utilitarians*, **Rationals** speak mostly of what new problems intrigue them and what new solutions they envision, and always pragmatic, they act as efficiently as possible to achieve their objectives, ignoring arbitrary rules and conventions if need be.

The 4 Temperaments

Guardian
Supervisor (ESTJ)   Inspector (ISTJ)
Provider (ESFJ)   Protector (ISFJ)

Artisan
Promoter (ESTP)   Crafter (ISTP)
Performer (ESFP)   Composer (ISFP)

Idealist
Teacher (ENFJ)   Counselor (INFJ)
Champion (ENFP)   Healer (INFP)

Rational
Field Marshal (ENTJ)   Mastermind (INTJ)
Inventor (ENTP)   Architect (INTP)

The Big Five

In psychology, the **Big Five personality traits** are five broad domains or dimensions of personality that are used to describe human personality, the five-factor model (FFM). The five factors are openness, conscientiousness, extroversion, agreeableness, and neuroticism. The acronym commonly used to refer to the five traits collectively is OCEAN. Beneath each global factor, a cluster of correlated and more specific primary factors are found; for example, extroversion includes such related qualities as gregariousness, assertiveness, excitement seeking, warmth, activity, and positive emotions.

The Big Five model is able to account for different traits in personality without overlapping. Empirical research has shown that the Big Five personality traits show consistency in interviews, self-descriptions and observations. Moreover, this five-factor structure seems to be found across a wide range of participants of different ages and of different cultures.

A summary of the factors of the Big Five and their constituent traits, such that they form the acronym OCEAN:

Openness to Experience
(*inventive/curious* vs. *consistent/cautious*)
Appreciation for art, emotion, adventure, unusual ideas, curiosity, and variety of experience. Openness reflects the degree of intellectual curiosity, creativity and a preference for novelty and variety a person has. It is also described as the extent to which a person is imaginative or independent, and depicts a personal preference for a variety of activities over a strict routine. Some disagreement remains about how to interpret the openness factor, which is sometimes called "intellect" rather than openness to experience.

Conscientiousness
(*efficient/organized* vs. *easy-going/careless*)
A tendency to be organized and dependable, show self-discipline, act dutifully, aim for achievement, and prefer planned rather than spontaneous behavior.

Extroversion
(*outgoing/energetic* vs. *solitary/reserved*)
Energy, positive emotions, assurgency, assertiveness, sociability and the tendency to seek stimulation in the company of others, and talkativeness.

Agreeableness
(*friendly/compassionate* vs. *analytical/detached*)
A tendency to be compassionate and cooperative rather than suspicious and antagonistic towards others. It is

also a measure of one's trusting and helpful nature, and whether a person is generally well tempered or not.

Neuroticism

(*sensitive/nervous* vs. *secure/confident*)

The tendency to experience unpleasant emotions easily, such as anger, anxiety, depression, and vulnerability. Neuroticism also refers to the degree of emotional stability and impulse control and is sometimes referred to by its low pole, "emotional stability".

Psychology Today's website enables you to take a 10-minute, 25-question test to assess your Big Five personality traits.

The Big M.O.

While personality tests like MBTI and Keirsey can tell you what you want to do, the **Kolbe A Index/Instinct Test** is designed to tell you what you *will* or *won't do*. It evaluates methods of operation based on natural instincts. This test enables the right person, the right project, and the right team to match up. It can be taken at www.kolbe.com.

While MBTI and Keirsey are useful for individuals looking for a better analysis of their personality, Kolbe is used by organizations in both hiring evaluations and in forming teams of compatible and complementary workers. Kolbe's web site touts the RightFit evaluation thusly:

> *RightFit is Kolbe's statistically proven hiring tool that helps companies screen and select the best job applicants. Instead of guessing how well a prospective employee will perform, RightFit helps you identify the required methods of operation, or*

profile, of the ideal candidate. The software then ranks each candidate on an "A" to "F" scale based on how well their individual instincts compare to the requirements for success in a given role. RightFit can also be used to select individuals who match the methods of proven high-performers, as well as individuals who can fill a critical gap on a team.

12 Kolbe Conative (Doing) Strengths

Everyone has a strength in each mode.

Diversity in the combination of strengths creates a multitude of MOs (methods of operation).

www.kolbe.com

Fact Finder	Follow Thru	Quick Start	Implementor
Simplify	Adapt	Stabilize	Imagine
Explain	Maintain	Modify	Restore
Specify	Systematize	Improvise	Build

There are four universal human instincts used in creative problem solving. These instincts are not measurable. However, the observable acts derived from them can be identified and quantified by the Kolbe A Index. These instinct-driven behaviors are represented in the four Kolbe Action Modes:

- **Fact Finder** - the instinctive way we gather and share information.

- **Follow Thru** - the instinctive way we arrange and design.
- **Quick Start** - the instinctive way we deal with risk and uncertainty.
- **Implementor** - the instinctive way we handle space and tangibles.

The Kolbe A Index result is a graphical representation of an individual's instinctive method of operation, or modus operandi (M.O.). The numbers in each Action Mode represent different points on a continuum, rather than relative values. Each point on the continuum indicates a positive trait. There is no such thing as a negative or "bad" Kolbe Index result.

You're Such a Character!

Martin Seligman and Chris Peterson are pioneers in the area of positive psychology. For decades, psychology has been focused to the point of obsession on the negative aspects of human personality. Seligman and Peterson have been working to shift that focus to understanding the upper reaches of human health, talent, and possibility.

As their first step in this process, Seligman and Peterson scoured every list of virtues they could find, from religious teachings to the Boy Scout Oath. They discovered that six broad virtues appeared on nearly every list: wisdom, courage, humanity, justice, temperance, and transcendence (the ability to forge connections to something beyond the self). The value of this list of six virtues is as an organizing framework for more specific *strengths of character*. There are several paths to each virtue, and different cultures vary in the degree to which they value each path. The value of the

491

classifications is as a guide to specific means of growth toward widely valued ends, without insisting that any one way is mandatory or even best.

Seligman and Peterson suggest there are twenty-four principle character strengths which lead to one of the six higher-level virtues. You can diagnose your strengths and take several other evaluations at the Authentic Happiness Testing Center at the site developed by Seligman, www.authentichappiness.org. Here are the virtues and their attendant strengths:

- WISDOM: curiosity; love of learning; judgment; ingenuity; emotional intelligence; perspective
- COURAGE: valor; perseverance; integrity
- HUMANITY: kindness; loving
- JUSTICE: citizenship; fairness; leadership
- TEMPERANCE: self-control; prudence; humility
- TRANSCENDENCE: appreciation of beauty and excellence; gratitude; hope; spirituality; forgiveness; humor; zest

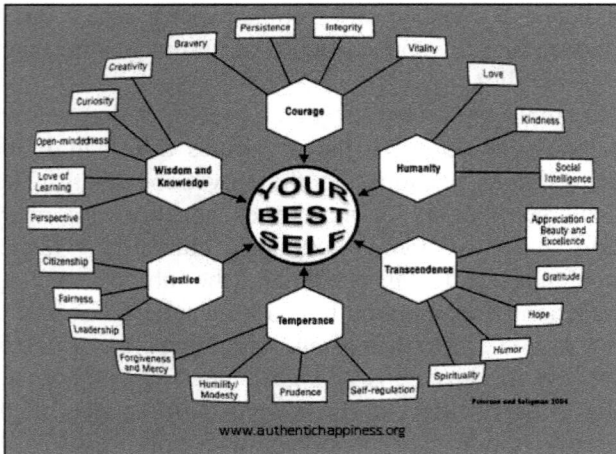

Everyone will have a different opinion on the relative value of each of these strengths, and there is no scale that determines the relative value of each. It is perfectly natural that we will give higher value to those strengths which we possess to a higher degree.

You're probably familiar with some version of the 80/20 principle. In most of our undertakings, including work, 80% of our results come from 20% of our efforts. If you think about the times you've been really productive, on a hot streak, in *flow*, you were accomplishing a lot with relatively little effort. In those situations, you felt great and it was easy to love your work. The other 80% of the time – well, that's another story.

One of the benefits of taking the kinds of evaluations listed above is finding out the 20% that will yield 80%. Some people may see taking such evaluations as a waste of time, but nothing is more wasteful than dedicating 80% of your time and effort for a yield of 20%. That's an outcome/input ratio of 1:4. You would do better to find the time to learn how to reverse that outcome/input ratio from 1:4 to 4:1.

As an example, take the character strengths test. There are 24 character strengths measured in this test. Your top 5 character strengths are the 20% that yield 80% of your results. It's important to know what those strengths are so you can fully utilize them to achieve your goals.

You'll also find out your greatest character weaknesses. We all have some, and it's not a good investment of time and effort to turn those weaknesses into strengths. However, by becoming aware of your greatest weaknesses, you can minimize the damage they might cause you. The weaknesses will likely never help you move forward; your goal is to keep them from moving you backward.

To Thine Own Self Be True

This is eHarmony's Mission Statement:
"To empower people with the knowledge and inspiration needed to grow and strengthen their most important relationships for a lifetime of happiness."
The Compatibility Matching System™ was developed and patented by eHarmony as a scientific approach to matchmaking. The 436-question relationship questionnaire creates a personality profile that describes you in areas like agreeableness, conscientiousness, openness, emotional stability, and extroversion. They also create a compatibility profile, outlining the type of person with whom you are most likely to develop a long-term relationship.

eHarmony's system was developed with personal matchmaking in mind, but its scientific approach to finding one's soul mate was a little out-of-the-box at the time. However, its likelihood of success seems greater than the traditional alternatives. Are you really likely to meet your perfect match just because you happen to work in the same office, live in the same building, or patronize the same bar on the same night?

Whether you're looking for a perfect mate or a perfect career, what you're looking for is compatibility. The most important factor for success in finding a good match is knowing who you are. The purpose of any personality test is not to tell you what you should be doing or who you should love. Its purpose is to give you some additional insight into who *you* are, in all your complex, unique beauty.

Please don't ever start telling yourself that "I should be a (fill-in-the-blank) because my personality test said so." It said no such thing. A personality test *might* indicate that you have certain traits that *might* be helpful in a certain line of work, but that's all.

If you have no clear idea of what you want for a career, and if you need a little guidance on what might be a good fit, a test like Myers-Briggs can be useful. If you think there's a field where you might want to work, but you don't know if it's a good match, taking the test might be a good starting point.

For example, you may have an interest in a sales position because you get to travel and meet people and because the potential money is good. However, your personality test indicates a low threshold for rejection, which might be a problem, as it could cause burnout. The test may also show you have a high level of persistence, which would be an asset in sales. This example illustrates how a personality test can offer guidance, but cannot determine whether you are suited for a job.

It's hard to be good at something that doesn't feel natural. Ultimately, you want to find something that feels like a natural fit, not a square peg in a round hole. It's your best chance for success *and* happiness.

WHAT DRIVES YOU?

My favorite definition of *inspire* is "to breathe life into." This definition has medical connotations, though it transcends the purely medical. This definition also makes it clearer that *inspire* is the opposite of *expire*, which in medical terms means to die. To be inspired, then, is the beginning of life for whatever you're inspired to do. By implication, when you are not inspired to do something, eventually that something will expire. First, we have inspiration; then to keep the spirit alive, we have respiration. Finally, without respiration, we have expiration.

When you are inspired to do something, you are pulled toward it, not pushed toward it. There is an irresistible draw to create something more than currently exists. Could Thomas Edison have created the electric light (not to mention thousands of other inventions) if he were not inspired, drawn irresistibly to create something that would transform mankind as much as any invention in history? Edison could certainly push himself (twenty-hour workdays were not uncommon), but he never felt the push; he only felt the pull, so he rarely tired or thought to give up.

Have you ever noticed that our most noble professions are given a term that is not bestowed on more mundane occupations? That term is *calling*. Calling is most closely associated with religious vocations, but a vocation can be any occupation to which one feels drawn. Most callings and vocations have something in common - their primary purpose is to serve others. Those with a true calling in any profession not only become the most successful in that profession, but

497

they are also sought out above others for their services. You would not seek out a doctor who was in it for the prestige or money. You would not seek out a priest who was in it for the power. You would not seek out a teacher for your child who was in it for the summer vacations. You want to know that the main reason those people are in those professions is because they were called into them by the opportunity to make life better for people like you.

When you're inspired, you have to channel a seemingly endless source of energy. Your body may tire, but your spirit never does. Rather than feeling like a donkey who is being prodded forward with a stick (and maybe a carrot), you feel like a dog who is tugging at the leash to run to the next adventure. To use another analogy, when you are inspired, you may not always know the best way to position the rudder, but your sails are always full.

When you're inspired, your passion burns with the steady intensity of Thomas Edison's successful light bulb. You find yourself thinking of ways to channel that passion to get the most out of it. When you're inspired, your passion becomes more than what you do - it becomes a large part of who you are. It also feels effortless.

Flipping Pyramids

Anyone who has ever taken a psychology course is familiar with Maslow's Hierarchy of Needs. Abraham Maslow developed his theory in 1943. The hierarchy is, in descending order:
- **Self-Actualization** (morality, creativity, spontaneity)

- **Esteem** (achievement, confidence, respect from others)
- **Love/Belonging** (friendship, family, sexual intimacy)
- **Safety** (physical security, employment, health, family)
- **Physiological** (breathing, food, water, sleep, sex)

Maslow theorized that, until one's needs are met at the lower levels, one cannot or will not devote energy to meeting needs at the higher levels. This assumption is valid - you can't focus on your job if you haven't had enough sleep or food; you can't focus on friendships if you are about to lose your job; you can't focus on becoming a more well-rounded person when a loved one is battling a life-threatening disease. The hierarchy of needs is one way of measuring how well we are achieving our full potential.

There is a similar hierarchy when we look at our work. If you are out of work, it can become a desperate struggle just to meet the physiological needs at the bottom of the hierarchy. When you do get a job, you hope it will pay enough to meet your physiological needs. You seek to stay with an employer and hopefully get some raises and promotions in order to fulfill your safety needs. However, when a job is just a job, it won't provide much more than these basic needs. Because these jobs neither demand much nor provide much, you may put your back into it, but not your heart and soul.

Most people aspire to have more than a job - they want a career. A career is a series of jobs that enables you to move up on the hierarchy of needs. (By the way, if you have a career, don't go on about it to people who just have jobs. It annoys them and makes you look like a snob.) A career will usually enable you to buy more of the things that people seek on the lower level of needs.

The most attractive aspect of a career is that it offers the opportunity to fulfill our esteem needs. If we did not consider esteem to be so highly valued, people would not work to earn a Ph.D. in English Literature for the opportunity to teach a core class at the local community college. They would go to a two-year trade school and learn plumbing, where they could then go out and charge $75 an hour for their services.

If you're lucky, a job leads to a career. If you're luckier still, your career becomes your vocation. A vocation is defined as an occupation or profession for which a person is especially suited or qualified. Someone who merely works in a job may be a square peg in a round hole. Someone who builds a career is likely to be a square peg in a square hole, though more careers are made by reshaping a round peg into a square one than by reshaping a square hole into a round one. With a vocation, you are not only a square peg in a square hole; you are the right size peg for that hole.

Finally, we have the pinnacle of the work hierarchy, the calling. We often think of callings in terms of religions, but a calling can be for any work that benefits others primarily and the worker secondarily. A calling is not work that one does for selfish reasons.

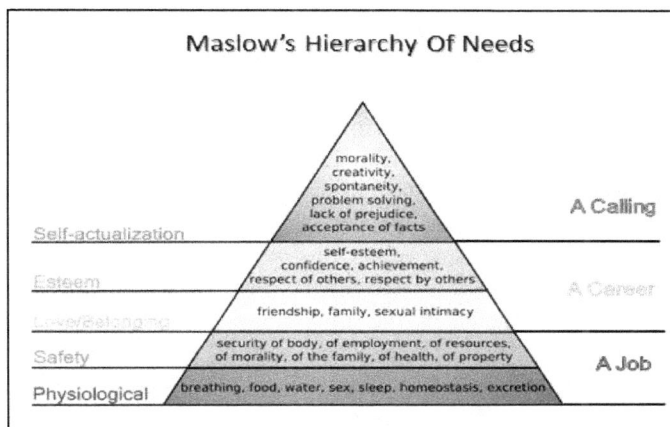

Maslow's Hierarchy Of Needs

When you merely have a job, you do the job for the pay. If there is any non-monetary benefit to the job, it won't keep you from leaving for a small raise in pay.

With a career, there are benefits beyond pay. You are unlikely to change careers if you could not make as much money in another career, even if you enjoyed the work more.

When you have a vocation, you continuously find it hard to believe that you actually get paid to do something you love. You are not about to give up the financial benefits, but they begin to assume secondary importance to what you receive beyond the paycheck.

Finally, a calling is work that you would pay money to others for the privilege of performing. You are so drawn to do that work, and you are so called by that work that it doesn't matter what you have to do in order to work in that field - you will do it. With a vocation, a person usually starts out with a skill set that makes that vocation a rewarding and easy choice. With a calling, a skill set may have to be acquired through years of training, and even then it might not be enough.

When viewed through the prism of Maslow's Hierarchy of Needs, most jobs take a bottom-up approach. The job promises to provide money in exchange for work, and that money can be used to supply one's basic needs. The reason most people can't get passionate about their jobs is that the job doesn't provide an opportunity to release their passions. Without passion for your work, the most you are likely to become in that work is "competent", which means you are capable of competing (but not necessarily winning).

A calling takes a top-down approach regarding the hierarchy of needs. A calling speaks to something inside the individual that promises to make them a better person, typically by providing the opportunity for that person to make the world a better place. A calling will provide you with the needs at the top of the hierarchy first. The more basic of needs get met as the effect of being passionate about the work leads to being more than competent in performing it. By excellently providing something of value to people, they then provide the means to meet all the basic needs.

Becoming your calling requires a top-down approach to Maslow's Hierarchy of Needs. You begin by realizing that you are not a human being having a spiritual experience; you are a spiritual being having a human experience.

The lower levels focus on feeding the physical needs alone. They can often do that at the expense of the soul and the mind. At the lower levels, there is no feeding of the soul; at most one can hope that the soul isn't being harmed by one's work. This is not to say that there is no value to work that provides only a paycheck. If a certain kind of work did not provide value to others, people would not pay for it, leading to its elimination.

The work you would most want to do, the work that you would do for no pay, the work that never seems like work, that work is your calling. It's possible to transform your current job into your calling, but it's tough working from the bottom up to make such a change. It's also not a good idea to quit your job, pitch a tent in the woods, and contemplate your true calling for the next year.

First look at your current situation and see if there is the potential to transform your job into a calling, to be pulled rather than pushed into getting up each day and going to work. In the meantime, do some soul-searching to ask yourself what kind of work you could do that:

a) would give you a sense of purpose;

b) would be within your capabilities at some point;

c) would enable you to meet your more basic needs as well.

It might take years to find your true calling, but the first step in finding your true calling is to realize you have one and to begin looking for it.

Motivation is Good; Inspiration is Better

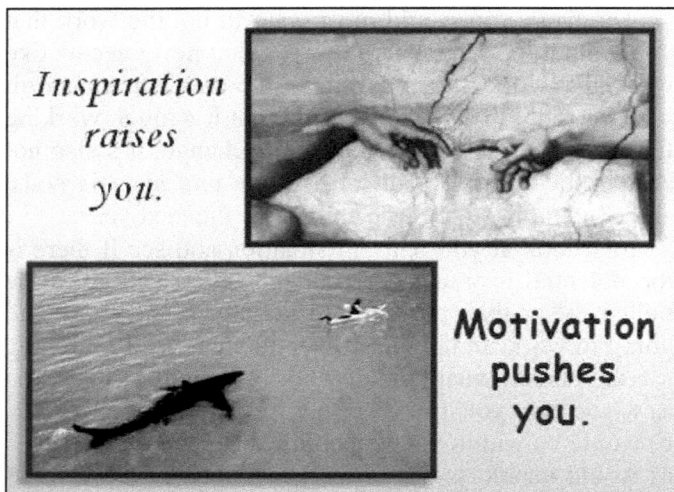

People are inspired to greatness; they are almost never motivated to it. Inspiration pulls you; motivation pushes you. It's just too exhausting to be pushed all the way to greatness. If you're merely motivated by family, friends, peers, greed, fear, competitors, enemies, or a thousand other "motivating factors," you may achieve greatness, but it will feel empty and, more importantly, it will be fleeting. Greatness built on motivation without inspiration is like a foundation that is made with concrete that has too much sand and not enough cement. It may look solid, but time quickly exposes the weakness, and whatever was built on that foundation soon collapses.

If you remember reading Mark Twain's *The Adventures of Tom Sawyer* in school, you may recall

Tom using psychology to get his friend Ben to whitewash the fence for him, a task that Tom despised doing. Tom seduced Ben to take over the task by acting as though he loved to whitewash and that he didn't think Ben was capable of doing the job properly:

"He had discovered a great law of human action, without knowing it – namely, that in order to make a man or a boy covet a thing, it is only necessary to make the thing difficult to attain. If he had been a great and wise philosopher, like the writer of this book, he would now have comprehended that Work consists of whatever a body is obliged to do, and that Play consists of whatever a body is not obliged to do."

There is a fundamental reason why money doesn't work as well as a motivator as most people might think. Money doesn't work as a motivator in practice as well as in theory because we tend to think of money as the cause, as the motivator, if you will. **Money isn't the cause; it's the effect.**

It is natural to think that if you are doing something for money, money is the cause of what you are doing. But money is the effect of what you are doing. A cause must first exist in order for you to be motivated by it. Money that you earn from work does not exist until you create it through your work.

When talking about money here, we are referring to the creation of wealth. You create wealth when you work to provide goods and services of value to others. The creation of wealth, as represented by money, is the effect of your work. At most, money as a motivator provides the opportunity to create wealth.

Frederick Herzberg was an American psychologist who greatly influenced business management with what is generally referred to as the Two-Factor Theory. Herzberg's theory states that people are not content with satisfaction at the lower levels of Maslow's hierarchy of needs. Individuals will also seek gratification of higher-level psychological needs related to achievement, recognition, responsibility, advancement, and the nature of the work itself.

Two-factor theory distinguishes between:

- **Motivators** (challenging work, recognition, responsibility, achievement) that give positive satisfaction arising from intrinsic conditions of the work itself and
- **Hygiene factors** (status, job security, salary, fringe benefits, work conditions) that do not give positive satisfaction, though their absence results in dissatisfaction. These factors are extrinsic to the work itself.

Essentially, **hygiene factors are necessary to prevent an employee from becoming dissatisfied. Motivation factors are needed to motivate an employee to higher performance.** Herzberg further classified workers' actions and how and why they do them. If you perform a work-related action because you *have* to, then that is classed as movement; if you perform a work-related action because you *want* to, then that is classed as motivation.

At some time in his youth, Frederick Herzberg probably read *The Adventures of Tom Sawyer*. Herzberg made a career and influenced business management practices by quantitatively proving what Mark Twain said - work consists of what you have to do and play consists of what you want to do.

What is the environment where you work? If the hygiene factors are lacking or inadequate, it can be hard for you to feel anything but dissatisfied. In such an environment, morale is low, turnover is high, and businesses that don't provide a minimum level of hygiene factors don't stay in business for long.

When a business is just starting up, the environment may be one where the hygiene factors are low, but the motivators are high. Hygiene factors are low because money is tight in most start-ups. The company can't offer security yet, but what they can offer is plenty of opportunity. It can be an exciting environment where everyone is excited about the prospect of building something from scratch as a team. That enthusiasm and dedication should translate into profits at some point. At that point, the employer needs to raise the hygiene factors to an acceptable level.

Old school business thinking was that as long as the business took care of the hygiene factors, it was up to the employees to find their own motivation. If management focused more on people than numbers, an unproductive environment could result. The main reason people stay in such jobs is that the hygiene factors there are better than the hygiene factors elsewhere. People get used to a certain level of salaries and benefits, and they are reluctant to give some of that up for intangibles like recognition and achievement.

The goal is a work environment that offers both the requisite level of hygiene factors and as many motivators as possible. What many business managers fail to recognize is that the way to get workers to be their most productive is to pay them enough that money is not an issue (which does not mean paying them more than anyone else or paying the employee as much as they demand) and then to provide as many motivators as possible.

To help get the proper perspective of money as a motivator, consider this situation. At your place of employment, you feel you are well-paid for the work you do. However, you just found out that two of your co-workers, neither of whom is more productive than you, both earn more than you. Would that news make you suddenly dissatisfied with your level of pay? What if you found out that those two co-workers were more satisfied with their jobs than you? Would you care? That bit of information would be unlikely to raise your level of dissatisfaction.

The situation just described illustrates a point - the best motivators are the ones that have no limits. When someone finds out that co-workers are paid more, they become dissatisfied because they believe that others' higher income must come at their own expense. When someone finds out that co-workers are more satisfied in their jobs, they do not become dissatisfied because satisfaction is not a finite resource. Satisfaction can be created in infinite quantities by those who will benefit most from its creation.

It is unlikely that a worker who found out that others were earning more would go to those co-workers and find out their secret of earning more in order to copy their practices and earn more, too. However, it is at least plausible that someone might approach co-workers who seem more satisfied, to find out their secrets, in the hopes of reaping greater satisfaction on the job, too.

We think of hygiene factors as motivators in part because of the Industrial Revolution. Before the

Industrial Revolution, work was arduous and often dangerous, but for the most part it wasn't routine. Two-thirds of the population worked in agriculture prior to the Industrial Revolution. That work had many drawbacks, but at least there was a certain variety to it.

Prior to the Industrial Revolution, there were no assembly lines. With the advent of the modern factory, tasks were broken down to their smallest elements, and workers would perform those smallest elements continuously.

If you worked at a Ford assembly plant in 1920, you could take pride that you were part of the team that built the Model T, the car that put America on wheels. However, your workday consisted of attaching the front bumper on the driver's side as each car came down the line. Your work involved six separate steps and had to be completed in 42 seconds because that was the pace of the moving assembly line. By the end of the year, you would have attached 171,428 bumpers to 171,428 Model T's. Work like that required a lot of outside direction and supervision. No one can stay self-motivated performing the same routine 86 times an hour, 8 hours a day, 250 days a year.

Non-routine jobs are far more common today. The pace of change requires that jobs evolve continuously to keep up with new technologies and competition. The push for productivity now has workers multi-tasking, as opposed to breaking work down into smaller and smaller increments. The variety of activities in the average workday today makes it easier for workers to maintain interest in their work. The number of workers putting in 10 and 12 hour workdays may be the result of the push for more productivity, but they could not be productive for 10 or 12 hours a day unless the work was able to hold their interest for that long a period.

One of the great motivators is autonomy. We all want to think we are the ones who decide what we are going to do. If you are a parent, you have probably used an If-Then scenario with your child at some time. They can be stated positively or negatively, as a carrot or a stick: "If you clean your room, we can go get ice cream. If you don't clean your room, you can't play any video games." If-Then rewards, and especially punishments, are perceived as reducing one's autonomy.

Autonomy is one of those intrinsic motivators. Intrinsic motivators are delicate things. They can be damaged by, of all things, extrinsic rewards. Bobby Jones was one of the greatest golfers of all time, winning thirteen major tournaments. He also co-founded Augusta National and the Masters Tournament. He was a lawyer by profession and only played golf as an amateur. When asked why he never turned pro, he replied, "When you play for money, it's not love anymore." The lesson of Bobby Jones is: **when people are doing something because of intrinsic motivators, don't muck it up by offering extrinsic rewards.** You will only hurt their performance.

Extrinsic rewards, like money, can send two seemingly contradictory signals at the same time. The first signal is that the task you are performing is valuable and that someone wants to demonstrate appreciation of you performing it with financial compensation. The second signal is that the task you are performing is inherently undesirable and that the only way to entice you to perform this undesirable task is to offer you financial compensation. We prefer the first signal simply because there is an intrinsic element to it: the recognition and appreciation of our performing a task well.

Extrinsic rewards, like money, tend to have a more addictive quality, compared to intrinsic rewards. We easily get used to whatever level of material comfort we currently enjoy, a trait known as adaptation.

We are capable of adapting to the change for the worse, but we certainly don't like it; furthermore, it clouds our attitude toward our work. Also, once we get paid for doing something, it's unlikely we will ever be willing to do it again for free. In such a case, we are willing to give up the good vibes of doing something for the joy of it if we are no longer getting paid to do it. It feels as if we are giving away something of value to someone who should be paying for it.

In order to feel motivated, we need to feel that the work we are performing has some importance, and we also need to feel a certain sense of urgency about it. A sense of urgency and importance isn't hard to come by if you're the attending physician in a hospital emergency room. It may be harder to generate those feelings when you're reviewing expense reports at your company.

There's a reason why every task at work needs to be done. If you don't see how your task fits into the big picture at work, you owe it to yourself to find out how the work you do makes a positive difference in people's lives. Your boss, if he/she is worthy of the position, knows you deserve such knowledge and that such knowledge can be a great motivator.

Your boss should also recognize that once you feel a sense of urgency and importance to your work, the best thing to do is free you to get the work done in the best way you see fit. If you are properly motivated about the purpose of your work, you are also properly motivated to do that work to the best of your ability and as efficiently as possible.

Master of Your Domain

Self-determination theory (SDT) is a theory of motivation developed by Edward L. Deci and Richard M. Ryan at the University of Rochester in the 1980's. SDT contends that humans have three innate psychological needs - competence, autonomy, and relatedness. The three needs cited in SDT can be defined as follows:

- **Competence**: to seek to control the outcome and experience mastery of a task
- **Autonomy**: the universal urge to be the causal agent of one's own life and to act in harmony with one's integrated self, though this action does not mean to be independent of others
- **Relatedness**: the universal desire to interact, be connected to, and experience caring for others

From the Self-Determination Theory web site:

*"Within SDT, the nutriments for healthy development and functioning are specified using the concept of basic psychological needs for autonomy, competence, and relatedness. **To the extent that the needs are ongoingly satisfied, people will develop and function effectively and experience wellness, but to the extent that they are thwarted, people more likely evidence ill-being and non-optimal functioning.** The darker sides of human behavior and experience, such as certain types of psychopathology, prejudice, and aggression are*

understood in terms of reactions to basic needs having been thwarted, either developmentally or proximally. " (emphasis mine)

Deci and Ryan's studies quantified that people who have their intrinsic needs met on the job are both healthier and, just as important, perform better over time, leading to higher compensation and more wealth. Those who focused on extrinsic rewards, especially money alone, felt more stress, felt less fulfillment and, in the long run, had less success and earned less than their counterparts who focused on intrinsic rewards and let the money take care of itself. Deci and Ryan and others who have followed have shown conclusively that **when you recognize that money is not the cause, but the effect, you end up with more money, and you are far happier on the way to attaining it.**

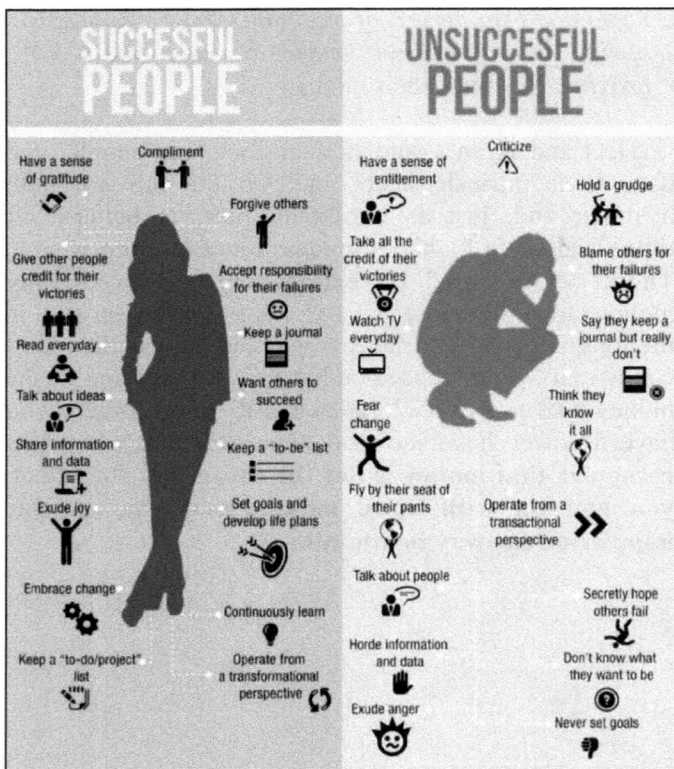

SUCCESFUL PEOPLE

- Have a sense of gratitude
- Compliment
- Forgive others
- Give other people credit for their victories
- Accept responsibility for their failures
- Read everyday
- Keep a journal
- Talk about ideas
- Want others to succeed
- Share information and data
- Keep a "to-be" list
- Exude joy
- Set goals and develop life plans
- Embrace change
- Continuously learn
- Keep a "to-do/project" list
- Operate from a transformational perspective

UNSUCCESFUL PEOPLE

- Have a sense of entitlement
- Criticize
- Hold a grudge
- Take all the credit of their victories
- Blame others for their failures
- Watch TV everyday
- Say they keep a journal but really don't
- Fear change
- Think they know it all
- Fly by their seat of their pants
- Operate from a transactional perspective
- Talk about people
- Secretly hope others fail
- Horde information and data
- Don't know what they want to be
- Exude anger
- Never set goals

More and more people are pursuing Master's degrees these days. Some are in programs because the job market isn't good for them. Some know they need more than a Bachelor's degree to be competitive in their field. Almost all of them seek what is implied by the title of the degree - they seek mastery of a subject.

As we have become more and more specialized in our jobs, mastery of the skills needed to perform our jobs has become more and more critical to our success. To be a jack of all trades is to be, by default in this era, a master of none. All trades require a level of mastery that makes it almost impossible for the average person to excel in more than a few areas.

We instinctively want to become highly skilled in a field for two important reasons. First, higher skill levels lead to higher compensation - ask any professional athlete. Second - and this reason is more important for most people - mastery leads to greater autonomy. **Mastery of your work skills leads to mastery of your life.**

When a job challenges us beyond our skill levels, we feel stressed. When a job doesn't challenge us at all, we become bored and disengaged. When we are challenged enough that we are fully engaged without being stressed, we are said to be in flow, or in sports parlance, in the zone. There is a sweet spot each of us has where we are energized by the challenge of our work, instead of being either debilitated or disinterested by it.

Because we have a tendency to get bored easily, mastery becomes a moving target. The rapid pace of change necessitates that we all continually upgrade our skills to remain competitive in the workforce. However, this rapid pace of change creates an externally imposed mandate to upgrade one's skills, which we are learning is a poor way to motivate people. We also have an intrinsic desire to upgrade our skills, in part because we don't want to become complacent and bored in our work. But mastery also feels good, and continuous improvement is the best way to maintain that good feeling.

It is never necessary to *be the best*; it is only necessary to *do your best*. When you do your best, you will occasionally be the best, too. Being the best is another one of those extrinsic factors - you are basing your mastery on a comparison to others. Because you can't control the skills and talents of others, you end up ceding your happiness and sense of worth to something beyond your control. Doing your best puts all the control with you, where it belongs. You set the standard; you do the evaluating; you hand out the rewards. And true mastery involves a commitment that, however good you are at something today, your goal is to be a little better tomorrow.

Motivation is more like respiration than inspiration. Motivation doesn't get us breathing, but it can help keep us breathing when breathing gets difficult.

Even when you're inspired, you still need motivation. Inspiration helps you produce a strategy; motivation helps you develop tactics. The best way to get and stay motivated is to find a cause that is bigger than just you.

We generally work harder to prevent disappointing others than to prevent disappointing ourselves. Look for intrinsic reasons to do something. Make the effort because it affects you in positive, intangible ways; not because others think you should do it or because someone or something is prodding you with carrots and sticks.

Finally, make sure you answer the why question before you worry about answering who-what-when-where-how questions. **The proper answer to the why question will provide inspiration *and* keep you motivated.** When you properly answer the why question, you will also find a lot of who-what-when-where-how questions begin to answer themselves.

Getting Along

Animals with bigger brains have more complex social networks, and we humans are at the top of that list. We have large frontal lobes because we have the largest social groups. We have the largest social groups because we could not survive without them.

When you look at humans as a species, it's obvious we did not become the dominant species on the planet because of any purely physical superiority. The only way we survived as a species, much less came to dominate, was because of our ability to develop and maintain complex social networks. What has worked for us as a species for thousands of years also applies to us as individuals. The better we are at developing connections with other people, the better our chances for survival, success, and ultimately, happiness.

Social networks are excellent at offering support when we need it. They are also excellent at providing constraints when we need those, too. There are the obvious examples, such as judicial systems that discourage criminal behavior that is detrimental to the group. There are also the less obvious examples, like posting your activities on Facebook, Youtube, etc.

Before engaging in activity that might be, at a minimum, embarrassing, we now think about the repercussions, should that activity end up on some social networking site. These same social networks help us stay on task when we make a commitment to positive change. If you tell all your friends on social media that you are going to lose ten pounds in the next two months, you know you will have to provide an accounting to them at the end of the period.

The best relationships are built on five attributes: respect, shared experience, mutual enjoyment of each other's company, trust, and reciprocity. The ability to establish and maintain all five of these attributes in a relationship is one reason why the number of meaningful relationships we can handle is limited. The importance of a relationship in our lives is also based largely on to what degree these five attributes are present.

When we are free to choose a relationship, the ability to respect someone is one of the first requirements. If we don't respect someone, it's unlikely we will want to establish any kind of relationship. Some relationships that are established for us, such as with our parents, assume a level of respect. Once we have the option of discontinuing such a relationship, the respect must be earned. The loss of respect for a person can be an instant relationship killer, such as when we discover a friend has been cheating on a spouse or a business partner.

Shared experiences bond people together, especially if the experience is profoundly positive or negative. A profoundly positive experience is something on the order of bringing a child into the world together, not merely taking a cruise together. Experiences that involved hardship, danger, or suffering are often the catalyst for our deepest friendships. Many a lifelong friend has been made on the battlefield. Misery truly does love company.

We want to have relationships when we enjoy spending time with someone. However, we have to spend a lot of time with people whose company we don't particularly enjoy. Such situations are especially true at work, where we don't get to choose our co-workers. The people we want to spend time with are those who share some of our interests and who also possess enough

518

social skills to make their presence something to be enjoyed, rather than merely tolerated.

Along with respect, trust must be present at the beginning of a relationship, or it is unlikely to form. Trust is greatest where the relationship is deepest. If a casual friend failed to keep a piece of shared gossip secret, the relationship would lose value, even though we might not feel compelled to end the relationship. On the other hand, if we found out our spouse had been unfaithful, a betrayal of trust on that level by someone that close is almost certain to irreparably damage the relationship.

Even in the strongest, most enduring, and most noble of relationships, certain rules, mostly unspoken, still apply. In order to maintain the relationship and reap its benefits, it is necessary to abide by these codes.

As a social construct, *reciprocity* means that in response to friendly actions, people are frequently much nicer and much more cooperative than what could be expected by the self-interest model; conversely, in response to hostile actions, reciprocity is frequently much nastier and sometimes quite brutal. Reciprocity encompasses the concepts of the Golden Rule, mutual back scratching, quid pro quo, and an eye for an eye.

Reciprocity is not the same as altruism or even gift giving. Altruism is helping those less fortunate, with the only reward being the positive feelings that result from the good deed. Gift giving is not typically based on need, but rather on the desire to make someone else happy. When a grandparent gives a gift to a grandchild, neither altruism nor reciprocity is a factor in that action.

Reciprocity is based both on the other party's intentions as well as the consequences of their actions. We actually feel a greater obligation to reciprocate when someone attempts to do us a favor that doesn't work out than we do for someone who inadvertently benefits us. Reciprocity is based on a trading of favors, as opposed to a formal negotiation or contract.

In addition to positive reciprocity, there is also negative reciprocity, which might be construed as retaliation or revenge. Negative reciprocity, unlike positive reciprocity, doesn't have the expectation of gain. Other than the pleasure of getting back at someone who has harmed you, the only other benefit to negative reciprocity may be to discourage such acts by the perpetrator or others in the future. In certain circles, such as the Mafia, to not retaliate when you've been wronged is taken as a sign of weakness and invites even worse abuses in the future.

Our instinct for reciprocity is so strong that a person will feel obligated to return a favor, even if the favor was unrequested, as was demonstrated in an experiment by Dennis Regan in 1971. Regan led subjects to believe they were in an art appreciation experiment with a partner, who was really Regan's assistant. In the experiment, the assistant would disappear briefly and bring back a soft drink for the subject. After the art experiment was through, the assistant asked the subject to buy a raffle ticket. In the control group the assistant behaved in exactly the same manner, but did not buy the subject a drink. The subjects who had received the favor, a soft drink, bought more raffle tickets than those in the control group, despite the fact that they had not solicited the drink or any favor from the assistant. Surveys completed by the subjects after they finished the experiment showed that whether they personally liked the assistant or not had no effect on how many tickets they bought.

One problem of reciprocity focuses on the unequal profit obtained from the concept of reciprocal concessions. The emotional burden to repay bothers some more than others, causing some to overcompensate with more than what was given originally. In the Regan study, subjects paid more money for the tickets than the cost of the unrequested soft drink. Whether it's unsolicited address stickers in the mail from some charity or flowers passed out by a religious cult at the airport, people who want something from us know that the best way to get it is to give us something that is unsolicited (and of lower value) first, and then wait for the reciprocity gene to kick in before making their sales pitch. Without our instinct for reciprocity, free samples might cease to exist.

In this world, we have *social norms* and *market norms*. Social norms involve the interactions between humans. They are about helping each other and getting along. They are the glue that holds a society together. They are biological. Market norms involve a bottom line. They are transaction-based. They can be precisely measured. They are mechanical.

We are all familiar with the old saying, "It's a pleasure doing business with you." Conducting business with people should be a pleasurable experience, but there should be clear boundaries where social norms rule and where market norms rule. In any business situation, there is a potential clash of social norms and market norms, and any attempt to mix the two can lead to real problems.

The first thing to realize is that **when social norms collide with market norms, social norms lose.** This collision almost always occurs when market norms invade the world of social norms. For example, many budding romantic relationships have come to a screeching halt because, at some point, the guy brought up how much he had spent on dates and that he wasn't getting anything in return. That one comment shifted the relationship from social norms to market norms.

In business relationships, market norms should rule. Certainly, every business should treat their customers and their employees with respect. But the business will have neither customers nor employees unless it maintains an acceptable bottom line. In the long term, all employees must be judged on their ability to add value to the business. All customers must be judged on whether they add to or subtract from the bottom line.

If you are an employee, the relationship with your employer should be based first on a fair exchange of labor for money. That said, social norms are one of the best ways to engender employee loyalty. We may stay because we need the paycheck, but we want to stay when we feel appreciated, which is a large purpose of social norms. You remember when an employer says "thank you" when distributing paychecks. Little things make a big difference.

In social relationships, social norms should rule. When you are invited to a friend's house for dinner, you bring a nice bottle of wine as a gift; you don't offer to "pay the tab" at the end of the evening. When your neighbor asks to borrow your lawn mower, you lend it with the expectation he will return the favor in the future (reciprocity); you don't charge him rent.

Social norms should always prevail when a higher calling is involved. People are more inclined to donate blood when cookies and juice are offered as a thank you than when cash is offered as compensation. If people want to do something for altruistic reasons, you will offend them and prompt them to withdraw support if you bring money into the equation. The good feeling we get when we do something to help others is priceless, so the worst thing one can do is attempt to put a price on it.

If you introduce market norms where social norms prevail, market norms will almost always win. But know that social norms may never return and that they never forget, either.

When someone makes a mistake with market norms, the typical result is a loss of business, but nothing more. People who are consistently bad with market norms may end up going out of business, but they probably won't become social pariahs.

Making mistakes with social norms can be far more costly. Our social network, our relationship support system, is undergirded by social norms. When we are clumsy with social norms, or when we attempt to replace social norms with market norms, we risk knocking that entire support system out from under us.

Not only do we risk relationship penalties from misuse of social norms, misuse of social norms can have a more devastating effect on our finances than misuse of market norms. You have to make a living from your friends because your enemies won't do business with you. Poor use of social norms can turn friends into enemies, with the result that you have no friends and no customers.

Social media has been called many things, but a couple of the more accurate descriptions are word of mouth on digital steroids and the world's largest referral program in history. Social media has become the most importance place for a business to be if they intend to stay in business. While it may be called social media, it is actually driven by market norms.

While keeping in touch with others' activities is a major driver of social media, the real reason for the popularity of social media is the almost endless opportunities for self-promotion. The whole purpose of LinkedIn is to enable people to promote themselves in the business environment. Twitter and Facebook enable us to promote ourselves both professionally and personally.

Over time, our social media postings paint a picture of us to others. We may not be aware of how often we may post on a particular topic, but we are keenly aware of Facebook friends who are obsessed with their pets, grandchildren, politics, or what they are having for lunch. These constant postings offer the opportunity for many people to get to know you better. Whether or not that's a good thing depends on what you're posting.

One of the more troubling trends with social media involves generations Y and Z, the young people who use social media in greater proportion for their socializing than older people. They may be more adept at communicating in a digital world, but for those relationships to have any real-world value, they must eventually take place in the real world, which means face-to-face. While social media may enable people, especially younger ones, to speak up in situations where they might remain silent in person (not necessarily a bad thing, either), the reliance on social media also seems to be hampering the ability to write and speak effectively in more traditional settings.

Goal(s)!

Since it was first published in 1989, Steven Covey's book *The 7 Habits of Highly Effective People* has sold more than 25 million copies worldwide. It ranks in the top ten best-selling non-fiction books of all time. Habit 2 is titled "Begin with the End in Mind." The author explains:

> *"To begin with the end in mind means to start with a clear understanding of your destination. It means to know where you're going so that you better understand where you are now and so that the steps you take are always in the right direction... we may be very busy, we may be very efficient, but we will also be truly* <u>*effective*</u> *only when we begin with the end in mind."*

Becoming inspired and motivated is like building the powertrain to the vehicle that will enable you to become successful and happy. The setting of goals is like building the steering and GPS systems that help steer you to your destination. Put in more primitive terms, **inspiration and motivation are your sails; goals are your rudder.**

Before you can set goals, you must first determine what your mission is. When you think of your mission, you should think in terms of a personal philosophy and set of values that don't change. Goals can and should change as needed. Goals adjust to the outer world and your inner changes; moreover, changing goals as needed enables you to stay true to your mission.

In recent years, American business has embraced the concept of SMART goals. The acronym stands for **S**pecific, **M**easurable, **A**chievable, **R**ealistic, and **T**ime-targeted. The concept of SMART goals contends that goals that are difficult to achieve and specific tend to increase performance more than goals that are not.

Setting SMART goals affects outcomes in four ways:

- **Choice**: goals narrow attention and direct efforts to goal-relevant activities and away from counter-productive or irrelevant activities.
- **Effort**: goals can lead to more effort, especially because a goal almost always exceeds the current level of performance.
- **Persistence**: Someone becomes more prone to work through the inevitable setbacks if pursuing a goal.
- **Cognition**: Goals can lead individuals to develop and change their behavior in the long run, even after goals are met.

Because SMART goals are specific, they avoid some of the biggest flaws in goal-setting - irrelevance and ambiguity. SMART goals can be very effective, but only if the goals themselves are worthwhile. Before goals, especially SMART goals, are created and implemented, everyone who is expected to meet those goals needs to believe that what they are working toward is worth the effort to get there. SMART goals presume a commitment; they don't create it.

The need to buy into a goal before attempting to achieve it is the reason for inspiration and motivation first. If you are setting goals only for yourself, becoming inspired and motivated can be fairly easy. If you have to inspire and motivate others, that's defined as Leadership. Leadership is in essence inspiring and motivating others to do what they would not do on their own. For our purposes, we will limit our discussion to personal goal-setting. If you are able to achieve your own goals, that's enough for now. Besides, you can't lead others to achieve goals if you're incapable of achieving your own goals.

SMART goals are most effective in steady-state situations, rather than ones that require major changes. SMART goals tend to focus on effects more than causes. They measures effects more than attempt to change behaviors. Since major outcome changes almost always require major behavioral changes first, setting up behavioral goals is a necessary prerequisite to setting up SMART goals.

You may think that setting small goals leads to less success because you aren't pushing yourself, but that isn't the case. **Small goals that get accomplished do more to spur us on than do large single goals that always seem to be over the horizon.** The positive reinforcement that achieving small goals provides enables us to continue making progress toward larger goals.

Research shows that small goals, known in psychology as proximal goals, have more effect than large goals, known as distal goals. In one study, elementary school students who did poorly in math were broken into two groups. One group was given the distal goal of completing seven thirty-minute math modules by the end of the seventh session. The other group was given the proximal goal of completing one module during each session. Both groups were functioning at the same math skills level at the beginning. On the final test, the distal goals group solved 45% of the problems; the proximal goals group solved 81%. The only difference in the two groups in this study was in the way the goals were presented. The distal group was thinking like a python, trying to swallow the problem whole; the proximal group was thinking like a piranha, biting the problem into small chunks. The results speak for themselves.

*"So, what are we aiming for, Timmy —
The Nobel Prize or 'Inspected by No. 7'?"*

Dean Karlan is an economics professor at Yale University. Along with colleagues Barry Nalebuff and Ian Ayres, he developed stickK.com. StickK.com offers you the opportunity, through "Commitment Contracts," to show to yourself and others the value you put on achieving your goals.

The four steps involved on stickK.com are:

1. **Select your goal.** Your goal can be anything you want. No guidance is offered on setting appropriate or attainable goals.

2. **Set the stakes.** You have the option of putting money on the line. If you don't succeed in meeting your goal, stickK will send your money to one of three options - a friend, a charity, or an "anti-charity," which is an organization you choose that is against what you stand for. The thought of

financially supporting the other side can be a powerful motivator.

3. **Get a referee.** Invite someone trustworthy to be your referee and report to stickK.com your success or failure.

4. **Add friends for support.** Your friends can supply support, peer pressure, or whatever you might need to help you meet your goal.

A study done in Scotland in 1992 demonstrated the healing power of written goals. A group of sixty patients who had hip or knee replacement surgery were studied during rehab. Movement is very painful after such surgery, but it is essential to get moving as soon as possible. Blood clots can form, and scar tissue can form in the joints, destroying flexibility.

Each patient received a booklet with his/her rehab schedule. In the back of the booklet were several additional blank pages with a heading: "My goals for this week are____:" The patients were asked to write down their personal rehab goals for each week, such as when and how far they planned to walk that week.

When the researchers followed up with the patients three months later, they found a profound difference between those who had written down weekly goals and those who hadn't. The patients who had written goals had begun walking nearly twice as fast as the ones who hadn't. They became mobile almost three times faster.

Many of the plans focused on how the patient would deal with pain or some other setback. These patients recognized that there would be times when meeting their goals would become especially difficult, so they dealt with the temptation to quit by having an action plan to get them past their worst moments.

Almost everyone responds better to positive reinforcement than the negative kind. For that reason, goals are more effective when stated in positive terms rather than negative ones. A goal that is stated in terms of what someone is moving toward, rather than what they hope to leave behind, will be more effective. For example, it's preferable to state a goal of becoming sober, as opposed to stating it as stopping drinking.

Writing down goals has been proven to increase the chances for success. Writing down goals creates a greater sense of clarity and commitment. However, clarity depends on how the goal is actually stated.

Most goals are so vaguely stated that it can be impossible to judge whether someone has succeeded or failed. Some of the goals people have made on stickK.com include "lose weight," "drink less," "start approaching attractive women," "eat/live clean," and "do whatever I want." These goals leave so much wiggle room that it can be easy for the individual to claim success. Any progress is to be encouraged, but progress isn't the same thing as victory.

Goals need to be quantifiable, which means that, whenever possible, a date and an amount of some kind should be part of a goal. The vaguely stated goals in the previous paragraph don't have any numbers attached to them, so it is difficult to measure progress, success, or failure. A referee for one of these people should insist that they come up with an amount and a date before agreeing to help.

For the person who wants to lose weight, referees should know how much weight and by what date. To aid progress, they should get a timetable of incremental weight losses and dates. Recall the elementary school math students who had their goals broken into seven individual modules, and they performed much better as a result. If an overall goal were to lose 30 pounds in 300 days, target dates for losing 5, 10, 15, 20, and 25 pounds should also be set. These sub-goals provide ongoing incentives while reducing procrastination. Missing a sub-goal should not be considered a failure, but rather a reminder that additional effort might be needed to reach the overall goal.

Very often we underestimate our own abilities. As a result, we set goals that are too modest. Goals should have a lot of flexibility to be adjusted upward and a lot less flexibility to be adjusted downward. The ability to adjust goals upward easily enables progress to occur as fast as possible. The ability to adjust goals downward uneasily reduces the tendency to want to backslide at the first sign of difficulty; but having the flexibility to adjust downward can also prevent complete abandonment of a goal. Even if a goal has to be adjusted downward, there is likely still an element of progress already, which should not go unclaimed.

If you have first discovered your inspiration, your motivation, and your mission before you start setting goals, then you should not have any goals that conflict with your personal values. Such goals are unlikely to be achieved, and even if they were, it would be a hollow victory.

In addition to not conflicting with personal values, goals should not conflict with each other. One way of avoiding conflicting goals is to have a clear priority of goals. A first priority might be to reduce spending and increase savings. There might also be a goal of exercising more and losing weight. Both of those goals can be worked on simultaneously. However, joining a health club to promote more exercise may increase

531

spending and reduce saving, which is in clear conflict with your first priority goal.

Psychologists Robert Emmons and Laura King have demonstrated in a series of studies that conflicting goals create three main problems:

- **Worry** - The effort to reconcile competing or conflicting demands creates stress.
- **Lower productivity** - Conflict leads to confusion, which leads to paralysis, or at least inefficiency.
- **Physical and mental health problems** - Greater anxiety and depression are most common emotional problems, which lead to poorer health overall.

If you hate having unfinished business, you probably don't procrastinate. The reason you hate unfinished business is the Zeigarnik effect, named after Russian psychologist Bluma Zeigarnik. Her studies demonstrated that unfinished business preys on our minds, while completing a task allows us to forget about it and move on.

When we have an uncompleted task or an unreached goal, it's like the seven-note musical riff commonly known as "shave-and-a-haircut...two-bits." (You might recognize it as the banjo riff from *The Beverly Hillbillies,* right before a commercial break.) Many a laugh has been induced where the last two notes are held in abeyance for what is only seconds, but seems like an eternity. Until we hear the last two notes, we can't move on.

Follow up studies have revealed another aspect of the Zeigarnik effect. When we have an unfinished task or unaccomplished goal, we can alleviate the distraction of it by making a written plan to complete the task or accomplish the goal. Once a plan is in place, our unconscious mind stops nagging our conscious mind and reverts to simple reminders to accomplish what has been promised.

Whenever we can take action that will help us achieve multiple goals simultaneously, it makes sense to do so. If dining out less often and eating at home will increase your savings and reduce your waistline at the same time, that's a double incentive to whip up something in the kitchen instead of making reservations. Viewed from another perspective, frequent dining out can reduce your wallet while expanding the butt that sits upon it.

Finally, every accomplished goal deserves a reward for reaching it. The reward should be proportionate with the difficulty of reaching that particular goal. Losing five pounds does not merit a new car, nor does losing one hundred pounds merit a mere bouquet of flowers. If a goal is worthwhile, the change resulting from its accomplishment will be rewarding. The act of accomplishment will also be rewarding. The additional reward is the motivation to keep going during the task of reaching the goal. During that time, when the hard work is being done but the rewards are not yet forthcoming, we need all the help we can get to keep us moving forward.

For most of us, peer pressure is most overwhelming in adolescence, but it is prevalent throughout our lives, in every group. Peer pressure is normally thought of in negative terms, and with good cause, especially when we think of teenagers doing reckless things because their peers goaded them into doing it. The parents of those teens might also be giving in to peer pressure. They might not be smoking pot or smashing mailboxes, but they might be going deeply into debt trying to maintain the lifestyle of their peer group.

Because the people with whom we associate can have a huge influence on our behavior, it's important to look at how they might be influencing the habits we develop. If our associates or co-workers have bad habits, there's a good chance we will develop some of those same habits. In general, if you hang around with people who behave better than you do, you will begin to behave better. The opposite, of course, is also true. Peer pressure exists, even when it isn't obvious.

Finding just one person who lives the way you want to live can be the turning point. In fact, far more people make major changes for the better because of a single person, not a single event. That single person might be a love interest, although those situations leading to long-term success are rarer than the romantic in us would like to believe. More often, the agent of change is a friend or colleague who is a positive role model, who supports your desire for change, and who introduces you to other people who can also serve as role models. Because these people believe in you, you begin to believe in yourself, and you begin to believe that you can become better.

80/20

It's unlikely you've ever heard of Vilfredo Pareto (1848-1923). He was an Italian engineer, sociologist, economist, political scientist, and philosopher. His greatest contribution is probably the theory that bears his name, the Pareto Principle. The reason you probably don't know of Pareto or his principle is because the more common name for the Pareto Principle is the 80/20 Rule.

Pareto developed his principle by making such diverse observations as 80% of the land in Italy was owned by 20% of the population, and 20% of the pea pods in his garden contained 80% of the peas. Across the spectrum of human endeavors, there is a consistent pattern that **20% of the input is responsible for 80% of the output.**

The 80/20 Rule is so important because, like many of the keys to success, it is counter-intuitive. We tend to think that equal inputs should have equal outputs. When identical efforts do not yield identical results, there is an unfairness to the system that must be rectified. Instead of focusing our efforts on the productive 20%, we spend too much time and effort in an almost always futile effort to lift the bottom 80% to the level of the top 20%. When the two groups do reach some level of parity, it is almost always the result of the top 20% being pulled down, rather than any success in lifting the bottom 80% up.

Joseph M. Juran was born in Romania in 1904. He emigrated to the U.S. in 1912, and his family settled in Minnesota. After graduating from college, Juran became an engineer at Western Electric. In 1941, Juran stumbled across the works of Pareto, resulting in a major shift in world economic power.

Expanding upon Pareto's principle, Juran developed a method of quality management that centered on the theory that 80% of quality problems are caused by 20% of the causes. Juran also argued that human problems - mainly a resistance to change - were at the core of most quality problems. Juran was also one of the first to recognize and analyze the cost of poor quality.

In the early 1950's, American industries weren't interested in Juran's theories. They were the world leaders, and there was a resistance to change. Japan was another story. They were rebuilding an economic base after the devastation of World War II. Japanese products at that time had a reputation for poor quality. In the 1950's and well into the 1960's, "made in Japan" was synonymous with "junk".

Juran became a guru to Japanese management. By the early 1970's, the quality of Japanese products was equal to or better than the competition from the rest of the world. At that time, all anyone had to do was drive a Toyota Corolla and a Ford Pinto back-to-back to see the genius of Joseph Juran. American business finally embraced Juran and his theories when ignoring them was no longer an option. Just as it took the Japanese nearly two decades to reap the rewards of Juran's theories of quality improvement, American businesses would spend the better part of two decades being uncompetitive before the quality gap narrowed appreciably.

If we know from Pareto that 20% of inputs create 80% of outputs, and if we know from Juran that 80% of problems are caused by 20% of causes, we also know that we can greatly improve who we are by focusing on these two areas.

We all have certain strengths that have served us well throughout our lives. These strengths probably came naturally to us. We tend to take them for granted, which is another way of saying we undervalue them. Also, we all have some glaring weaknesses that tend to erase much of the progress that our strengths could be providing to us.

To become as efficient as you can become, your efforts should be focused as follows:

1. Recognize, develop, and utilize your strengths to their fullest advantage. "Lead with your strength" is not just some slogan; it is practical advice.
2. Recognize your most glaring weaknesses and then work to minimize the damage they do to you. You are unlikely to turn a glaring weakness into a strength, nor is it a good use of your limited time, energy, and willpower to try. You can, however, reduce such a liability substantially.
3. Recognize your remaining mild strengths and weaknesses for what they are and largely ignore them. The return on investment from trying to improve in these areas is almost non-existent. Your time is much better spent on steps 1 and 2.

Good Enough is Often Better

People whose goal is perfection in every decision are known as *maximizers*. Maximizers tend to be frustrated and unhappy because reality almost never meets their goals and expectations. They will spend a great deal of time on the decision-making process, and they will make some excellent decisions as a result. Unfortunately, they will never fully enjoy the fruits of their labors because their assessment is based on relative standards, not absolute ones. Their assessment is based relative to perfection, which is impossible to achieve.

Satisficers are the opposite of maximizers. They do not expect perfection from themselves, and they don't expect their decisions to be perfect. Satisficers set absolute standards, and when those standards have been met, they won't spend additional resources for incremental improvements. Satisficers are well aware of the point of diminishing returns; maximizers blow way past that point because they are obsessed with perfection.

Maximizers may make some better individual decisions than satisficers, but they also don't make some decisions that need to be made. They are preoccupied with making the best decision every time. Satisficers may give up a little on the quality of their decisions, but they more than make up for it in quantity. Satisficers will take care of all the business that needs to be taken care of and will still have a life.

Maximizers also suffer from an affliction that satisficers do not – buyer's remorse. Maximizers pay a price in mental anguish that satisficers rarely do. They also usually end up worse off financially than satisficers. Satisficers see the big picture and know when it's time to allocate resources to more productive endeavors. Maximizers are micro, not macro, and so they lose out on many opportunities because they can't see past their current obsession. Going back to the 80/20 rule, **satisficers are for more likely than maximizers to focus on the 20% of inputs that generates 80% of outcomes and ignore the rest.**

Success and failure have an emotional connection because two of our most powerful emotions are linked closely to them - success with happiness and failure with sadness. We naturally assume that when we are successful at something, happiness will immediately ensue. We also expect failure to bring sadness.

Because it is easier to generate negative emotions than positive ones and because we expect to feel sad when we fail, our expectations of sadness are almost always met. Ironically, one of the keys to success is to not let failure sadden you to the point of becoming discouraged. People like Thomas Edison failed far more often than they succeeded, yet ultimately such people are hailed as being extremely successful.

Success generating happiness is a much trickier proposition. People equate success with happiness, and they often use the terms synonymously. Achieving success can often prove disappointing, though. For example, a young woman may have a goal of reaching a certain management level at work. She may work long hours and make many sacrifices to climb the corporate ladder. Once the big promotion finally is received, she may experience more emptiness than elation. She may have the title, the salary, and the corner office. However, the rush of happiness she was expecting as part of the package isn't there because, contrary to popular expectations, happiness is not standard equipment on success. Also, because happiness did not come automatically, she can be left feeling not merely neutral but sad because her expectations were so unmet.

Success and failure are travelling companions. As you journey toward a goal, you will inevitably encounter both along the way. Harvard business professor Rosabeth Moss Kanter, who has studied many business organizations, observed: "Everything can look like failure in the middle." If you understand that failures along the way are an inevitable part of long-term success and if that recognition enables you to control the negative emotions that come along with those failures, you are much more likely to persevere to the point of eventual success.

When we begin a new challenge, we start out with many positive emotions - hope being perhaps the strongest of them all. Hope is an essential emotion in getting any project off the ground, but as Sir Francis Bacon observed, "Hope is a good breakfast, but it is a poor supper." Once the initial excitement at the beginning of the journey has waned and the long slog toward the finish line is all there is at the moment, we can become like kids in the back seat on a long drive - "Are we there yet? Are we there yet? Are we there yet?"

When a goal becomes closer to realization, our emotions improve, with confidence of success leading the way. There is a U-shape to the emotional pattern we encounter when we work toward a long-term goal - hope and anticipation at the beginning, confidence and pride toward the end, but a cornucopia of negative emotions in the middle, including but not limited to, anger, cynicism, depression, despair, impatience, stress, and uncertainty.

The onset of negative emotions is much less likely to slow us down, and they are also likely to be fewer and of lower intensity if we anticipate their arrival and prepare accordingly. Think about the pattern of going to college. At the beginning, you were full of hope and enthusiasm for this grand new experience you were about to have. Toward the end, you were focused on completing your degree with the pride and anticipation of becoming a college graduate. However, in between, there were three (or four or five) years of eight o'clock classes, boring lectures, ridiculously long term papers, and stressful weeks of final exams. For many college students, the hardest period begins around the second semester and lasts until the middle of junior year. In the second semester, there is not yet enough experience to have adjusted to the daily grind. By junior year, the student is both used to the daily grind and can see the light at the end of the tunnel. When students fail to complete their degree, that failure is not usually because of a lack of intelligence or even discipline, but rather an inability to handle the march through the valley of negative emotions.

What these students experience in that middle period is *growth*. The growth mindset is simply acknowledging that there will be failures, setbacks, bad feelings, and the rest. The growth is in the acceptance of all the negatives and then rising above them, even getting psyched up at the challenge of conquering the drudgery that comes with any job.

Knowing that we will face valleys along the way to our goals can actually make us optimistic. Knowing that failure is going to cross our path on the journey to success, we are more likely to seek it out and confront it, rather than fearing and avoiding it. It isn't the obstacle that we choose to face head-on that defeats us; it's the object that blindsides us because we refuse to acknowledge it.

The value of being an optimist has been articulated beautifully by Daniel Kahneman, the renowned psychologist and Nobel laureate:

> *"If you were allowed one wish for your child, seriously consider wishing him or her optimism. Optimists are normally cheerful and happy, and therefore popular; they are resilient in adapting to failures and hardships, their chances of clinical depression are reduced, their immune system is stronger, they take better care of their health, they feel healthier than others and are in fact likely to live longer. Optimistic individuals play a disproportionate role in shaping our lives. Their decisions make a difference; they are the inventors, the entrepreneurs, the political and military leaders - not average people."*

One of the keys to achieving anything worthwhile is persistence, and two of the benefits of an optimistic temperament are persistence in the face of obstacles and resilience in the face of setbacks. **If the first step in achieving a goal is the belief that you can and will achieve that goal, optimism is the first, most important tool to have in your kit.**
Optimism can be viewed as a cornucopia of positive emotions molded into a single personality. Those positive emotions and optimism have a convoluted cause and effect pattern. When you possess positive emotions like confidence, enthusiasm, and inner peace, it's easy to be an optimist. Going the other way, if you are a natural optimist, positive emotions like confidence, enthusiasm, and inner peace seem to pour forth like a natural spring. Whether you are a natural-born optimist or have made yourself into one, once you are one, the positive emotions seem almost self-generating.
Optimism can be taken to the extreme, though. Daniel Kahneman also points out that the blessings of optimism are offered only to individuals who are only mildly biased and who are able to accentuate the positive without losing track of reality. The overly optimistic person is likely to take excessive risks. How many fortunes have been lost because people refused to accurately assess or even acknowledge the downside potential of an investment? Every economic bubble that bursts is testament to the dangers over over-optimism. It is important to believe that you can handle a worst-case scenario, but in order for that belief to have value, you first have to be able to accurately gauge what the worst-case scenario actually is.

WHAT ARE YOU THINKING?

In the 1984 movie *Moscow on the Hudson*, Robin Williams plays Vladimir Ivanov, a Soviet musician who defects to the U.S. The first third of the movie shows his life in Moscow – no freedom to choose where he will work or where he can go and waiting in long lines to get basic necessities like toilet paper.

When he goes to an American supermarket for the first time, Vladimir asks the manager where the "coffee line" is. He is informed there is no line, but that coffee is on aisle two. As he walks down the aisle, he recites the brand names he sees: *"Taster's Choice, decaffeinated, Maxwell House, El Pico, Chock Full o' Nuts, Espresso, Cappuccino, Café France, Sanka, Folgers, Café Caribe, coffee, coffee, coffee ,coffee, COFFEE!"*, at which point he passes out from hyperventilation.

The unbearability of no choice caused Vladimir to leave family, friends, and everything familiar for the chance to choose. His collapse in aisle two was a natural response when he became overloaded with choices (this was pre-Starbucks, too). In this situation, the effort required to make the right choice was totally out of whack with the potential benefits. Not to mention, Vladimir's choosing skills were underdeveloped.

Your life's work is a different story. The potential benefits make the effort of choosing wisely both necessary and worthwhile. Reading some books, taking some tests, and learning more about who you are and what you want is a small price to pay to discover a career direction that will provide more than a paycheck for the rest of your life.

Risk and Reward

Change involves risk, which is why people have a reluctance to change, especially a change as important as their job. However, such risks are necessary because **risk and reward move in the same direction.** In order to earn a greater reward, you must be willing to assume greater risks. We understand this correlation when it comes to investing, but it also applies in other areas of life. Everyone who has ever been single understands that the reward of having a date on a Saturday night involves the risk of being rejected when you ask for a date.

Understanding your risk tolerance is essential in determining the rewards you will seek. **Your rewards are determined by your risk tolerance, not the other way around.** Commissioned sales people earn some of the highest incomes in any line of work. A lot of people would love to earn such an income. However, the risk of an income that can fluctuate wildly, in a job where a slump might cost you that job, is too much risk for most people to accept. That kind of pressure is one reason why such jobs have a high turnover rate.

There can be a huge difference between perceived risk and actual risk. We base decisions on our perceived risk. If we overestimate the risk, we are likely to freeze when we should act. If we underestimate the risk, we will act when we should freeze. Learning the facts about the risks we are taking narrows the gap between perceived and actual risk. We will still act based on perceived risk, but the closer our perception is to reality, the better our decisions will be.

People become more risk averse, perhaps too risk averse, when they are deciding among potential gains. The opposite is also true. When attempting to avoid a loss, we may be willing to accept too much risk to avoid the loss.

There is truth to the old saying that there is no one as free as someone with nothing left to lose. Let's say you've just lost your job; your home has been foreclosed on, and your spouse has left you. The risks involved in packing up your remaining possessions and heading off to another state or country, with no promises of anything, to start a new life and a new career in a new place seem small compared to the potential reward. On the other hand, if you still had your job, your house, and your spouse, making such a move with nothing solid at the other end would not likely happen. This form of loss is why, as people age and become established and successful, they tend to become more conservative. It's not political; it's psychological.

Psychological profiles, like those you get from the Myers-Briggs test, can be helpful in determining how much risk is within your comfort zone. While we can't change our essential personality, experience affects our perception of risk. Remember the first time you tried to dive off the diving board? You may have struggled for weeks to make that head-first plunge into the depths below. Once you succeeded, you asked yourself, "What was I so afraid of?" The best way to become less risk averse and a better judge of actual risk is to incrementally increase the risk you will take.

The Devil You Know

Despite our seemingly permanent contempt for politicians, incumbents are re-elected over 80% of the time. Our willingness to keep sending back the same people we vilify is an example of status quo bias. **When**

there isn't a clearly superior alternative, we choose to stick to the status quo – the devil we know. Even when there is a better alternative out there, we often stick with the status quo because of the inconvenience of making the change and of that nagging uncertainty the change won't be for the better.

This status quo bias can lead us to not make job and career changes, even though we believe it would be better for us if we did. The idea of saying goodbye to co-workers, to familiar surroundings, to our daily routine is a lot to overcome. Who wants to go through the trouble of building all that up again when you have it here now?

Status quo bias can work the other way, though it occurs less frequently. Sometimes we develop a bias *against* the status quo. This bias tends to occur when we are bombarded with messages indicating our current situation isn't good enough. The goal is to stir discontent and to have us buy the product or service being offered. It takes a fairly high level of dissatisfaction for most people to dump the status quo. Those sales pitches are designed to ratchet up that level to the point of taking action.

At some point, you may have reached a tipping point with your job. At that point, you went from seeing the job in overall positive terms to seeing it in overall negative terms. The tipping point may have been reached as a result of a change in bosses, a change in job duties, or a change in physical environment. There may have also been a change in you. You outgrew the job. Your priorities changed as a result of a change outside of work (marriage, parenthood, etc.). Whatever the reasons, you are now focused on the CONS of your job instead of the PROS.

"We're tunneling out after lunch – pass it on."

As you evaluate your current job situation, get out a sheet of paper and write PROS and CONS at the top of the page. Draw a line down the middle. Under the PROS column list everything positive about your job. List everything negative in the CONS column. Discuss your list with friends and family who can offer additional perspective (Bosses and gossipy co-workers should not be consulted.) This exercise will help you get the status quo into proper perspective.

(sample follows)

Current job

PROS	CONS
short commute	bad neighborhood
good 401(k) plan	below-average salary
good health insurance	no life insurance
nice co-workers	obnoxious boss
no weekend work	some unpaid overtime
liberal sick leave	limited vacation time
low stress level	limited advancement
work is pleasant	work isn't stimulating

Trade-Ups and Trade-Offs

It's the Curse of the Desirable. It doesn't matter if you are desirable as a teammate, a lover, or an employee. If you are desirable, you have more choices available to you. Unfortunately, having more choices can actually make it harder to make the right choice.

If you are choosing between your current job and one other job, it's fairly easy to do a side-by-side comparison and determine which one is best for you. However, if you have your current job and three potential new jobs to choose from, the choices increase arithmetically, while the trade-offs increase geometrically.

These trade-offs are known as opportunity costs. Accepting one job costs you the opportunity to accept another job. The more choices you have, the higher the opportunity costs associated with that choice. When you go to Baskin-Robbins, you get 31 choices. That's good. You must reject 30 of them. That's bad.

The weight associated with rejecting alternatives tends to decrease our satisfaction with the choice we make. As we compare jobs, there's a tendency to start taking the best aspects from all these job opportunities and to create an ideal job out of them. This composite becomes the standard to which any choice we eventually make is compared. No real job can compare to that composite we make.

Once you've made your list of the PROS and CONS of your current job, prioritize each column. Prioritizing means listing in descending order what you like most and hate most about your job. The items at the top of the PROS list are items you definitely want to have at your new job. To lose those could make the new job worse by comparison, despite other improvements over the current situation.

The items at the top of your CONS list you don't want to take with you. However, some of those items may be part of almost any job (things like set hours or a dress code). It's important to discern the CONS items that are common to most any job and those that are unique to your current situation. The latter group you want to leave behind as much as possible.

If you think you will find a job with all the PROS of your current job (plus a few more) and none of the CONS, wake up. Unless you stumble across a job that constantly feeds your ego and wallet, while allowing you to avoid any contact with humans displaying negative traits, you are going to have trade-offs.

When evaluating PROS and CONS, think of them as chess pieces. The PROS are your team; the CONS are the opponent. When you prioritize the list, you assign a rank to each item. Some are queens; some are knights, and some are pawns. The items at the bottom of the list are pawns. In chess, you readily exchange one of your pawns for one of your opponent's pawns; so it should be with the low items on the list. Getting rid of a minor CON is consolation for getting rid of a minor PRO.

The bigger pieces require more consideration. Are you willing to trade off your top PRO to get rid of your top CON (an exchange of queens)? The top items on your list may also have greater ramifications for others. For example, the top PRO may be a large salary, but the top CON may be constant travel. Someone with small children at home would have to weigh the impact of such trade-offs on family as well.

When we are evaluating a new job versus our current one, there is a tendency to underestimate the CONS of the new job. This underestimation occurs in part because we never know all the CONS of a job until we spend some time on that job. Also, when we are anxious to make a job change, there is a natural tendency to play up the PROS and play down the CONS to justify the decision to make the job change. It's important to be aware of this tendency for two reasons – first, you don't want to make a job change based on an erroneous evaluation. Second, awareness of this tendency can reduce your chances of "buyer's remorse", after you settle into your new job and realize it isn't a paid Utopia.

Going Solo

You're suffocating. There are the endless, useless meetings, the moronic co-workers, the bi-polar boss, the time-sapping emails, the lack of direction, the lack of progress, and the lack of purpose. Sometimes you feel you just can't take another day of it. You want to spread your wings and fly like an eagle and not waste another day with these turkeys.

Don't start flapping your wings yet. Before you take the tremendously huge step of venturing out on your own, there are a lot of questions to answer and a lot of work to be done.

The first thing you will need to do is determine your motives for wanting to go on your own. If the main motivation is to get away from something – if you feel pushed in that direction, Stop! That push may be sufficient motivation to give two weeks' notice, but it will not be sufficient motivation to succeed in an environment where the failure rate hovers around 75% in the first year.

Negative emotions are a drain of energy, not a source of energy. It is negative emotions that push you away from your current situation. To succeed in starting a business from scratch, you need positive emotions, which are a source of energy. You get that energy when you feel pulled toward something; when it feels like a calling, your destiny.

If you are going to fly solo, you need to be pulled, not pushed to do it. You have to *need* to do it, not merely *want* to do it.

Low, Medium, or High Risk?

There are different methods to being on your own, with different risks and benefits. One of the first things to determine is which method is appropriate for you and your circumstances.

At the low end of the risk scale is the ***independent contractor***, someone found commonly in technical fields. They are often sub-contracted by an agency and will work for a single company until a project is completed or until the funding dries up.

An independent contractor often has the worst of both worlds. They have to look and act like employees of the hiring party, as many outside of the company don't know they aren't employees. While they may have slightly more flexibility than an employee in the method of completing a task, they are still under the control of the hiring party. Their duration of contract is at the discretion of the hiring party, and there is no safety net when they find themselves suddenly without work. There are also none of the employee benefits like health insurance, 401(k) plans, paid vacation, etc. Lack of benefits is why an independent contractor is often paid more on an hourly basis than an employee counterpart.

An independent contractor arrangement can work well for someone who wants a more flexible work arrangement, or for someone who is already retired, or for someone who has a working spouse, where in such cases necessities like health insurance are already provided.

Next up on the risk-reward scale is the *small business owner*, which is a more complex structure than an independent contractor.

When you start a small business, you first need a business plan. That plan will include a market analysis of potential customers and competition, marketing and sales plans, expense and income projections, pro forma financial statements, and physical housing for the business.

You will need all this information in order to get financing to help get your business off the ground. Conventional outside financing will require this data and more, and they will charge an interest rate commensurate with the risk, which they consider to be high. If financing is coming from private sources (like family), you still need to have a solid business plan, since they also need to have their interests protected. You don't want to lose your family, as well as your business, through a faulty plan. Even if all the money to start a business is coming out of your own pocket, you owe yourself the same due diligence you would owe to a third-party lender.

The business owner, unlike the independent contractor, has the opportunity to build something of market value, something with the ability to someday generate income without the direct labor of the owner. That growth generally takes many years and a lot of dealings with customers, employees, and creditors in the interim. There is more long-term potential for wealth than being an independent contractor, but there is a longer gestation period.

At the top of the risk-reward continuum is the *entrepreneur*. While many, if not most, people who are out on their own consider themselves to be entrepreneurs, few actually meet the true definition.

It's Not What They Do; It's Who They Are

Every entrepreneur I've ever met, regardless of their enterprise, takes a cue from the commander of another Enterprise, Captain Kirk. The entrepreneur longs to "boldly go where no man has gone before."

The entrepreneur, more than anyone else, is a person with *vision.* Our history is replete with them – Benjamin Franklin, Thomas Edison, Henry Ford, and Steve Jobs, to name a few. They each had ideas for a future no one could even imagine. After their genius and determination made their vision reality, we all wondered how the rest of us could have missed something so obvious. The entrepreneur has a right brain that puts the rest of us to shame.

off the mark .com   by Mark Parisi

DEREK, SENSING A TREND, DECIDES TO CASH IN.

What makes a great entrepreneur? According to Silicon Valley venture capitalist John Doerr, the best ones are "missionaries, not mercenaries."

"Mercenaries have a lot of drive, they're opportunistic and always pitching their latest deal, whereas missionaries are more passionate and strategic. Mercenaries are sprinting and often have in their organizations an aristocracy of founders, whereas the missionaries are in it for the long run, obsessing on customers, not competition. They try to build a meritocracy—a loud, noisy place where the best ideas can get on the table."

Most entrepreneurs demonstrated their tendencies at an early age. They would often start a business like mowing lawns, baby-sitting, or delivering newspapers. These early enterprises are also where most of them learned about money and its importance in making and sustaining a successful business.

Entrepreneurs are competitive by nature, but their competition is most often themselves. They are less interested in how they are doing compared to others than how they are doing compared to the standards they have set for themselves.

Entrepreneurs don't worry much about what others think. They recognize that most people don't possess their sense of vision, so those opinions aren't of much value. Entrepreneurs value integrity; they will do business on a handshake, and they feel strong associations with people who share their work ethic. Henry Ford and Thomas Edison were close friends because they were so similar.

Entrepreneurs don't retire. **You retire from what you do, not from who you are.** When one venture has reached the desired level of success, they start looking for the next challenge. Often, they have different projects going on simultaneously.

Entrepreneurs work hard; they give their all to their endeavors, but they are actually better than most when it comes to maintaining balance in their lives. They value time with family, and they can usually afford leisure activities that are out of reach for most people.

Entrepreneurs are satisficers, not maximizers, which means they recognize when effort has reached the point of diminishing returns, and they move on. They know instinctively when it's "good enough" and are satisfied. A maximizer will obsess about something until it's perfect. The entrepreneur recognizes that perfection is not the goal; the goal is maximum productivity.

Entrepreneurs are, above all, agents of change.

A Calculated Leap of Faith

Unfortunately, there is no standardized test you can take to determine if you are an entrepreneur, or even if you should go into business for yourself. That's a call you have to make after some serious introspection. Many people take such a leap and fail, not because they had a bad idea, but because they didn't make sure there were the tools in place to enable them to succeed. It's sad to see someone fail when they take a leap they shouldn't have taken. It's sadder still to see someone who should have taken that leap, but couldn't bring themselves to do it. They and the world are worse off for that great idea that never got its chance.

It starts with an idea. The idea must be something that is unique and/or better than what is currently out there. Sometimes the idea is amazing in its simplicity. Ray Kroc's idea was that, for the low-priced dining out experience, consistency is more important to the consumer than getting the best meal. The product he created was McDonald's.

The product of your idea must be able to be described in terms of benefits to the consumer. The tendency of the producer is to focus on the features of a product. However, you should **begin with intended benefits to the customer and let the features evolve to meet those benefits.** The customer seeks benefits, not features, so focus your product's promotion on benefits.

Know your target market, not just demographically, but psychologically. You certainly need to know the hard numbers of your market – age, income, location, etc. That information tells you the *breadth* of your market. You also need to know the emotional reasons they want your product. That information tells you the *depth* of your market, which is important to be able to assess consumer loyalty. If there is no emotional attachment to your product or service over another's, you will lose to the lower price or new features of a competitor.

Other than coming up with a killer idea, the single biggest obstacle to launching a successful enterprise is cash flow. A great idea may generate investors, but for every budding entrepreneur with too much investment capital, there are a thousand with too little.

A well-thought out business plan can give you an idea of the business' cash flow needs, and that business plan is essential to lure bona fide investors. However, a business plan is an estimate at best. There is a tendency to underestimate expenses and start-up delays and to overestimate the speed and volume of income. A good business plan should be able to stand up to the scrutiny of someone less optimistic (more realistic?) than you.

It isn't just the cash flow of the business; the cash flow of your household needs serious planning. At the very least, you are likely to be giving up a part of the household income to make this leap. That loss will require a downward adjustment in household expenses to keep the household financially solvent. If you are stopping a paycheck that was providing 50% of your household income and if your expenses were already at 90% of your household income, where will you make the necessary cuts to balance the budget? Too often, people cover this shortfall with an increase in personal debt. When the income from the business doesn't materialize quickly or sufficiently enough, the debt load can send the budding entrepreneur into personal bankruptcy.

There is an old saying - Overnight success takes

557

about fifteen years. Experience proves that time frame is about right. Sure, the Google Guys became billionaires in less than half that time, but let's stick to reality here.

There are going to be trade-offs getting your idea off the ground. You will have to make allocation decisions about time, money, energy, production, marketing, research, and other things you can't yet imagine. This volume of decision making means one of your most important skills is the ability to make a decision and then let it run.

There is a decision hierarchy, and at the top of that hierarchy are decisions affecting your life, as well as the lives of your family. If you have a family and if they are not willing to make the sacrifices necessary to make your venture succeed, you are at a fatal disadvantage. It's hard enough making this transition, even with the full support of those closest to you. If you can't convince them that this venture is worth the sacrifice, how will you convince others?

So, before you put together a business plan, you need to put together a *life plan*. Start with the kind of life that makes you feel happy and fulfilled. Yes, those are fuzzy terms, but you know what makes you feel that way. The desire for happiness and fulfillment is also the best motivator one could have.

As you put together your life plan, here are some questions you should ask yourself (and ask yourself any other questions you feel are relevant):

- What kinds of activities give me the greatest sense of satisfaction?
- What do I have to offer that other people want and need?
- With what kind of people do I enjoy spending time?
- How much money do I need (not how much money do

I want)?
- Where would I choose to live?
- What are my obligations to others?
- How can I meet those obligations and still fulfill my dreams?
- If I found out I had one week to live, what would I most regret that I didn't do.
- If I found out I had six months to live, what would I make sure I did in that remaining time?

Any business venture you put together should have as its primary goal the ability to help you achieve your life goals. Simply stated, **your work supports your life, not the other way around.** When we get swamped by the details and demands of our work, we can easily forget the proper order of things.

Whatever business you create, make sure it is one that reflects you and your values. Your business should appear as an extension of you, which will make it easier for you to run the business, rather than having the business run you.

Burning Bridges

The more non-reversible a decision seems, the more difficult it becomes to make, which is one reason why making a major new commitment, like marriage or a new job, is so hard.

There can be a great temptation when you leave a job to take a few parting shots at annoying co-workers, and especially at your soon-to-be-ex-boss. Don't do it! First, it serves no purpose other than juvenile ego gratification. Second, you may need some of these people in the future – as references, as contacts, maybe even as customers.

Third, knowing you didn't burn the bridge back to your old job can make the decision to take a new job a little easier to make. The bridge back makes it possible for you to move forward with less fear.

At this point, a disclaimer is needed. While keeping bridges intact can enable you to make a needed change, there is a psychological toll. (In the journey of life, all bridges are toll bridges.) Having options, especially the option of returning to the status quo, can keep us from making the psychological commitment to succeed at our new job.

Consider the phrase "til death do us part." The weight of a commitment like that should make one cautious in saying "I do." Those who take it seriously are more likely to do what it takes to make the marriage succeed than those who view divorce as an easy option if things don't work out according to plan. **The downside to options is that we are less likely to commit the necessary effort to succeed at the option we've chosen.** When his junior officers doubted they could press on in the Battle of the Bulge, General Patton sternly admonished them saying, "If we are not victorious, let no one come back alive!" That's commitment!

In the short term, we tend to regret the things we did that didn't turn out well more than we regret the things we didn't do that might have turned out well. Yet, over time, we regret more the things we *didn't* do more than the things we did. We chastise ourselves over our sins of omission more than over our sins of commission. When we don't take advantage of the opportunity of a lifetime, even though that opportunity involves risks, we often spend the better part of a lifetime regretting our lack of faith and courage.

If you ask old people about their biggest regrets, they'll tell you of the trips they didn't take, the time they didn't spend with their kids, the "I Love You" they didn't say when they had the chance. When you are contemplating a major life change like a new career, it can be very useful to ask the advice of someone much older and wiser than you. If there are such people in your life who do not have a personal stake in your contemplated change, see what they think about your plans.

Finally, don't think you will kick yourself for the rest of your life if you attempt to make a better life for yourself, and it just doesn't quite work out as planned. In such a case, you may have some regrets in the short term, but over time, you will be glad you took the risk. Failure in a noble cause is still noble.

WHERE DO YOU THINK YOU'RE GOING?

The best-selling book *Good to Great* chronicles what companies do to go from being merely good to being great. The first thing great companies do is to get the right people on the bus and the wrong people off the bus. Then those people decide where to take the bus. The point in *Good to Great* is that the selection of the right employees to ride the "bus" is the biggest factor in an organization's success.

Also, average companies give employees something to work on. Great companies give employees something to work toward. Great companies offer a place to go, not just a plan to follow.

Catch the Right Bus

You're being invited onto the bus. Hopefully, you are being invited onto more than one bus. How do you know if the drivers are competent, if the other passengers are easy to get along with, if the bus is well-maintained, and if the bus is going where you want to go, and if it is even seeking your input as to its destination?

Too often, in the excitement of receiving a job offer, we don't ask these and similar questions about our new situation. We assume everything is fine because we so badly want it to be.

You need to evaluate a new employer even more than they need to evaluate you, and here's why. You will be one of dozens, hundreds, maybe thousands of employees at your new job. Your individual impact, especially in the early years there, will not be earth-shaking. On the other hand, you are about to decide on the one job you will have for the foreseeable future. The job will provide you not only with an income, but also with future opportunities for growth and a sizeable part of your personal identity. You've got more on the line in this merger than they do. You owe it to yourself to evaluate them at least as hard as they evaluate you.

Before you can say yes to a job offer, you should be able to answer these questions about the job and the employer:

- Why am I here?
- Why should I go with you instead of your competitor?
- What can I do for you?
- What problems of yours can I help solve?
- What kind of organization are you?
- Do you have the corporate personality and values that fit with mine?
- Can you afford me? In other words, can you pay me enough to beat the competition, but still have it be less money than my new boss makes?
- What does this job involve?
- What are the skills a top employee in this job would have to have?
- Do I want to work with these people?
- Is the product or service your company produces something that can make me proud?
- Are you a leader in your field, or at least aspire to be?

Revolving Doors

As you decide if a company is one you want to join, one of the best tools to use is the company's retention ratio or turnover ratio. These are simply opposite ratios of each other – retention ratio states the percentage of employees who stayed over the last year; turnover ratio states the percentage who left. From here on we'll refer to turnover ratio only. A company's Human Resources department should be able to provide you with data on turnover ratios for the industry and your particular job and how they compare to that average.

An employer's turnover ratio may tell you more than any other statistic about the work environment there. When a company is trying to get you onboard, they will tell you all the good things about the company – salary, benefits, opportunity, pleasant work environment, etc. The turnover ratio tells you with total objectivity whether the people in charge know what they're doing. People leave bosses more than they leave companies or jobs. When the bosses don't know what they're doing, the employees are keenly aware of it, and they don't stick around.

Turnover ratios vary widely by industry, so it's important to know the turnover ratio for the industry you are entering. The average employee turnover rate nationally is about 15%, which means 15% of positions have to be filled every year. That rate also means the average employee changes jobs every 7 years. As a rule, the higher the level of training and education required for a position, the lower the turnover ratio tends to be. When you invest a lot of years to reach a position, you don't walk away on a whim.

A low turnover ratio will imply the following about a company (A high ratio will imply just the opposite.):
- Management is competent and communicates clear expectations to the employees.
- Management provides feedback to employees and makes them feel valued.
- Employees feel free to speak their mind and criticize

within the goal of making improvements in the company, product, or service.

- Employees are encouraged to demonstrate skills and talents, even if they are outside their normal duties.
- Raises and promotions are merit-based with criteria for them clearly stated.
- If an employee's behavior or performance becomes unacceptable, they are terminated quickly, to protect the morale of the other employees.

While some turnover is desirable because it brings new people and ideas into the organization and keeps everyone from ending up at the top of the pay scale, organizations want to have a low turnover ratio. Replacing an employee costs a company, on average, three months' salary of the replacement. For top executive positions, it can cost a year's salary or more. The only reason a company would want to have a high turnover ratio is to keep salaries as low as possible by having many employees at the bottom of the pay scale. Productivity and morale would both be poor at such a place. Avoid such organizations altogether.

Are You Worth It?

The amount that you can be paid for your work is directly affected by the price that can be obtained for the product or service you produce. That price falls within a range. The producer's cost creates the floor of price. Any business that charges a price that is less than its cost of production won't be in business for long. Labor costs are typically the highest single business expense. For most businesses, they comprise at least half of total expenses, and can be as high as ninety percent in service industries. For that reason, changes in employee compensation have a major impact on pricing. The higher the compensation structure, the higher the price floor must be to be a profitable venture.

The value of the product or service to the consumer creates the ceiling of price. Sometimes that value can be objectively measured. If a service you provide saves a customer $1,000, paying only $500 for that service is an obvious, objective gain for the customer. Sometimes the value is more subjective. A Starbucks coffee is considerably more expensive than a Waffle House coffee. Those who value only the coffee aren't likely to pay the higher Starbucks price. However, there's a subjective value to the Starbucks experience, at least for many people. That experience creates value for those Starbucks customers; at least enough value to justify the price premium of Starbucks over its competitors.

When a new product or service is created, the perceived value is likely to be high. Pricing at this stage is governed by the ceiling more than the floor. Businesses frequently lose money in the early stages of a product/service life cycle because they are recouping development costs and sales volume is starting at zero. There is also little or no competition at this stage, so prices can be raised until there is measurable sales resistance.

Any highly profitable business enterprise will draw competitors like bees to flowers. New competitors will typically compete on price, driving down prices and profitability. As downward pressure on prices continues, profit margins get squeezed. Since raising prices under these conditions will decimate sales, profitability is increased by reducing costs – lowering the floor. Since labor costs are typically the biggest cost, employee compensation is affected, by wage and hiring freezes, or by layoffs and wage reductions under severe conditions.

Competition, and barriers to entry by competition, are key factors in determining profitability, and hence the wage structure. Brain surgeons make more than janitors for two main reasons. First, the value of having a brain tumor removed is greater than the value of having your office cubicle cleaned. Second, the arduous path to become a brain surgeon means there are few qualified to do it. In other words, brain surgeons don't have cut-throat competition for business. The path to becoming a janitor is far less arduous. There are so many potential janitors out there that wages will never be any higher than is necessary to attract enough janitors to meet the demand for them.

The professions that offer the best chances for higher incomes and relative job security are those that offer real value to the customer (objectively and subjectively measured) and that can't easily attract competitors and imitators. By the way, competition comes in many forms, from people in another country to software that hasn't been invented yet. If it can be done cheaper, eventually it will be.

Money and More

If you are reading this book with the purpose of learning how to get paid more, this is the section of interest to you. But remember, **more money will not make you love a job, any more than it would make you love a person.** Money is one way your employer demonstrates their appreciation of your contributions. Money can enable you to buy more stuff, but money has very little connection to job satisfaction. If you think you will love a job you hate if you are just paid more, you're fooling yourself. The rush of a raise will soon fade. You will spend up to your new income level and then feel even more trapped in a job you now hate even more. You will realize you sold out instead of doing something you love.

The purpose of a company's compensation system is, or should be, to get and keep the best people. It should not attempt to get right behavior from the wrong people.

For the average employee, benefit costs as a percentage of total compensation run around 30%. That figure means that if a company is paying an employee $35,000 a year, they are also paying another $15,000 for the benefits that employee receives.

There are legally mandated insurance and benefits a company must provide and pay for in whole or part. These mandates include social security, workers' compensation, and unemployment insurance.

The most common employee benefits offered by small businesses are:
- Paid Vacations; offered by 75% of small businesses.*
- Employee Health Insurance Plan; 61%
- Paid Sick Leave; 59%
- Disability Insurance; 41%
- Education Reimbursement for Job; 39%
- Pension Plan; 30%
- Life Insurance; 29%
- Dental Insurance; 24% *

*provided to full-time staff with at least 1 year's service.

Benefits can be broken down into two broad categories: nice-to-have and need-to-have. Need-to-have benefits include any insurance coverage and retirement plans. Retirement plans are so important and complex they are covered in a later chapter.

Health insurance is probably the single most important benefit to the majority of U.S. workers. No one, regardless of age or health, can afford to be without it. Health insurance is often the main reason employees don't leave a company. They may have a medical condition that would preclude them from coverage at a new job or out on their own.

The complexities of different types of coverage are beyond our scope here. Here is what you need to know – any company worth working for should make group health insurance available for employees and have it available for a reasonable premium. **You must have this coverage.** To go without health insurance when it's available, to put that kind of financial risk on yourself and your family, with the only benefit being the saving of the insurance premium, demonstrates a level of irresponsibility that should make you unacceptable to any decent employer.

Disability insurance pays you in the event you are unable to perform your job due to injury or illness. It is one of those benefits that younger people don't give much thought. However, if you become disabled and can't work, your income goes away, but your expenses don't go away. In many cases, expenses increase significantly with a disability. At least if you die, your expenses die with you. The loss of income without the loss of expenses is why disability insurance is even more necessary than life insurance. There's another reason, too. If you are under forty, you are twenty times more likely to be disabled before reaching retirement age than you are to die.

Long-term disability insurance (which usually begins

570

six months after being disabled and can cover from three years up to age sixty-five) is relatively inexpensive. It typically pays about two-thirds of what your salary was at the time of the disability. (If they paid more than two-thirds, you'd be less motivated to get well and return to work.) Because of the risk of becoming disabled and the cost if you do, you should enroll in this coverage if your employer makes it available. Generally, all but the smallest organizations offer this coverage as part of their benefits package.

Life insurance is necessary if there are others who depend on your income. Dependent children and non-working spouses certainly fit that description. The death benefit from life insurance would be used by your survivors to replace the income lost by your untimely demise.

Employers, through an insurer, often offer life insurance at a lower price, known as group rates. There may be a requirement by the insurer that a minimum percentage of employees sign up to have the coverage available. The insurer doesn't want only higher-risk employees getting the coverage and messing up all their risk calculations.

There is usually a small amount of coverage (perhaps one year's salary) that you can get without any medical exam. Higher amounts of coverage may require you to qualify medically. Each company and each insurer will vary on what they offer and how they offer it.

The advantages of group life insurance through an employer are lower premiums compared to getting the coverage on your own and no qualifying medical exam for at least some of the offered coverage. The disadvantage is that you typically can't take the coverage with you when you leave. The insurer may offer you coverage on an individual policy, but that's not usually any different than what you could get on the open market.

Dental coverage is excluded from most health insurance policies, which is why you see it offered separately. For all the reasons you need health insurance, you need dental insurance, too.

For both dental and health insurance, policies that pay for preventive care, such as regular dental cleanings and exams, are better. An employer who encourages employees to take care of themselves demonstrates concern for the employees' well-being. They are also protecting their investment, as healthy employees are more productive employees.

Paid vacation and sick leave policies don't vary as widely from company to company as other benefits, in part because everyone seems to check those out first. In asking about benefits, you should ask about vacation and sick days last. Otherwise, it may look like you want to get away from the job before you even have it.

Before you get excited at the prospect of extra vacation time, check to see how many hours a week you'll be expected to put in at your new job. When you're paid a salary, as opposed to an hourly wage, it's much easier for your boss to squeeze you for more hours. If you're working fifty hours a week, you would need an extra ten weeks of vacation to be even with someone working forty hours a week. Giving you an extra week of vacation to squeeze ten more weeks of work out of you is a good deal for your employer, but not for you.

Any company that encourages continuing education by paying for it gets a gold star. Good employers recognize that offering tuition reimbursement and the like is not an expense, it's an investment.

Because of the pace of change now, it is essential that all employees at all levels continuously expand their base of knowledge. The employees who take advantage of such benefits not only keep up to date and are more secure in their current jobs, they can also accumulate credentials necessary for the next job up the ladder.

Many companies provide reimbursement for education expenses after you satisfactorily complete a class or a program. That's perfectly acceptable and to be expected. In business you pay for results, not for mere effort.

Profit-sharing and ESOP's (employee stock ownership plans) are nice to have, but don't put too much weight on them. Profit as defined for profit-sharing plans can be rather fuzzy, and management often has a lot of discretion in deciding if there will be profit-sharing each year.

Look to see if there is a solid history of corporate profitability and if the company has shared that with employees as agreed. Whatever you do, don't base any decisions, whether to accept a job or even making up a budget, on the assumption that profit sharing will materialize. If it comes, let it be a pleasant surprise.

ESOP's give you the chance to buy stock in your employer company, usually at a discount of 10-15%. There is often a requirement that you hold the stock for a minimum period; you can't buy, sell immediately and reap a quick profit. It's important to remember that you already have a lot invested with your employer. It's wise not to put too many eggs in one basket. It's much more important that you fully fund your retirement program (need-to-have) than participate in an ESOP (nice-to-have).

How They Rank & How They Rank 'Em

U.S. News & World Report - January, 2015

Choosing an occupation is personal, and of course, there is no ideal way to determine the best job overall. Still, U.S. News' Best Jobs rankings offer job seekers an intuitive method to compare professions based on components that matter most: salary, the number of expected openings, advancement opportunities and career fulfillment. The result of our efforts is a list of jobs ranked according to their ability to meet those employment concerns.

The Best Jobs methodology is divided into two components: how U.S. News selects jobs to profile, and how those jobs are ranked against each other.

Selecting the Jobs

To identify professions that should be included in the 2015 rankings, we started with data on jobs with the greatest hiring demand, or in other words, the highest projected number of openings from 2012 to 2022, as categorized by the U.S. Bureau of Labor Statistics. The jobs at the top of the list were then selected for the 2015 Best Jobs analysis and rankings.

Ranking the Jobs

U.S. News ranks jobs in an overall list and in six mutually exclusive, occupational industry lists: Best Business Jobs, Best Creative Jobs, Best Construction Jobs, Best Health Care Jobs, Best Social Services Jobs and Best Technology Jobs. Professions are ranked based on our calculated overall score, which combines several components into a single weighted average score between 0 and 5.

The overall score is calculated from seven component measures, and for each measure, jobs receive a score between 0 and 10. Here are the component measures and their weights in computing the overall score:

-10-Year Growth Volume (10 percent)
-10-Year Growth Percentage (10 percent)
-Median Salary (30 percent)
-Job Prospects (20 percent)
-Employment Rate (20 percent)
-Stress Level (5 percent)
-Work-Life Balance (5 percent)

About the Component Measures

1. 10-year growth volume. Growth volume, according to the BLS, is the total number of new jobs that should be created for an occupation in a 10-year timespan. For example, the BLS projects the United States will add 23,300 new dentist jobs between 2012 and 2022.

Why is it important?
An occupation with significant job growth is likely to have many new job opportunities in the future. This is also a crucial factor, because we use the BLS' projected growth volume to select the jobs we'll rank each year.

How is this score calculated?
We translate job growth volumes from a number to a score of up to 10 points. Those occupations expected to grow by 500,000 openings or more received the highest score: 10. Occupations with job growth numbers

between 200,000 and 499,999 earned 8 points; between 100,000 and 199,999 earned 6 points; less than 100,000 openings earned 4 points; and any occupations for which numbers were expected to decrease received 2 points.

2. 10-year growth percentage. This is an occupation's employment percentage growth over the course of 10 years. For example, the BLS estimate of 23,300 new dentist jobs between 2012 and 2022 equates to 15.9 percent.

Why is it important?
The 10-year growth percentage measures how rapidly an occupation is expanding. A high growth rate indicates strengthening demand for this type of worker. The BLS predicts that total employment is projected to increase 10.8 percent between 2012 and 2022. Those jobs with higher percentages are growing faster than average. Growth percentage is also important to our methodology, because the growth rate is used to select the jobs we'll rank each year.

How is this score calculated?
We translate job growth percentages from a number to a score of up to 10 points. Occupations for which the projected growth rate increased by 30 percent or more earned the total possible 10 points; those for which growth increased between 20 and 29 percent earned 8 points; where growth increased between 10 and 19 percent, the job earned 6 points; and where growth increased by 9 percent or less, the job earned 4 points. Any occupations that saw growth decrease received 2 points.

3. Median salary. This is the median salary earned by someone employed in a given occupation, according to BLS.

Why is it important?
Most people prefer higher salaries.

How is this score calculated?
We translate median salary from a dollar amount to a numerical score using the following formula: salary score = the square root of the median salary divided by 40. We set a maximum salary score of 10 points.

4. Employment rate. The percentage of people in an occupation who are currently employed.

Why is it important?
It's more challenging to get a job in an occupation with high unemployment.

How is this score calculated?
We translate unemployment rates, recorded for each profession, to a 10-point scale. For example, if a job's unemployment rate is 4 percent or less, it earned the full possible 10 points; a job with unemployment between 4.1 percent and 6 percent earned 8 points; between 6.1 and 8 percent earned 6 points; between 8.1 and 10 percent earned 4 points; and those jobs with unemployment higher than 10 percent earned 2 points.

5. Future job prospects. This rating indicates the ease of landing a job in the future, based on the number of openings versus the number of job seekers. For example, the BLS predicts nurse practitioners will be in high demand, particularly in underserved inner cities and rural areas, so this job has an excellent job prospect rating. By contrast, the BLS projects there will be more students graduating from law school each year than there are jobs available. Competition for open positions for lawyers will be competitive, so this occupation received a lower job prospect rating.

Why is it important?
If you want to pursue a career in which the BLS projects it will be easier to find employment over the next 10 years, aim for one with a higher job prospect rating.

How is this score calculated?
We translate the BLS "descriptive rating" to a score of up to 10 points. A job that received an "excellent" prospect rating earned 10 points; a job that has a "good" rating earned 8 points; a job with a "favorable" rating earned 6 points; and an occupation with a "keen competition" rating earned a score of 4. Jobs for which prospects weren't identified or for which prospects varied were considered not applicable for a prospect score by U.S. News.

6. Stress level. This rating indicates the amount of day-to-day stress someone might experience while working in an occupation.

Why is it important?
The level of stress an individual feels in his or her job can lower quality of life, negatively affect health and alter someone's opinion of the work he or she does.

How is this score calculated?

Based on interviews and extensive research, our editors assign qualitative stress-level ratings to each occupation. These ratings are intended to represent the average stress level for the occupation, and it's important to note that stress varies significantly among individuals and their specific job circumstances.

These qualitative stress-level ratings are translated on a 10-point scale. A stress level rating of "High" translates to 2 points (the lowest score); a rating of "Above Average" translates to 4 points; a rating of "Average" translates to 6 points; "Below Average" to 8 points; and "Low" translates to 10 points (the highest score).

7. Work-life balance. This rating captures how much any profession will affect lifestyle.

Why is it important?
Finding the appropriate balance between career, ambition, health, family and leisure activities can improve job performance.

How is this score calculated?
Based on interviews and assessment of literature, U.S. News editors assign qualitative work-life balance ratings for each occupation. Similar to stress level, it's important to note that work-life balance may vary significantly among individuals and with specific job circumstances.

Our qualitative work-life balance ratings are translated to scores on a 10-point scale. A rating of "High" translates to 10 points (the highest score); a rating of "Above Average" translates to 8 points; a rating of "Average" translates to 6 points; a rating of "Below Average" translates to 4 points; and a rating of "Low" translates to 2 points (the lowest score).

U.S. News & World Report 100 Best Jobs 2015

1. Dentist
2. Nurse Practitioner
3. Software Developer
4. Physician
5. Dental Hygienist
6. Physical Therapist
7. Computer Systems Analyst
8. Information Security Analyst
9. Registered Nurse
10. Physician Assistant
11. Web Developer
12. Diagnostic Medical Sonographer
13. Occupational Therapist
14. Market Research Analyst
15. Marketing Manager
16. Accountant
17. School Psychologist
18. Mechanical Engineer
19. Occupational Therapy Assistant
20. Operations research Analyst
21. IT Manager
22. Civil Engineer
23. Cost Estimator
24. Esthetician
25. Financial Adviser
26. Logistician
27. Pharmacist
28. Medical Equipment Repairer
29. Dietitian and Nutritionist
30. Speech-Language Pathologist
31. Computer Systems Administrator
32. Radiologic Technologist

33. Insurance Agent
34. Database Administrator
35. Marriage and Family Therapist
36. Epidemiologist
37. Construction Manager
38. Substance Abuse Counselor
39. Elementary School Teacher
40. Bookkeeping, Accounting and Auditing Clerk
41. Licensed Practical/Vocational Nurse
42. Optician
43. High School Teacher
44. Loan Officer
45. Middle School Teacher
46. Physical Therapist Assistant
47. Business Operations Manager
48. Pharmacy Technician
49. Home Health Aide
50. HR Specialist
51. Respiratory Therapist
52. Nail Technician
53. Lawyer
54. Medical Secretary
55. Maintenance and Repair Worker
56. Veterinarian
57. Meeting, Convention and Event Planner
58. Sales Manager
59. Personal Care Aide
60. Administrative Assistant
61. Sales Representative
62. Massage Therapist
63. Computer Programmer
64. Veterinary Technologist and Technician
65. Financial Analyst
66. Hairdresser

67. Dental Assistant
68. Management Analyst
69. Financial Manager
70. Clinical Social Worker
71. Medical Assistant
72. Medical Health Counselor
73. Police Officer
74. Recreation and Fitness Worker
75. Public Relations Specialist
76. School Counselor
77. Computer Support Specialist
78. Real Estate Agent
79. Plumber
80. Clinical Laboratory Technician
81. Architect
82. Surgical Technologist
83. Auto Mechanic
84. Compliance Officer
85. Exterminator
86. Child and Family Social Worker
87. Art Director
88. Preschool Teacher
89. Interpreter and Translator
90. Security Guard
91. Paralegal
92. Executive Assistant
93. Taxi Driver and Chauffeur
94. Paramedic
95. Customer Service Representative
96. Sheet Metal Worker
97. Bill Collector
98. Office Clerk
99. Teacher Assistant
100. Receptionist

CNN/Money 100 Best Jobs 2015

	JOB TITLE	MEDIAN PAY	10-YR. JOB GROWTH
1.	Software Architect	$124,000	23%
2.	Video Game Designer	$79,900	19%
3.	Landman	$103,000	13%
4.	Patent Agent	$126,000	13%
5.	Hospital Administrator	$114,000	23%
6.	Continuous Improvement Mgr.	$96,600	12%
7.	Clinical Nurse Specialist	$89,300	19%
8.	Database Developer	$88,200	23%
9.	Info. Assurance Analyst	$96,400	37%
10.	Pilates/Yoga Instructor	$62,400	13%
11.	Clinical Applications Specialist	$84,300	25%
12.	Portfolio Manager	$123,000	27%
13.	Dentist	$152,000	16%
14.	User Experience Designer	$89,300	18%
15.	Auditing Director	$132,000	13%
16.	Real Estate Development Mgr.	$107,000	12%
17.	IT Program Manager	$122,000	15%
18.	Project Control Specialist	$86,600	19%
19.	Pharmacist in Charge	$125,000	15%
20.	QA Coordinator (RN)	$69,300	19%
21.	Strategy Manager	$112,000	19%
22.	Product Development Director	$131,000	12%
23.	Physical Therapy Director	$87,900	23%
24.	Emergency Room Physician	$274,000	19%
25.	Product Analyst	$67,800	32%
26.	Rehabilitation Services Mgr.	$86,900	23%
27.	Health Information Mgt. Dir.	$81,900	23%
28.	Product Mgt. Director	$148,000	13%
29.	Practice Administrator	$78,300	23%
30.	Facilities Director	$97,500	12%
31.	Accounting Director	$103,000	13%
32.	Software QA Manager	$110,000	15%

33.	Orthopedic Surgeon	$410,000	23%
34.	Clinical Services Director	$77,600	23%
35.	Clinical Pharmacist	$117,000	15%
36.	Anesthesiologist	$340,000	24%
37.	Biomedical Engineer	$82,400	27%
38.	IT Security Consultant	$110,000	37%
39.	Telecom. Network Engineer	$90,500	15%
40.	Technical Consultant	$101,000	23%
41.	Customer Service Director	$103,000	12%
42.	Payroll Director	$99,000	12%
43.	Private Banker	$86,500	27%
44.	Operations Director	$108,000	12%
45.	Risk Management Director	$121,000	12%
46.	Construction Manager	$88,700	16%
47.	R & D Engineer, IT	$108,000	20%
48.	Business Development Dir.	$136,000	13%
49.	Proposal Manager	$87,600	13%
50.	Financial Accounting Mgr.	$74,500	13%
51.	Career Services Director	$62,700	12%
52.	Hand Therapist	$83,000	36%
53.	Strategic Planning Director	$139,000	12%
54.	Internal Auditing Manager	$101,000	13%
55.	Consulting Manager	$130,000	19%
56.	Alumni Affairs Director	$64,200	15%
57.	Finance & Administration Mgr.	$74,300	12%
58.	Analytics Manager	$109,000	27%
59.	Nursing Manager	$82,400	23%
60.	Web Analyst	$72,300	25%
61.	Health Care Administrator	$81,000	23%
62.	Business Development Mgr.	$99,600	13%
63.	Regional HR Manager	$84,900	13%
64.	Athletic Director (University)	$70,500	15%
65.	Product Marketing Specialist	$67,600	32%
66.	Implementation Consultant	$91,800	19%
67.	Network Architect	$122,000	15%
68.	Nursing Informatics Analyst	$69,400	25%

69.	Research Analyst	$64,400	32%
70.	Assisted Living Director	$56,400	23%
71.	IT Network Engineer	$79,100	12%
72.	Business Mgr., eCommerce	$82,600	12%
73.	Assoc. Partner, Consulting Svc.	$196,000	19%
74.	Healthcare Consultant	$108,000	13%
75.	Contract Administration Mgr.	$77,400	12%
76.	Regional Property Manager	$80,600	12%
77.	Principal Architect	$132,000	17%
78.	Practice Manager	$63,900	23%
79.	Analytics Director	$142,000	13%
80.	Civil Engineer	$77,400	20%
81.	Lead Physical Therapist	$84,700	36%
82.	Financial Reporting Manager	$96,800	12%
83.	Database Admin. (DBA) Mgr.	$120,000	15%
84.	Marketing Consultant	$90,700	32%
85.	Biostatistician	$98,800	27%
86.	Athletic Coach	$47,000	15%
87.	Financial Analysis Manager	$99,800	16%
88.	Content Strategist	$80,000	32%
89.	Transportation Engineer	$78,100	20%
90.	Information Tech. Auditor	$88,200	25%
91.	Assisted Living Administrator	$55,500	23%
92.	Systems Analyst	$83,800	25%
93.	Tech Support Engineer	$75,400	20%
94.	Public Relations Director	$90,500	13%
95.	Auditing Manager	$90,900	13%
96.	Program Mgt. Dir. Human Svcs. $55,500	13%	
97.	Environ. Health/Safety Dir.	$114,000	15%
98.	Database Administrator	$89,100	15%
99.	Structural Engineer	$80,400	20%
100.	Clinical Lab Supervisor	$66,900	30%

Happiness Index: Top 200 Careers with the Highest Job Satisfaction Ratings

Methodology: The following career ratings represent averages taken from the responses of 13,871 MyPlan.com users during registration in 2014. Users were asked to rate how happy they were in their current occupation by indicating that they were either "Very Happy," "Happy," "Mixed / Neutral," "Not Happy," or "Miserable". The scores below are normalized on a 100-point scale with 0 being "Miserable" and 100 being "Very Happy".

1.Singers	91.7
2.Municipal Fire Fighters	90.0
3.Aircraft Assemblers - Structure, Surfaces, Rigging & System	83.3
4.Pediatricians — General	80.0
5.College Professors — Communications	79.2
6.Educational, Vocational & School Counselors	78.8
7.Managers of Animal Husbandry Animal Care Workers	78.6
8.Criminal Investigators & Special Agents	77.5
9.College Professors — Psychology	76.9
10. College Instructors - Vocational Studies	76.7
11. High School Teachers - Vocational Studies	76.3
12. Coaches & Scouts	75.0
13. College Professors — Business	75.0
14. Veterinary Technologists & Technicians	72.9
15. Chief Executives	72.4
16. Physician Assistants	72.2
17. Supervisors/Managers of Tactical Operations Specialists	71.4
18. Rehabilitation Counselors	70.8
19. Clergy	70.8
20. College Professors - Philosophy & Religion	70.8
21. Private Detectives & Investigators	70.8
22. College Instructors — Education	70.4

23. Self-Enrichment Education Teachers	70.0
24. Middle School Teachers - Vocational Studies	70.0
25. Athletes & Sports Competitors	70.0
26. College Professors — History	70.0
27. Arbitrators, Mediators & Conciliators	70.0
28. Mental Health Counselors	69.0
29. Actors	67.9
30. Commercial & Industrial Designers	67.9
31. Skin Care Specialists	67.5
32. Bus Drivers — School	67.2
33. College Instructors — Medicine & Health Specialties	66.7
34. Managers/Supervisors of Police & Detectives	66.7
35. Chiropractors	66.7
36. Lodging Managers	65.9
37. Physical Therapists	65.8
38. Court Reporters	65.6
39. Operating Engineers/Construction Equipment Operators	65.6
40. Emergency Medical Technicians (EMT) & Paramedics	65.5
41. Financial Examiners	65.4
42. Cost Estimators	65.0
43. Recreation Workers	65.0
44. College Professors — English Language & Literature	64.5
45. Instructional Coordinators	64.4
46. Medical Equipment Preparers	64.3
47. Dispatchers (except police, fire & ambulance)	64.3
48. Tax Preparers	64.3
49. Education Administrators — College	64.1
50. Operations Research Analysts	63.9
51. Photographers	63.9
52. Wholesale & Retail Buyers	63.8
53. Dietitians & Nutritionists	63.6
54. Occupational Therapists	63.6
55. Technical Directors & Production Managers	63.6
56. Correctional Officers & Jailers	63.3
57. Massage Therapists	63.3
58. High School Teachers	63.2

59. Chefs & Head Cooks	63.2
60. Librarians	62.9
61. Mechanical Engineers	62.8
62. Medical & Health Services Managers	62.8
63. Statisticians	62.5
64. Packers & Packagers	62.5
65. Inspectors, Testers, Sorters, Samplers, Weighers	62.5
66. Social Science Research Assistants	62.5
67. Pharmacists	62.5
68. Counseling Psychologists	62.5
69. Dental Hygienists	62.5
70. Copy Writers	62.5
71. Construction Managers	62.5
72. Materials Engineers	62.5
73. Creative Writers — Authors, Poets & Lyricists	61.8
74. Art Directors	61.7
75. Middle School Teachers	61.6
76. Substance Abuse & Behavioral Disorder Counselors	61.6
77. Environmental Scientists & Specialists	61.5
78. Mental Health & Substance Abuse Social Workers	61.5
79. Medical & Public Health Social Workers	61.1
80. Bus Drivers - Transit & Intercity	61.1
81. Managers/Supervisors of Landscaping Workers	61.1
82. Education Administrators — Elementary & High School	60.7
83. General & Operations Managers	60.7
84. Directors - Religious Activities & Education	60.5
85. Computer Operators	60.4
86. Helpers — Installation, Maintenance & Repair Workers	60.0
87. Internists — General	60.0
88. Construction & Building Inspectors	60.0
89. Musicians	60.0
90. Surveyors	60.0
91. Loan Interviewers & Clerks	60.0
92. Radar & Sonar Technicians	60.0
93. Licensed Practical & Licensed Vocational Nurses	60.0
94. Medical & Clinical Laboratory Technicians	59.7

131.	Managers/Supervisors of Agricultural Workers	56.3
132.	Mechanical Drafters	56.3
133.	Airfield Operations Specialists	56.3
134.	Aerospace Engineers	56.3
135.	Managers/Supervisors of Construction/Extraction Workers	56.1
136.	Construction Carpenters	56.1
137.	Management Analysts	55.9
138.	Family & General Practitioners	55.8
139.	Storage & Distribution Managers	55.8
140.	Social & Community Service Managers	55.7
141.	Airline Pilots, Copilots & Flight Engineers	55.6
142.	Electrical Repairers — Commercial & Industrial Equipment	55.6
143.	Payroll & Timekeeping Clerks	55.4
144.	Editors	55.4
145.	Managers of Mechanics, Installers & Repairers	55.4
146.	Nuclear Medicine Technologists	55.0
147.	Occupational Health & Safety Specialists	55.0
148.	Plumbers	55.0
149.	Industrial Production Managers	55.0
150.	Graphic Designers	55.0
151.	Electrical & Electronic Equipment Assemblers	55.0
152.	Merchandise Displayers & Window Trimmers	55.0
153.	Maintenance Workers — Machinery	55.0
154.	College Professors — Engineering	55.0
155.	Medical Assistants	54.7
156.	Elementary School Teachers	54.7
157.	Pharmacy Technicians	54.7
158.	Financial Managers, Branch or Department	54.6
159.	Sales Engineers	54.4
160.	Cooks — Restaurant	54.3
161.	Construction Laborers	54.3
162.	Marketing Managers	54.3
163.	Opticians — Dispensing	54.2
164.	Film & Video Editors	54.2
165.	Preschool Teachers	54.0
166.	Public Relations Specialists	53.8

167.	Managers of Production & Operating Workers	53.8
168.	Sales Representatives — Wholesale & Manufacturing	53.7
169.	Police Patrol Officers	53.6
170.	Structural Metal Fabricators & Fitters	53.6
171.	Radio & Television Announcers	53.6
172.	Speech-Language Pathologists	53.3
173.	Helpers - Production Workers	53.2
174.	Manicurists & Pedicurists	53.1
175.	Sales Representatives — Technical & Scientific Products	53.0
176.	Computer, Automated Teller & Office Machine Repairers	52.8
177.	Eligibility Interviewers - Government Programs	52.8
178.	Landscaping & Groundskeeping Workers	52.8
179.	Fitness Trainers & Aerobics Instructors	52.8
180.	Medical & Clinical Laboratory Technologists	52.8
181.	Veterinarians	52.8
182.	Accountants	52.7
183.	Food Service Managers	52.1
184.	Aircraft Mechanics & Service Technicians	52.1
185.	Claims Examiners — Property & Casualty Insurance	52.1
186.	Security Guards	52.1
187.	Bill & Account Collectors	51.9
188.	Hosts & Hostesses — Restaurant, Lounge & Coffee Shop	51.7
189.	Dancers	51.7
190.	Personal Financial Advisors	51.5
191.	Managers/Supervisors of Office & Administrative Workers	51.4
192.	Bookkeeping, Accounting & Auditing Clerks	51.3
193.	Concierges	51.3
194.	Managers of Food Preparation & Serving Workers	51.1
195.	Loan Officers & Mortgage Brokers	51.0
196.	Purchasing Managers	51.0
197.	Civil Engineers	50.9
198.	Personal & Home Care Aides	50.6
199.	Painters - Construction & Maintenance	50.0
200.	Pharmacy Aides	50.0

Forbes Ten Happiest Jobs – 2011
1. Clergy
2. Firefighters
3. Physical Therapists
4. Authors
5. Special Education Teachers
6. Teachers
7. Artists
8. Psychologists
9. Financial Services Sales Agents
10. Operating engineers

Forbes Ten Happiest Jobs – 2015
1. School Principal
2. Executive Chef
3. Loan Officer
4. Automation Engineer
5. Research Assistant
6. Database Administrator
7. Website Developer
8. Business Development Executive
9. Senior Software Engineer
10. Systems Developer

Forbes Ten Most Hated Jobs – 2011
1. Director of Information Technology
2. Director of Sales and Marketing
3. Product Manager
4. Senior Web Developer
5. Technical Specialist
6. Electronics Technician
7. Law Clerk
8. Technical Support Analyst
9. CNC Machinist
10. Marketing Manager

Forbes Ten Most Hated Jobs – 2015
1. Security Guard
2. Merchandiser
3. Salesperson
4. Dispatcher
5. Clerk
6. Research Analyst
7. Legal Assistant
8. Technical Support Agent
9. Truck Driver
10. Customer Service Specialist

As you review these listings, you may notice inconsistencies. Jobs may be ranked high on one list and low on another. The list of happiest and unhappiest jobs had an almost complete turnover in just four years. Jobs that people default into because they don't have better options aren't likely to have a high ranking. Because you're a unique individual, you could probably find a job in the bottom ten of a list and rank it higher personally than a job in the top ten of a list. Rankings like these may be more useful as a guide to jobs you want to avoid rather than jobs you want to pursue.

You will need to research the position you are seeking to know what the salary range is for that position. You also want to know the employer's situation. You are looking for information on how urgent it is for them to fill this position, the quantity and quality of the competition, and who is in the position to offer you the job and its salary without someone else's approval.

If it can be arranged, it is best to have two meetings – one to clarify the job responsibilities, and a second meeting to discuss the compensation package. Because of the importance of both topics, you want to come across as thorough and thoughtful.

Do not accept a job offer without sleeping on it. Even if the offer is beyond your wildest expectations, it's not going anywhere overnight. If they want you today, they'll still want you tomorrow. You need that time away from them to process the offer and to see if there is room to negotiate. (There usually is.)

When contemplating how high they might go, you can be sure that they won't pay you more than what your new boss makes, so you know your ceiling is somewhere below that figure. How much below may be hard to tell. If you state your minimum salary just below their maximum salary, you can negotiate and still end up at the high end of the salary range for that position.

There is an additional advantage in having gone over all the job responsibilities prior to negotiating salary. In order to get a higher salary than they are offering, you may want to see what additional responsibilities you are in a position to accept. It is important to approach this and every negotiation from a win-win perspective. If the company feels like they are getting a top-flight employee with an eagerness to assume responsibility, they shouldn't mind paying a competitive salary for such a person.

One more thing – companies will want to know your salary history. It is not in your interest to provide that information. If your current salary is considerably lower than what this new job typically pays, the company may try to low-ball you on salary. If you are making a career change that involves less pay, the company may be concerned you can't make the adjustment, and will soon leave for more money. If they press you, politely but firmly point out:

- The old salary was for the old job. The new salary is for the new job. It's apples and oranges.
- Their benchmark is what other prospective employers will pay. That's their competition, not your old job.
- You've researched this position; you know what the salary range is, and it's not a problem for you.

Copyright 2001 by Randy Glasbergen.
www.glasbergen.com

GLASBERGEN

"You can name your own salary. I call mine Tiny Tim."

WHAT ARE THEY SAYING ABOUT YOU?

Three seconds. One-one-thousand, two-one-thousand, three-one-thousand. That's it. That's how much time it takes to evaluate you.

Of course, someone as complex as you cannot be evaluated in a mere three seconds. Nevertheless, in that brief period, people who are in a position to offer you the job of your dreams, to forever change your life for the better, may blow you off because your jewelry is tacky.

It's not fair, but we all do it. We have so many potential interactions with people in a typical day that we have to set up screening mechanisms to protect ourselves. Someone who conducts interviews for a corporation sees hundreds, if not thousands of job applicants a year. More than most, these people need quick methods to carve the unqualified applicants from the herd.

In those first three seconds, you will be scoped out from head to toe. Your grooming, demeanor, mannerisms, and body language will all be evaluated. If you appear to match the corporate culture, you'll still be in contention.

You have to make several first impressions. The assistant of the person interviewing you will have a first impression, and the interviewer will want to know about it. Blow it with the assistant, and you might as well go home. Every person you meet will each have a first impression, and they will talk to each other; what you show them better be consistent. The worst impression any of them have may become the dominant one. This is a screening process, after all. You may even be scrutinized via security cameras while you wait in the reception area or walk to the next interview. You're under a microscope the minute you set foot on their turf.

If you're young and just starting your working life, you will quickly learn that in the adult world, "popular" doesn't exist. No one was ever voted most popular at any Fortune 500 company. **Popularity is replaced in the working world by** *competence.* Competence means being able to do your job to at least the minimum level of expectations. The root word of competent is *compete*, and to be competent means you are able to compete with others who are doing the same thing.

Competence breeds confidence. If you want to be self-confident in your work, you must first become competent in your work. If you want others to be confident in your work, they must be able to see evidence of your competence in your work. Regardless of how popular you may have been in high school, it won't mean a thing in the workplace if you can't be counted on to do your job.

Your Life On a Page

To get to the interview, you must first survive the initial screening of your cover letter and résumé. You aren't writing a résumé for you – you are writing it for the readers. Put yourself in the readers' shoes – they look at dozens of résumés every day, and they are looking for something to disqualify it quickly.

First rule: No Typos! A résumé with spelling, grammar, or punctuation errors is totally unacceptable. You have word processors, spell check, and all kinds of software to help you. Also, always proof a paper copy of anything you send out; don't just proof what's on the computer screen. There are often errors we only catch when we see it on paper.

If you send a résumé with errors, it will end up in the trash, regardless of your qualifications. The reader will assume such carelessness is typical of your work and will automatically disqualify you from further consideration.

Because résumés tend to be scanned rather than read, it should be no more than one page. **Edit ruthlessly.** Tweak your résumé for each reader. That doesn't mean major rewrites, but different employers are looking for different characteristics. Since you will have researched any company you send a résumé to, you should have an idea what they value most and what they are looking for in a new hire. Something as simple as setting key words in bold type so they stand out can cause your résumé to be read, rather than merely scanned.

Don't put personal information (age, religion, hobbies, etc.) on your résumé. Education, work experience, skill sets, and **what you offer them** are what need to be on there.

One last most important rule about your résumé – **Never lie.** If the lie is caught before you're hired, you won't be. If it's caught after you're hired, you'll be fired. Lies are easy to catch because so much of your history is available, often just by going online. And even if you're never caught, you're still doomed to fail. No relationship built on a lie ever succeeds.

Sartorial Perfection

"You're wearing that?!" This criticism-as-question is bad enough on Saturday night, but it's the last thing you

should hear when dressing for a job interview. When selecting your ensemble for any business meeting, but especially for a job interview, remember the old medical dictum, "First, do no harm."

There is an old adage that you don't dress for the job you have, but for the job you want. **If you don't look the part, you aren't likely to get the part.** The first thing to find out is what the prescribed attire is for your desired position in that particular company. Because companies can vary widely on what they consider appropriate dress, you may see accountants in one company in three-piece suits and their counterparts in another company in jeans. It's up to you to find out the dress code before the interview. Ask someone in their Human Resources department if you're not sure. It is also better to err on the side of being overdressed if there's any doubt about what's appropriate to wear.

Make sure your clothing is clean, spot-free, and pressed. Don't wear anything with frayed cuffs or collars. Understated colors and patterns are best. Make sure that everything you put on is coordinated. The goal is to have the interviewer notice only you, not your clothing. You don't want to compete for the interviewer's attention with your own ensemble.

For everyone, but especially women, do not wear anything that could be considered sexually provocative, unless sex is part of the job description. An outfit that might be attractive in a social setting can be very distractive in a business setting. Know the difference.

Be the epitome of hygiene. Bathe or shower before you go. Use deodorant. Brush your teeth and use mouthwash. Shave. Tame your hair. Unkempt may be the style, but you don't want to give anyone the chance to associate the word sloppy with you. Make-up should be applied with the idea of hiding flaws, rather than enhancing beauty. And nix the perfume and cologne. At best, it's another distraction. At worst, the interviewer could be allergic, ending the interview before it begins.

Lastly, no visible tattoos or body piercings, unless you're certain the interviewer has them, too. The higher up you go in the interview process, the older and more conservative the interviewer tends to be. Freedom of expression is fine, but you don't want to express yourself right out of contention.

The Unsaid

One of the reasons that people are evaluating you before you are even introduced is that 80-90% of our communication is non-verbal. Some key areas of non-verbal communication are:

- **Promptness** – Like Shakespeare said, better three hours too soon than one minute too late. Nothing short of Armageddon is an acceptable excuse. **Get your ass there on time!**
- **Eye Contact** – Failure to make eye contact indicates you are weak, submissive, and dishonest. You may be none of those things, but that's the message you send when you don't look them in the eye. If making eye contact is difficult, look at their nose or mouth. Unless their face is within a foot of yours, they can't tell the difference.
- **The Handshake** – The proper grip is somewhere between dead fish and pro wrestler. Three pumps and release. One hand only unless you're consoling someone. Also, maintain eye contact when shaking hands.
- **Your Face** – Who doesn't love a smiling face? It

indicates warmth, friendliness, and most important in an interview, affiliation. (Don't worry; your teeth look just fine.) Besides, a smile begins with the eyes, which is why eye contact is important. You smile with your eyes - your mouth just goes along for the ride.

- **Posture** – Erect (but not rigid) posture indicates strength, health, and self-confidence. Head up, shoulders back. Lean forward slightly when sitting to indicate you are attentive and interested in what the other person is saying.
- **Proximity and Touching** – In American culture, our personal space is about two feet in all directions. In formal situations like a job interview, everyone should respect everyone else's personal space, which is one reason not to wear provocative clothing or scents for an interview. It can be perceived as an invitation into your personal space, which one doesn't do in a business environment.
- **Gestures** – Because we are naturally nervous in an interview situation, there is a greater tendency to rock, tap feet, twitch, and gesture with our hands more than usual. Even if you're a bundle of nerves inside, you want to give the impression of quiet self-confidence and serenity. Proper posture helps, as does taking regular deep breaths to relax you. Try not to have anything in your hands during the interview (it promotes fidgeting). Keep your hands folded in your lap as much as possible. Occasional hand gestures are fine; just try not to look like a marionette on meth when you're making them.
- **Gum** – Don't even think about it.

"I've told you why I need a dog. Now suppose you tell me what makes you think you might be that dog."

The Said

At this point, you have managed to run the gauntlet of screenings to enable you to sit down and actually have an interview. The first thing to recognize is the difference between an interview and an interrogation. In an interview, the interviewer is gathering information that the interviewee (you) generally wants the interviewer to have. In an interrogation, the interviewer is trying to extract information that the interviewee wants to keep hidden. An interrogation is an adversarial relationship. An interview should be a mutually beneficial one, which is why being truthful about everything prior to the interview is so important. **You want to keep the interview from becoming an interrogation.**

The prefix *inter* means between or among. In an interview, both parties should be gaining a better *view* of each other, which means **you should be asking questions as well.** Asking questions is a sign of interest and intelligence. Research the company and the position you're seeking before the interview. The information you gather should generate some questions. Your research will also help you generate more substantive questions, demonstrating your diligence. Have your questions written down so you can remember to ask all of them, which will also show you're organized.

Two bits of advice, though. First, don't attempt to take control of the interview. Wait until the topic is on one of your questions before asking it. You may need to wait until the end of the interview to ask many of your questions. You should always be given the opportunity to ask questions before the interview concludes. Second, ask your questions in a manner that doesn't put the other person on the defensive. If you can ask a question in terms of seeking clarification or illumination on a topic, it is less likely to be viewed as confrontational.

Just as the nervousness of the situation can make us more fidgety, nerves cause us to answer too quickly and to speak at too fast a pace. **Before answering any question, take a breath.** That three second pause indicates you are giving thought to the question, not just blurting out anything. It's amazing the dumb things we *don't* say if we give ourselves three seconds to run it through our brain before it comes out of our mouth. If they ask you twenty questions in the interview, all of these pauses will add one additional minute to the interview - time well spent.

Taking a few seconds to collect our thoughts also cuts down the use of fillers – *you know, like, umm, dude*, etc. You must be conscious of your use of these phrases and make a conscious effort to eliminate them from your speech. The habit of using them usually develops in the teen years. You don't want the interviewer to think your communication skills haven't improved since tenth grade.

Slower speech is clearer speech. Proper enunciation makes your words easier to understand. If you are asked more than once to repeat something because they couldn't understand you, you've got a problem. Making the conscious effort to slow down your speech may make it sound agonizingly slow to your ear. However, to the person you are trying to impress, it sounds just right.

An accent is anything that doesn't sound like you. Accents, regional and foreign, may require special attention. It takes time to modify a strong accent. Pacing is very important in these situations. A fast speaking pace, combined with an unfamiliar accent will be very hard to understand. Be aware if people are having a problem understanding you because of your accent. Slowing down and enunciating can overcome a lot of the problem.

It's getting harder and harder to find proper grammar in popular culture. Remember your high school language arts classes? If you paid attention in those classes, the interview is the payoff. If your grammar is on the atrocious side, keep your answers short and simple to make it less obvious. You may also consider only jobs where communication skills are not a high priority.

A Class Act

Everyone has at his/her disposal what is arguably the single most effective tool to get people to like you and want you on their team. Strangely enough, relatively few people bother to use this tool. I'm referring to good manners.

The importance of good manners on a macro scale is best stated in the book *How Good People Make Tough Choices:*

> *"Three great domains of human action are positive law, free choice, and manners. Manners operate in the domain between positive law and absolute freedom. It is the domain of obedience to the unenforceable. We enforce the law upon ourselves. This ethical middle ground is constantly at risk of encroachment from both sides.*
>
> *When ethics collapses, law rushes in to fill the void. Regulation is necessary to sustain human interaction. Certain behaviors must be followed, if not voluntarily, then by compulsion."*

Good manners on a micro scale are not about which fork to use at dinner. Good manners are about something simpler, yet more difficult to follow: The Golden Rule – Do unto others as you would have them do unto you.

Good manners are based on the axiom that first you give, then you get. If you treat people with consideration first, you can expect consideration in return. If you give someone consideration, but don't receive it in return, that should tell you something about the other person's character and whether you would want to work with him/her.

Good manners require you to be other-centered, rather than self-centered. Before you speak or act, you think about how your words or actions will be received by others. You consider their feelings and sensibilities. If you think your words or actions might offend someone, you make a determination whether the situation warrants such behavior. Feeling better at someone else's expense is not only not a justification, it's bad manners. Even when the other party is guilty of bad manners or worse, there is no need to sink to their level. **High principles and good manners are not mutually exclusive.**

As a practical demonstration of your good manners, it is imperative that you **send a hand-written Thank You note to everyone with whom you interview.** An e-mail is not sufficient for something this important. An e-mail takes almost no effort and gets lost among the dozens of e-mails your interviewer gets every day. It takes five minutes to hand write a three sentence Thank You note and address the envelope. (Get the interviewer's business card so you have the address.) You will be amazed at how such a small effort on your part can help you get what you want. If 90% of the interviewees don't bother to send a Thank You note, but you do, you've just given yourself an edge over 90% of the competition. What other five minute task gives you that kind of competitive advantage?

Face Time

Technology can be wonderful for keeping in touch with people who are at a distance, but technology has also caused interference with the ability and desire to communicate face to face. We seem all too eager to let electronic communication supersede good old-fashioned conversation.

There is no communication involving technology that will ever be better than face-to-face communication. Webinars have a place, but the more important the meeting, the less appropriate they are. If there is bad news to be delivered, it is always better (though harder for the messenger) to tell the affected people in person, rather than informing them electronically. The 2009 movie *Up In the Air* explored the delicate process of telling people they are losing their jobs. An unsuccessful attempt to perform this task via computer screens in the film illustrated the intangible benefits of face-to-face communication.

Networking is still the best way to land a good job in the right field. But make no mistake – networking is a face-to-face process. LinkedIn, Facebook, chat rooms, and any other electronic social media are not true networking. Networking involves meeting with people, pressing the flesh, schmoozing, shaking hands, patting backs, smiling, gesturing, and all the hundreds of other ways humans communicate with each other using more than typed words. Even the telephone at least enables the other person to hear your voice inflections, which can communicate more than a text message. Even a telephone call isn't as good as face time because you cannot see or touch the other person. **The more of your senses that can be involved with the communication, the more effective that communication will be.**

If you are looking for leads in all the traditional places, you aren't likely to turn up anything but leftovers from all the others who have been picking over the same territory. **The best first contacts in a job search are the people who know you best**, and these people are also the people you see the most on a face to face basis. You may not think these close contacts have other contacts of their own, but you'd be surprised how quickly such a network spreads out. Also, because these people know you and like you, they are more likely to expend some serious effort on your behalf to connect you with someone who can get you that ideal job.

Some of the best sources for help in your job search are people you have worked with on some altruistic level. These are people you work with at a place of worship, a Rotary Club or other civic organization, or any activity where you have involved yourself for the benefit of others. Your contacts there have seen you at your best, and they are likely to have contacts that can help you. More important, they are likely to want to help you because they have seen you helping others.

Whenever you have the opportunity to spend time with people face to face, take advantage of it. Never forego an opportunity to communicate with someone who is in your presence to communicate with someone who is not in your presence. The quality of face to face communication cannot be matched by *any* electronic device, now or ever.

What's Out There on You?

You've almost made it. You survived all the screening processes. You had a great interview, following the advice laid out here, and now you're waiting for the call saying they want to hire you.

Your potential employer has another step to take first. They will call and confirm prior employment history, and they may call some of your references, which is no problem because you've been totally honest about everything.

They will also check you out on Google, Intelius, Facebook, Instagram, Snapchat, and any other website that might have information about you.

There are two groups of sites they will look at, so you need to look at them first. Check out information about you that has been generated by others. Websites like

Intelius can list any criminal record. Any organization to which you belong (or belonged) may have information about you on their website. Google yourself to see what is out there that others can learn about you. If there is incorrect information about you out there, contact the website in question and request they correct or delete the information. If there is incorrect potentially harmful information out there, you may need to be pre-emptive and let your potential employer know about it up front. Making them aware of it and documenting the errors may save some awkward questions later and will make you look like you're on top of everything.

Nothing on any of those sites may be as harmful as what you may have put out there yourself. Websites like Facebook are not targeted to potential employers, but potential employers are looking at them to learn more about job candidates. Many people aren't getting hired because of what is posted out there.

Frank revelations (often with pictures) about drugs, sex, drinking, and other improprieties will not commend you to any employer. Even if some of the claims are merely posturing to impress peers, it won't make any difference. At the very least, it would demonstrate extremely poor judgment on your part. An employer would also be concerned that co-workers, customers, and competitors might see it, hurting you and your employer.

If there's anything out there about you on any personal website, and if you aren't willing to print it out and submit it along with your résumé, then you need to shut it down. The issue isn't about freedom of expression; it's about not shooting yourself in the foot when opportunity knocks. If you want to work with mature adults, you have to prove you are one of them.

There is something else that almost all potential employers will look at, and you might not even think they would bother. **Part of the background check for job applicants now includes obtaining a copy of the applicant's credit report.** Since the employer is paying you, rather than being paid by you, wanting to see your credit report doesn't seem to make sense. However, there are actually some good reasons for employers to check out this part of your life.

While it's true that the employee runs a financial risk if the employer has financial problems, those risks are generally limited to pay earned, but not yet received. The employer runs a much greater risk if the employee has financial problems. Theft from the employer is the most common risk. Theft may entail stealing property from the employer. The greater risk is the theft of money from the employer, primarily through fraud. This risk is high because one can often steal funds from the company electronically, which is harder to catch than someone loading merchandise into the trunk of a car. Also, theft from fraud can go on for years, and its detection may only come after thousands of dollars have been stolen and spent.

An employee with financial problems also presents the risk of a frivolous lawsuit against the employer. The employee overburdened with debt is more likely to look for a lawsuit, any lawsuit, to provide a quick cash settlement and a way out of debt. Even if the lawsuit is baseless, the cost of defending a lawsuit gives the employee hope that the employer might settle out of court.

Finally, your credit report can give the potential employer (who hardly knows you at this point) some insight into how you manage your affairs. If your credit report indicates that your management of your personal business affairs is a disaster, they will not be confident that your management of their business affairs will be any better. Even if there is no chance for you to steal from the company, mismanagement of your own money is a huge strike against you when competing against others for a plum job. Next to a shining (and accurate) résumé, a shining credit report is one of the best arrows to have in your quiver when you're hunting down a new job.

Fingernails on a Blackboard

The annals of TV history are full of them – the irritating co-worker. You have Dwight Schrute from *The Office*, Mimi Bobek from *The Drew Carey Show,* and Ted Baxter from *The Mary Tyler Moore Show,* to name a few. We find them funny for two reasons. First, we don't have to work with them. Second, they either don't know or don't care that they are such a drain and strain on their co-workers.

We've all known people like these at work. What we may almost never know is, are we one of those fingernails-on-a-blackboard personalities? It is unlikely you have been blunt enough to disclose their defects to such a person in your office. Is it possible you are such a person, and no one has yet been blunt enough to point it out to you? You don't want to find all this out at your exit interview, after you finally made the case for them to can you.

An irritating manner or personality may not be enough to get someone fired on its own, but it can serve as incentive to get the employer digging for something less subjective as grounds for termination.

Here are just a few of the many ways you can sour the office environment and make yourself a target for termination:

- Having loud telephone conversations
- Not cleaning up after yourself in the staff kitchen
- Showing up late for work or for meetings
- Looking at a co-worker's computer screen over his or her shoulder
- Taking supplies from a co-worker's desk
- Neglecting to say please and thank you
- Wearing too much perfume or cologne
- Chewing gum (or anything else) loudly
- Taking the last of something without replacing it
- Talking behind someone's back
- Asking someone to lie for you
- Blaming someone else when you are at fault
- Taking credit for someone else's work
- Asking a subordinate to do something unrelated to work, i.e. run errands
- Trying to convert others to your political or religious beliefs
- Opening someone else's mail
- Sending unwanted email
- Telling offensive jokes
- Smoking in common areas
- Not pulling your own weight
- Complaining about the company, boss, or co-workers
- Having a condescending attitude toward others
- Maintaining a sloppy, unsanitary work area
- Conducting a side business at your main job
- Being under the influence of anything at work
- Gossiping, especially about bosses or co-workers
- Sexual impropriety (by their definition, not yours)
- Discussing personal problems during business hours

Individually, none of these actions would likely get an otherwise competent employee fired. But an accumulation of them, especially in combination with other more serious offenses, almost certainly will. If nothing else, such activities are a drain on co-workers' productivity and morale That's not something a good employer will tolerate for long.

Condemned by Your Own Hard Drive

If your employer is looking for solid cause to terminate you, they can probably find the smoking gun on your office computer.

Take email. Not only is there a log of how much company time you spend on email, there are the emails themselves. Emails of a personal nature are a misuse of company time. Emails that speak negatively about your boss, co-workers, or the company are real trouble. Gossip used to center around the water cooler; now it flies around via email. Before sending any email, either from the company computer or about your company from any computer, ask yourself if you would send that email if you had to copy your boss on it. If you wouldn't want your boss to see it, don't send the email; it'll come back to haunt you.

Emails are not the only thing on your hard drive. There is also a complete record of your downloads – every site and how much company time you wasted there. You may be able to explain going to Amazon to order a birthday gift for your nephew. You won't be able to explain away even one minute spent on a porn site.

What you say about your company and co-workers away from the job can get you fired, too. Many people post work-related entries on personal blogs. Even if it is a personal blog, access to it is still unlimited. Any confidential information about the company or an employee that ends up on a blog is cause for dismissal.

Think of blogging as a public speaking engagement where you have no idea who might be in the audience and every word is recorded. That thought might keep you from blurting out something that will cost you your job. One last thing – never drink and blog.

Even the most obtuse of employees must have some inkling that they might have crossed the line when they performed the deeds that caused the axe to fall. The last thing you want to have happen in your career is to lose your job over something that, in retrospect, all you can say is "What was I thinking?!"

Resume' or Eulogy?

When the wealthiest man in town passed away after a long life, the citizens gathered for the requisite memorial service. Two old friends who had known the deceased for many years were talking. One asked the other, "Do you have any idea how much he left?" The other gentleman replied, "I know exactly. He left it all."

What makes for an outstanding resume' generally makes for a second-rate eulogy. It's ironic. We expend so much effort creating an impressive resume'. Once we're gone, what's on that resume' isn't what people remember about us.

On your resume', you get the opportunity to highlight your personality type, your temperament, and your conative (doing) strengths to your advantage. And you should. But a resume' doesn't lend itself to highlighting your character strengths. If you attempt to highlight the six virtues that Seligman and Peterson studied (wisdom, courage, humanity, justice, temperance, transcendence), you may come across as egotistical. These virtues must be inferred by the reader of your resume'.

It's another irony that the traits of yours that must be only implied on your resume' are actually the traits that employers are really seeking. Smart employers know that skills can be taught, but that virtues are instilled. They also know if they haven't been instilled in you by the time you send them your resume', they can't make the effort to instill them in you.

In his book, *The Road to Character*, David Brooks refers to the part of us that focuses on our resume' as Adam I and the part that focuses on our eulogy as Adam II. He makes these observations:

- Adam I wants to conquer the world.
- Adam II wants to obey a calling to serve the world.
- Adam I asks how things work.
- Adam II asks why things work.
- Adam I wants to venture forth.
- Adam II wants to return to his roots.
- Adam I achieves success by winning victories over others.
- Adam II builds character by winning victories over himself.
- Adam II lives by an inverse logic. You have to give to receive. You have to conquer your desire to get what you crave. Success leads to the greatest failure, which is pride. Failure leads to the greatest success, which is humility and learning.

Brooks also notes that our culture teaches us to promote ourselves and to master skills for success, but doesn't encourage us to learn humility, sympathy, and self-confrontation, which are necessary to build character. A vocation is not found by looking inside and finding your passion. It is found by looking outside and asking what life is asking of us. Working on your career builds a resume'; working on a calling builds a eulogy.

One of the most important books of the 20th Century was *Man's Search for Meaning*, by Viktor Frankl. Frankl was an up-and-coming psychiatrist in Vienna in the late 1930s. He was also Jewish, and his punishment for being Jewish was to be sent to Auschwitz and later Dachau concentration camps. Viktor Frankl's wife, mother, and brother died in the concentration camps – he and his sister were the only family members to survive the Holocaust.

Man's Search for Meaning offers two important perspectives. It serves as a journal and recollection of the daily life in the concentration camps from the perspective of a trained psychologist. It also offers insight into what is most important in life, which too often only becomes clear after great loss.

Here are some of Frankl's perspectives on what we should really want in life:

- Life is not a quest for pleasure or power, but a quest for meaning.
- There are three possible sources for meaning: in work, in love, and in courage during difficult times.
- The way in which a man accepts his fate and all the suffering it entails gives him ample opportunity – even under the most difficult circumstances – to add a deeper meaning to his life.
- Suffering ceases to be suffering at the moment it finds a meaning, such as the meaning of a sacrifice.
- Pleasure is, and must remain, a side-effect or byproduct, and is destroyed and spoiled to the degree to which it is made a goal in itself.

- It did not really matter what we expected from life, but rather what life expected from us. Our answer must consist, not in talk and meditation, but in right action and in right conduct.
- Woe to him who, when the day of his dreams finally came, found it so different from all he had longed for.
- Sometimes the frustrated will to meaning is vicariously compensated for by a will to power, including the most primitive form of the will to power, the will to money.
- A human being is not one in pursuit of happiness, but rather in search of a reason to become happy.

Exactly two months before he was assassinated, Dr. Martin Luther King, Jr. gave a sermon that became known as "The Drum Major Instinct". It was a prophetic sermon. It also serves as a great lesson on how we should think about the mark we want to leave on this world. Here is the conclusion to that sermon:

"Every now and then I guess we all think realistically about that day when we will be victimized with what is life's final common denominator—that something that we call death. We all think about it. And every now and then I think about my own death and I think about my own funeral. And I don't think of it in a morbid sense. And every now and then I ask myself, "What is it that I would want said?" And I leave the word to you this morning.

If any of you are around when I have to meet my day, I don't want a long funeral. And if you get somebody to deliver the eulogy, tell them not to talk too long. And every now and then I wonder what I want them to say. Tell them not to mention that I have a Nobel Peace Prize—that isn't important. Tell them not to mention that I have three or four hundred other awards—that's not important. Tell them not to mention where I went to school.

I'd like somebody to mention that day that Martin Luther King, Jr., tried to give his life serving others.

I'd like for somebody to say that day that Martin Luther King, Jr., tried to love somebody.

I want you to say that day that I tried to be right on the war question.

I want you to be able to say that day that I did try to feed the hungry.

And I want you to be able to say that day that I did try in my life to clothe those who were naked.

I want you to say on that day that I did try in my life to visit those who were in prison.

I want you to say that I tried to love and serve humanity.

Yes, if you want to say that I was a drum major, say that I was a drum major for justice. Say that I was a drum major for peace. I was a drum major for righteousness. And all of the other shallow things will not matter. I won't have any money to leave behind. I won't have the fine and luxurious things of life to leave behind. But I just want to leave a committed life behind. And that's all I want to say.

If I can help somebody as I pass along,
If I can cheer somebody with a word or song,
If I can show somebody he's traveling wrong,
Then my living will not be in vain.
If I can do my duty as a Christian ought,
If I can bring salvation to a world once wrought,
If I can spread the message as the master taught,
Then my living will not be in vain.

When it's time for your memorial service, no one is going to praise you for your impressive resume' or your wealth accumulation. They will hopefully praise you for your contributions to a better world, for which you may have been rewarded with material comfort. However, no one sucks up to the deceased, rich or not.

You are going to live a long, full productive life. People will be lined up to say good things about you at the end of that long, full productive life. What do you want them to say?

Think about the different groups of people you will come close to in your life. Start with family members. What would you want your siblings to say about you? More important, what would you want your children to say about you? What do you want your professional colleagues to say about you? Think about your professional qualities, your work ethic, and your contributions to your profession.

What will your friends say? Not at the podium, but in small groups after the others have gone. What they say then is the real measure of what they thought of you and your impact on their lives.

What about those other people who don't necessarily fall into one of the above categories? These people could be from your church, your Rotary Club, your hobby group, or any other service or social organization which included you.

What would you want all these people to say about you? What accomplishments would you like them to be able to list? More important, what personal character traits of yours would you want them to be able to testify by examples from your own life? Would there be consistency in their perceptions of you?

Once you have thought of the things you would like

people to say at your funeral, think about the work you must do between now and then to make those words ring true. Then get to work.

If You Don't Remember Anything Else...

- Lifelong learning and adaptability will be required for all the good jobs in the future.
- Your right brain, the creative, crazy half, will be your most important tool.
- A passion for what you do is absolutely vital to both success and happiness at work.
- You are likely to have a far longer lifespan than most, if not all of the companies you will work for.
- Need vs. Want = Require vs. Desire. Know the difference.
- Increased ability to change jobs also means less job security.
- The job should be changed to fit you; you don't change to fit the job.
- Tests like Myers-Briggs can be very useful in assessing what kind of work might be a good fit.
- Tests like Myers-Briggs don't have all the answers.
- Your satisfaction at work is based on factors you select.
- More money won't make you love a job you hate.
- Don't subordinate the mission to the money.
- The money follows the mission.
- If you plan to strike out on your own, be pulled, not pushed into it.
- Some people will let geography determine where they will work. Others prefer to choose who they will work with first and let that choice determine where they will live. To each his/her own.

- Companies and jobs are global and mobile. Your competition is in the next hemisphere, as well as the next cubicle.
- Risk and reward move in the same direction. A change for greater rewards will likely have greater risks.
- Charge for your output, not your input, which means charging by the project, not by the hour. This method benefits those who produce and punishes those who don't.
- Your risk tolerance determines your reward. Your desired reward does not determine your risk tolerance.
- Status quo bias impedes our ability to make objective comparisons between our current and potential jobs.
- Comparing the pros and cons of different jobs in writing can help clarify the better fit for you.
- As the number of job choices increase arithmetically, the anxiety over making the right decision increases geometrically.
- The best places to work focus on getting the best people in place first and then keeping them there.
- Benefits should be looked at very closely when comparing job offers. Benefits packages can easily offset a lower salary.
- Take your time making a decision to accept a job offer. If they want you today, they'll want you tomorrow.
- *Why* is an essay question, not multiple-choice. It is a question answered with opinions and feelings, not just facts. Thought is a prerequisite to answering *Why*.
- To ask *Why* is not to question the legitimacy of something. It is a search for elaboration, illumination, and confirmation.
- When you compete against others, no one wants to help you. When you compete against yourself,

everyone wants to help you.

- Money is not the cause of our work; it is the effect of our work.
- All legitimate work deserves respect because it provides goods and services to our fellow man, making their lives better.
- The right work is a source of energy, not a consumer of our energy.
- The right work does wonders for our self-esteem.
- Work supports your life, not the other way around.
- We can most help our fellow man, thus ourselves, when we are doing the work for which we are best suited.
- Work is one of the best ways to leave the wood pile higher than you found it.
- You need to work and save so that the senior you can live with the independence and dignity you deserve.
- Work provides one of the best ways to leave a legacy of meaning.
- Don't just work on your resume; work on your eulogy.

WORKING WORDS OF WISDOM

Showing up is 80% of life.

-Woody Allen

Work for your future as if you are going to live forever, for your afterlife as if you are going to die tomorrow.

-Arabian Proverb

Nothing is really work unless you would rather be doing something else.

-James M. Barrie

Initiative is to success what a lighted match is to a candle.

-Orlando Battista

Action without study is fatal. Study without action is futile.

-Mary Beard

When you come to a fork in the road – take it.

-Yogi Berra

If you don't know where you're going, you'll end up somewhere else.

-Yogi Berra

The more men, generally speaking, will do for a dollar when they make it, the more that dollar will do for them when they spend it.

-William J. H. Boetcker

Should we measure you by what you have, or by who you are?

-John Bogle

What the wise man does at the beginning,
the fool does at the end.

-Warren Buffett

There are three *i*'s in every cycle:
first the innovator, then the imitator, and finally the idiot.

-Warren Buffett

There is dignity in work only when it is work freely accepted.

-Albert Camus

Set me a task in which I can put something of my very self, and it is no longer a task; it is joy; it is art.

-Bliss Carman

Success is getting what you want.
Happiness is wanting what you get.

-Dale Carnegie

Every man is the son of his own works.

-Cervantes

Never stand begging for that which you have the power to earn.

-Cervantes

He who sacrifices his conscience to ambition burns a picture to obtain the ashes.

-Chinese Proverb

Courage is the first of human qualities because it is the
quality which guarantees all the others.

-Winston Churchill

An optimist sees an opportunity in every calamity;
a pessimist sees a calamity in every opportunity.

-Winston Churchill

If you mean to profit, learn to please.

-Winston Churchill

We make a living by what we get;
we make a life by what we give.

-Winston Churchill

Nothing in life is to be feared. It is only to be
understood.

-Marie Curie

Genius is one percent inspiration and ninety-nine percent
perspiration.

-Thomas Edison

Imagination is more important than knowledge.

-Albert Einstein

Not everything that can be counted counts.
And not everything that counts can be counted.

-Albert Einstein

The best augury of a man's success in his profession is
that he thinks it is the finest in the world.

-George Eliot

It is not half as important to burn the midnight oil as it is
to be awake in the daytime.

-E. W. Elmore

Poor men seek meat for their stomachs;
rich men seek stomachs for their meat.

-English Proverb

By the work one knows the workman.

-Jean de la Fontaine

Profit is a byproduct of work; happiness is its chief
product.

-Henry Ford

If a man empties his purse into his head, no one can take
it from him.

-Benjamin Franklin

The best investment is in the tools of one's own trade.

-Benjamin Franklin

By failing to prepare you are preparing to fail.

-Benjamin Franklin

Work has a greater effect than any other technique of
living in the direction of binding the individual more
closely to reality; in his work, at least, he is securely
attached to a part of reality, the human community.

-Sigmund Freud

Work is love made visible.

-Kahlil Gibran

Success is simple.
Do what's right, the right way, at the right time.

-Arnold Glasow

Beware of wishing for anything in youth, because you
will get it in middle age.

-Goethe

A clever person commits no minor blunders.

-Goethe

When you hire people who are smarter than you are,
you prove you are smarter than they are.

-R.H. Grant

All problems become smaller if you don't dodge them
but confront them. Touch a thistle timidly and it pricks
you; grasp it boldly and its spines crumble.

-Admiral William F. Halsey

All man's gains are the fruit of venturing.

-Herodotus

There can be no freedom without freedom to fail.

-Eric Hoffer

There is no education in the second kick of a mule.

-Ernest Hollings

The important thing is not so much where we stand,
as in what direction we are moving.

-Oliver Wendell Holmes

Change is not made without inconvenience, even from worse to better.

-Richard Hooker

To escape criticism – do nothing, say nothing, be nothing.

-Elbert Hubbard

We work to become, not to acquire.

-Elbert Hubbard

We must dream of an aristocracy of achievement arising out of a democracy of opportunity.

-Thomas Jefferson

The chains of habit are too weak to be felt until they are too strong to be broken.

-Samuel Johnson

The future is purchased by the present.

-Samuel Johnson

He that never labors may know the pains of idleness, but not the pleasures.

-Samuel Johnson

Don't think of retiring from the world until the world will be sorry that you retire.

-Samuel Johnson

Don't compromise yourself. You're all you've got.

-Janis Joplin

Amateurs hope; professionals work.

-Garson Kanin

Happiness is not attained through self-gratification,
but through fidelity to a worthy purpose.

-Helen Keller

The surest way to be happy is to seek happiness for
others.

-Martin Luther King, Jr.

They copied all they could copy,
but they couldn't copy my mind;
And I left them sweatin' and stealin',
a year and a half behind.

-Rudyard Kipling

Unless the job means more than the pay it will never pay
more.

-H. Bertram Lewis

What kills a skunk is the publicity it gives itself.

-Abraham Lincoln

The heights by men reached and kept,
Were not attained by sudden flight,
But they, while their companions slept,
Were toiling upward in the night.

-Henry Wadsworth Longfellow

If you would hit the mark, you must aim a little above it.
Every arrow that flies feels the attraction of earth.

-Henry Wadsworth Longfellow

The most effective way to cope with change is to help create it.

-L.W. Lynett

There is no security on this earth; only opportunity.

-General Douglas MacArthur

There are three ingredients in the good life:
learning, earning, and yearning.

-Christopher Morley

Ill-luck is, in nine cases out of ten, the result of taking pleasure first and duty second, instead of duty first and pleasure second.

-Theodore T. Munger

Life is like a game of cards. The hand you are dealt represents Determinism. How you play it is Free Will.

-Jawaharlal Nehru

He who has a Why to live can bear almost any How.

-Friedrich Nietzsche

You never get a second chance to make a good first impression.

-Will Rogers

Even if you're on the right track, you'll get run over if you just sit there.

-Will Rogers

When you cease to make a contribution, you begin to die.

-Eleanor Roosevelt

Far better it is to dare mighty things, to win glorious
triumphs, even though checkered by failure, than to take
rank with those poor spirits who neither enjoy much nor
suffer much, for they live in the gray twilight that knows
not victory nor defeat.

-Theodore Roosevelt

To be without some of the things you want
is an indispensable part of happiness.

-Bertrand Russell

A goal without a plan is just a wish.

-Antoine de Saint-Exupery

Failures are divided into two classes – those who
thought and never did, and those who did and never
thought.

-John Charles Salak

Do not choose to be wrong for the sake of being
different.

-Lord Samuel

The only place where success comes before work is a
dictionary.

-Vidal Sassoon

Success is not the key to happiness.
Happiness is the key to success.
If you love what you are doing, you will be successful.

-Albert Schweitzer

Why not go out on a limb? Isn't that where the fruit is?

-Frank Scully

It is the mind that makes the body rich.

-William Shakespeare

The test of a vocation is the love of the drudgery it involves.

-Logan Pearsall Smith

The trouble with the rat race is that even if you win, you're still a rat.

-Lily Tomlin

Endeavor so to live that when you die, even the undertaker will be sorry.

-Mark Twain

Good manners consist of concealing how much we think of ourselves, and how little we think of the other person.

-Mark Twain

It is easier to do a job right than to explain why you didn't.

-Martin Van Buren

Hell is the state in which we are barred from receiving what we truly need because of the value we give to what we merely want.

-Virgil

The best is the enemy of the good.

-Voltaire

Work banishes those three great evils, boredom, vice and poverty.

-Voltaire

Everything I did in my life that was worthwhile I caught Hell for.

-Chief Justice Earl Warren

The world of achievement has always belonged to the optimist.

-J. Harold Wilkens

Education is not the filling of a pail, but the lighting of a fire.

-W.B. Yeats

It's better to burn out than to rust.

-Neil Young

REFERENCES

Baldridge, Letitia; *Letitia Baldridge's New Complete Guide to Executive Manners;* Rawson Associates, 1993

Belsky and Gilovich; *Why Smart People Make Big Money Mistakes*; Simon and Schuster, 1999

Bolles, Richard; *What Color is Your Parachute?;* Ten Speed Press, 2006

Branham, Leigh, *The 7 Hidden Reasons Employees Leave;* AMACOM, 2005

Collins, Jim; *Good to Great;* Harper Collins, 2001

Covey, Stephen; *Seven Habits of Highly Effective People;* Franklin Covey Co., 1990

Daniels, Aubrey, *Bringing Out the Best in People;* McGraw-Hill, 2001

Fitzhenry, Robert, ed.; *The Harper Book of Quotations;* Harper Perennial, 1993

Frederickson, Barbara L.; *The Value of Positive Emotions*; 2003; *American Scientist*

Friedman, Thomas; *The World is Flat;* Farrar, Straus and Giroux, 2006

Goodman, Ted, ed.; *The Forbes Book of Business Quotations;* Black Dog and Leventhal, 1997

Haidt, Jonathan; *The Happiness Hypothesis*; 2006; Basic Books

Harford, Tim; *Adapt*; 2011; Farrar, Straus and Giroux

Harford, Tim; *The Logic of Life*; 2008; Random House

Heath, Chip & Heath, Dan; *Switch*; 2011; Broadway Books

Heathfield, Susan, *The Awesome Power of Goal Setting;* Heathfield Consulting Associates, 2006

Heathfield, Susan, *Top Ten Ways to Retain Your Great Employees;* Heathfield Consulting Associates, 2006

Iyengar, Sheena; *The Art of Choosing*; 2011; Twelve Publishing

James, William; *The Principles of Psychology*; 1890, 1950; Dover Publications

Jansen, Julie; *I Don't Know What I Want, But I Know It's Not This;* Penguin Books, 2003

Kahneman, Daniel; *Thinking, Fast and Slow*; 2011; Farrar, Straus and Giroux

Kidder, Rushworth; *How Good People Make Tough Choices;* Quill, 2003

Kritzell and Logan; *Reinventing Your Career;* McGraw-Hill, 1997

Koch, Richard; *The 80/20 Principle*; 1998; Currency

Lore, Nicholas; *The Pathfinder;* Fireside, 1998

Martin, Judith; *Miss Manner's Guide for the Turn-of-*

the-Millenium; Fireside, 1990

McCormack, Mark*; What They Don't Teach You at Harvard Business School;* Bantam Press, 1988

McKay, Dawn Rosenberg, *How to Get Fired;* Careerplanning.com, 2006

McKay, Dawn Rosenberg, *Toward a More Civil Workplace;* Careerplanning.com, 2006

Paul, Margaret, PhD, *Do I Have To Give Up Me To Be Loved By You?;* Harper Collins, 1989

Pink, Daniel, *Free Agent Nation*; Warner Business Books, 2001

Pink, Daniel H.; *Drive*; 2009; Riverhead Books

Stanley, Thomas J. & Danko, William D.; *The Millionaire Next Door*; 1996; Pocket Books

Tieger and Barron-Tieger; *Do What You Are*; Little, Brown, 2001

Tracy, Brian, *Goals-How to Get Everything You Want;* Berrett-Koehler, 2003

WEB SITES
authentichappiness.org
homebusinessmag.com
humanmetrics.com
Kolbe.com
monster.ca
myersbriggs.org
psychologytoday.com

psych.rochester.edu/SDT
stickK.com
teamtechnology.co.uk